The New Class Society

The New Class Society

Goodbye American Dream?

Second Edition

Robert Perrucci
and Earl Wysong

ROWMAN & LITTLEFIELD PUBLISHERS, INC.
Lanham • Boulder • New York • Oxford

ROWMAN & LITTLEFIELD PUBLISHERS, INC.

Published in the United States of America
by Rowman & Littlefield Publishers, Inc.
A Member of the Rowman & Littlefield Publishing Group
4720 Boston Way, Lanham, Maryland 20706
www.rowmanlittlefield.com

PO Box 317
Oxford, OX2 9RU, United Kingdom

British Library Cataloguing in Publication Information Available

Library of Congress Cataloging-in-Publication Data

Perrucci, Robert.
    The new class society : goodbye American dream? / Robert Perrucci and Earl
Wysong.— 2nd ed.
    p. cm.
    Includes bibliographical references and index.
    ISBN 0-7425-1937-6 (cloth : alk. paper) — ISBN 0-7425-1938-4 (pbk. : alk. paper)
    1. Social classes—United States.   2. United States—Social conditions—1980–
I. Wysong, Earl, 1944–   II. Title.
HN90.S6 P47   2002
305.5'0973—dc21   2002001368

Printed in the United States of America

♾™ The paper used in this publication meets the minimum requirements of
American National Standard for Information Sciences—Permanence of Paper
for Printed Library Materials, ANSI/NISO Z39.48-1992.

Contents

Tables and Figures

TABLES

FIGURES

Preface to the Second Edition

"*My second day as chairman, a plane that I lease, flying with engines I built, crashed into a building that I insure, and it was covered with a network I own.*" Those words were spoken on September 11, 2001 by Jeff Immelt, the new head of General Electric Corporation, following the terrorist attack on the World Trade Center in New York City.

In one sense Mr. Immelt's words express, in his way, the shock Americans felt as they watched the horrific events unfold on live television that bright September morning. But in another sense, the information conveyed by the remarks of GE's CEO reveal, perhaps inadvertently, the recent, extensive growth and consolidation of corporate power in the United States. General Electric is no longer simply a major corporation producing consumer durables for American households. Today GE is a massive, global firm involved in the aviation, insurance, real estate, securities, and mass media industries with annual revenues of $130 billion (2000). As Mr. Immelt's remarks indicate, the company's interests are clearly linked to many sectors of the U. S. economy and to many places around the world.

It was the interconnectedness features of modern multinational companies that were of special interest and concern as we completed the manuscript for the first edition of *The New Class Society* some five years ago. At that time we presented what we continue to believe is a fresh and compelling analysis of a newly emerging class structure. It is based on our view that a number of large, powerful organizations—such as GE and others—have begun to span and dominate the economic, political, and cultural institutions of our society in new ways that both shape and legitimate growing class inequalities.

Although many changes have occurred in the United States over the past half-decade, many inequalities that are part of the emerging new class structure have either remained unchanged or have been exacerbated by recent events and policies. As we move into the early 2000s, we believe that class, gender, and racial inequalities are increasingly linked and require explicit attention and analysis. The second edition has been extensively revised to reflect our efforts to develop a more unified approach for analyzing these issues. We have added new sections throughout the book which identify and explore how complex organizational structures are implicated in the creation and perpetuation of class, gender, and racial inequalities. We remain committed to our distributional model of class structure, but we have expanded it in ways that we believe extend our understanding of how the organizationally based distribution of resources that are critical to class membership can also be applied to understanding gender and racial inequalities.

As we complete the second edition of our book, the future continues to rush away from the present in ways that render even our most recent research findings and information summaries somewhat dated by the time they appear in print. Even so, we remain convinced that the class polarization trend we described in the first edition is continuing and remains a constant, threatening feature of the social landscape. Moreover, we see little evidence that mainstream institutional leaders are willing to change the organizational structures and public policies that are leading our nation toward an increasingly divided, two-class future. Our decision to add the subtitle *Goodbye American Dream?* to the second edition reflects our concern regarding the forces dividing our society along class lines. The question mark appended to the subtitle is less a statement of uncertainty about the trends that we have identified, and more of an expectation that a social movement in support of greater class equity will develop in the twenty-first century.

More than two hundred years ago the framers of the U. S. Constitution sought to erect boundaries to contain what their experiences had taught them was the most powerful and pernicious organizational structure of their time: the central government of the nation-state. The document they crafted did not anticipate the rise of powerful, private multinational firms with levels of economic, political, and cultural resources that rival or exceed those of many nation-states today. At the heart of the U. S. Constitution were guarantees protecting citizens' political rights against a powerful (and potentially abusive) nation-state and democratic participation in shaping the national government. Although the elite class membership of the founders and the limitations they established to democratic participation by gender and property ownership are well known, they did establish important precedents in the areas of citizenship rights and democratic participation. We believe the challenge for the twenty-first century is to extend citizenship rights and democratic participation into the economic and cultural arenas. Such changes would provide citizens with opportunities to begin the process of reigning in the powers of the large, private corporations (and corporate-government confederations) that have been responsible for polarizing the class and opportunity structures over the last 30 years in the United States. We believe that only through the vigorous extension of democracy into the "private sphere" and the establishment of both political and economic citizenship rights can the American Dream be redeemed.

Preface to the
First Edition

The dawning of industrial capitalism in England in the eighteenth century was accompanied by severe and often violent dislocations in the lives of agricultural workers. Land that had for generations been held in common and used for grazing animals was enclosed for use in sheep raising, an industry that was essential to the capitalists who owned the burgeoning textile industry. Peasant villages were destroyed, and agricultural workers were forced off the land. Deprived of their jobs and the means of making a living through agriculture, dislocated peasants were also faced with a hostile government eager to serve the needs of a powerful new capitalist class. The enactment of vagabondage laws and poor laws forced displaced peasants—men, women, and children—into the factories where they found long hours, extremely harsh working conditions, and low wages. A modern-day economist looking at this transition from a feudal agricultural society to an industrial capitalist society might describe it as an example of "creative destruction"—the painful but necessary "shock therapy" that often accompanies technological and economic change.

The experiences of eighteenth-century peasants bear a striking resemblance to those of manufacturing workers in the United States in the 1970s and 1980s. Forced out of their high-wage manufacturing jobs, their unions under attack by both government and corporations, workers were forced into the burgeoning service industries where they found low wages, no benefits, and exploitative working conditions. The "end of welfare" legislation of 1997 has the ring of eighteenth-century vagabondage and poor laws, forcing displaced and threatened workers to accept increasingly onerous working conditions and wages.

The experiences of the eighteenth-century peasant and the late-twentieth-century blue-collar worker were both a part of a larger transformation in the structure of class inequality taking place in the respective historical periods. The post–World War II period in the United States provided economic growth for society and consumer prosperity for millions of Americans. The idea of America as a middle-class society gained prominence as the sons and daughters of working-class Americans went, in increasing numbers, to college, into high-wage skilled jobs, and into the professions. Then something happened: Beginning in the 1970s and continuing into the 1980s, the once powerful high-wage auto, steel, textile, rubber, and consumer electronics industries went into a tailspin. Competition from the Far East and Europe led to a wave of plant closings in the United States and the transfer of manufacturing jobs to lower-wage areas abroad. Millions of high-wage, blue-collar jobs disappeared, and the existence of middle-class, blue-collar "aristocrats" became a fiction. The rapid introduction in the 1980s of advanced computer technology and information systems helped facilitate the dramatic "downsizing" of millions of white-collar middle-management employees by major U.S. firms. This trend continues to be encouraged by ongoing waves of corporate mergers and acquisitions.

This book is about the transformation of the mid-century "middle-class" American society into a bifurcated and polarized two-class society. This "new class society" consists of a privileged class made of 20 percent of the population and a new working class composed of the other 80 percent. A person's position in the new class society is determined by access to four types of scarce resources, which together we call generative capital: consumption capital, investment capital, credentialed-skill capital, and social capital. The privileged class is composed of those who have access to these resources over time, which means that they are stable and predictable. The new working class, in contrast, has limited access to generative capital, and their resources have become more unstable and unpredictable. Moreover, the privileged class uses its resources to maintain and legitimate the new class society. This is achieved through its control of large-scale organizations and institutional networks in the areas of the economy, politics, and culture.

The first two chapters set the stage for the book by providing the lens of class analysis for viewing American society. Chapter 1 introduces our "new class" theoretical model, compares our approach with previous class analysis traditions, and describes the main features of what we view as the emerging new class society. In chapter 2 the ideals of the American Dream are contrasted with the major features of the new class society. It documents recent notable class trends and introduces two "hidden" class realities explored in detail in later chapters: conflicting class interests and the organizations that maintain and legitimate the class system.

The middle section of the book (chapters 3 through 7) examines how the privileged class maintains and extends its advantages by holding positions of dominance in the major institutional sectors of U.S. society. The global economy, government policy, education, and the information industry are examined as settings in which class inequalities are created and reinforced. These chapters use material reported daily in the media to demonstrate how class interests and privileged-class power are used to make decisions about jobs and wages, health care and social security, taxes and television, and the education of the next generation of Americans.

In the final chapter we consider the prospects for both continuity and change of the new class society. It reviews current class-based imbalances in institutional power; it revisits the populist movements of the past as a potential guide to understanding future challenges to class inequalities; and it explores the emerging struggle between privileged-class policies that would reinforce class inequalities and challenges from working-class organizations to such policies.

Acknowledgments

There are a great many steps between the completion of a manuscript and a published book. First you have to find someone who believes in what you are trying to do. We are indebted to Dean Birkenkamp for his strong support of this project and for sharing in our effort to present a fresh view of class in the United States. He encouraged us to undertake a second edition and to extend our analysis to examine the connections between class, gender, and race. Several people at Rowman & Littlefield helped to bring the second edition to completion: Gretchen Hanisch, Alison Sullenberger, copyeditor Chris Thillen, and production editor Jehanne Schweitzer. Tony Faiola continued his fine work on the graphics in the book. Joyce Webb was helpful in printing multiple versions of several chapters.

1

Class in America

My momma always said that life is like a box of chocolates. You never know what you're gonna get.

—*Forrest Gump*, 1994

The lead character of the popular film, Forrest Gump illustrates that despite limitations of intellect, his pure heart, guileless character, sincerity, hard work, and positive mental attitude enable him to prevail over life's hardships. Gump's disarming qualities defrost the cynicism of a heartless world and open the path to material success, social respect, and personal fulfillment. His achievements appear to affirm his momma's homily, reinforce belief in the American Dream, and give testimony to the pervasive ideological belief that all men are created equal.

However, movie ideals often clash with social realities. Is life really like a box of chocolates—unpredictable and capricious in detail but essentially rewarding to the pure of heart? Consider the contrast between fictional experience Forrest Gump and the real-life experiences of Jim Farley.

Jim Farley's fellow workers at Federal Mogul Corporation's roller bearing plant on the east side of Detroit called him Big Jim—not so much because of the size of his body, they said, as because of the size of his heart.

They liked the soft-spoken yet tough manner in which he represented them as a union committeeman. And they liked his willingness to sit down over a shot and a beer at the nearby Office Lounge and listen to the problems they had with their jobs, their wives, or their bowling scores.

Jim Farley had come North from eastern Kentucky, because mechanization of the mines and slumping demand for coal made finding work there impossible. The idea of leaving behind the mountains where he had grown up for the punch-in, punch-out factory life in a big city like Detroit didn't appeal to him much—but neither did the

1

thought of living on relief, like so many unemployed miners in his hollow and most others in Pike County. . . .

Federal Mogul announced that it would be phasing out its Detroit operations by early 1974 and moving bearing production to a new plant in Alabama. Farley, say those who knew him, became a different man almost overnight—tense, moody, withdrawn. A month after the announcement he suffered a heart attack. Physically, he recovered rapidly. Mentally, things got worse. His family and friends called it "nerves." . . .

With close to 20 years at Federal Mogul, the thought of starting all over again—in an unfamiliar job, with no seniority and little hope for a decent pension—was not pleasant. But Farley had little choice. Three times he found work, and three times he failed the physical because of his heart problem. The work itself posed no difficulty, but none of the companies wanted to risk high workers' compensation and health insurance premiums when there were plenty of young, strong workers looking for jobs.

As Farley's layoff date approached, he grew more and more apprehensive. He was 41 years old: what would happen if he couldn't find another job? His wife had gone to work at the Hall Lamp Company, so the family would have some income. But Farley's friends were being laid off, too, and most of them hadn't been able to find work yet either—a fact that worsened his outlook.

Farley was awake when Nancy left for work at 6:15 A.M. on January 29, but he decided to stay home. His nerves were so bad, he said, that he feared an accident at work. His sister-in-law Shirley stopped by late that morning and found him despondent. Shortly before noon he walked from the kitchen into his bedroom and closed the door. Shirley Farley recalls hearing a single click, the sound of a small-bore pistol. She rushed to the bedroom and pounded on the door. There was no response.

Almost 20 years to the day after Jim Farley left the hills of eastern Kentucky, his dream of a secure life for his family was dead. And so was he.[1]

Most people would see Jim Farley's death as an unnecessary personal tragedy. Here was a man with severe psychological problems who simply could not cope with the stress of job loss. "Millions of people lose a job in this lifetime, but they don't commit suicide" might be the typical response. There is a strong tendency to see unemployment as individual failure and the inability to "bounce back" as further evidence of that failure.

But there is another way to look at Jim Farley's death, one that recognizes a long chain of life experiences that produce patterns of predictable hardship and limited opportunities. Farley's chances in life are powerfully shaped by his social-class location, which constrains opportunities. His life is like that of millions of others who barely finish high school and move through half a dozen different jobs hoping to find one that will provide a decent wage and long-term security. Yet, just as the class structure constrains the lives of people like Jim Farley, it confers numerous advantages and opportunities on others. The same class structure that shapes laws denying workers a right to a job gives companies like Federal Mogul the right to do what they wish with their property. They can close a plant with little or no consideration of their workers or the community. In fact, tax laws may provide incentives for closing plants and building new ones in countries with lower-wage workers. The conditions leading to Jim Farley's death some twenty-five years ago have now spread across the land. Millions of workers in stable, high-wage jobs in America's basic industries have been told they are no longer needed. Thousands of plants are closed and sit empty in steel towns along the rivers of the Monongahela Valley in Pennsylvania. They were among the first to go in the dramatic reshaping of America's class structure which eliminated the middle-class worker, and they were soon followed by similar dislocations in the auto, textiles, glass, and electronics industries.

After the flight of manufacturing to foreign shores, corporate America's appetite for profits began to turn to its white-collar labor force. Suddenly, the giant corporations like IBM, AT&T, and GM discovered "downsizing" or "rightsizing" or "restructuring," in which the use of new technology and new work organization resulted in a 10–20 percent reduction in employees. The 1990s brought the global economy, and it became the corporate "bogeyman," disciplining workers with the constant threat of further shutdowns and layoffs to allow American firms to compete with other firms and other workers across the globe.

What are we to make of America's love affair with Forrest Gump? Why the attraction to the Gump myth in the face of the harsh realities? Maybe believing that life is like a box of chocolates leads to an expectation of sweet (but mixed) outcomes and makes predictable class-based disappointments and hardships easier to bear. After all, during the Great Depression of the 1930s, Hollywood produced some of its most upbeat and fanciful films.

To make sense of Jim Farley's death (and maybe even the popularity of Forrest Gump) we need to recognize that the American class structure in the past thirty years has been dramatically altered. What we are seeing is not a temporary aberration that will be soon put right but a fundamental shift in the distribution of economic and political power that constitutes the class structure. To understand the declining fortunes of millions of Jim Farleys and the corporate decisions of thousands of Federal Moguls, it is necessary to examine the workings of class structure and how it shapes the lives of workers, the decisions of politicians, and the actions of corporations.

INEQUALITY

The real news is that the median wage—the take-home pay of the worker smack in the middle of the earnings ladder—is still less than it was before the last recession. At the same time the upper reaches of America have never had it so good.

—Robert B. Reich, *Nation*, February 16, 1998

Most Americans have a keen sense of the presence of inequality. We learn about it in many ways on a daily basis, from our observations of people, homes, cars, neighborhoods, and news accounts of the "rich and famous." There is good evidence that we start to learn about inequality at a very early age and accumulate additional knowledge throughout our lives.[2]

If we were to talk with a group of "average" Americans about their awareness of social differences among people in our society, we might hear something like the following:

> It's those ballplayers and movie stars that make all the money. Millions of dollars a year for playing a game or acting like a jerk in front of a camera. Then there's the rock stars getting rich off the videos they sell to kids.
>
> The middle class is getting a screwing. The honest, hard-working slob who pays taxes, tries to raise a family, and has a helluva time making ends meet. It used to be that hard work would pay off with a steady job, a house of your own, and a decent car. But you can forget about that happening today.
>
> There are lots of people in this country who are called poor, because their income is below some official poverty line. Some of these people are probably in bad shape through no fault of their own. But there's a lot who just don't want to work, who would rather get a government check and food stamps. I would rather take a minimum-wage job than lose my self-respect by taking handouts.

Most Americans are aware of different forms of inequality. They know about income inequality and the patterns of discrimination against women and racial and ethnic groups. This awareness can be traced to stories in the mass media or what they may have learned in courses in high school or college. Knowledge of inequality is often conveyed in stories about the gender gap in salary, or the homeless, or the number of children or older Americans living below the poverty line. But what about the social arrangements that produce inequality and are responsible for its persistence? A pervasive form of inequality cuts across age, race, ethnicity, and gender to confer privilege on a minority of Americans while relegating the rest to varying degrees of insecurity, need, or despair. This is class inequality, a structured system of unequal rewards that provides enormous advantages to a small percentage of people in the United States at the expense of the overwhelming majority. Inequality is contained within a class system that resembles a game of monopoly that is "rigged" so that only certain players have a chance to own Park Place, and a great many others go directly to jail.

The discussion of class in America is a taboo subject because of the national reluctance to examine how the class system of the United States operates on a day-to-day basis. We do not learn from our schools or media how a privileged but organized minority of Americans is able to amass a disproportionate share of our national wealth and to transmit that privilege across generations to create a permanent economic, political, and social elite class. This structured class inequality is both the cause and the consequence of the ability to control important resources such as money, education, votes, or information. And for this system to work, the majority of disadvantaged Americans must be persuaded to believe that the way things work out for people is fair. This is done by distracting attention from class inequality and focusing the national spotlight on conflict between Blacks and Whites, women and men, gays and straights, pro-choice and antiabortion partisans.

American society is complex. It contains a diverse population of people of different races, ethnic origins, and religions. The people are divided across a complicated and shifting political spectrum spanning liberalism, the radical right, the religious right, conservative, libertarianism, and democratic socialism. Politics are played out across a dizzying array of interest groups concerned about the environment, abortion, flag burning, animal rights, prayer in schools, gun ownership, sexual harassment and sexual lifestyles and hundreds of other groups that are for or against something. Some of these interest groups confront each other over their different ideas on rights, justice, and freedom—or what we might call the "pursuit of happiness." However, most of the interest groups try to use the powers of government to aid them by changing tax law, funding health care, or reducing air pollution. This means that to be successful interest groups have to lobby members of Congress. And government, with its millions of employees and thousands of agencies and departments, oversees the use of a $1.6 trillion budget, a task that entails taking money from most people and giving some of it to other people.

The day-to-day operation of this society is made possible by the 130 million Americans who are in the labor force. The work they do is described in the ten thousand occupations listed in the *Dictionary of Occupational Titles*. The economy, often described as if it were separate from the rest of society, is made up of thousands of establishments where people make a living, from the multinational General Motors with 386,000 employees worldwide (in 2000) to the family-owned Korean grocery in Brooklyn.

Many of those Americans who are still socially alert and concerned about how our society works read newspapers and magazines, watch news programs on television, or belong to an interest group. But the socially aware are probably also overwhelmed by this entity we call society (a nineteenth-century French sociologist called it "the Great Being"). The complexity, the contradictions, the madness of modern life lead the average American to alternate between anger, involvement, and frustration and often finally to withdraw into some safe haven or escapist activity.

Everyday life has become so complicated that we have created a host of new occupations for people whose job it is to keep us informed about the workings of "The Great Being." These jobs are found in what is humorously referred to as the "hot-air sector" of our economy, where "experts," "pundits," and "advocates" give us an hour-by-hour, blow-by-blow account of the number of jobs created or lost, the strength or weakness of long-term bonds, the creeping or waning inflation, and the international crisis of the week involving famines, floods, and "ethnic conflicts" (although the Russian bear has been caged, the world is still portrayed as a dangerous place). We get some relief from the hot-air sector by tuning in on the "drop your pants in public" talk shows like the Jerry Springer Show. The daily accounts of murder and mayhem (especially gang violence and drive-by shootings) are presented as if they are happening in our own city or on our own block. This image of complexity is intimidating and keeps millions of Americans from taking an active interest in civic life.

Amid all this complexity and contradiction and conflict, is it any wonder that most Americans have lost confidence in their elected officials, corporations, schools, or unions? Is it any wonder that fewer than four in ten citizens vote in presidential elections? Americans seem to be constantly off balance, unsure about what to believe, suspicious of every leader who promises a "better way," and ultimately cynical about the possibilities for change. Escape may be the only way out, or so it seems. If we have the money, or credit cards, we can escape into consumerism. If not, there is television, booze, or drugs.

But there is another way to look at American society; it is a view that is rarely presented in newspapers, discussed on television, or taught to our school children. This view says that it is possible to understand how society works and how the pursuit of happiness becomes available to some but not to others; that amid all the complexity, one can find stable and enduring patterns in our collective lives. The stable and enduring pattern that is the focus of this book is the new class system.

MAPPING THE CLASS STRUCTURE:
PAST TRADITIONS AND NEW REALITIES

Mapping the U.S. social class structure and defining what *class* means in America have always been difficult and slippery tasks. Academic sociologists, journalists, and pundits have applied a variety of contrasting images and approaches to these topics. The use of such varied approaches has contributed to confusion and inconsistencies in academic and public arenas concerning the nature of the American class structure and how *class* can best be defined. Even so, poll data indicate that most Americans recognize the existence of a clearly identifiable, patterned U.S. class structure as well as the reality and importance of class inequalities. Survey findings suggest that Americans tend to view class structure in terms of a cakelike image, with groups of people organized into layers and stacked in a ranking system that ranges from low to high across gradual and shaded degrees of class differences. Such a view implies that the people grouped together within each layer are part of a specific social class and that class location is based on the possession of similar shares of important resources. This image appears to include the notion that class is partly a function of economic factors as well as cultural and lifestyle differences among people.

Sociological models of class structure and definitions of social class have sought to achieve greater precision and clarity than public views and images. But whereas some academic maps and definitions are similar to public perceptions, others are strikingly different. Although past sociological efforts to map the class structure and define class have not been uniform, they have tended to be organized around one of two distinct traditions or approaches—the production model and the functionalist model.

The production model is a kind of single-factor approach in which people's positions in the production process (and their possession of economic wealth) occupy center stage. It views class structure as organized on the basis of the relationship people have with the means of production: People tend to be either owners of productive wealth, like factories, offices, malls, airlines, rental properties, small businesses, or nonowners—workers.

This approach is grounded in the work of Karl Marx. But some contemporary sociologists (neo-Marxists) have refined and extended the original two-class model to reflect the reality that the production and corresponding occupational structures are much more complex today than they were in the 1880s.[3] Recent sociological variations of this approach move beyond the two-class model to produce a multilevel image of class structure with a relatively short list of levels or classes. However, unlike the public image of classes shading into one another because of gradually shifting economic and lifestyle differences, Marxian production models view the class structure as more sharply divided by wealth inequalities that reflect people's positions in the production process. In these models, classes are typically labeled as owners, managers, small employers, workers, and the poor (or underclass). In each instance, class position is based on a person's location in the production process—which also closely corresponds to the possession of wealth and to the occupational roles people perform. Owners (big and small) set policy and control the production process; managers assist owners and act as "order givers" who oversee the production process and often accumulate portions of productive wealth themselves; workers are "order takers" and typically do not share in the ownership of productive wealth (or at most own only very small portions); the poor are excluded from both ownership and most forms of desirable work. (But according to this model some segments of the poor may be used by owners and managers from time to time, as a force to pressure workers into accepting lower wages or less desirable working conditions.)

The functionalist model was partly inspired by Max Weber's view that social stratification is a complex, multidimensional phenomenon and cannot be understood on the basis of a single factor. Unlike the Marxian production model, in which ownership and control (or the lack of it) are critical to producing the class structure (and defining class), the functionalist approach provides a cakelike image of the class structure, and views the layers (classes) as organized according to variations in the levels of prestige. Prestige levels are viewed as reflecting a combination of several qualities individuals possess. These include the level of importance attached by cultural values to different occupational categories individuals occupy, educational levels they attain, and variations in their incomes. Although money does matter somewhat in some functionalist models, prestige, especially occupational prestige—not wealth per se—is the critical factor shaping the class structure and locating people within it. According to functionalist models, occupations requiring advanced formal education such as teaching and social work confer high levels of prestige on people who work at them, even though their income levels may be lower than some factory or business occupations requiring less education.

As noted, functionalist models encourage a layer-cake view of the class structure. In contrast to production-model views of sharp class divisions based on production positions and economic wealth, functionalist models envision a multilayer class structure with shaded degrees of prestige and income dividing the social classes. Thus, functionalist models are somewhat similar to the public image of class structure. But functionalist models often completely omit references to class and substitute the term *socioeconomic strata* as a way of describing the layered rankings of people possessing similar levels of prestige and economic resources. The strata that make up the class structure are typically arranged by functionalist models into descriptive class categories that are further subdivided. For example, the highest class is often divided into upper-upper-class and lower-upper-class groupings with the same *upper-* and *lower-* prefix designations applied to the middle and lower classes as well. Approached in this way, class structure takes on a kind of shaded, layer-cake image with classes more akin to statistical categories than groupings of real people.[4]

BEYOND TRADITION: NEW CLASS REALITIES AND THE DISTRIBUTIONAL MODEL

> If calling America a middle-class nation means anything, it means that we are a society in which most people live more or less the same kind of life. In 1970 we were that kind of society. Today we are not, and we become less like one each passing year.
>
> —Paul Krugman, *Mother Jones*, November–December 1996

The production and functionalist models differ in many respects, but both emphasize the importance of occupation as a key factor in determining class location—although for different reasons. As we have seen, the production model emphasizes the links between occupation, production position, and class, whereas the functionalist model emphasizes the links between occupation, prestige, and class. Although both models have made useful contributions in analyzing class inequalities in the past, their focus on the occupationally linked factors of production and prestige is inadequate to the tasks of both describing and understanding the emerging realities and complex dimensions of the New American Class System.

To more fully understand the origins, nature, and dynamics of the new class system, in this book we develop and apply a new model of class analysis. Our model builds in part on some features of, but is also distinct from, the production and functionalist models of the past. We refer to our approach as the distributional model of class analysis, and it includes at least four major features that distinguish it from previous models of class analysis.

The first distinctive feature of our model is our view that the emerging new class system is organizationally based. This means that the class structure is viewed as increasingly organized around and through large, organizational structures and processes that control the distribution of several forms of valuable economic and social resources. We maintain that large organizations—through various levels and groups of "gatekeepers" within them—direct, channel, and legitimate the distribution of these resources to individuals and groups. Occupations are still important in our approach, not simply because of their role in production but because of the organizations in which their work is conducted. Lawyers are not important as lawyers; they are important because of the firms in which and for which they do their work. This view is directly linked to the second important feature of our approach: We define classes as collectivities of individuals and families with comparable *total resources over time*. Class location reflects the extent to which people possess combinations of four forms of generative economic and social resources: investment, consumption, skill, and social capital (discussed later). People possess variations in these forms of capital in large measure owing to the nature and extent of the links they have to upper-level authority positions within corporate, government, and cultural structures. Thus, we view the class structure as being largely shaped by the distribution of organizationally controlled forms of capital that, held in greater or lesser amounts, determine the class locations of individuals and groups.

A third major feature of our approach concerns the idea that large organizations are centrally involved in legitimating the distributional processes as well as the class inequalities that arise from them. As we will see in later chapters, this means that large organizations are key sources for generating various forms and kinds of idea systems and explanations that justify the distribution of the four forms of capital to various individuals and groups as fair and legitimate. The fourth and final major feature of our approach rests on our assertion that the U.S. class structure is increasingly polarized by class inequalities into two broad class divisions. This leads us to argue that the new class system more closely approximates a double-diamond image of class structure than the cakelike, stacked-layer images evoked by earlier models of class analysis.

Our distributional model takes into account the reality that large organizations dominate the economic, political, and cultural landscapes today and through complex distributional structures and processes shape the nature and details of the new American class system. In this system, social classes consist of collections of real people (not statistical categories) who hold similar levels of, and have similar access to, the four forms of generative capital. These forms of capital are distributed to class members through organizationally based structures and processes that, as we will see, are dominated by privileged groups who themselves possess high levels of all four forms of capital.

GENERATIVE CAPITAL AND
CLASS STRUCTURE

Our image of a double-diamond class structure is based on the way that vital life-sustaining resources are distributed and the availability of these resources over time. In some societies the most important resource is land, because it allows one to grow food to eat and to exchange the surplus food for housing, health care, and seeds to grow more food. Peasant farmers in Central America are permanently impoverished because most land is held in large estates. These estates produce coffee or cotton for export; that is, they produce for foreign exchange or money. Peasants, without land, face the choice of starvation, working for the owner of a large landholding, or moving to the city in search of work.

In American society today, capital is the main resource used in exchange for what we need and want, and it is found in four forms: consumption capital, investment capital, skill capital, and social capital. We call these resources *generative capital* because they can produce more of the same resource when invested, or they can contribute to the production of another resource (e.g., social capital can produce investment capital).

Consumption Capital

Consumption capital is usually thought of as income—what we get in our wages and salary, unemployment check, social security, or welfare check. The lucky people have enough of it to buy food and clothing, pay the rent or mortgage, and make payments on the furniture or car. The really lucky people have a little money left over. But for most people, there is plenty of month left over when the money runs out.

When thinking about how much consumption capital families have and how they spend it, we immediately recognize that food can mean lobster or macaroni and cheese; clothing can mean second-hand from the thrift shop or name brands and fashionable labels. People vary in their weekly or monthly consumption capital, and two families with the same monthly income may choose to spend it in very different ways.

Figure 1.1 describes the distribution of income among families in the United States in 1999. About 15 percent of the families had incomes above $100,000 per year. At the other extreme, 22 percent of families had annual incomes below $25,000. The general pattern of the distribution of family income over the last thirty years reveals an increase in the proportion of families with upper levels of income, and a decrease in the families with middle-level income. In 1969, about 4

Figure 1.1   Money Income of Families, 1999

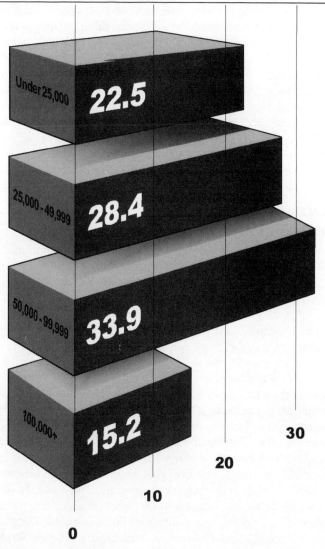

Source: Mishel, Bernstein, and Schmitt, 2001

percent of families had incomes of $100,000 or more. This percentage increased to 7.5 percent in 1989, and to over 15 percent in 1999. Across this same time period, middle-level incomes ($25,000–50,000) declined from 41 percent of families in 1969, to 34 percent in 1979, to 31 percent in 1989, and finally to 28 percent in 1999. About one-quarter of all families across the four time periods had incomes below $25,000, putting many Americans in the category of "working poor."[5]

Consumption capital is closely linked to position in the system of production, or occupation. Some jobs pay a lot more than others, but there is also large variation in the incomes of people with the same occupation. Salaries of lawyers, professors, or engineers may vary from upper six figures at the high end to incomes barely above the national average for wage and salaried workers (e.g., $31,000 in 1998). Thus, position in the system of production is important, but it does not tell us the full story when considering the question of income. Attempts to map the class structure by using only occupational categories or occupational prestige rankings will invariably combine persons who are getting vastly different returns on their educational assets. The salaries of lawyers, professors, or engineers will be due partly to their occupation and partly to the particular organizations in which they do their work (in addition to other resources discussed later).

Investment Capital

Investment capital is what people use to create more capital. If you have a surplus of consumption capital (the money left over when the month runs out), you can save it and earn interest each month. You can buy a house, or you can invest in stocks or bonds and earn dividends and capital gains. You can buy an old house, a "fixer-upper," renovate it, divide it into apartments, and collect rent. If your annual rent receipts exceed the combined cost of mortgage payments, property taxes, insurance, and maintenance costs, you will earn a profit.

If you have a great deal of investment capital, you can live off returns on investments in stocks or investments in a business. If you own a business, it probably means that you will employ others and will have to decide how much to pay workers and whether or not to provide them with health insurance or retirement plans. The less you need to pay them, the more you will have for yourself.

The varied ways in which investment capital is used produce wealth, which provides power and independence and is a major source of well-being for families. Wealth is determined by the total current value of financial assets (bank accounts, stocks, bonds, life insurance, pensions) plus durable assets such as houses or cars, minus all liabilities such as mortgages and consumer debt. Thus, we can describe a family's wealth in terms of *total net worth* (financial assets, plus durable assets, minus liabilities) or *total financial wealth* (only financial assets). The distinction is important, because financial assets can generate income (interest, dividends) but durable assets like homes or cars are "lived in" or for "driving around."

The level of wealth inequality in the United States is much greater than the level of income inequality. Much less is known about wealth than about income distribution in the United States, but wealth is probably a more significant indicator of inequality because of its role in transmitting privilege across generations. Some sociologists have described wealth inequality as "the buried fault line of the American social system."[6] Figure 1.2 presents the shares of total net worth and total financial wealth in 1983, 1989, 1992, and 1998 for the top 1 percent, the middle 19

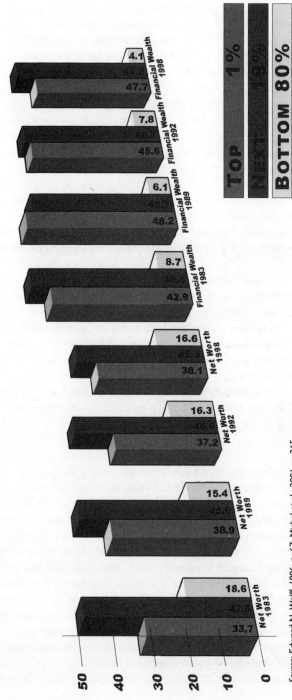

Figure 1.2   Percentage Shares of Total Net Worth and Total Financial Wealth, 1983–1998

Source: Edward N. Wolff, 1996, p. 67; Mishel et al., 2001, p. 265.

percent, and the bottom 80 percent of households. It is clear that there is enormous disparity in wealth controlled by the top 20 percent of the population compared with that of the bottom 80 percent. The privileged classes in 1998 controlled 83.4 percent of total net wealth and 96.0 percent of financial wealth—both figures representing increases over 1983. Wealth provides security, well-being, independence, and power to a privileged minority in American society, who can use that wealth to advance their privileged-class interests. The members of this privileged class have accumulated wealth while in positions that are at the intersection of an occupation and an organizational position. Consider the case of a new Ph.D. in business from the University of Chicago who received a starting salary of at least $100,000 at Columbia University, while another Ph.D. recipient from an obscure business school may receive $50,000 for a starting salary at a less prestigious university.[7] This same new Ph.D. from the University of Chicago received comparable offers from Harvard, Duke, and the University of North Carolina. This is clearly a case of elite universities preparing their graduates for positions in elite universities, and paying salaries that serve to enhance the salaries of everyone else at those elite universities.

Those with significant wealth are likely to be the corporate elite, top managers, doctors and corporate lawyers, members of Congress, White House staff, cabinet officials, professors at elite universities, media elite, "talking heads" on television, and assorted cultural elites. They are Democrats and Republicans, conservatives and liberals, Christians and Jews, pro-choice and antiabortion, radical feminists and Promise Keepers. They have a common commitment to keeping 80 percent of the population "bamboozled" while pretending to represent their interests. They have a common bond, which is high income, job security, and wealth, and they will rig the rules of the game in order to preserve and extend their privilege.

Skill Capital

Skill capital is the specialized knowledge that people accumulate through their work experience, training, or education. Skilled plumbers learn their craft through apprenticeship programs and years of on-the-job experience. Skilled doctors learn their craft primarily in medical schools, but their skills are developed further through work experience.

Skill capital is exchanged in a labor market, just as investment capital is used in connection with a financial market. Both plumbers and doctors try to get the highest return for their skill in the form of wages or fees, and they do this through collective associations like labor unions (United Auto Workers) or medical societies (American Medical Association). When skill capital is organized in the form of collective associations, there is greater likelihood of job security or high wages. Workers with unorganized skills (i.e., nonunion) or with low levels of skill are more vulnerable when dealing with employers or clients.

The most important source of skill capital in today's society is located in the elite universities that provide the credentials for the privileged class. For example, the path into corporate law with six-figure salaries and million-dollar partnerships is provided by about two dozen elite law schools where the children of the privileged class enroll. Similar patterns exist for medical school graduates, research scientists, and those holding professional degrees in management and business. After the credentialed skill is provided by elite universities, the market value of that skill (and its income- and wealth-producing capability) is protected by powerful corporations and professional associations. People in high income- and wealth-producing professions will seek to protect their market value not only for themselves but also for their children who will enter similar fields.

Social Capital

Social capital is the network of social ties that people have to family, friends, and acquaintances. These ties can provide emotional support, financial assistance, and information about jobs. Social capital is used by immigrants in deciding which communities they will settle in when they come to the United States. These same immigrants use social capital to get settled and to find jobs. Social ties are also used by doctors, lawyers, and other professionals to facilitate their affiliations with more or less prestigious organizations where they will begin to "practice" their work.

The basis of social ties can be found in school ties and in kinship, religious, and political affiliations. For example, graduates of elite universities often become the new recruits at national law firms, major corporations, foundations, and government agencies. A study by the Office of Management and Budget reports that 40 percent of foreign service professionals in the State Department come from eight Ivy League colleges. Another example is found in a story in the *New York Times* (November 10, 1995) about some of the appointments made of new lawyers to join the staff of New York State's new attorney general. One new employee is the daughter of the best friend of the state's U.S. senator; she is paid $75,000 a year. Another employee just admitted to the bar is the daughter of another lawyer who served on the attorney general's election committee; she is paid $60,000 a year.[8]

But social capital is used for more than just getting high-paid secure jobs. It is also used to solidify class interests by making sure that people marry within their corporate or professional class. For example, consider the type of "personal ad" that appears in many upscale magazines for the young urban professional:

Join the Ivy League of Dating. Graduates and faculty of the Ivies, Seven Sisters, Johns Hopkins, M.I.T., Stanford, U. of Chicago, CAL Tech, Duke, U.C. Berkeley, Northwestern, meet alumni and academics. The Right Stuff! Call XXX–XXX–XXXX.

One has to wonder what the "right stuff" is. These ads may appeal to people who are simply trying to meet someone on their intellectual level; but they could instead join MENSA, an association of people with high IQ. More likely it is an effort to match same-class individuals with credentialed skills. This is the way to get dual-earner-household doctors, attorneys, and corporate elites or the "mixed marriages" of doctors and fashion designers or artists who become the "darlings" of *People* magazine fare.

Although everyone has at least a minimal level of social capital, it should be clear that access to different forms of social capital (like consumption, investment, and skill capital) is distributed very unequally. Having a family member able to loan you $100 or a friend who works in a retail store and can tell you about a job opening is not the same as being a member of a fraternity or sorority at an elite university. Social capital refers to current memberships people hold in social networks that are linked to varying levels of organizational power, prestige, and opportunities. Individuals can be connected by strong ties (e.g., family members) or weak ties (e.g., acquaintances) to formal and informal social networks that are associated with varying levels of organizational resources and power. A person's position in these social networks provides access to information and opportunities that can be converted into important financial and social benefits. For example, the extent of investment capital owned or controlled can be the result of holding high positions in large organizations; paid and unpaid leadership positions in economic, political, or cultural organizations can be used to advance personal careers or provide opportunities for relatives and friends. Thus, social capital must be viewed as a class-linked resource that both protects and advances privilege and provides a barrier for those "upstarts" seeking to expand their generative capital.

GENERATIVE CAPITAL AND POWER

The residents of one zip code—10021—on New York City's Upper West Side contributed more money to Congress during the 1994 elections than did all the residents of 24 states.

—Ellen Miller and Randy Kehler *Dollars and Sense*, July–August 1996

The distribution of these scarce and valued resources—consumption capital, investment capital, skill capital, and social capital—is the basis for class inequality among individuals and families in America. This inequality is revealed when resources are converted into economic power, political power, and social power. Economic power is based on the resource of money (consumption capital and investment capital), and it usually is used to provide food, shelter, and clothing. People who have more economic power can buy more things and better things and thereby make their lives more comfortable and enjoyable. Money can be converted into other valued things like health care, which enables those with more money to live longer and healthier lives. Money can protect people when unfortunate or unforeseen events occur, like an earthquake, tornado, or flood. Recovering from these

RALL copyright © Ted Rall. Reprinted with permission of Universal Press Syndicate. All rights reserved.

natural disasters and from human disasters like unemployment or illness is possible when you have economic power. Money also has the special quality of being transferable to others and can also be used to transmit advantage.

Consumption capital can be used to procure social capital. For example, families with money can use it to help secure the futures of their children by purchasing special experiences through travel, tennis lessons, scuba diving, dance, and creative arts in the hope that such experiences will foster or strengthen social relationships with others having similar experiences. It is also done by buying entry into prestigious educational institutions that provide their students with lifelong advantages. Families who buy elite educational degrees for their children are using their consumption capital to develop both social capital and skill capital. Graduates of elite universities have a special advantage in converting their credentialed skill capital into better jobs. They establish the social contacts that can be used later in life to solidify or enhance their social position. Many families, recognizing the payoff that comes with a degree from an elite college, prepare their children with SAT prep courses in the eighth grade and private school education. In 2000–01, Harvard University received 19,009 applications for 1,650 places in the entering class. Those lucky enough to be selected can expect annual costs of

$35,400 per year for tuition, fees, room and board, and personal expenses. Clearly, these families are using their consumption capital to invest in the education of their children.

Three out of four families in the United States have very little economic power. Even so-called middle-class families on the "brink of comfort" (as they are sometimes described; see *New York Times* story by Charisse Jones, February 18, 1995) find themselves in a constant struggle to make ends meet. There are thousands of anecdotal stories about how people struggle to meet family expenses, but the most systematic evidence is provided by the U.S. Department of Labor in its preparation of a consumption budget for an average married couple with two children.[9]

Monthly Budget for Family of Four (1998 dollars)

Housing	$793	27.3%
Utilities	247	8.5
Furnishings	109	3.7
House operations	73	2.5
Food	555	19.1
Auto	558	19.2
Clothing	137	4.7
Health care	165	5.6
Entertainment	207	7.1
Other	64	2.2

This monthly budget totals $2,908, or $34,896 annually. In order to have this much money to spend each month, the household's gross annual income (before taxes) would have to be about $40,000. Moreover, this budget assumes one wage earner, because a number of monthly expenditures would increase with two wage earners. Less than one-half of American families earn enough money to live by the U.S. Department of Labor budget, and when they do, they are often two-earner families. Two people working full-time, each earning about $10 per hour, will have a combined annual gross income of about $41,000. If two people with children are working to make this income, then you will have to add childcare to the consumption budget, which can be from $100 to $300 a week. This middle-class budget for a family on the "brink of comfort" will produce nothing for savings, and little for retirement beyond social security taxes. If one or both of the wage earners in this family should experience unemployment for a month or longer, the family would be in serious difficulty.

If the hypothetical family just described is on the brink of comfort, what must things be like in a female-headed household with one or two children where the mother brings home about $1,000 a month from a $7.00-an-hour job as a retail clerk? This family is sitting on the official poverty line, or maybe one paycheck above or below it. Clearly, a household budget for three or four persons of $1,000 a month generates no economic power.

The problem facing three of every four families in the United States is not simply that they are just making ends meet—whether on $30,000 a year or $12,000 a year—but that their consumption capital is limited, unstable, and unpredictable. They cannot count on these resources over time in any predictable way, and if they should experience any period of joblessness they will face a serious crisis. Possession of stable and secure resources over time is the key to economic power. The predictability of resources allows people to plan and save in order to provide for the future. They can think about buying a home, sending a child to college, saving for retirement, or starting a business. Most American workers have very unstable incomes, even if they are sometimes earning what seems like a "high" salary. For example, take the case of the United Auto Worker employed in a General Motors assembly plant. During periods of peak production and heavy overtime, a worker might earn $5,000 per month. This is a $60,000-a-year job, assuming that the monthly salary continues all year. But that's the rub. When overtime disappears and production schedules are cut back because of overproduction, that $60,000 may be quickly cut to $40,000; or layoffs might reduce that income even more; at worst, the plant may be shut down and production moved to a lower-wage area in the United States or some other country—which is exactly what happened to hundreds of thousands of high-wage blue-collar workers in the 1970s, 1980s, and 1990s.

Political power is the result of collective actions to shape or determine decisions that limit or enhance peoples' opportunities. The tenants of a housing project can combine their time to collect signatures on a petition calling on the housing director to provide better services. Corporations in a particular sector of the economy can combine their money (economic power) to hire lobbyists who will seek to influence members of Congress to support or oppose legislation that will affect those corporations. Individuals and organizations with more economic power have a different set of opportunities for exercising political power than groups without economic power.

The clearest examples of how collective economic power can be converted into political power are in the area of corporate welfare—the practice of congressional action that provides billions of dollars in federal loans and subsidies to specific industries. More than $100 million a year goes to corporations like McDonald's, Pillsbury, and Sunkist to help them advertise their products in foreign countries. The Pentagon provides another $100 million a year to a group of semiconductor firms to help them compete internationally. This money goes not to small, struggling firms but to giants like Intel and National Semiconductor Corporation.[10] The total annual corporate welfare bill just from business tax preferences from the federal government was estimated at $195 billion in fiscal 2000.[11]

Groups with little economic power usually try to exercise political power through mass mobilization of persons with grievances. Bringing together hundreds or thousands of persons for a march on city hall conveys a visible sense of a perceived problem and an implied threat of disruption. The capacity to disrupt may be the only organized weapon available to those without economic resources. Such actions usually get the attention of political leaders, although it does not always produce the results desired by aggrieved groups.

Social power involves access to public services and the interpersonal networks that can be used to solve many of the day-to-day problems that confront most families. Public services like police, fire protection, and public transportation can provide people with the security to use public space for living, leisure, and getting to and from work, stores, and day-care facilities. Interpersonal networks consist of the informal groups and formal associations that are available in a community for persons with certain interests and concerns. The availability of community groups concerned about the presence of toxic waste dumps, the spread of crime, and the quality of the schools in their community provides opportunities for people to learn about many things in addition to toxic waste, police protection, and education. Such groups often provide links to information about jobs, or how to approach a local banker for a loan, or how to obtain information about financial aid for college students.

Opportunities to develop social power vary widely across groups. People who have jobs that provide little flexibility in their work schedules or are physically demanding may have little time or inclination for participating in community groups at the end of a hard day. Similarly, some jobs offer more opportunities than others to develop the interpersonal networks that can be drawn upon to help a family member find a job or to help in finding good and affordable legal assistance.

There is considerable evidence from social research that Americans with greater economic resources, and those holding upper managerial positions in organizations, are more likely to actively participate in a variety of community affairs.[12] These active participants accumulate information about community affairs and social contacts that can be used to advance or solidify the interests of one's social group. Some of the key players in this process of accumulating social power have been identified as women from professional families who are out of the labor force and have the discretionary time for civic affairs.[13]

An interesting example of how social power operates among the privileged classes is provided by the case of the Morrison Knudsen Corporation.[14] It happened that the chairman's spouse started a private charity organization to provide young women with alternatives to abortion. The spouse served as unpaid executive director of the charity and was apparently successful in obtaining donors to support its activities. The success of the charity could perhaps be traced to the fact that five of the charity's directors are the spouses of directors of Morrison Knudsen, and three of the directors of the charity are senior executives of the corporation. Thus, the spouse of the board chairman of Morrison Knudsen was able to use her social power to put together a charity organization capable of drawing upon the political and economic power of directors from the privileged elite. Such opportunities would certainly not be available to a community organization trying to oppose the location of toxic waste sites in their area or one trying to get the local police to be more responsive to the concerns of local citizens.

CLASS STRUCTURE AND CLASS SEGMENTS

The combination of capital and power can be used to describe the class structure of American society. One popular way of describing the class structure of a society is with a physical or geometric shape or image. The shape or image conveys the relative proportions of people in a society who have some valued thing, like money or education. The pyramid (figure 1.3), for example, illustrates a class structure in which a small percentage of a society (10 percent) has a great deal of the commodity, another 30 percent has a little less, and the majority (60 percent) has the least amount of the valued commodity.

Another frequently used image is the diamond (figure 1.4), which provides a different picture of the way valued things are distributed. The diamond image says that a small percentage (10 percent) of a society has a lot of something, another small percentage (10 percent) has very little of something, and most of the people (80 percent) are in the middle, with moderate amounts of the valued commodity.

In each of these class structures, the class positions of people can be simply designated as upper class, middle class, or lower class. Thus, the pyramid image represents a society in which most persons are lower class, and the diamond image represents a middle-class society. If asked to choose between the two societies depicted here, most people would probably choose the society represented by the diamond image, because most of the people are in the middle class. If you chose to live in the pyramid society, you would have a 60 percent chance of being in the lower class.

However, before choosing one of these societies in which to live, you might want a little more information. You might want to know about the particular attribute or characteristic that puts people in each class. Is it something they are born with, like skin color or physical size, or is it some characteristic they learn or acquire, like being a good hunter or a skilled craft worker? You might also want to know something about how people in each class live, in terms of basic necessities, material comforts, physical security, and freedom. Finally, it might be important to know if it is possible for people to change their class position within a lifetime or across generations, or if there are opportunities for their children to rise above the class into which they were born.

Thus, the image of a society as pyramidal or diamond-shaped provides an overall view of how people in that society are distributed on some valued characteristic or attribute. But it does not tell about the society's "rules" for determining or changing their class position.

Let us try to make all this a little more concrete by examining American society. Most efforts to portray the American class structure have focused on occupations

Figure 1.3   Pyramid Diagram of Class Structure and Class Segments

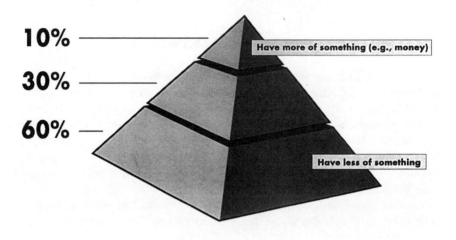

as the main determinant of the class structure and of people's positions in that structure. Occupations have been classified according to the public's opinion of the social standing or prestige associated with being a public school teacher, or a dentist, or a mechanic, or a machine operator. When large numbers of Americans are asked to rate occupations on a scale ranging from "excellent" to "poor" in social standing, they consistently place U.S. Supreme Court Justice, physician, and corporate manager at the top of the list; at the bottom are garbage collector, filling station attendant, and janitor. The prestige hierarchy of occupations has remained pretty stable in studies done over several decades and in different countries.[15] This has led some analysts to see occupational prestige as the basis of class structure in American society. They also assert that the term *class* is not meaningful because prestige is determined according to a continuous system of rankings of occupations, without any sharp boundaries or divisions between occupations.

However, if you look behind these prestige rankings to ask what it is that people are actually ranking, you will find that what is being evaluated is not simply the prestige of an occupation but also its income and power. In our society, the occupational structure as embedded in organizations is the key to understanding the class structure, and a person's occupation is one aspect of class position. But how do the hundreds of different occupations combine to create a structure of distinct classes with different amounts of economic, political, and social power? What aspects of occupations determine their position in the class structure?

People often speak of their occupation or their job as what they do for a living. An occupation or job describes how a person is related to the economy in a society or what one does in the process of the production of goods and services. An oc-

Figure 1.4   Diamond Diagram of Class Structure and Class Segments

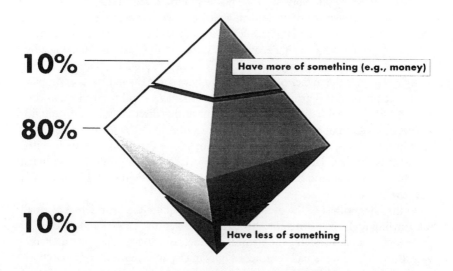

10% ────────── Have more of something (e.g., money)

80% ──

10% ────────── Have less of something

cupation or job provides people with the means to sustain life ("to make a living"); and the sum total of the work done by people in their occupations or jobs is the wealth generated by the economic system. In one sense there is a parallel or symmetric relation between the availability of jobs and the amount of wealth that is generated. The more people in a society are working at making a living, the better the economic health of the total society. But there is also a sense in which there is an asymmetric relationship between the well-being of working people ("how much of a living they make") and the total wealth that is generated. Some people contribute more to the total wealth than they receive for their work, as in the case of some workers whose wages are a fraction of the value of their products when they are sold. And some people may receive ten or twenty times more in income for their work than that received by others. So although there may be 130 million Americans involved in occupations and jobs for which they are compensated, their amount of compensation varies widely according to how they are related to the production process. There are a variety of ways in which people are related to the production process in today's economy.

The Privileged Class

The activity of some people in the system of production is focused on their role as owners of investment capital. Such a person may be referred to colloquially as the "boss" or, in more respectful circles, as a "captain of industry," an "entrepreneur," or a "creator of wealth," but in the language of class analysis they are all owner-employers. The owner may actually be the sole proprietor of the XYZ Corporation and be involved in the day-to-day decisions of running that corporation. But ownership may also consist in the possession of a large number of shares of stock in one or several corporations in which many other persons may also own stock. However, the ownership of stock is socially and economically meaningful only when (1) the value of shares owned is sufficient to constitute "making a living," or (2) the percentage of shares of stock owned relative to all shares is large enough to permit the owner of said shares to have some say in how the company is run. Members of this group (along with the managers and professionals) control most of the wealth in America. The point of this discussion is to distinguish owners of investment capital from the millions of Americans who own shares of stock in companies, who own mutual funds, or whose pension funds are invested in the stock market. The typical American stock owner does not make a living from that ownership and has nothing to say about the activities of the companies they "own."

On the lower rungs of the owner-employer group are the proprietors of small but growing high-tech firms that bring together venture capital and specialized knowledge in areas involving biomedical products or services and computer software forms. These are "small" businesses only in Department of Commerce classifications (less than $500,000 in sales), for they bear no resemblance to the Korean grocer, the Mexican restaurant owner, or the African American hair salon found in many American cities. They are more typically spin-off firms created by technical specialists who have accumulated some capital from years of employment in an industrial lab or a university and have obtained other investment capital from friends, family, or private investors.

A second activity in the system of production is that of manager, the person who makes the day-to-day decisions involved in running a corporation, a firm, a division of a corporation, or a section within a company. Increasingly, managers have educational credentials and degrees in business, management, economics, or finance. Managers make decisions about how to use the millions of dollars of investment capital made available to them by the owners of investment capital.

The upper levels of the managerial group include the top management of the largest manufacturing, financial, and commercial firms in the United States. These managers receive substantial salaries and bonuses, along with additional opportunities to accumulate wealth. Table 1.1 presents a typical pattern of "modest" compensation for the officers of a large firm in 2000. We refer to this compensation as "modest" because it is far below the multimillion-dollar packages of compensation for CEOs at IBM, AT&T, Disney or Coca-Cola (which range from $20 million to $50 million). But such distinctions are probably pointless, because we are describing executives whose wealth is enormous in comparison with others not in their class. For example, the top CEO in the group just listed also owns 100,000 shares of stock and has options for another 100,000 shares in the corporation he heads. The value of these shares fluctuates with the market value of the stock, which in the summer of 2001 was $31 a share, or about $3 million for the 100,000 shares.

Table 1.1   Compensation for Corporate Executives (2000)

Position	Annual Compensation	Bonus	Stock Awards
President and CEO	$745,385	$450,000	$2,028,125
Executive vice pres.	299,897	119,000	745,000
Executive vice pres.	273,846	120,000	558,750
Senior vice pres. and General Counsel	242,885	34,000	447,000
Senior vice pres. and CFO	275,192	128,000	558,750
Vice president	342,029	174,760	—
Executive vice pres.	322,400	5,000	—

Source: Based on data from the Annual Report and Proxy Statements, Great Lakes Chemical Corporation, 2001, Indianapolis, Ind.

The lower levels of the managerial group carry out the important function of supervising the work done by millions of workers who produce goods and services in the economy. The success of this group, and their level of rewards, is determined by their ability to get workers to be more productive, which means to produce more at a lower cost.

Professionals carry out a third activity in the economic system. This group's power is based on the possession of credentialed knowledge or skill, such as an engineering degree, a teaching degree, or a degree in public relations. Some may work as "independent professionals," providing service for a fee, such as declining numbers of doctors, dentists, and lawyers. But most professionals work for corporations, providing their specialized knowledge to enhance the profit-making potential of their firm or of firms that buy their services. The professional group is made up of university graduates with degrees in the professional schools of medicine, law, business, and engineering and in a variety of newly emerging fields (e.g., computer sciences) that serve the corporate sector. The possession of credentialed knowledge unifies an otherwise diverse group, which includes doctors who may earn $500,000 a year and computer specialists who earn $60,000 a year.

The potential to accumulate wealth is very great among certain segments of professionals. The mean net salary in 2001 for all physicians surveyed in one report was $196,000. There were great differences between the incomes of family practice physicians, who averaged $145,496 in 2001, and specialty physicians such as radiologists and oncologists, who averaged $255,223.[16] Unfortunately, these averages hide the salaries of graduates from elite medical schools and those affiliated with the most prestigious hospitals. Also absent is information about doctor's entrepreneurial activities such as ownership of nursing homes or pharmaceutical firms.

Similar opportunities for high income exist among lawyers, where partners at the nation's elite law firms average $335,000 and associates average $80,000 (1998). Even law professors at prestigious law schools have a chance to amass a small fortune while teaching and practicing law or consulting. A recent *New York*

Times story reported that a professor at Harvard Law School gave the school a bequest of $5 million.[17] The *Times* reported that the professor is "not one of the school's prominent moonlighters" and is "unlike Prof. Alan M. Dershowitz, the courtroom deity who has defended Leona Helmsley and Mike Tyson and is on the O. J. Simpson defense team." So how did the professor do it? By "writing and consulting."

Professors at elite universities who are in selected fields like law, medicine, business, biomedical engineering, or electrical engineering have opportunities to start high-tech firms and to consult for industry in ways that can significantly enhance income. Even "modest" activities, like becoming an outside director for a bank or industrial firm, can be very rewarding. A colleague in a business school at a Big Ten university who is a professor of management has been on the board of directors of a chemical corporation for twenty years. His annual retainer is $26,000. He gets an additional $1,000 a day for attending meetings of the board or committee meetings and $500 a day for participating in telephone conference meetings (the board meets six times a year, and committees convene from one to six times a year). Each nonemployee director gets a $50,000 term life insurance policy and a $200,000 accidental death and dismemberment insurance policy. After serving on the board for a minimum of five years, directors are eligible for retirement benefits equal to the amount of the annual retainer at the time of retirement. Retirement benefits begin at the time of the director's retirement from the board and continue for life.

Why does the president of this university, or its board of trustees, allow a professor to engage in such lucrative "outside activities"? Maybe it's because the president, whose annual salary is $200,000, holds four director positions that give him more than $100,000 a year in additional income.

Professionals in elite settings not only make six-figure salaries, but they have enough "discretionary time" to pursue a second line of activity that may double or triple their basic salaries. Not a bad deal for the professional class.

Not everyone with a credentialed skill is in the privileged professional class. We exclude from this group workers like teachers, social workers, and nurses, who despite their professional training and dedication fail to get the material rewards accorded to other professionals. Moreover, they are usually labeled as "semiprofessions," implying that they somehow fall short of the full professionals. This may be due to the fact that most of these "semiprofessionals" are women, and that their services do not provide direct benefits to the privileged class. They deal with people in nonproductive roles as students, patients, or human service clients, and they deal mostly with people without much in the way of consumption or investment capital. We also exclude university professors at nonelite schools. They are excluded because of the large number of faculty at hundreds of nonelite colleges and universities who make modest salaries; and many of them are not even employed in tenure track positions. We also exclude the thousands of attorneys working for legal services agencies, franchise law firms, and in public defender positions. Professionals in these positions are excluded because of limited job security, modest levels of income, and little investment capital. Thus, we distinguish between elite and marginalized professional groups, with only the former being in the privileged class.

The New Working Class

Finally, there is the large majority of Americans—employees who sell their capacity to work to an employer in return for wages. This group typically carries out their daily work activities under the supervision of the managerial group. They have limited skills and limited job security. Such workers can see their jobs terminated with virtually no notice. The exception to this rule is the approximately 14 percent of workers who are unionized; but even union members are vulnerable to having their jobs eliminated by new technology, restructuring and downsizing, or the movement of production to overseas firms.

This working group also consists of the many thousands of very small businesses that include self-employed persons, and family stores based on little more than "sweat equity." Many of these people have been "driven" to try self-employment as a protection against limited opportunities in the general labor market. But many are attracted to the idea of owning their own business, an idea that has a special place in the American value system: It means freedom from the insecurity and subservience of being an employee. For the wage worker, the opportunities for starting a business are severely limited by the absence of capital. Aspirations may be directed at a family business in a neighborhood where one has lived, such as a dry-cleaning store, a beauty shop, a gas station, or a convenience store. Prospects for such businesses may depend upon an ethnic "niche" where the service, the customer, and the entrepreneur are tied together in a common cultural system relating to food or some personal service. The failure rate of these small businesses is very high, making self-employment a vulnerable, high-risk activity.

Another sizable segment of wage earners, perhaps 10–15 percent, has very weak links to the labor market. For these workers, working for wages takes place between long stretches of unemployment, when there may be shifts to welfare benefits or unemployment compensation. This latter group typically falls well below official poverty levels and should not be considered as part of the "working poor." The working poor consists of persons who are working full time at low wages, with earnings of about $12,000 a year—what you get for working full time at $6.00 an hour.

Table 1.2 summarizes these major segments of Americans with different standing in the current economy. The groups are distinguished as (1) those who own capital and businesses; (2) those who control corporations and the workers in those corporations; (3) those who possess credentialed knowledge that provides a protected place in the labor market; (4) the self-employed, small business-owners

Table 1.2   Class Structure in America

Class Position	Class Characteristics	Percentage of Population
Privileged Class		
Superclass	Owners and employers. Make a living from investments or business ownership; incomes at six- to seven-figure level, yielding sizable consumption and investment capital.	1–2%
Credentialed Class		
Managers	Mid- and upper-level managers and CEOs of corporations and public organizations. Incomes for upper-level CEOs in seven-figure range, others six figures.	13–15%
Professionals	Possess credentialed skill in form of college and professional degrees. Use of social capital and organizational ties to advance interests. Incomes from 100K to upper-six figures.	4–5%
New Working Class		
Comfort class	Nurses, teachers, civil servants, very-small-business owners, and skilled and union carpenters, machinists, or electricians. Incomes in the $35–50K range but little investment capital.	10%
Contingent Class		
Wage earners	Work for wages in clerical and sales jobs, personal services, and transportation and as skilled craft workers, machine operators, and assemblers. Members of this group are often college graduates. Incomes at $30K and lower.	50%
Self-employed	Usually self-employed with no employees, or family workers. Very modest incomes, with high potential for failure.	3–4%
Excluded class	In and out of the labor force in a variety of unskilled, temporary jobs.	10–15%

who operate as solo entrepreneurs with limited capital; and (5) those with varying skills who have little to offer in the labor market but their capacity to work.

These segments of the class structure are defined by their access to essential life-sustaining resources and the stability of those resources over time. As discussed earlier, these resources include consumption capital, investment capital, skill capital, and social capital. The class segments differ in their access to stable resources over time, and they represent what is, for all practical purposes, a two-class structure, represented by a double-diamond (see figure 1.5). The top diamond repre-

Figure 1.5   Double-Diamond Diagram of Class Structure and Class Segments

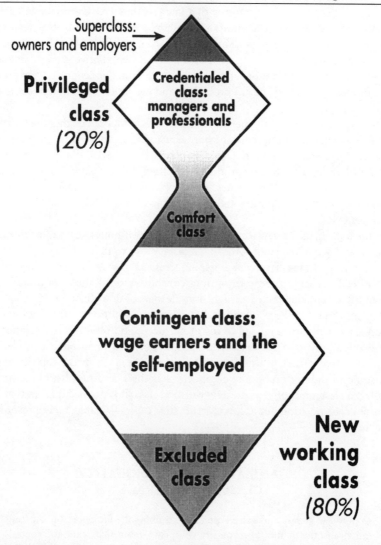

sents the privileged class, composed of those who have stable and secure resources that they can expect will be available to them over time. This privileged class can be subdivided into the superclass of owners, employers, and CEOs, who directly or indirectly control enormous economic resources, and the credentialed class of managers and professionals with the knowledge and expertise that is essential to major industrial, financial, commercial, and media corporations and key agencies of government. The bottom diamond is the new working class, composed of those who have unstable and insecure resources over time. One segment of this class has a level of consumption capital that provides income sufficient for home owner-ship and for consumption patterns that suggest they are "comfortable." Thus, we label this segment the comfort class, represented by school teachers, civil servants, social workers, nurses, some small-business owners, and skilled union-ized carpenters, machinists or electricians. Despite their relatively "high" incomes ($35,000–60,000), the comfort class is vulnerable to major economic downturns or unforeseen crises (e.g., health problems) and has limited investment capital to buffer such crises.

The largest segment of the new working class is composed of the wage earners with modest skills and unpredictable job security. This group includes, for exam-ple, machine operators in manufacturing plants, bank clerks, and the supervisors who could be displaced by new production technology, computerized information systems, or other "smart" machines. Their job insecurity is similar to that of the growing segment of temporary and part-time workers, thereby making them the contingent class.

At the bottom of the new working class are those without marketable skills who move in and out of the labor force in temporary jobs or in seasonal employment. They are the excluded class, who either are treated as "waste," because they are no longer needed as either cheap labor or as consumers, or fill the most undesirable jobs in restaurant kitchens or as nighttime cleaners of downtown buildings.

It is important to keep in mind that a person's location in the double-dia-mond class structure is related to his or her occupation but not determined by that occupation (as is the case in the production and functionalist models of class, discussed earlier in this chapter). Some lawyers are in the top diamond, and some in the bottom. Some engineers, scientists, and professors are in the privileged class, and some in the new working class. It is not occupation that de-termines class position but access to generative capital—stable, secure resources over time.

ORGANIZATIONS AND INEQUALITY: CLASS, GENDER, RACE

> As powerful as race and racism are in determining the life chances to African Americans, the politics of inequality will play a more significant and central role, both inside the black community, and in its relations with other groups. In short, class matters, and the battle for economic fairness will in many respects be the most fundamental factor in the future of African-American politics.
>
> —Manning Marable, *The Black World Today,* February 22, 2000

While our primary concern is with examining the nature and consequences of the new class structure in the United States, we also recognize that inequality has many faces. It is our view that a wide array of class as well as gender and race-based forms of inequalities exist in American society, and that they are grounded in and linked to large organizations, especially corporations, and the resources that they control.

As we noted earlier, social class membership reflects peoples' possession of four forms of generative capital. We also pointed out that access to and possession of various levels of all types of generative capital depend on the nature, level, and types of organizational affiliations that individuals hold. For example, an individual might hold an upper-level executive or managerial position with a corporation. The dollar value of this affiliation is expressed through the consumption capital (i.e., salary) and investment capital (e.g., stock options) held by that individual. Organizational affiliations that generate high levels of consumption and investment capital would also be likely to produce high levels of social capital through informal and formal social and business ties to other individuals with similar types and levels of organizational affiliations.

But class inequality, with its oppositional groupings of privileged and working classes, is not the only structure of dominance found in contemporary American society. There is also gender inequality and racial/ethnic inequality, which establishes oppositions between women and men, and between persons of color and Whites. Sometimes gender and racial/ethnic inequalities are expressions of class inequality, in that poor women and poor African Americans and poor Hispanics are denied access to opportunities for a good education and good jobs. In these cases, gender and racial/ethnic inequalities reinforce class inequality by placing women, Blacks, and Hispanics with low incomes, limited educational credentials, and no influential social connections in subordinate positions in the economic, political, and cultural sectors. However, sometimes gender and racial/ethnic inequalities affect the lives of women and non-Whites for reasons other than class inequality. When women or African Americans with educational credentials or work experience are denied good jobs, or promotion opportunities, it may be simply because of discrimination based on gender or race.

It is our view that understanding the structures and processes that undergird the origins and reproduction of class as well as gender- and racial/ethnic-based forms of inequality must begin with a focus on organizations. To clarify and illustrate how organizationally based factors underlie and are critical to all three forms of inequality, we begin by considering this question: What factors facilitate or impede people's access to organizational affiliations with stable, resource-rich organizations at the levels and types of links (e.g., occupation) that yield the high levels of all (or most) forms of generative capital associated with privileged class membership? The short answer to our question involves organizational policies and practices that structure the processes by which people gain access to organizational affiliations at various levels and types. Organizational policies and practices that shape and guide the affiliation process (especially where employment decisions are concerned) are routinely claimed by policy-making and policy-executing organizational representatives to operate according to principles of meritocracy.

However, substantial evidence documents that such policies actually function as class-, gender-, and racial-biased gatekeeping mechanisms.[18]

We view organizational policies and practices governing affiliation processes as being comprised of two "inequality scripts," one formal, the other informal. At the formal level, these scripts identify the organizational roles (e.g., career positions) and specify the formal credentials necessary to access the roles (e.g., educational level or experience). The informal level represents the covert dimension of affiliation decisions made by organizational gatekeepers. At this level, informal qualifications including class background, gender, and racial/ethnic membership enter into affiliation decisions. In most organizations we are likely to find not one, but several inequality scripts. Hiring practices for positions at the nonprivileged class level are likely to be handled by middle-level managers in personnel or human resources departments. Filling affiliations at the privileged class level, such as hiring/promoting senior executives, are typically directed by senior, privileged-class members of the organization.

Upper-level positions, or positions on career ladders to the top, are typically filled via inequality scripts that selectively advantage the children, friends, and associates of current members of the privileged class. High-level positions are compensated by high incomes, are linked to long career ladders within the organization, and typically require elite educational credentials. Persons from privileged-class backgrounds are most likely to successfully negotiate the organizational affiliation process and "fit" into these organizational roles that demand and yield high levels of generative capital. This is the case because they benefit indirectly from various forms of family "sponsorships" and "investments" that frequently result in elite educational credentials.

Abundant evidence exists that women and Blacks especially have been negatively affected by organizationally based inequality scripts in at least two respects. First, working-class women and Blacks have historically been more likely than working-class White males to be employed in smaller and less capitalized organizations, resulting in lower wages, fewer benefits, and greater job insecurity.[19]

Second, even when working-class women and Blacks have been able to get jobs with resource-rich organizations, they are often employed in gender and racially segregated jobs. There is substantial evidence that the American workplace is segregated by gender and race. Women comprise 95 percent of nurses, but only 22 percent of doctors; 98 percent of dental assistants, but only 10 percent of dentists; 98 percent of secretaries; 86 percent of elementary school teachers; 97 percent of receptionists; and 78 percent of cashiers.[20] The top occupations for Black and Hispanic men are truck driver, janitor, security guard, assembler, construction laborer, farm worker, cook, and gardener. The occupations with the highest levels of gender and racial segregation are also those with the lowest incomes.[21]

Third, when women or people of color rise to privileged-class positions, the promotion process often includes an invisible "glass ceiling" and/or tokenism.

These features are evident in studies that have documented the disproportionate representation of White males versus women and Blacks in accessing organizational affiliations at privileged-class levels.[22] Women in management positions are often viewed as having dual commitments to work and family, and thus as less suitable for fast-track careers. Some have suggested that women in upper management often forgo high-demand, high-reward positions, selecting instead mommy-track options that permit them to get less demanding work assignments (less travel, no night or weekend assignments), in return for more time outside of work.[23] However, even if these decisions are viewed as "choices," they are made by women who know that if they want to have a career they will still have to work the "second shift" at home. African Americans who have benefited from affirmative action policies to attain upper-management positions in corporations are often placed in racialized positions involved with Black consumer markets or dealing with politically based community issues.[24]

In everyday life, gender and racially based forms of inequality are more often reported in the mainstream media—and often more visible and more readily identifiable at personal levels—than class-based inequality. The persistence of tradition-based, informal social scripts organized around social identity hierarchies based on gender and race help sensitize and reinforce individual and collective attention to inequalities in these areas. Traditionally, these informal scripts have "assigned" White males to positions of dominance vis-à-vis women and Blacks. The informal evidence that appears to support these scripts and the male privileges written into them help create resentment and divisions among working-class men, women, and people of color.

The gender- and race-based inequalities and grievances experienced in everyday life make it more difficult for working-class men, women, and people of color to recognize their common *class interests* as members of the working class. Also, the immediate and personalized experiences of gender- and race-based inequalities tend to distract most members of the working class from the organizationally based sources of critical class, gender, and racially based inequalities and grievances. Most people fail to recognize that such inequalities are grounded in and linked much more closely to the organizationally based inequality scripts that create and perpetuate class divisions than to informal, micro-level social scripts. Even though we view class-, gender-, and race-based inequalities as organizationally based and driven, we also view class inequalities as qualitatively different from gender and racial grievances. This is the case because we believe class inequalities transcend gender and racially based grievances and have the potential to unite all members of the new working class in efforts to promote changes that would reduce all three forms of inequality.

In our view, a focus on social class is central to understanding major features and trends in our society today. Gender and racial inequalities are real and far from unimportant as features and experiences. But returning to class provides us with a unifying image of structured inequality.

THE NEW AMERICAN
CLASS STRUCTURE DEFINED

The gap between the haves and have-nots is greater now than at any time since 1929.

—Edward N. Wolf, *Top Heavy: The Increasing Inequality of Wealth in America and What Can Be Done about It,* 1996

Figure 1.5 provides a picture of the new American class structure as a "double diamond," divided between the privileged and those lacking the privileges that come with money, elite credentials, and social connections. This two-class structure is composed of approximately 20 percent privileged Americans and 80 percent nonprivileged Americans. Members of the employer, managerial, and professional classes have a stable income flow, employment stability, savings, pensions, and insurance. Their positions in the economy enable them to use their resources to accumulate more resources and to ensure their stability over time. The new working class has little in the way of secure resources. Their jobs are unstable, as they can be eliminated by labor-replacing technology or corporate moves to offshore production. Only marginal professionals and craft workers possess some skills that provide short-term security, but even their skills are being eroded by new technology, the reorganization of work, and the decline of union power.[25]

This image of class structure in American society is based on three important principles that define the new American class structure and how it works in practice.

Class Structure Is Intergenerationally Permanent

One of the most significant aspects of class structures is their persistence over time. The inequality that a person experiences today provides the conditions that determine the future. This aspect of class structure is rarely discussed by the media or even by scholars devoted to the layer-cake image of inequality. In fact, most discussion of class structure views that structure, and one's place in it, as temporary and ever changing. The belief in equality of opportunity states that regardless of where a person starts out in life it is possible to move up through hard work, motivation, and education. Similarly, the overall structure is viewed as changing, as revealed in statistics on the median income, the expanding middle class, or the declining percentage of the population living below the poverty line. In short, the popular image of class differences is that they are temporary and constantly changing. But in fact, nothing could be further from the truth when it comes to the new class system in the United States.

The "rules of the game" that shape the class structure are designed to reproduce that structure. Let's consider a few of those "rules" and how they work.

First, our legal system gives corporations the right to close down a plant and move the operation overseas, but it does not give workers a right to their jobs. Owners and employers have property rights that permit wide latitude in making decisions that impact on workers and communities. But workers' jobs are not viewed as a property right in the law. The protected right to a secure job would provide workers with a stable resource over time and modify their vulnerable situation in the class system.

Second, people in privileged classes have unrestricted opportunities to accumulate wealth (i.e., extensive consumption capital and investment capital). The accumulation process is based on tax laws that favor the rich, a variety of loopholes to avoid taxes, and an investment climate that enables the rich to get richer. The share of net worth and financial wealth going to the top 20 percent of the population is staggering (see figure 1.2). One out of five Americans owns almost everything, while the other four are on the outside looking in.[26]

This extraordinary disparity in wealth not only provides a clear picture of the polarized two-class structure; it also provides the basis for persistence of that structure. Because inheritance and estate laws make it possible to do so, wealth is transmitted across generations, and privilege is thereby transmitted to each succeeding generation. At the end of May 2001, the United States Congress passed a new tax bill that included the elimination of the federal estate tax, thereby enabling the privileged class to transmit their wealth without tax penalty. This was part of President Bush's tax reform proposal that will provide significant tax reduction for people with six-figure earnings, but only modest reductions for middle- and low-income families. Moreover, there were no reductions in payroll taxes, including those supporting Social Security and Medicare, which account for a much higher percentage tax on lower-income families than on those in upper-income brackets.

Another feature of the American class structure that contributes to its permanence is the sheer size of the privileged class. It consists of approximately 20 million households, or between 40 million and 50 million people. A class of this numerical size, with its associated wealth, is able to fill all the top positions across the institutional spectrum. Moreover, it is able to fill vacant positions or newly created positions from among its own members. Thus, recruitment of talented women and men from the nonprivileged class will become increasingly rare.

Third, the so-called equality of opportunity in America is supposed to be provided by its system of public education. Yet everyone who has looked at the quality of education at the primary and secondary levels knows that it is linked to the class position of parents. Spending per pupil in public schools is tied to property taxes, and therefore the incomes of people in school districts. Schools in poor districts have the poorest physical facilities, libraries, laboratories, academic programs, and teachers.[27] Some of the children who survive this class-based public education are able to think about some sort of postsecondary education. But even here the game is stacked against them.

Going to college is based on the ability to pay the costs of tuition, and, unless living at home, room and board. Even at low-cost city colleges or state universities, the expenses exceed what many working-class families can afford. On the other hand, even if college attendance were not tied to ability to pay, it is not likely that many youngsters from low-income families would think of college as a realistic goal, given the low quality of their educational experience in primary and secondary grades.

Thus, the "rules of the game" that are the foundation for the class structure are designed primarily to transmit advantage and disadvantage across generations. This persistence of structure exists even when there are instances of upward social mobility—the sons and daughters of working-class families who move into the professional classes. This upward mobility occurs in a very selective way and without changing the rules of the game. For example, when the birthrates among the privileged class fail to produce enough children to fill all the high-level, organizationally based professional positions for doctors, lawyers, engineers, computer specialists, and managers, it may become necessary to recruit the most talented young men and women from the working class. The most talented are identified through special testing programs and curriculum tracking and are encouraged to consider advanced education. "Elite" colleges and universities develop special financial and academic programs for talented working-class students, and a variety of fellowship programs support those with financial need. Upward mobility is made possible not by changing the rules of the game but by "creaming" the most talented members of the working class. The creaming process has the dual effect of siphoning off potential leaders from the working class and supporting the belief in equality of opportunity and upward mobility.

There Is No Middle Class

The functionalist view of class structure, as noted earlier, presents a "layer-cake" image of class differences. There are six or eight classes made up of groups of occupations that differ in prestige, education level, or income. These differences between classes are not sharp and discontinuous but gradual shadings of difference between one class and another. The layer-cake image encourages a belief in a "center" or a "middle class" that is large and stands between the upper and lower classes. The different groups in the middle may think of themselves as being "better off" than those below them and may see opportunities to move up the "ladder" by improving education, job skills, or income.

This image of class structure is stabilizing, in that it encourages the acceptance of enormous material inequality in American society because of the belief that anyone can improve his or her situation and become one of the "rich and famous." It also encourages greater attention to the small differences between groups and tends to ignore the large differences. For example, many Americans are hardworking men and women who often work two jobs to make ends meet but are limited by these low-wage and no-benefit jobs. These people are often most hostile to the welfare benefits provided for people who are just below them in income. A working poor person gets $12,000 a year for full-time work, whereas a welfare family may get the same amount in total benefits without working. However, these same working poor rarely have their hostility shaped and directed toward the rich, who may be more responsible for the low wages, limited benefits, and inadequate pensions of the working poor.

The belief in a middle class also allows politicians to proclaim their support for tax breaks for what they call the middle class while debating whether the middle class includes those with incomes up to $250,000 a year or only those earning $100,000.

In our conception of class structure, there can be no middle class. Either you have stable, secure resources over time, or you do not. Either you have a stable job and income, or you do not. Either you have secure health insurance and pensions that provide adequate income, or you do not.

Classes Have Conflicting Interests

In the functionalist, layer-cake theory of class structure, each class is viewed as having more or less of some valued quality or commodity such as education, occupational skill, or income. Members of each class may aspire to become members of classes above them, and they may harbor negative opinions and prejudices of those in classes below them. But classes, in this theory, are not fundamentally opposed to one another. Of course, there is often discussion of why members of certain classes might support or oppose particular political candidates because of their social or economic policies. But these alliances or oppositional views are seen as linked to shifting issues and are not tied to class interests.

Our view is more closely aligned with the central ideas of Marxist class analysis, which stresses the role of exploitation and dominance in class relations. We see in the United States today the two large classes of privileged and working-class Americans having fundamentally different and opposed objective interests, so that when one class improves its situation the other class loses. The advantages of the privileged class, expressed in its consumption capital, investment capital, skill capital, and social capital, are enjoyed at the expense of the working class. Any action to make the resources of the working class more stable—by improving job security or increasing wages and pensions, for example—would result in some loss of capital or advantage for the privileged.

Given the existence of oppositional interests, it is expected that members of the privileged class will work to advance their interests. As employers they will seek to minimize worker wages and benefits and to fight efforts by workers to organize. As media owners, filmmakers, and writers they will produce cultural products and information that undermine efforts by the working class or African Americans to organize and advance their interests. Think, for example, about how the media and opinion makers are quick to cry "class warfare" whenever a social critic such as Ralph Nader points to the wealth of the privileged. Think also about how the opinion makers react to African Americans like Al Sharpton or Louis Farrakhan when they seek to occupy positions of leadership, or social critics like Noam Chomsky when they criticize U.S. policies. They are usually ignored or marginalized by media and opinion makers.

These three principles—class structure has intergenerational permanence, there is no middle class, and classes have conflicting interests—provide a basis for understanding the central defining features of the American class structure. We have, in effect, tried to answer the question, What is class inequality? In the next chapter we address the question, How does class inequality work?

NOTES

1. Don Stillman, "The Devastating Impact of Plant Relocations." *Working Papers* (July–August 1978): 42–53.

2. Cecelia Burns Stendler, *Children of Brasstown: Their Awareness of the Symbols of Social Class* (Urbana: University of Illinois Press, 1949); Robert G. Simmons and Morris Rosenberg, "Functions of Children's Perceptions of the Stratification System," *American Sociological Review* 36 (1971): 235–49; Scott Cummings and Del Taebel, "The Economic Socialization of Children: A Neo-Marxist Analysis," *Social Problems* 26 (December 1978): 198–210; Anthony M. Orum and Roberta S. Cohen, "The Development of Political Orientations among Black and White Children," *American Sociological Review* 38 (1973): 62–74; Jeannette F. Tudor, "The Development of Class Awareness in Children." *Social Forces* 49(1971): 470–76.

3. For an orthodox Marxian view, see Charles H. Anderson, *The Political Economy of Social Class* (Englewood Cliffs, N.J.: Prentice Hall, 1974). For a sophisticated neo-Marxian analysis, see Erik O. Wright, *Classes* (London: Verso, 1985), and *Interrogating Inequality* (London: Verso, 1994). Wright's early analysis emphasizes ownership and control of the means of production and control of labor as the defining conditions for determining class location; his more recent work adds control of organizational assets and ownership of skill assets.

4. For a good example of the functionalist multidimensional model of class, see Dennis Gilbert and Joseph A. Kahl, *The American Class Structure* (Chicago: Dorsey Press, 1987). For an approach that emphasizes the status or prestige of occupations, see Peter M. Blau and Otis D. Duncan, *The American Occupational Structure* (New York: Wiley, 1967).

5. Data not shown. See Lawrence Mishel, Jared Bernstein, and Joh Schmitt, *The State of Working America, 2000–2001* (Ithaca, N.Y.: Cornell University Press, 2001), p. 83.

6. Melvin Oliver, Thomas M. Shapiro, and Julie E. Press, "'Them That's Got Shall Get': Inheritance and Achievement in Wealth Accumulation," in *Research in Politics and Society*, vol. 15, ed. Richard E. Ratliffe, Melvin Oliver, and Thomas M. Shapiro (Greenwich, Conn.: JAI Press, 1995).

7. Katherine S. Mangan, "A Shortage of Business Professors Leads to 6-Figure Salaries for New Ph.D.'s" *Chronicle of Higher Education* 47 (May 4, 2001): A12–13.

8. Clifford J. Levy, "New York Attorney General Remakes Staff by Patronage," *New York Times*, November 10, 1995.

9. David S. Johnson, John M. Rogers, and Lucilla Tan, "A Century of Family Budgets in the United States," *Monthly Labor Review* (May 2001): 28–45.

10. This estimate was provided by the Cato Institute and reported in Stephen Moore, "How to Slash Corporate Welfare," *New York Times*, April 5, 1995.

11. U.S. Congress, House Committee on the Budget, *Unnecessary Business Subsidies*. 106th Congress, 1st sess., 1999, Serial 106–5.

12. See Alan Neustadtl and Dan Clawson, "Corporate Political Groupings: Does Ideology Unify Business Political Behavior?" *American Sociological Review* 53 (1988): 172–90; Robert Perrucci and Marc Pilisuk, "Leaders and Ruling Elites: The Interorganizational Bases of Community Power," *American Sociological Review* 35 (December 1970): 1040–57; Robert Perrucci and Bonnie L. Lewis, "Interorganizational Relations and Community Influence Structure," *Sociological Quarterly* 30(1989): 205–23; and David Knoke, *Organized for Action: Commitment in Voluntary Associations* (New Brunswick: Rutgers University Press, 1981).

13. Arlene Kaplan Daniels, *Invisible Careers: Women Civic Leaders from the Volunteer World* (Chicago: University of Chicago Press, 1988).

14. Diana B. Henriques, "Ties That Bind: His Directors, Her Charity." *New York Times*, March 21, 1995.

15. Robert W. Hodge, Paul M. Siegel, and Peter H. Rossi, "Occupational Prestige in the United States: 1925–1962," in *Class, Status, and Power*, ed. Reinhard Bendix and Seymour M. Lipset (New York: Free Press, 1966); Robert W. Hodge, Donald J. Treiman, and Peter H. Rossi, "A Comparative Study of Occupational Prestige," in Bendix and Lipset, *Class, Status, and Power*.

16. Michael Romano, "2001 Physician Compensation Report," *Modern Health Care*, August 13, 2001, 30–34.

17. David Herzenhorn, "The Story behind the Generous Gift to Harvard Law School," *New York Times*, April 7, 1995.

18. Richard L. Zweigenhaft and G. William Domhoff, *Diversity in the Power Elite: Have Women and Minorities Reached the Top?* (New Haven: Yale University Press, 1998).

19. Barbara Reskin and Irene Padavic, *Women and Men at Work* (Thousand Oaks, Calif.: Pine Forge Press, 1994), Chapter 4; Donald Tomaskovic-Devey, *Gender and Racial Inequality at Work* (Ithaca, N.Y.: ILR Press, 1993), Chapter 4.

20. Randy Hodson and Teresa A. Sullivan, *The Social Organization of Work*, 2d ed. (Belmont, Calif.: Wadsworth, 1995), Appendix, Table 1.

21. Reskin and Padavic, *Women and Men at Work*, p. 120.

22. Ibid., Chapter 5.

23. Felice N. Schwartz, "Management Women and the New Facts of Life," pp. 415–21; Arlie Hochschild and Anne Machung, "The Second Shift: Working Parents and the Revolution at Home," pp. 376–90, in Amy S. Wharton, ed., *Working in America* (Mountainview, Calif.: Mayfield Publishing, 1998).

24. Sharon M. Collins, "The Marginalization of Black Executives," *Social Problems* 36(October, 1989): 317–31.

25. Harley Shaiken, *Work Transformed: Automation and Labor in the Computer Age* (New York: Holt, Rinehart and Winston, 1985); David F. Noble, *Forces of Production: A Social History of Industrial Automation* (New York: Knopf, 1984).

26. Edward N. Wolff, *Top Heavy: The Increasing Inequality of Wealth in America and What Can Be Done about It* (New York: Twentieth Century Fund, 1996).

27. Jonathan Kozol, *Savage Inequalities: Children in America's Schools* (New York: Harper, 1991).

2

Separate Realities:
The Dream and the Iceberg

To the C students I say, You, too, can be President of the United States.

—George W. Bush, Yale University Commencement Address,
Nation, June 11, 2001

Strange and Ugly things are about to happen.

—Hunter S. Thompson, *Generation of Swine*, 1988

"The fruit doesn't fall far from the tree." Prior to the first three decades of the post–World War II period, this aphorism linking children, parents, and social class stood at the intersection of commonsense observations and social science research.[1] From wealthy elites to White trash, personal experiences, popular culture, and sociological data supported the widely shared consensus that social class tends to "run in families." But following World War II, real wages (adjusted for inflation) for working-class Americans began trending in an upward direction. At the same time, the postwar period witnessed improving opportunities for advancement from the working class into more prestigious occupations.[2] For members of the newly forming blue- and white-collar middle-income groups of the 1950s and 1960s, these patterns provided a reassuring vision of a comfortable and secure future for themselves and their children. Improving living standards combined with traditional beliefs in the open-ended economic and social opportunities in America contributed to an enthusiastic, shared embrace of the American Dream as a cultural ideal among members of virtually all social classes.[3] The American Dream is predicated on the belief that humble class origins are not destiny. It is grounded in the faith that American society offers equal and unlimited opportunities for upward mobility for those who embrace a strong work ethic, regardless of class ori-

41

gins. Although the details of the dream vary, Americans typically envision it as including economic comfort and security (an above-average and secure income), higher educational levels (for themselves and their children), a rewarding job, home ownership, and personal freedom.[4]

The U.S. mainstream media generate a steady stream of reports conveying the impression that the American Dream is alive, well, and within reach. In 1999, for example, the booming stock market energized high-profile coverage of the "Everyone's Getting Rich" theme by TV programs such as CNN's *Talkback Live* and by magazines including *Money* and *Newsweek* cover stories.[5] Although the 2000–2001 market meltdown tempered this exuberant storyline, media promotion of the dream-as-within-reach continues. In 2001 CBS news anchor Dan Rather published *The American Dream*. His book focused on the expansive opportunities America supposedly offers all citizens and provided compelling vignettes of individuals who, through commitment and perseverance, achieved individualized versions of the dream. The book's message was clear: Freedom and opportunity exist in abundance in the United States, allowing the dream to be realized by those with courage, ambition, and a strong work ethic.[6] As an updated variation of the Horatio Alger tales more than a century ago (discussed in chapter 6), Rather's book illustrates the ongoing media promotion of and popular interest in this topic.

In reality, and somewhat paradoxically, the dream runs both parallel with and counter to the general trend whereby children tend to replicate the class ranking of their parents. For privileged-class families, the dream offers a reassuring sense of continuity: The advantaged positions of parents can and will be passed on to, and extended by, their children. For working-class families, the dream represents a possible future of reward, fulfillment, and affluence—especially for their children. To some extent, the early post–World War II period seemed to provide middle-income families with evidence that the dream was within reach. Thus, among members of the nonprivileged classes, the dream has resonated powerfully as a mythic cultural ideal and—at least for a time—as an attainable reality. Today, however, there is growing evidence that opportunities for realizing the American Dream, especially for those in the new working class, are being shredded by powerful economic, political, and cultural forces that are part of the emerging, iceberg-like new class society.

The purpose of this chapter is threefold. First, we clarify our iceberg metaphor and consider the taboo nature of class analysis. Second, we identify three important "above the waterline" trends associated with the new class system that are at odds with the ideals of the American Dream. Third, we consider two dynamic dimensions of the new class system (discussed in detail in later chapters) that we view as submerged "beneath the waterline" of conventional social analysis—conflicting class interests and the structures and processes that maintain and legitimate the class system. Bridging and blending elements of critical sociology, trend analysis, and popular culture, this chapter explores the social geography and dynamic forces at the heart of the new class society. It previews themes of power, greed, betrayal, deception, heartbreak, resistance, and hope that are central to the story of social class in America. As we will see, it is an edgy and twisted tale previewing a long, strange trip intended for travelers, not tourists.

THE THREE-THOUSAND-MILE ICEBERG

The first lesson of sociology ... [is] the importance of class consciousness.

—Charles H. Anderson, *Toward a New Sociology*, 1974

Like a huge iceberg stretching coast to coast across the American social horizon, the new class society combines a dramatic profile of sharply defined and disturbing visible features with a submerged and hidden mass of potentially society-wrecking forces and consequences. Compared with the social structure of the recent past, the new structure is sharply leaner in the middle, larger and much meaner at the bottom, and increasingly "secessionistic" among the privileged few at the top. In the terms of figure 1.5, it is a structure that combines privilege, security, and affluence for those in the upper diamond with increasing peril, insecurity, and eroding incomes for those in the lower diamond.

Recent political events and public opinion trends suggest that many Americans are interested in class inequality issues and increasingly aware of some of the most visible features of the class iceberg. The trail of evidence supporting this view includes, for example, widespread public interest in and support for the class-based politics of Ralph Nader during and after the 2000 presidential campaign.[7] It continues in the form of grassroots interest in and support for progressive political challenges to the expansion of global capitalism as manifested by organized citizen action efforts in 2001.[8] Further evidence is apparent in recent demonstrations mounted in opposition to unfettered corporate-controlled global trade, as illustrated by large-scale protests in 1999 (Seattle), 2000 (Washington, D.C.) and 2001 (Quebec City, Canada).[9] Recent national poll results indicating growing public disenchantment with the rich and large corporations represents yet another aspect of growing public concern regarding class inequalities.[10]

Coexisting with public interest in class inequalities are contrarian social trends and developments that suggest many Americans are confused, divided, and distracted where such issues are concerned. These tendencies are considered in detail in chapter 7, but high levels of public interest in escapist forms of popular culture, especially those promoted by the mass media, illustrate this point. Mushrooming TV-driven celebrity-lifestyle reports, survivor, weak-link, "reality" programming, *WWF SmackDown*, millionaire-style game shows, and 24–7 sports coverage involve working-class audiences in a kind of parallel universe of entertainment where fantasies are realized and the grim realities of class inequalities recede from view. Other forms of evidence indicative of confusion about or distraction from class inequality issues can be found in high levels of public involvement in escapist or passive forms of consumer-oriented activities including recreational shopping, religious fundamentalism, websurfing, legalized gambling, and diversionary films.

The existence of mixed forms of evidence where class inequality is concerned suggests that Americans generally lack a consistent focus on, or clear understanding of, the submerged dimensions of the class iceberg—including conflicting class interests, the structures and processes that legitimate the class system, and the possibilities for changing it.[11] We think the paradoxical trends of interest/concern and confusion/distraction stem, at least in part, from the taboo nature of social class in America.

SOCIAL CLASS: THE LAST TABOO

> People in the United States don't like to talk about class.... Class is not discussed or debated in public because class identity has been stripped from popular culture.
>
> —Gregory Mantsios, *Race, Class, and Gender in the United States*, 1995

Mainstream American social institutions today openly address a wide range of issues that until recently have been considered taboo as topics for public discussion. Despite the expanding inventory of previously censored cultural and lifestyle issues (e.g., sexual orientation, abortion, rape, family violence, race and gender inequalities), social class analysis remains the last taboo. In fact, as far as class analysis is concerned, a virtual blackout exists among mainstream social institutions, and few public forums exist for wide-ranging discussions of the nature and consequences of social-class structures and inequalities. It is one topic that has been consistently marginalized and ignored by the schools, the mass media, and by most political leaders.

Class analysis is not a curricular theme or topic at the primary or secondary level and is seldom included in university-level courses.[12] In the print media, newspaper editors have little interest in, or sympathy for, working-class interests or issues. Majorities ranging from 54 percent to 60 percent of editors report that they side with business in labor disputes and also on business-worker conflicts involving issues such as minimum-wage increases and plant-closing legislation.[13] Every major U.S. daily newspaper includes a separate business section, but none includes a separate "class" or even "labor" section, and none of the 1,483 daily U.S. newspapers includes a regular commentary column written by a socialist or social democrat.[14] A similar situation exists in the electronic media, as illustrated by a study of the three network television evening news programs, which found the networks devote only 2 percent of total airtime to workers' issues.[15]

Politicians typically avoid class-based rhetoric—especially the use of language and policy labels that might openly emphasize or reveal the conflicting economic and political interests of working-class versus privileged-class members. This is the case because political candidates who violate what amounts to an unwritten rule against framing class inequalities as legitimate public policy issues risk being accused of promoting divisive and disruptive "class warfare" by privileged-class-based mainstream media pundits and their class cousins, "responsible" public officials, politicians, and business leaders.[16]

During the 2000 election, Green Party presidential candidate Ralph Nader experienced the full range of media and political sanctions that accompany violations of the unwritten class rule. Nader was initially ignored and then later castigated by most mainstream media outlets, especially for "interfering with the . . . two party system."[17] Reporters often sought to discredit Nader by painting him as "out of touch" with mainstream voters and by pointing out that he favored rhetoric that *USA Today* said sounded like "the early 1900s Socialist halls in New York."[18] Politically, Nader was not only excluded from the presidential debates by a commission reflecting the wishes of both major parties, he was even "banned from the debate audience."[19] In a comment that in many ways illustrated recurring media efforts to both demonize and trivialize Nader's candidacy, *Crossfire* commentator Bill Press asked, "What could be scarier . . . than Freddie Krueger meets *The Blair Witch 2* in *The House on the Haunted Hill?* Two words: Ralph Nader."[20] It is interesting to note that in many ways, the negative media and political treatment afforded Nader as a progressive populist candidate paralleled what had occurred four years earlier during the reactionary populist presidential campaign of Pat Buchanan.[21]

Al Gore, the centrist Democratic presidential candidate in 2000, was also reminded of the risks associated with even minor violations of the unwritten class rule. In a speech to the Democratic Convention, Gore pledged to take the side of working families against "powerful forces and powerful interests." The next day Ronald Brownstein, a *Los Angles Times* reporter, wrote: "In a time of peace and prosperity, Al Gore is betting that Americans want to go to war." "By using the word 'war,' Brownstein was echoing the Bush campaign's denunciation of the Gore speech as 'class warfare.'"[22] But unlike Nader, Gore's campaign was never centered around working-class-based grievances, interests, policies, or themes. However, even occasional populist-like rhetorical references in a few of Gore's speeches were sufficient to earn the enmity of privileged-class media pundits. After the election, Chris Matthews of *MSNBC* and *CNBC* expressed a sentiment that appeared to be widely shared by mainstream media reporters and pundits: "Al Gore . . . ran a negative campaign based on resentment, especially class and economic . . . that the American people just . . . wanted to tune out." Looking back on the 2000 election results, the mainstream media consensus appeared to be: "Al Gore ran too far to the left."[23]

Mainstream media and political establishment-driven hostility to Nader's class-based campaign themes, the parallel critique of Gore's tepid and transient use of

populist language, and the sanctions imposed on both candidates stem from privileged-class control over these institutions. The sanctions imposed on Nader and
Gore for violating the "no class rule" are likely to serve as sobering lessons to
wannabe candidates in future campaigns. The 2000 elections made it clear that
candidates who invoke strong or even weak forms of class analysis as campaign issues or as the basis for public policy proposals violate a powerful, privileged-class-
enforced taboo. Candidates who call attention to class-based inequalities become
predictable lightning rods for attacks from privileged-class members in the media,
political, and business arenas.

Only two exceptions exist to the political taboo on class issues. First, it is acceptable to discuss the "middle class." Because large numbers of Americans identify themselves as middle class, references to this group actually serve to disguise
and mute class differences because the term is so inclusive—it includes nearly
everyone. When the mainstream media profile middle-class problems, as in the
New York Times 1996 "Downsizing of America" series, it creates public interest and
a large market. However, such accounts do not address conflicting class interests.
For example, the central message of the *Times* series was one not of class interests
but of individual effort: "The lesson, heard again and again, [is] that while government and business can do some things, in the end workers have little to fall
back on but themselves."[24]

More recently, many mainstream media reports have focused on how new economic uncertainties and problems are affecting middle-class workers, investors,
consumers, and families. The content and images of such reports are obviously intended to appeal to middle-income readers and viewers beset by rising economic
anxieties. Profiles of middle-class families and individuals coping with mounting
job losses and shrinking stock portfolios were at the heart of page-turning
Newsweek and *Time* cover stories in 2001.[25] Like the earlier *Times* "Downsizing" series, the recent wave of media dispatches on the latest middle-class economic concerns avoids any attention to how such conditions might be grounded in
conflicting class interests. Instead, these accounts tend to parallel the individual-
level focus of the "Downsizing" series.

The second exception to avoidance of the class issue includes mass media
glimpses into the lives of the privileged class as well as tours of the excluded
class. Television programs often take viewers to both destinations. The glamour
of life at the top is routinely showcased on tabloid-style TV "newsmagazine"
(e.g., *Access Hollywood, Entertainment Tonight, EXTRA!*) profiles of wealthy
show business, sports, and occasional charismatic corporate elites. The grim realities of life-at-the-bottom experiences turn up on occasional PBS or cable TV
documentaries concerning homelessness, welfare, and related issues. However,
these inside looks at the extremes do not involve class analysis. Instead, they
serve as models or morality tales, the first to aspire to and the other to avoid. The
two models are never presented as causally related: One is not rich because the
other is poor.[26]

The taboo nature of class is a product of institutional biases that discourage and deflect media and public discussions of class issues—especially conflicting class interests. These biases are grounded in privileged-class interests in encouraging public silence on, or even confusion about, class issues. Members of the superclass have an especially strong interest in not having public attention called to their class-based advantages or to broader class inequalities, because a close examination of the origins of and basis for these inequalities—including the wealth, power, and privileges of this class—might call the entire class system into question.[27]

Superclass preferences for avoiding public discussions of class inequalities are paralleled by the interests of credentialed class members in maintaining their own positions of comfort and security. Allied with and following the lead of their superclass sponsors, many credentialed class members are rewarded for helping to keep class analysis out of the arena of public discourse. In their roles as government officials, organizational managers, media producers, and community leaders, credentialed class professionals often pursue organizational policies and practices that have the effect of deflecting public attention away from class inequalities and class-based analysis of social issues and problems.[28]

Individuals and groups proposing higher taxes on the wealthy are attacked by many credentialed-class political leaders and media editors as advocating destructive and divisive "class warfare."[29] Whether the topic is taxes, income, educational opportunities, or other class-based inequalities, privileged-class advantages and working-class disadvantages are topics to be avoided, not discussed.[30] Social inequalities (when they are considered) are most often framed by credentialed-class leaders as problems of gender, race, or other cultural-ethnic divisions—or perhaps the result of personal or genetic flaws (e.g., a "predisposition" to problems limiting achievement, such as alcoholism, drug use, or mental illness).[31] Class analysis is out of the picture.

Although privileged-class interests are major factors underlying the class taboo, we do not see a "class conspiracy" driving the neglect of class issues in public discourse. Rather, we see the superclass and its credentialed-class allies as bound by shared cultural assumptions, values, experiences, worldviews, and organizational memberships.[32] These shared qualities lead to strong, common commitments to maintaining the economic, political, and cultural status quo.[33] Such views lead members of these two classes (and most Americans) to explain material and social success (or failure) on the basis of factors other than class-based resources.[34]

Despite the taboo driving public neglect of class analysis, it has become virtually impossible for workers and their families, politicians, reporters, and even privileged-class members to ignore several class-related trends that are transforming the nature of social geography and social experiences in the United States today. Although these trends are increasingly obvious and growing in significance as subjects of public commentary and even political discourse, they are only the most visible and obvious features of the social-class iceberg today.

ABOVE THE WATERLINE:
NEW CLASS-SOCIETY TRENDS

Globalization, heightened immigration, the decline of unions, and the ongoing shift from manufacturing to services all continue to press down the wages of middle- and low-income workers.

—Aaron Bernstein, *Business Week,* April 23, 2001

While American society has always been divided by substantial class inequalities, recent developments in the economic, political, and cultural arenas have produced substantial changes in the U.S. class system. Three important class-related trends fall above the waterline of the class iceberg in the sense of being increasingly visible and obvious sources of growing public concern and commentary: (1) class polarization, (2) downward mobility, and (3) class secession.

Class Polarization

We are now the "two nations" predicted by the Kerner Commission thirty years ago. Only the dividing line . . . is class.

—Patrick Buchanan, *The Great Betrayal,* 1998

Class polarization refers to the growing division of the United States into two main classes: the privileged class and the new working class. This trend is the result of four convergent developments that have become increasingly evident since the early 1970s. First, a pattern of growing income inequality has placed increasing numbers of persons and families in the upper- and lower-income ranges, with declining numbers in the middle. Second, a corresponding pattern of falling real wages for most working Americans has eroded living standards for all but those in the highest income groups. Third, a pattern of shrinking fringe benefits for more and more workers has emerged, particularly in the areas of health care and pensions, resulting in ever higher levels of economic insecurity among middle- and low-income groups. Finally, the increasing use of contingent, contract, temporary, and part-time workers by a wide range of employers has contributed to a growing "contingency workforce" characterized not only by low pay and prestige but also by vanishing-point levels of job security.

Once upon a time—and not too long ago—the material realities of life for middle-income Americans were such that references to this group by social scientists and journalists as the "middle class" were understandable, if overstated. Of course, as is often the case with class issues, the precise meaning of this concept was (and is) somewhat elusive and subject to debate. Even so, since the end of World War II, for most mainstream academic researchers as well as for the American public, middle-class status has typically been associated with an identifiable core of economic and social resources. These include "respectable" jobs (mid-level prestige or higher), stable, mid-level (or higher) incomes, security benefits (health care, pensions), and participation in conventional social institutions such as churches, schools, community groups, and other voluntary organizations.[35]

For the first three decades of the post–World War II period, most academic definitions and popular perceptions of an American middle class were grounded in an economic reality whereby a majority of middle-income individuals and families possessed stable jobs and experienced gradually rising real incomes.[36] The reinforcement of these core features among middle-income groups by additional material resources anchored middle-class status (e.g., expanding levels of employer-provided benefits including health care, life and disability insurance, vacation time, and pensions).[37] This stable resource base made it possible for many middle-income families, over time, to increase their stock of investment capital (by homeownership and investment savings), skill capital (by additional education and by sending children to college), and social capital (using more free time to participate in various social groups and organizations). The material and social resources of middle-income Americans, combined with widespread egalitarian cultural beliefs of America as a middle-class nation, were reflected in subjective class-identification studies that from the 1940s through the 1980s consistently found majorities of Americans identifying themselves as members of the middle class or upper middle class.[38]

In short, the middle-income–middle-class linkage was predicated on workers' access to organizational resources that went beyond income alone. In post–World War II America, job stability and rising real wages combined with other forms of economic and social resources typically available to middle-income households produced a large group that could readily realize a modest version of the American Dream. The resource base of middle-income Americans at this time could even provide a platform for upward mobility, especially for their children. However, "sometime around 1973, the American dream stopped working. That's the year that the real (inflation-adjusted) hourly wage for nonsupervisory workers— almost three-quarters of the workforce—peaked. Since then, it's fallen."[39] As real wages fell, other major structural changes in this period transformed the national economy in ways that produced a "crisis of the American Dream."[40]

Although not causes in and of themselves, as the most visible features of the class polarization process, the four convergent developments cited earlier in this section offer a starting point for understanding the extent to which the material realities of the U.S. middle-income group have been transformed. An examination of these developments, in conjunction with the evidence concerning the distribution of consumption capital (income) and related material resources in the last thirty years, supports our view that a polarized new class system has emerged— minus a middle class. (A portion of what has been called the middle class is best understood as part of the comfort-class segment in our model.) To many who considered themselves part of the middle-class, the period since the early 1970s brought the "end of the world"—as they knew it.

Many may not agree with our view that America has no middle class; but national polls reflect a growing public awareness of major changes in the class system. In a significant shift from previous studies of class membership perceptions, by the mid-1990s a majority (55 percent) of Americans identified themselves not as members of the middle class but as members of the working class.[41] As the new century began, most sociologists also agreed that at the very least, the middle class is under siege or declining. Many introductory sociology college texts now include discussions of the declining or disappearing middle class as a separate topic, typically in chapters dealing with stratification or class inequalities.[42]

Declining Middle Incomes and Wages

Although all U.S. national income studies include middle ranges, middle-income levels do not necessarily translate into middle-class status. Moreover, as we noted in chapter 1, even the numbers of what are often called middle-income Americans have declined since the 1970s. The realities of shrinking numbers of middle-income workers and declining real wages for average wage earners over the past three decades are reflected in a variety of recent income studies.

One study that examined the distribution of total employment by per hour wage levels from 1973 through 1999 documented decreases in the size of mid-level wage groups and increases in the size of the lowest and highest wage groups (all per-hour wages reported in 1999 dollars). The proportion of workers in three middle-income wage groups (from $8.19 to $24.57 per hour) declined from 67.8 percent of all workers in 1973 to 61.3 percent in 1999. In contrast, the percentage of workers in the lowest wage group ($8.19 or less per hour) increased from 23.6 percent of all workers in 1973 to 26.8 percent in 1999; the highest-wage worker group (over $24.57 per hour) grew from 8.6 percent in 1973 to 12.0 percent of all workers in 1999.[43]

As might be expected, changes in the distribution of low-, middle-, and high-wage jobs were paralleled by shifts in the distribution of annual incomes. Our chapter 1 summary of annual U.S. family income trends over the past thirty years revealed that the percentage of middle-income Americans declined sharply, while the percentages in the top and bottom income groups increased. Using more expansive definitions of middle income, other recent studies have found similar patterns over the past thirty years. Underscoring the shift toward greater income inequality over the last thirty years, the U.S. family income "Gini ratio" (a measure of income inequality whereby zero equals total equality and 1 equals total inequality) increased from .356 in 1973 to .430 in 1998.[44]

The last 30 years witnessed not only declining proportions of middle-income workers and families but also reductions in real earnings for many Americans. Average per-hour real wages (in 2000 dollars) declined for production and nonsupervisory workers (about 80 percent of the workforce) from $14.37 in 1973 to $13.61 in 2001. Thus, in 2001 the average weekly earnings of production and nonsupervisory workers amounted to $544.40 (40 hours at $13.61 per hour). If a worker earned this amount for 52 weeks, her income would have been $28,309. This amount was $1,581 *less* in real income (adjusted for inflation) than the $29,890 annual income a worker in the same classification would have earned in 1973 (at $14.37 per hour in 2000 dollars).[45]

As the middle-income group was shrinking and real wages falling for many workers, shifts in income inequality also occurred *within* the new working class, especially along the lines of gender and racial/ethnic membership. This trend is reflected in hourly wages shifts within occupational sectors and in changes in median family incomes. In blue-collar and service occupations (about 50 percent of all male workers and 25 percent of all female workers), men fared less well than women in average hourly wage rate changes over the past thirty years. Male blue-collar and service wages *fell* from $15.51 and $12.89 per hour in 1973 to $13.90 and $11.01 in 2000 (all amounts in 2000 dollars). By contrast, female wages in these areas remained virtually unchanged, standing at $9.48 and $8.14 per hour in 1973 and moving only slightly to $9.49 and $8.00 in 2000 (well below male wages). Wages in white-collar jobs (47 percent of male workers and 73 percent of female workers) increased for both groups. Average hourly wages (in 2000 dollars) for white-collar male workers rose from $20.58 in 1973 to $22.69 in 2000; female white-collar wages increased from $12.49 in 1973 to $15.13 in 2000 (also well below male wages).[46]

Within the new working class, workers of color, as a group, experience the greatest income inequalities. This pattern is evident in comparisons of median family income trends by race and ethnicity. White median family income rose from $45,311 in 1973 to $50,106 in 1999 (in 1999 dollars). Black median family income also increased from $24,837 in 1973 to $30,053 in 1999, but obviously still lagged far behind White income. Hispanic median family income actually *fell* from $30,761 in 1973 to $30,262 in 1999. Median family income changes are especially interesting in that they occurred during a period when the annual number of paid working hours logged by married couples in all racial and ethnic groups increased sharply. In White married households with children (head of household age 25–54) the total average annual hours worked (husbands and wives combined) increased from 3,302 in 1979 to 3,689 in 1998. Among Black married couples, working hours increased more than for Whites, rising from 3,227 in 1979 to 3,843 in 1998. Hispanic married couples also increased their hours, though by less than for Blacks and Whites, moving from 3,082 hours in 1979 to 3,415 in 1998. (One full-time job at 40 hours per week multiplied by 50 weeks would equal 2,000 hours per year.)[47]

The evidence concerning income trends supports the conclusion that there has been a growing polarization of income in the United States. Using census bureau information, the Economic Policy Institute (EPI) provides a useful way of illustrating the extent of inequality concerning income redistribution in the United States. The EPI reports the shares of aggregate (total) national income received by U.S. families divided into five quintile groups, arrayed by income levels from the lowest 20 percent to the highest 20 percent.

Drawing upon EPI and census bureau data, figure 2.1 summarizes several aspects of family income levels and redistribution trends in recent years. First, it illustrates, using side-by-side comparisons, the shares of national income received by families in each quintile group for 1980 and 1999. Second, the first line at the bottom of the figure reports the percentage changes in family income shares from 1980 to 1999 for each quintile group. Finally, the last line at the bottom of the figure provides a summary of 1999 family income ranges for each quintile (in 1999 dollars).[48]

During the 1980–1999 period, each quintile group experienced changes in the percentage of aggregate income received, ranging from highly positive to highly negative. The top 20 percent experienced a 15 percent increase in its share of national income (from 41.1 percent in 1980 to 47.2 percent in 1999), whereas the other four quintiles all experienced decreases in their shares of national income. These ranged from a modest loss of 6 percent for the fourth quintile (dropping from 24.4 percent to 23 percent) to a whopping 19 percent loss for the bottom quintile (dropping from 5.3 to 4.3 percent). The changes in income shares for these five groups reflect the reality that income was redistributed over the 1980–99 period—in an upward direction.

The income ranges reported as the last line of figure 2.1 provide a context for considering the impact of upward income redistribution. The income range for the bottom quintile in 1999 included all families with incomes up to $22,826 (in 1999 dollars). This means not only that families in this group have the lowest incomes but also that they will be most affected by income losses because they have the fewest resources to begin with. Yet this group suffered the greatest loss in income share during the 1980–99 period. The income ranges for the second quintile ($22,826 to $39,600), the middle quintile ($39,600 to $59,400), and the fourth quintile ($59,400 to $88,082) provided these groups with greater cushions (compared with the bottom quintile) to absorb income losses. Of course, the top quintile, with an income range of $88,082 and up, needed no cushion; it increased its income share by 15 percent.

The growing gap between top and bottom income groups is even more evident when we compare changes in the shares of income *after federal taxes.* According to a 2001 Congressional Budget Office (CBO) study, in 1981 the after-tax income share received by the top 5 percent of U.S. households was 19.2 percent, while the bottom 40 percent received only 17.7 percent. In 1997 (the most recent year for which data were available), the after-tax income share of the top 5 percent ($245,900 average after-tax annual income, 1997 dollars) had grown to 25.8 percent, but the bottom 40 percent share had shrunk to 15 percent ($17,500 average after-tax annual income). Under the 2001 tax law, the CBO projected the after-tax income share received by the top 5 percent would remain constant, but that the bottom 40 percent income share would be *reduced* to 14.9 percent.[49]

Top-earning groups have far outdistanced average wage earners over the past two decades, but the very highest paid groups have done the best. In 2000, "cash

Figure 2.1 Family Income Shares and Changes, by Quintile Group, 1980–1999

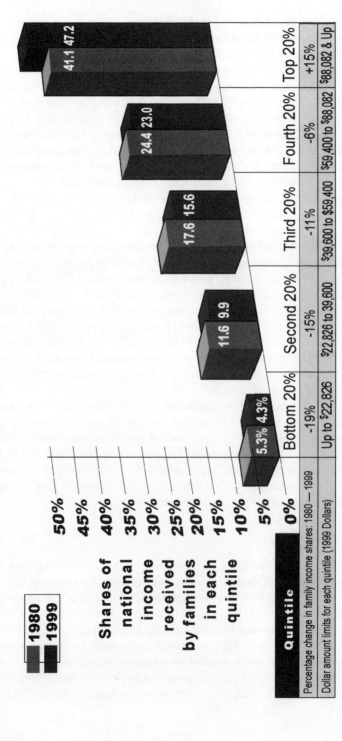

Quintile	Bottom 20%	Second 20%	Third 20%	Fourth 20%	Top 20%
Percentage change in family income shares: 1980 — 1999	-19%	-15%	-11%	-6%	+15%
Dollar amount limits for each quintile (1999 Dollars)	Up to $22,826	$22,826 to 39,600	$39,600 to $59,400	$59,400 to $88,082	$88,082 & Up

Source: Economic Policy Institute, "Family Income Share, Limits," pp. 1, 7.

compensation for the CEOs at 365 of the largest U.S. companies increased 18 percent in 2000 [over 1999]." The total annual average pay for CEOs in the top 365 firms in 2000 averaged $13.1 million (cash compensation plus bonuses).[50] Over the past twenty years, the average annual compensation of corporate CEOs at major U.S. firms increased by over 900 percent from $1.3 million in 1980 to $13.1 million in 2000 (in 2000 dollars). At the same time, the average annual incomes of production workers actually *decreased* by 1.3 percent from $28,950 in 1980 to $28,579 in 2000.[51] Minimum-wage workers did even worse. They experienced a 20 percent decrease in their real average incomes, dropping from about $13,062 in 1980 to $10,088 in 2000.[52] If production and minimum-wage workers had received 900 percent pay increases (like CEOs) since 1980, in 2000 their annual incomes would have been $260,550 and $90,792 respectively.

In 1980 total annual CEO compensation was 45 times what production and nonsupervisory workers earned. But like the Energizer Bunny, the CEO group kept going and going. In 1990, the CEO-to-average worker pay ratio grew to 96:1. It jumped to 236:1 in 1996 and then skyrocketed to 458:1 in 2000.[53] According to *Business Week*, in 2000 two CEOs, with overlapping tenure at Citigroup, were the highest paid: John Reed, $293 million, and Sanford Weill, $224 million. Eight other CEOs received total pay of more than $100 million dollars in 2000. In addition to skybox-level incomes, the value of stock options many CEOs receive can dwarf the economies of small nations. At the end of 2000, Lawrence Ellison, Oracle CEO, held $3.4 billion in unexercised stock options. Three other CEOs held over $1 billion each in such options and six others held options worth from $371 to $848 million.[54]

Few minority members or women become CEOs. One study found that minorities make up only about 1 percent of *Fortune* 500 top executives.[55] *Business Week*, in an analysis of 825 companies, found that women accounted for only 171 of the 4,341 highest-paid executives and less than 1 percent of the CEOs in 2000. When women get to the top, they earn less than men. "For the top 20 highest-paid male executives, total compensation averaged $138.5 million [in 2000], while the 20 best-paid females barely eked out $11.2 million apiece."[56]

Losses in Benefits

Although executives are doing well, members of the new working class, as we have seen, generally find their incomes shrinking. In recent years, the falling incomes of many workers have also been matched by reductions in fringe benefits. During the 1979–94 period (adjusted for inflation), "the average value of benefits including employer-provided health insurance, pension plans, and payroll taxes grew [by] just $.04 per year." More recently, fringe benefits for average-wage, private-sector workers (i.e., employer-paid pension plans, insurance [health and life], and payroll taxes [the employer portion of Social Security and unemployment taxes], declined from 19.3 percent of workers' total compensation in 1990 to 17.6

percent in 2000. Also in this period (1990–2000), employee benefits fell from an average of $3.76 to $3.34 per hour (in 1999 dollars).[57]

Reductions in pension and health care coverage over the past several years illustrate the extent to which workers' benefits have fallen. The proportion of workers covered by employer-provided pensions has declined and so has the quality of such plans, which tend to fall into two categories. First, defined-benefit plans "guarantee a worker a fixed payment based on pre-retirement wages and years of service; these are generally considered the best plans from a worker's perspective." Second, defined-contribution plans provide for employer contributions to an individual worker's retirement account (to which workers often can add).[58]

The proportion of full-time private sector workers in medium and large firms (100 workers or more) covered by defined-benefit pension plans fell from 84 percent in 1980 to 50 percent in 1997. For workers in small firms, such coverage declined from 20 percent in 1990 to 15 percent in 1996.[59] The proportion of all private sector workers covered by all types of employer-provided pension plans declined from 51.1 percent in 1979 to 49.2 percent in 1998. Male workers in the private sector saw pension coverage (of all types) fall from 56.2 percent (1979) to 50.9 percent (1998). Minority members fared even worse. For Black and Hispanic workers, pension coverage fell from 46.4 and 38.3 percent (1979) to 42.4 and 28.4 percent (1998). By contrast, the percentage of women workers covered by employer-provided pensions in the private sector rose from 42.8 percent in 1979 to 46.8 percent in 1998.[60]

The fact that the proportion of workers covered by all types of employer-provided pensions declined only slightly in the 1979–98 period "was most likely due to the expansion of 401(k) and other 'defined contribution' pension plans." The share of workers in such plans rose from 13 percent in 1975 to 42 percent in 1997. Under these plans, retirement income depends upon the investment options provided by employers and upon investment decisions workers make over time. In both cases, workers are often presented with substantial limitations and uncertainties that can make retirement income problematic and unpredictable. "Therefore, the shift from traditional defined-benefit plans to defined-contribution plans represents an erosion of pension quality."[61]

Regarding health care, the share of workers covered by employer-provided health care plans, where employers pay amounts ranging from partial to full premiums, declined from 70 percent of private sector workers in 1979 to 63 percent in 1998. This trend affected all groups of workers. From 1979 to 1998, health care coverage for male workers fell from 75 to 66 percent and from 62.2 to 58.6 percent for female workers. During the same period, coverage for Whites fell from 71.6 to 66.4 percent; Black health care coverage dropped from 64.1 to 58.4 percent and coverage for Hispanics fell from 60.9 to 44.6 percent.[62]

Parallel with declining health care coverage were increased premium costs for workers, and increased percentages of workers were required by employers to help fund their health care plans. The increase in health care premiums paid by workers rose from an average of $122 per month in 1996 to $145 per month in 1999.[63] The proportion of full-time private sector workers in medium and large firms (100 workers or more) required to make contributions for self medical coverage increased from 26 percent in 1980 to 69 percent in 1997; for family medical coverage the percentage of workers required to make contributions increased from 46 percent in 1980 to 80 percent in 1997.[64]

Growing Contingent Work

Workers' wages and benefits fell in part due to the growing use by employers of more non-full-time workers to reduce labor costs. The alternatives to full-time employment include a number of work arrangements variously referred to by researchers and journalists as "contingent" or "nonstandard" work.[65] Despite the lack of comprehensive trend data on contingent work,[66] different forms of information suggest that employers are employing more workers outside of full-time work arrangements.[67] In 1999 about 25 percent of all U.S. employees were contingent workers, meaning they were employed in "nonstandard work arrangements." This category includes regular part-time work, independent contractors, and all other forms of nonstandard work (temps, on-call, contract firms). The distribution of contingent work follows familiar patterns of gender- and minority-based inequalities. Women made up 56.7 percent of temporary workers in 1999 and Black, Hispanic, and younger workers (16 to 24) were overrepresented in substandard temp and on-call work. Contingent workers "generally earn less and receive fewer fringe benefits than workers with similar skills in regular full-time jobs." Wages average about 20 percent less (per hour) for women and men working part-time or as temps compared with similar workers in full-time jobs. Regarding benefits, in 1999 only 8.5 percent of temporary workers received employer-provided health insurance and only 5.8 percent were included in employer pension plans.[68]

The trend of increasing contingent work has been paralleled by declining levels of unionization among U.S. workers. The share of U.S. wage and salary workers who are union members fell from 24 percent in 1973 to 13.5 percent in 2001.[69] The falling rate of unionization directly lowers wages and fringe benefits for many workers as unionized jobs disappear. Also, as union rates decline, "there is less pressure on non-union employers to raise wages (a 'spillover' or 'threat effect' of unionism."[70]

Increasing contingent work and falling unionization rates have contributed to reductions in job stability. The percentage of workers reporting long-term job tenure (10 or more years on their current job) declined from 41 percent in 1979 to 35.4 percent in 1996. As the proportion of workers in long-term jobs fell, the median years of tenure held by workers with the same employer also declined over the last thirty years.[71] More recent data suggest a continuation of mid-1990s job instability trends as 2001 witnessed a record pace of layoffs and rising unemployment that intensified as the year ended.[72]

Mainstream media reports suggest that increasing job insecurity simply reflects the new nature of work life in the global economy and that workers can actually benefit from such trends.[73] In reality, worker access to long-term jobs is important because such "jobs . . . are the kinds of employment situations that provide workers with the best potential for sustained wage growth, good fringe benefits, and a feeling of employment security."[74] However, more workers are finding stable, long-term employment more difficult to find. It is apparent that the trends of declining incomes and fringe benefits are related to the growth of contingent work, declining unionization levels, and diminished job security for more and more members of the new working class. These developments combined with sharp increases in income and wealth for members of the privileged class have generated a growing division of the United States into a society of haves and have-nots: class polarization.

Downward Mobility

> Most Americans have a lower net worth [today] than they did . . . when this greatest stock market rally in history began.
>
> —Bob Harris, *EXTRA!* July–August 1999

Downward mobility is one type of vertical movement possible in class-stratified societies. Vertical social mobility refers to movements by individuals or groups up or down across class boundaries and often involves generational comparisons. Intergenerational vertical mobility occurs when an individual rises above or falls below the class ranking of his or her parents (e.g., an individual with working-class parents rises as an adult to membership in the superclass). Intragenerational vertical mobility occurs when an individual rises above or falls below the class ranking he or she held at an earlier point in adult life without reference to his or her parents' class ranking (e.g., a physician who—for whatever reasons—falls to a position as a laborer). Social mobility also can be horizontal, as might occur when an adult worker moves from one occupation of average prestige and pay to another with similar prestige and pay levels.[75]

When sociologists track vertical social mobility, those using functionalist models typically utilize a combination of income, job prestige, and educational attainment as indicators of class. Production model advocates are more likely to focus on an individual's role in the production process (laborer, manager, owner) as a guide to class rank. Functionalist model studies of vertical social mobility in the United States in the 1960s and 1970s using occupational prestige rankings as indicators of class position found substantial occupational mobility occurring mainly in an upward direction. By contrast, production model studies focusing on capitalist property ownership as an indicator of class found little evidence of intergenerational mobility into the "capitalist property ownership class" in the 1980s and

1990s.[76] More recent research using functionalist model approaches suggests that upward intergenerational social mobility in the 1990s was becoming more difficult in the United States—especially for the poor.[77]

Downward mobility refers to the experience of falling in terms of social class membership. The concept has been used as way of summarizing the economic, social, and psychological losses many middle-income (or above) workers have experienced due to job losses related to economic restructuring in the United States. The label spotlights the "falling from grace" experience of middle-income workers displaced from their jobs and often discovering they could not find new work that would replace the income, health, pension, and job security benefits of their former jobs. For many workers, the results of job loss include sharp, permanently impaired living standards, diminished long-term economic security, anger, self-doubt, depression, guilt, and dislocated personal relationships.[78]

Downward mobility was initially used by researchers to describe the job displacement experiences of blue-collar workers (jobs lost due to plant closings, automation, or layoffs). More recently, the term has also been applied to diverse groups of workers, including managerial and professional white-collar employees who have lost their jobs due to corporate "restructuring" or "downsizing" (permanent staff reductions claimed necessary for efficiency). As a result of social science research and media coverage of factory closings and related job losses from the 1980s to the present, downward mobility entered the public lexicon as a label for what came to be a high-profile, savage, and persistent social trend.[79]

The personal effects of downward mobility have figured prominently in mass media reports on this topic. Examples include the *New York Times* "Downsizing of America" series and book (1996) and more recent (2001) cover stories in *Newsweek* and *Time*.[80] Stories of downward mobility made (and still make) for compelling first-person media reports, and as a social trend downward mobility is hard not to notice. The reality and fear of downward mobility have served, and continue to serve, as major sources of anxiety, grief, dislocation, and frustration for millions of American workers and their families.

Research findings using functionalist or production model approaches tend to support the conclusion that downward mobility became an increasingly common experience for large numbers of American workers and their families in the 1980s and 1990s.[81] Although our distributional model does not include a middle class, we agree that downward mobility may be one effect of job losses among middle-income groups and that the phenomena represents an important and persistent social trend. From the perspective of our model, we would view downward mobility as occurring when members of class segments in the upper portion of the new working class (e.g., the comfort class) experience substantial, job-related resource losses involving consumption capital and economic power. When such losses shift workers and their children into the depths of the contingent or excluded class segments, then we would say downward mobility has occurred.[82]

It is clear that downward mobility is largely driven by job losses due to displacement and downsizing. However, three related developments also increase the extent to which downward mobility is experienced by workers and their families: declining numbers of middle-income families or households, declining real wages, and downward intergenerational drift among young adults raised in middle-income (or upper-middle-income) families who cannot find jobs that will allow them to replicate their parents' income levels or living standards.

Down by Work: Lost Jobs

One study estimated as many as one-fifth to one-third of all workers experienced downward mobility in the 1980s due to job displacement.[83] Such estimates are not surprising given that from 1979 to the mid-1990s, more than 43 million jobs were eliminated in the United States due to displacement and downsizing.[84] And despite the fact that more new jobs have been created than have been eliminated since 1979, most new jobs (over 70 percent) involve low-paying work in the retail, health, and temporary services fields.[85] Low unemployment rates at the end of the 1990s masked the reality that job losses continued to mount as 3.3 million workers were laid off during 1997–99.[86] In the manufacturing sector, which is highly unionized, 2.5 million jobs were lost during 1979–99, and 700,000 more jobs in that sector disappeared in the period from July 2000 through May 2001.[87] According to Challenger, Gray and Christmas, an outplacement firm, job cuts announced by U.S. employers through early September 2001 exceeded 1.1 million. This was "up 83% from last year's 12 month tally and far above any annual total in the past dozen years."[88] Job losses accelerated following the September 11 terrorist attacks. As the economy slid into recession, the U.S. Labor Department reported employers "cut work forces by 415,000 [in October], the most job losses in a single month since May 1980."[89]

Down by Money: Lost Income

The income consequences of job displacement are typically disastrous for what were formerly middle-income wage earners. Workers displaced from the auto, steel, meatpacking, and aerospace industries in the mid-1980s reported income losses of about 44 percent compared with their pervious earnings in the first two years after being laid off.[90] In the mid-1990s, of 2.2 million full-time workers laid off in 1993 and 1994, only two-thirds had found full-time work by 1996. More than one-half of this group was earning less than what their previous jobs paid, and more than one-third experienced pay cuts of 20 percent or more. The average weekly median earnings for this group declined about 14 percent, but older full-time workers (late fifties and early sixties) who found new jobs experienced pay decreases averaging 37 percent.[91]

During the 1997–98 period, 4.2 million workers permanently lost their jobs due to plant closings and other forms of job displacement. Of that group, 1.9 million workers lost jobs they had held for 3 years or more. A study of the latter group found that by early 2000, 23 percent of the long-tenured displaced workers were working full time at lower pay relative to earnings from lost jobs, 11 percent were working part-time or were self employed, and 21 percent were unemployed or had left the labor market. As was the case in earlier studies, displaced older workers (45–64) experienced the greatest losses in earnings.[92] A recent study by Koeber and Wright found a similar pattern of older age-greater income loss. Their research involving 2,424 displaced workers revealed that for males over 50, average weekly earnings declined by $98—from $743 (past job) to $644 (current job); for females over 50, average weekly earnings declined by $44—from $419 (past job) to $375 (current job).[93]

In addition to income losses related to job displacement, the thirty-year pattern of falling real wages for average workers further reinforces the downward mobility drift experienced by many workers. This trend is evident by the decline in average real wages for production and nonsupervisory workers which fell from $13.91 per hour in 1973 to $13.24 per hour in 1999 (in 1999 dollars).[94] It is also evident by more recent data showing that over the last two decades of the twentieth century, the average annual real income (adjusted for inflation) of production and non-supervisory workers actually declined by $371—dropping from $28,950 in 1980 to $28,579 in 2000 (in 2000 dollars).[95]

Down by Age: Lost Living Standards

The extent of recent downward intergenerational mobility is difficult to determine, in part because of definitional issues concerning the meanings of *class*, *generations*, and *downward mobility*. Despite these problems, recent income-based research findings and poll data indicate that by objective measures and subjective impressions, young workers today are finding it difficult to match the living standards achieved by older workers in the previous generation.

Two intergenerational income studies from the late 1990s produced similar findings: Young U.S. adult workers in the 1990s earned substantially lower real incomes (on average) than those of comparable young workers in the recent past. One study found the 1979 median weekly earnings (in all occupational categories) for young adults (25–34 years old in 1979) averaged $545 (1996 dollars). By contrast, in 1996 the median weekly earnings for young adults (25–34 in 1996) averaged $463 (1996 dollars).[96] A second study examined the average real incomes of unmarried 18- to 29-year-old workers in three time periods (reported in 1994–95 dollars). Before taxes, the average income of young single workers was $22,413 in 1972–73, $21,928 in 1984–85, and $19,891 in 1994–95. This study found that real earnings of young adult workers in 1994–95 were 11.3 percent lower than those of young adult workers in 1972–73, and that more than 80 percent of the total decline occurred between the 1984–85 and 1994–95 periods.[97]

More recent comparisons of entry-level wages for high school educated workers also indicate sharp income drops have occurred across generational lines. Per-hour average entry-level wages for high school graduates (in 1999 dollars) declined for males from $12.42 in 1973 to $9.27 in 1999; female high school grads' entry-level wages dropped from $9.09 in 1973 to $7.89 in 1999. Among college educated workers, entry-level real average hourly wages for males remained virtually flat over the last 26 years ($16.46 in 1973/$16.74 in 1999). In contrast, college educated women did experience some real growth in entry-level wages ($13.80 in 1973/$14.65 in 1999). Despite some modest wage gains among college-educated workers, the fact remains that there has been a "dramatic erosion of wages since 1973 . . . among young workers."[98]

Reports of low wages among young workers are not surprising. In 1999 only 50 percent of young workers (ages 18–34) without college degrees (73 percent of all young workers) held full-time, permanent jobs, according to a nationwide poll conducted for the AFL-CIO.[99] Given the kinds of jobs young workers hold, generational income comparisons, and wage trends among young workers, it appears that downward intergenerational mobility is a relatively common experience among young adults today.

Downward Mobility: Social Consequences and Popular Culture

The consequences of the downward mobility experience (from all causes) for millions of new-working-class members and their families over the past three decades include a growing sense of insecurity and pessimism among middle-income Americans. These trends are reflected in public attitudes, lifestyle choices, and even the popular music of today's youth. In a mid-1990s National Opinion Research Center poll, 67 percent of Americans agreed that "the lot of the average man is getting worse," and 38 percent felt it is "not fair to bring a child into the world."[100] A more recent survey conducted for the Council for Excellence in Government found only 30 percent agreed that "in today's society, the American dream [is] achievable for all those willing to work for it."[101]

Consistent with American workers' pessimistic views concerning economic opportunities, marriage rates and traditional family lifestyles have declined. In 1970, married couples with a child (or children under age 18) accounted for 50 percent of all U.S. families and 40 percent of all U.S. households. But in 1999, the proportion of traditional families (married couples with children under 18) had declined to 35 percent of all families and to 24 percent of all households. During the same period, nonfamily households as a share of all households increased from 19 percent in 1970 to 31 percent in 1999.[102] In short, shrinking income and benefit levels for many members of the new working class have increasingly placed traditional lifestyles and the economic security associated with the American Dream out of reach for many workers.

"The world is a vampire—Set to drain [you]" sang Smashing Pumpkins, a popular Generation X alternative rock band from the mid-1990s. This grim take on the life chances of the young is not an isolated image. It is a theme frequently echoed in the lyrics of popular music today. Sometimes cynicism and pessimism are seamlessly woven together. In a later verse of the same song, the band sings, "Despite all my rage I am still just a rat in a cage." In short, the band—and their youthful audience—know that they're being used, and they don't like it. But they do not offer any emancipatory vision or see any alternatives to a life of rage in the cage.

Contemporary popular music often conjures up a bleak, iron-cage imagery of the world as viewed by youth. They appear to feel trapped in a predictable, down-sized, dead-end society. But they also appear unsure of what to do about it, other than to shop. For many youth, rebellion and authenticity are displayed and achieved by embracing the subculture of cool: consuming "alternative" music, clothes, styles, and "rebel" attitudes (e.g., post-punk, thug, gangsta) promoted by clever liberation marketing styles of hip corporations.[103] Messages encouraging re-sistance to or liberation from the forces driving downward mobility do appear in some youth music.[104] However, the content more typically reflects rather narrow, self-absorbed concerns and frustrations of youthful angst as well as "images of confinement"—illustrated by Radiohead's 2001 album, *Amnesiac.*[105] Such issues are often expressed through defiant lyrics and video images emphasizing attitude, style, and gesture, as in rage rock, hip-hop, and rap. In short, the children of post–World War II middle-income Americans appear trapped in a subcultural zeitgeist that reflects their feelings of increasing anxiety and frustration about a downward-trending class system they were born into and are trapped by, but that does not provide them with the experiences or knowledge necessary to under-stand, influence, or reshape it.

Class Secession

The United States is in some ways becoming a medieval society, in which people live and work in the modern equivalent of castles—gated communities, apart-ment buildings with doormen and office buildings with guards.

—Keith Bradsher, *New York Times*, July 23, 2000

As income erosion, economic insecurity, and downward mobility increase among the new working class and are manifested in a tight spiral of community tensions and social problems, the privileged class is increasingly distancing itself from pub-lic institutions in ways that suggest not simply more suburbanization but rather class secession. Of course, the very wealthy have always separated themselves from the nonwealthy through exclusive neighborhoods, clubs, and schools. However, what Robert Reich terms the "secession of the successful" combines traditional forms of physical and social separation and increasing numbers of privately pro-vided services with an ideology that encourages and legitimates hostility to public institutions serving members of nonprivileged classes.[106] In short, this trend involves a separatist social identity and a secessionistic mentality.

One measure of the increasing physical separation of the privileged class from the working class is the growing number of home-owner associations, which typically govern details of home and property maintenance in neighborhoods and communities that are physically separate and sometimes walled off from surrounding areas. The Community Association Institute estimates that 190,000 community associations existed in 1996 and that they were growing at the rate of about 10,000 per year.[107] These organizations are typically initiated by developers to supervise upscale housing developments. Membership is usually mandatory for home owners. An association board of directors (appointed first by the developer and later elected by home owners) enforces developer-designed codes, covenants, and restrictions regarding property use, maintenance, and services; and each home buyer must sign a contract in which they agree to abide by the association's rules. Association-provided services are financed by membership fees and may range from basics like trash collection to maintenance of parks, recreation sites, private security guards, and even lobbying activities. The latter service logically follows the reality that associations are private concerns representing groups with narrow, private interests. Thus, associations lobby state and local governments on various issues such as zoning decisions and tax relief for services they already provide—like garbage collection.[108]

Of all community associations, those that govern physically walled and gated upscale residential developments are among the fastest growing. In 1987 there were an estimated twelve thousand U.S. gated communities, but by 1998 the number had grown to thirty thousand with a total population of 8 million Americans. Developers estimate that eight of ten new urban projects today are gated.[109] In the suburbs the numbers are more difficult to determine, but regional data suggest that gated suburban communities are also growing in numbers. "In communities like San Antonio, Texas, one in three new homes being built is in a gated community. The national number is expected to double in the next five years."[110]

The combination of high income, physical isolation, and privately provided services in gated communities encourages what political scientist Evan McKenzie refers to as an "ideology of privatism—an ideology that overlays and reinforces sentiments favoring exclusiveness, exclusion, and isolation." In his study of home-owners' associations, McKenzie maintains that this ideology, when combined with the physical isolation that "privatization for the few" produces, can lead to "an attenuated sense of loyalty and commitment to public communities." As a result, he believes there could be "a gradual secession from the city . . . [with the city becoming] financially untenable for the many and socially unnecessary for the few. Certainly this steady secession would make the lives of those who remained in the city increasingly difficult."[111]

The expansion of private, class-segregated communities, the erosion of privileged-class support for mixed-class, public institutions (residential neighbor-

Copyright © Lloyd Dangle. Reprinted with permission.

hoods, municipal services, public schools), and the crystallization of a secessionist ideology supporting these trends are apparent to commentators from different points on the political spectrum today. Conservative Charles Murray sees current income trends "producing something very like a caste society" in which the wealthiest 10 or 20 percent of the population will simply "bypass the social institutions it doesn't like."[112] He explains that when public services fall apart, the privileged class will retreat to private enclaves complete with private services like schools and police—as in the gated community model.

Writing from a liberal perspective, Robert Reich sees members of the privileged class as increasingly identifying with private rather than public interests in terms of where their allegiances lie—producing both secessionistic ideas and consequences. Top executives of American firms declare that "their job is to maximize shareholder returns, not to advance public goals."[113] Mainstream reporters and media publications also openly acknowledge the realities of growing class segregation. A mid-1990s *Newsweek* cover story offered the following view of class secession from the political center: "Increasingly the [privileged class] is choosing to live in ways that minimize its mixing with . . . [other classes]. . . . Sometimes it just moves farther out into the suburbs, or higher up the high rise. But increasingly often it chooses to live in a walled and gated community guarded by private security forces."[114]

BENEATH THE WATERLINE:
CONFLICTING CLASS INTERESTS

Inequality is on the rise. . . . It is time to build an economic fairness movement to act as a countervailing force to the power of concentrated wealth and large corporations.

—Chuck Collins and Felice Yeskel,
Economic Apartheid in America, 2000

Although the class iceberg thrusts some obvious features of the system into view, with the right kind of conceptual sonar gear we can also peer beneath the waterline. There we can glimpse some hidden features of the new class society. To begin, we view the preceding three trends as closely related to, and reflective of, conflicting class interests. Contrary to the "win-win" language and imagery so prevalent in media accounts of business and labor relationships, we see superclass corporate owners and their credentialed-class allies as having interests that are fundamentally opposed to those of working-class Americans. It is our view that privileged-class interests trend in the direction of preserving and extending class-based economic, political, and cultural inequalities. Such interests translate into a privileged-class agenda centered on maintaining and enhancing the wealth, power, privilege, and security of the superclass and of its credentialed-class allies. This agenda is pursued through privileged-class dominance of the major economic, political, and cultural organizations of society.[115]

Protecting Privilege

Large corporations and corporate-generated wealth are at the heart of conflicting class interests and privileged-class power. The economic resources controlled by major U.S. corporations are staggering. Although the total U.S. "corporate population" consists of nearly 5 million firms with total annual receipts of $15.9 trillion (1997), a relatively small number of huge companies dominate the U.S. economy as well as all major sectors of American business.[116]

The 500 largest firms (the *Fortune* 500) represent only .0001 (one-thousandth of 1 percent) of the nearly 5 million U.S. corporations. This small group received $7.2 trillion in revenues in 2000—an amount that represents nearly one-half of all annual U.S. corporate revenues.[117] In the manufacturing sector, 601 U.S. corporations (out of over 2,255 firms) had assets exceeding $1 billion in 1999. The combined assets of these firms represented 77 percent of the total assets held by all U.S. manufacturing companies. The net profits earned by the top 601 corporations in 1999 ($209 billion) accounted for 80 percent of all net profits earned by all U.S. manufacturing corporations that year.[118] Looking only at assets, the twenty largest commercial banks (out of 8,580) held $3.3 trillion in assets in 2000 which represented approximately 58 percent of all banking assets.[119] The ten largest insurance companies (mutual and stock firms) held $1.3 trillion in assets in 2000 which amounted to about 46 percent of all assets held by all insurance companies.[120] Large U.S. companies not only dominate the national economy, but also play increasingly dominant roles in the global economy since many are multinational firms with subsidiaries scattered around the globe.[121]

Most giant U.S. corporations are largely owned and controlled by a small number of superclass elites who are assisted by their credentialed-class allies. In general, the superclass includes the top wealth-owning and income-receiving groups in the United States—including the 271 U.S. billionaires in 2001.[122] It comprises the wealthiest 1 percent of U.S. households which, in 1998, owned 47.7 percent of all common stock, and the next wealthiest 9 percent which, in the same year, owned 38.5 percent. (The bottom 90 percent owned only 13.9 percent.)[123] As wealth and income shade downward, this class gradually merges into the credentialed class.

In terms of income, superclass members are typically found among the 480,000 taxpayers (individuals and families) filing returns with incomes more than $500,000 (in 1998).[124] Members of the credentialed class are found in the second-from-the-top income tier—including most of the 2.4 million taxpayers filing returns with annual incomes of $200,000 or more (in 1999).[125] The credentialed class also includes many individuals from households with pre-tax incomes of $144,299 or more, which was the average income for the top 20 percent of U.S. households in 1999 (in 1999 dollars).[126]

Members of the superclass who are actively involved in organizational governance occupy top positions of power and authority in the largest and most powerful economic, political, and cultural organizations in the society. Such superclass executives—along with their credentialed-class subordinates—are considered, by social science researchers, to form the heart of an American "power elite." Members of this group play active, corporate officer and board member roles and occupy public-policy-influencing positions in public and private organizations—and have been the focus of research documenting this group's membership, power, and self-conscious and cohesive nature.[127]

Various forms of data concerning income levels and sources illustrate that the higher the income, the lower the percentage derived from salaries and wages and the greater the percentage derived from dividends, interest, and other forms of corporate-based compensation. In 1999, 67 percent of income for households in the top 20 percent income group came from wages or salaries, while 30 percent came from investment capital income of various types. But for the top 1 percent income group, only 42 percent of income was derived from wages and salaries, and 58 percent came from investment capital income.[128] Moreover, reports on executive compensation reveal that salaries (plus bonuses) represent only a small portion of CEOs' annual incomes. For example, the salary plus bonus incomes for the ten top-paid U.S. CEOs in 2000 averaged $6.9 million. But this figure represents only 4.5 percent of the average total pay for this group in 2000—$154.2 million, including exercised stock options and other forms of long-term payments.[129]

The incomes of credentialed-class managers and white-collar professionals who assist superclass elites in sustaining the corporate project are nowhere near those of superclass members, but they are still substantial. In Washington, the salary received by members of Congress has often been viewed as the top of the middle class and thus, as the floor of the upper-middle class.[130] In 2001 that was $145,100.[131] This figure represents an approximate baseline minimum for privileged-class managers and professionals—especially in large private sector firms. In 2000, the total annual compensation for the chief financial officers (CFOs) at the largest U.S. firms averaged $2.77 million; the pay at top firms averaged $932,000 for controllers and $927,000 for treasurers. Although CFO pay declines substantially outside the largest firms, the median annual compensation for CFOs in organizations of all types and sizes (corporate, government, nonprofits) was still a respectable $109,319 in 2000.[132]

From newly rich corporate officers to the oldest American family fortunes, sky-box-level incomes and wealth are clearly linked to the ongoing production of corporate profits. Privileged-class corporate officers understand this connection. Therefore, superclass members actively involved in corporate governance, along with a select group of upwardly mobile credentialed-class members groomed by superclass sponsors, work diligently to ensure the continued financial health, power, and survival of the corporate enterprise. At the highest levels of wealth, the corporate basis of immense personal wealth is clearly illustrated by CEO fortunes linked to specific firms. Examples include Bill Gates's $58.7 billion Microsoft-based fortune, Warren E. Buffett's $32.3 billion Berkshire-based empire, and Philip H. Knight's $4.3 billion Nike-based holdings.[133] Large corporations are clearly the engines that generate the income and wealth of the superclass and also of its credentialed-class allies.

As a result of privileged-class ownership and control of large firms, the class interests of this group are served in three ways. First, much of the value of the goods and services produced by workers is distributed through corporate-based channels and practices to superclass corporate owners and to their credentialed-class allies. The heart of this process is simple and increasingly transparent today. It begins with corporations paying workers far less (in wages and benefits) than the market value of what they produce. The difference between wages paid and the market value of what workers produce is retained as profits. The process concludes with the retained profits being distributed to CEOs and managers as salaries, bonuses, and stock options, and to stockholders, as dividends. When the U.S. fast-food industry pays most of its workers at or near minimum wage rates of $5.15 per hour (2001) and provides virtually no paid fringe benefits, it is not surprising that in 1997 McDonald's could easily afford an $8.1 million compensation package for CEO Michael R. Quinlan.[134] Similarly, when Nike pays its Indonesian workers $1.20 per day to make shoes that sell for $125 per pair in U.S. markets, it's no surprise that Nike CEO Phil Knight was paid $2.8 million in 2000 and is a billionaire.[135]

Second, the corporate-derived income and wealth of the privileged class are used as class-based resources for penetrating and controlling government to develop and reinforce a body of law and public policies that legitimate privileged-class dominance and institutionalize class inequalities. Such arrangements make class-based social inequities and biases in the economic and political order favoring the privileged class appear to be "normal" or even "natural." Also, control of government allows the privileged class to actively pursue public policies that serve its immediate interests—such as tax cuts (primarily benefiting higher income groups), reducing the size of government (fewer business regulations means more profits), and welfare cuts (creating a larger pool of low-wage workers, using the poor as scapegoats). Third, privileged-class control of public-opinion-shaping institutions such as the state, the mass media, and the educational system is used to ignore, conceal, marginalize, contest, disguise, or misrepresent issues and information that would expose class-based inequalities and legitimate class-based grievances of workers.

We believe the interests of the new working class, in contrast with privileged-class interests, trend in the direction of reducing existing class-based economic, political, and cultural inequalities. This means, first, that workers have economic interests in receiving a larger share of the value of the goods and services they produce in the form of higher wages as well as more extensive and secure fringe benefits. Such outcomes would occur at the expense of superclass owners of productive property and their credentialed-class allies by reducing profit margins. Second, workers also have political interests in contesting privileged-class control of government in order to use law and public policies on behalf of the working class as instruments for reducing economic and political class inequalities. For example, workers' opportunities and economic security would be enhanced by an expansion of social spending for education, a national health care system, and additional protections for the environment. Third, at the cultural level, workers also have interests in using the mass media and schools to expose class-based inequalities and to legitimate the class-based grievances of workers.

Our view of the existence of conflicting class interests does not mean that we see the privileged and working classes as equally aware of or equally well organized to work toward the active realization of their interests. To the contrary, as the later chapters illustrate, we see privileged-class members as much more conscious of their collective class interests, more cohesive in pursuing them, and in possession of much greater (and more unified) organizational resources than the working class. The net result is that compared with the working class, the privileged class is much more aware of, and able to effectively pursue and realize, its common class interests.

Class War in America

> Our business and political class . . . declared class war twenty years ago, and it was they who won. They're on top.
>
> —Bill Moyers, *Nation*, November 19, 2001

Nowhere is the reality of conflicting class interests, privileged-class consciousness, and the overwhelming power of superclass-dominated organizational resources more apparent than in the story behind the transformation of the American class system in the period from the 1970s to the present. The trends of class polarization, downward mobility, and class secession are the direct result of policy decisions made and sponsored by superclass-controlled organizations over the past thirty years that collectively represent nothing less than total class war. Although varying explanations exist for the current configuration of the American class system, none approaches the explanatory power of a class-war analysis. Although the details of the story are complex, the main actors, events, and policies underlying it are stunningly simple. They are fundamentally grounded in conflicting class interests and linked to the dynamics of an almost totally one-sided class war sponsored and directed by the superclass and driven by corporate resources.

The story behind today's new class society begins in the late 1960s and early 1970s. Several working-class political movements initiated during this period led to an expansion of New Deal–based national policies that effectively increased opportunities for—as well as the economic, occupational, and physical well-being of—working-class Americans. Such policies included numerous Great Society programs such as Medicare and Medicaid, as well as several new federal regulatory acts in six major areas, including consumer products, discrimination in employment, traffic safety, consumer finance, job safety, and the environment.[136] Among these acts were groundbreaking measures such as the 1966 Coal Mine Safety Act, the 1969 National Environmental Policy Act, and the 1970 Occupational Health and Safety Act. For workers, the net effect of the progressive legislation enacted in the 1960s and early 1970s was a welcome expansion of the welfare state.

Members of the superclass viewed pro-worker policy developments with fear and loathing: "The expansion of the welfare state in the 1960s and 1970s created panic among the U.S. capitalist class."[137] This reaction was undoubtedly magnified by the parallel trend of declining corporate profits during this period.[138] The superclass response was a concerted, large-scale mobilization for total class war. At the heart of this effort was the conscious creation of a two-pronged political and economic strategy for the purpose of waging class war on a scale unprecedented in American history. The following sections introduce two key dimensions of this class war, both of which are explored in more detail in later chapters.

The Political Dimension of the Class War

In the political and public policy arenas, the superclass dramatically expanded the organizational and resource base undergirding its political lobbying and policy-influencing capacity. The list of heavyweight superclass-promoted lobbying developments that emerged during this period begins with the Business Roundtable. Organized in 1973 by John Harper, head of Alcoa Aluminum, and Fred Borch, the CEO of General Electric, it included two hundred CEOs from the largest banks and corporations, and it remains one of the most formidable corporate lobbying organizations today.[139] In that same year, to further beef up superclass political pressure on Congress, the National Association of Manufacturers moved to Washington, D.C. Also, the number of corporations represented by registered lobbyists grew dramatically, from 175 in 1971 to 650 in 1979, and membership in the Chamber of Commerce more than doubled, from 36,000 in 1967 to 80,000 in 1974.[140] The 1970s and 1980s also witnessed the development and growth of an extensive corporate-funded network of conservative "think tanks" aimed at influencing public policy with conservative ideas and policies such as "supply side" economics and "welfare reform."[141]

To help fund the political campaigns of candidates favorable to privileged-class business interests, the number of corporate political action committees (PACs) grew from 89 in 1974 to 1,206 in 1980.[142] Business mobilization of PACs continued throughout the 1980s and 1990s, with corporate and related trade association PACs totaling 2,746 in 2000 and accounting for 53 percent of the $579.4 million disbursed by all PACs in 1999–2000.[143] In addition to the expansion of corporate PACs, the amounts of money from business-based political contributions of all types also increased dramatically, as election expenditures for all Congressional candidates spiraled up from $342.4 million in 1981–82 to $765.3 million in 1995–96, and rising to $1 billion in 1999–2000.[144]

In the 1999–2000 election cycle, a record total of $3 billion was spent on federal elections (compared with $2.4 billion in 1996).[145] The increasing cost of political campaigns has led to an ever greater dependence—especially at the national level—by both Republicans and Democrats on high-dollar contributions from both wealthy individuals and corporate PACs. Funds from these sources include both "hard" and "soft" money, with the former subject to federally regulated limits on amounts donated, whereas the latter is largely free from donation limits and loosely regulated in terms of how the monies may be spent.[146] In the 2000 election cycle (January 1, 1999 through December 31, 2000) hard and soft campaign contributions (primarily from wealthy individuals and corporate PACs) to both major parties and federal candidates totaled $2.6 billion, split 58 percent for Republicans and 42 percent for Democrats.[147] The tilting effect of privileged-class dominance of national election funding in favor of candidates supporting the interests of this class was evident in 2000, when business contributions of all types to all federal candidates totaled fifteen times more than donations by organized labor (up from 11 to 1 in 1996).[148]

The political mobilization of superclass-funded organizations hit the jackpot with the election of the Ronald Reagan and George Bush administrations. Their record of strong support for superclass-based corporate interests and hostility to welfare-state programs is well known. As David Stockman, the architect of Reagan's economic policies, put it, "The Reagan Revolution required a frontal assault on the American welfare state."[149] Superclass interests received further boosts in the 1994 and 1996 congressional elections as Republicans captured, and then retained control over, both houses of Congress. Led by then House Speaker Newt Gingrich, conservative Republicans openly pledged to dismantle the New Deal and Great Society social legislation. The process began in earnest with the highly publicized "Contract with America" and achieved notable success with the passage of welfare "reform" legislation in 1996—with support from many Democrats and President Clinton.[150]

The superclass scored big again in 2000 with the coup-like selection of President George W. Bush as a result of the 5–4 Supreme Court ruling on the Florida election results and with the installation of a Republican-dominated Congress.[151] In the early 2000s, the superclass policy agenda of the 1990s continued with renewed energy. Political juice and superclass money turned first to cutting taxes—mainly for the rich—which led to the $1.35 trillion tax cut bill promptly passed with Republican and Democratic support and signed by President Bush in 2001.[152] Then, as the U.S. economy sank into recession following the September 11, 2001 terrorist attacks, the Bush administration won House passage of a $100 billion "economic stimulus" bill. Key features of the bill clearly favored superclass interests. If passed by the Senate, the bill would repeal the corporate alternative minimum tax and refund alternative minimum income taxes paid by major corporations over the past 15 years. This means that rebates would be sent to IBM ($1.4 billion), General Motors ($833 million), General Electric ($671 million), and Enron ($254 million). The bill would also enhance expense write-offs for business capital assets, reduce the 27 percent individual tax rate to 25 percent in 2002 (four years earlier than under current law), and cut long-term capital gains tax rates from 20 percent to 18 percent.[153] Social Security "reform" was yet another front-burner policy initiative pushed by the Bush administration with superclass backing (as we will see in chapter 5).

Republican officeholders are typically the most openly enthusiastic supporters of privileged-class interests. But the social, labor, and trade policies of the Clinton administration illustrate the political reality that many Democrats also routinely support policies favored by the privileged class. It is clear that today Democrats seldom act as the champions of or advocates for the interests of the new working class. For example, following Vermont Senator Jim Jeffords's decision to drop his Republican Party affiliation in June 2001 to become an independent, Democrats assumed majority control of the U.S. Senate. Many mainstream pundits and media reports presented these developments to the public as if they constituted a political earthquake.[154] However, the changes prompted other, more astute political observers to note that nothing had really changed because both parties represent the same privileged-class interests. Reporters Cockburn and St. Clair observed, "With Democrats now controlling the Senate, life can proceed exactly as it did in the Clinton era, with roughly the same judicial appointments, the same savage posture towards the poor, the imprisoned and the condemned, and the same open-handed generosity towards the corporations."[155] Indeed, the consequences of intensified business-driven political lobbying along with increased privileged-class funding of both major political parties have included the increasingly transparent conversion of large segments of the Democratic Party into a political force reflecting the hegemonic power of superclass-based corporate interests. As Ralph Nader has commented, "Now we have a two-party convergence—one might call it a collaboration or a conspiracy—against the broader political wishes of the American people."[156]

The Economic Dimension of the Class War

In the economic arena, superclass corporate elites dictated policies aimed at increasing profits by waging war on workers' wages. Domestically, this has involved the use of government to establish and maintain a hard line against workers' rights and wage demands. Reagan's 1981 firing of striking air-traffic controllers established a tough, antilabor policy trend that continued with his appointments of antilabor members to the National Labor Relations Board and with other actions such as his threat to veto the High-Risk bill of 1986–87, which would have mandated government protection for high-risk workers' health.[157]

The pro-business, antilabor policies of the Reagan administration that benefited the economic and political interests of the privileged class were continued and extended by the Bush, Clinton, and Bush W. administrations. In each administration we find evidence of strong support for policies aimed at reducing worker and union rights, social spending, governmental regulations on businesses, and taxes on corporations and wealthy individuals; we also find each administration supporting a growing list of "free trade" agreements.[158]

Internationally, the "globalization strategy" of U.S. firms involved the use of technological innovations to facilitate the transfer of manufacturing jobs to Third

World nations. During the 1980s and 1990s, credentialed-class corporate managers and professionals designed and executed the increasing use of various new technologies, including satellite communication, computers, standardized production procedures, and containerized shipping, as the technical basis for the globalization of production. These developments accelerated the "capital flight" transfer of production facilities from the United States to nations such as Mexico, Indonesia, and China, which in turn made the use of cheap Third World labor ever more feasible and profitable. Numerous U.S. firms, including General Motors, Ford, Zenith, and Converse, located more and more of their production facilities in Third World nations, and some "U.S." companies, such as Nike (headquartered in Beaverton, Oregon) produce virtually all of their products in Third World nations. In 1997, U.S.-headquartered multinational firms and foreign affiliates controlled by U.S. firms employed nearly 28 million workers—many of them in Third World nations.[159]

The transformation of the manufacturing sector by corporate globalization strategies has accelerated the development of a postindustrial, service-based economy—and hastened the drift toward class polarization. Over the past thirty years the proportion of U.S. workers engaged in manufacturing fell from 33.1 percent in 1970 to a projected 11.6 percent in 2008. This decline has been paralleled by a sharp increase in service-sector employment, rising from 62.5 percent of all workers in 1970 to a projected 74.4 percent in 2008.[160] The service economy trend intensifies class divisions because of the corporate-generated, two-tiered labor market that is especially evident in the service sector. This system consists of firms utilizing a small group of high-paid "core" workers, such as managers, professionals, computer programmers, and other "symbolic analysts," and a very large group of moderate-to-low-paid "peripheral" workers—viewed as less central to organizational needs and goals.

The differences in pay and benefits for the two groups are closely linked to differences in levels of skill and social capital. Variations in these resources tend to reflect the prestige of the educational credentials workers possess as well as their social ties to organizational leaders (social capital). Thus, workers' possession of these class-based capital resources influence their proximity to corporate and organizational power and their access to the limited number of well-paid positions. Peripheral workers occupy a spectrum of jobs ranging from modestly paid occupations such as teachers and police officers to much lower paid positions such as cashiers, guards, personal care and home health aides, and janitors—which are projected to be among the occupations with the largest job growth in the 1998–2008 period.[161] However, even modestly paid service workers find themselves continuously subject to wage and benefit pressures as employers increase contingent-labor staffing policies.[162] At the bottom, as we noted earlier, the lowest-paid service workers are increasingly linked to large organizations through temporary agencies as contract or contingent laborers.[163]

With superclass interests as a dominant force in the national government, sig-

Copyright © Lloyd Dangle. Reprinted with permission.

nificant features of the welfare state benefiting the new working class have been—
and are currently being—dismantled. The minimal levels of economic security
that national social policies afforded workers and the poor in the past are increasingly disappearing. At the same time, the combination of superclass-sponsored government-corporate attacks on unions, along with the globalization
process, has led to a continuous erosion of workers' wages, benefits, and rights.
These developments have been accompanied by corporate layoff and downsizing
policies that have led to the disappearance of many blue- and white-collar middle-income positions. The end result of these class-war-driven policies and practices has been the emergence of the increasingly polarized and hardened new
class society.

BENEATH THE WATERLINE: CLASS MAINTENANCE AND LEGITIMATION

To maintain their power and privilege, elites have learned to ... exploit nonelites without their realizing they are being exploited.

—Harold R. Kerbo, *Social Stratification and Inequality*, 2000

The second hidden dimension of the class iceberg involves the structures and processes that maintain and legitimate the new class society. Of course, elite classes in stratified societies have always devoted a portion of their considerable resources to legitimating and reinforcing the class system, thereby ensuring their continued possession of disproportionate levels of wealth, power, and privilege. However, the problems of maintaining and legitimating the emerging new class society have been rendered more complex by the extreme inequalities of the system and the tension between these class realities and the relentless, media-driven promotion of the American Dream as a cultural ideal.[164] Thus, the current class maintenance and legitimation strategies, structures, and policies combine sophisticated extensions of approaches used in the past with emerging, innovative forms of control and distraction.

The Class-Power-Network Model

Our perspective on how the new class system is maintained and legitimated is based on an organizational model of class interests and power. It views large firms as repositories of superclass resources and also as dominant sources of power in virtually all sectors of society. According to this approach, privileged-class leaders use corporate-based resources to create, fund, and control extensive, overlapping organizational networks within the economic, political, and cultural social arenas. These networks consist of organizations linked by various connections such as interlocked board members, shared public policy interests, and common goals—including the maintenance and legitimation of concentrated privileged-class power and wealth.

In the economic arena, network examples include superclass-controlled trade associations and peak corporate groups—such as the Business Roundtable. Superclass-funded public policy "think tanks," lobbying organizations, and PACs are examples of organizational networks within the political arena. In the cultural arena, network examples include superclass-funded foundations, civic and cultural organizations, and elite university boards of trustees. We view these interlocked organizational networks as directed by privileged-class leaders who use them to pursue strategies and objectives that reinforce the shared economic, political, and cultural interests of their class. These include legitimating corporate autonomy, power, and profit maximization as well as maintaining the organizational structure of the new class system so as to perpetuate the advantaged positions, interests, and privileges of the superclass and its credentialed-class allies. However, we also believe the organizations within these networks typically present public facades that disguise or deemphasize their privileged-class biases and the ways in which they function as surrogate actors for privileged-class interests.

Although the class-power model views superclass leaders as participating in conscious and deliberate activities to protect privileged-class interests, it is not based on a conspiracy theory of power. We do not view superclass leaders as a group that secretly conspires to promote its interests and maintain class inequalities. Rather, following G. William Domhoff, we view the coordinated, interest-supporting activities of superclass leaders and their credentialed-class allies as grounded in a complex structural system that is populated by a relatively homogeneous group that is similar in many important respects. Privileged-class leaders tend to have similar elite educational backgrounds, to be officers of large, interlocked firms, and to be members of a small number of elite social and cultural organizations. The class-based shared family, business, and social experiences of this group lead to shared common values, worldviews, and commitments to maintaining the status quo.[165] From where privileged-class leaders stand, life is good and the system works. The shared culture of the superclass leads not to conspiracy but rather to an authentic boosterism for the corporate model and the "magic of the market." There's no need for a conspiracy when the most common question among privileged-class leaders is, "Why change what works? (for us!)."

Dominant Class-Power Networks

Figure 2.2 illustrates the main features of our class-power-network model. At the top, the model views the dominant class power base as grounded in the organizationally active superclass members and their credentialed-class allies (the power elite). This group is centrally involved in directing and coordinating the three overlapping corporate-based dominant power networks. Strategies for class maintenance and legitimation extend downward through four basic social institutions: the national economy, the state, media and culture, and the educational system. The following five chapters consider in detail how the maintenance and legitimation strategies identified by the model are linked to organizational policies and practices directed by privileged-class leadership. And they illustrate how these strategies and related policies serve privileged-class interests—especially by helping to perpetuate and legitimate structured inequalities within the new class society.

By focusing on the top half of the model, we can begin to see how the abstract notion of superclass dominance is channeled through real organizations that collectively merge into powerful networks. From the top down, the dominant power networks pursue superclass interests through corporate-based activities penetrating the four routine institutional structures of society. As we will see, the corporate

Figure 2.2   Class-Power Network Model

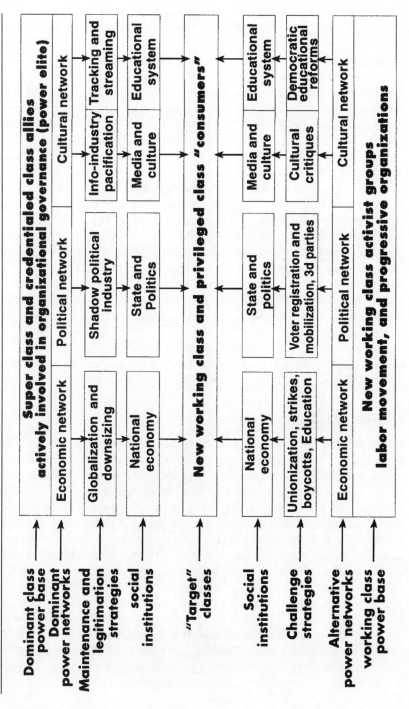

practices and public policies that emerge from these structural linkages weave legitimation, co-optation, distraction, and coercion into a dense organizational web that sustains the new class system's inequalities.

Members of the new working class find themselves as targets of the dominant power networks depicted by the model. Specific public policies, programs, business practices, and cultural ideas maintaining and legitimating superclass interests, the corporate empire, and class inequalities in the new class system are routinely and repeatedly directed at working-class members (and privileged-class consumers) through the four basic social institutions shown in the model.

For members of the working class, the cumulative effects of lives lived under superclass-dominated social institutions encourage public acceptance of class hierarchies, extensive corporate power, and the inequalities associated with these arrangements. Oligopolistic corporate control of the economy (e.g., aerospace, auto, electrical, media industries), corporate-funded bashing of big government (Rush Limbaugh), and corporate-media sponsored celebrations of the free enterprise system (e.g., *Fox News Channel*) produce patterns of ideas and experiences that constantly remind the working class that private businesses are "good" and public enterprises are "bad" (or at best inefficient).[166] In short, working-class behaviors and attitudes are shaped in ways that promote public acceptance (ideological legitimation) of class inequalities. Such outcomes ensure that the distribution of capital resources in the new class society remains relatively unchallenged and unchanged—with a small number of highly rewarded positions reserved for members of the privileged-class top diamond and those in the new-working-class bottom diamond restricted to positions with much lower rewards.

Alternative Class-Power Networks

Of course, the top portion of figure 2.2 is only part of the story. At the bottom of the figure we find an alternative class-power base grounded in new-working-class activist groups. The labor movement along with other progressive groups such as many women's rights, civil rights, environmental, and gay rights organizations form the heart of three overlapping alternative power networks. These alternative networks challenge—with varying degrees of vigor and with limited resources—the strategies, policies, and messages of the dominant power networks within the economy, the state, the media, and the schools. The alternative-network dimension of our model underscores the point that we do not equate superclass dominance in the economic, political, and cultural arenas with total control. On one hand, inequalities embedded in the new class society are largely maintained and legitimated by the actions, policies, and ideas orchestrated by superclass-sponsored and credentialed-class-managed organizations within the dominant power networks. But on the other hand, these activities and ideas are subject to challenges by alternative-power-network actors in the economic, political, and cultural arenas, with labor unions serving as the core alternative organizational force.

Our inclusion of trade unions as a key feature of the alternative power networks does not mean that we view unions as speaking with a single voice for workers or that we view all unions as consistent advocates for workers' common class interests. We recognize the labor movement includes diverse and sometimes contradictory trends and actions. Even so, among organizational alternatives to corporate power, trade unions possess the greatest concentration of human and economic resources and represent the most significant alternative organizational force countering corporate dominance. But this recognition does not diminish the importance of other organizations in the alternative power networks—some of which are linked to leaders and funding sources associated with privileged-class backgrounds. Some of these individuals and groups might—in some sense—be considered "class traitors" by more conventional privileged-class members. Such organizations include women's rights groups (e.g., National Organization for Women [NOW]), civil rights groups (e.g., National Association for the Advancement of Colored People [NAACP]), public interest groups, (e.g., Ralph Nader's numerous organizations), alternative, pro–new-working-class national circulation magazines (e.g., *Nation, Progressive, Mother Jones, In These Times*), progressive research and policy groups (e.g., Economic Policy Institute), and some religious organizations. These groups, often in conjunction with trade unions, are frequently involved in challenging the strategies, objectives, and policies of the Dominant Power Networks.

Inequality and Inequity

The efforts of alternative power network groups to promote economic, political, and social policy changes that would reduce class-, gender-, and racial/ethnic-based inequalities call attention to the distinction between inequality and inequity. *Inequality* refers to the objective reality (factually verifiable) that various distinct and identifiable groups (e.g., class, gender, racial/ethnic groups) receive unequal shares of various forms of scarce and valued resources distributed within the society. For example, much of the evidence presented thus far concerning differences in the distribution of consumption and investment capital illustrates that the highly unequal economic and political outcomes people experience in the United States are often based on their membership in class, gender, and racial/ethnic-based groups.

Inequity refers to a subjective judgment that the unequal access to scarce and valued resources experienced by groups distinguished by class, gender, and/or racial/ethnic membership is unfair and unjust. This concept interprets the organizationally based policies and practices used as the bases for unequally distributing scarce and valued resources as fundamentally flawed in the sense that they arbitrarily privilege some groups over others and thereby violate basic standards of fairness in the distributional process. Thus, people who observe class and other group-based forms of inequality through the lens of inequity view organizational policies and practices that produce highly unequal resource outcomes for such groups as requiring substantial revision and change.[167] From an inequity perspective, class, gender, and racial inequalities in areas such as the distribution of income, wealth, health care, economic security, educational and occupational opportunities are not viewed simply as reflections of merit-based distributional processes; rather, they tend to be viewed as evidence of fundamental biases and flaws embedded in a variety of distributional processes which perpetuate unfair economic, political, and cultural advantages of existing privileged-class groups at the expense of nonprivileged-class groups.

Almost by definition, a worldview of class (and other) inequalities based on an inequity interpretation necessitates and legitimates changes in the economic, political, and cultural arenas aimed at substantially narrowing the current range of inequalities. This is the orientation and approach taken by most individuals and groups that are part of the Alternative Power Networks. While most participants in these networks are unlikely to envision total equality as a realistic goal, the pursuit of *equity*—the distribution of scarce and valued resource in a fair and just manner—does appear to be a widely shared objective among the members of these Networks.

Of course, it is possible to argue that substantial inequalities are legitimate and justified. For example, contemporary justifications of class inequalities are often grounded in Herbert Spencer's late nineteenth century ideology of social Darwinism. Spencer celebrated the supposed superiority of the wealthy, viewed the poor as inferior and deserving of their fate, and justified class inequalities on the basis of a pseudoscience of "survival of the fittest."[168] Echoes of Spencer's views still resonate in the United States today—especially among the privileged class. For example, research evidence indicates that individuals with higher-class backgrounds are more likely than those with lower backgrounds to view people with higher-level occupations and educations as deserving greater incomes than people with lower-level occupations and educations.[169]

BACK TO THE FUTURE: THE ICEBERG, THE DREAM, AND THE DETAILS

Titanic came around the curve, into the Great Iceberg. Fare thee, Titanic, Fare thee well.

—Leadbelly (H. Ledbetter), "Fare Thee Well, Titanic," 1912

As the Titanic disaster reminds us, icebergs can be treacherous—especially the huge frozen mass below the waterline. Our exploration of the hidden portion of the class iceberg is also fraught with danger, though not of the physical sort. Because of the taboo nature of class, few people venture below the waterline of conventional social analysis. Down there, visibility is limited. The images are murky.

The dangers abound of miscommunication, misunderstanding, and charges from "respectable quarters" that it is unproductive or even un-American to make the trip: Better to stick with the dream than explore the iceberg. Even so, we'll take our chances. We think the potential rewards are worth the risks, and we invite you to join us.

The remainder of this book represents a tour of territory that for most Americans is familiar and yet, in many ways, unknown. Our class-power-network model serves as the basic map for exploring the hidden features of the new class society. As we will see, the dominant power networks are not abstract, ivory-tower inventions but real organizational webs of power that we encounter daily. By tracking the interests, strategies, and activities of privileged-class-dominated organizations, the model helps us understand how this class dominates organizations, public policies, programs, ideas, and social behavior in the economic, political, and cultural arenas.

Like a magnifying glass, the model serves as a lens bringing into focus the details of the ways in which the dominant power networks have created and work to maintain and legitimate the new class society. Using this lens, we will discover how the web of power spun by the dominant power networks attempts to control the production and enforcement of ideas about, debates over, attention to, and the enactment of class-relevant laws and public policies as well as the production and distribution of values and beliefs related to personal fulfillment, the mass consumption of goods and services, and the uses of work and leisure time. The cultural dimension of the dominant power networks has become increasingly important to the legitimation process, because the cultural network includes potent organizations (media, schools) that disseminate ideas, information, and images that help legitimate the new class system and serve as vehicles for distracting public attention away from the many inequalities of the system.

The class-power-network model will also help us see and better understand another important dimension of the class iceberg—the "underdogs" of class conflict. The alternative-power-networks portion of the model provides us with a map for understanding how dominant-power-network strategies, policies, programs, and ideas favoring privileged-class interests are contested and challenged in specific terms by real organizations and real people. These challenges are grounded in an agenda emphasizing fair play, an end to arbitrary class inequalities, and greater opportunities for all Americans to actually achieve the American Dream—and thereby bring about a class-iceberg meltdown.

NOTES

1. See, for example, Seymour M. Lipset and Reinhard Bendix, *Social Mobility in Industrial Society* (Berkeley: University of California Press, 1959); Harry J. Crochett Jr., "The Achievement Motive and Differential Occupational Mobility in the United States," *Ameri-*

can *Sociological Review* 27 (1962): 191–204; Reinhard Bendix and Frank W. Howton, "Social Mobility and the American Business Elite—II," *British Journal of Sociology* 9 (1958): 1–14.

2. Peter Blau and Otis D. Duncan, *The American Occupational Structure* (New York: Wiley, 1967); David L. Featherman and Robert M. Hauser, *Opportunity and Change* (New York: Academic Press, 1978).

3. Beth A. Rubin, *Shifts in the Social Contract* (Thousand Oaks, Calif.: Pine Forge Press, 1996), 7–8; John E. Farley, "What's in the American Dream," in *Sociology* (Englewood Cliffs, N.J.: Prentice-Hall, 1990), 99.

4. George J. Church, "Are We Better Off?" *Time*, January 29, 1996, 37–40; Everett Carll Ladd and Karlyn H. Bowman, "The Nation Says No to Class Warfare," *USA Today*, May 1999, 24–26.

5. *EXTRA!Update*, "Everyone's Rich in Media-Land . . . But You?" August 1999, 4.

6. Dan Rather, *The American Dream: Stories from the Heart of Our Nation* (New York: William Morrow, 2001).

7. William Greider, "Nader and the Politics of Fear," *Nation*, March 12, 2001, 15–18; The Editors, "The Nader Campaign and the Future of U.S. Left Electoral Politics," *Monthly Review*, February 2001, 1–22.

8. "Opposing the World Trade Organization," "Fighting Permanent Normal Trade Relations Status for China," "Opposing Harmful Trade Measure for Africa," "Monitoring Harmonization and Other Trade Issues," *Public Citizen News: Annual Report 2000*, March–April 2001, 10–12; Lori Wallach, "Corporate Protectionism," *Public Citizen: Special Anniversary Issue* 21 (2001): 10–11, 27.

9. Seth Ackerman, "Prattle in Seattle," *EXTRA!* January–February 2000, 13–17; Rachel Coen, "Whitewash in Washington," *EXTRA!* July–August 2000, 9–12; David Moberg, "Tear Down the Walls: The Movement is Becoming More Global," *In These Times*, May 28, 2001, 11–14.

10. For poll examples, see Andrew Kohut, "Globalization and the Wage Gap," *New York Times*, December 3, 1999, A29; Bob Burnett, "Publisher's Notes," *In These Times*, March 19, 2001, i; John Omicinski, "Public in Poll Supports Church, Police, Military," *Indianapolis Star*, June 26, 2001, A3.

11. Andrew Levison, "Who Lost the Working Class?" *Nation*, May 14, 2001, 25–32.

12. Charles E. Hurst, *Social Inequality* (Boston: Allyn and Bacon, 1995), 308–10.

13. David Elsila, Michael Funke, and Sam Kirkland, "Blaming the Victim: The Propaganda War against Workers," *UAW Solidarity*, April 1992, 11–17.

14. John W. Wright, ed., *The New York Times Almanac 2001* (New York: Penguin, 2000), 384; Robert W. McChesney, *Rich Media, Poor Democracy* (Chicago: University of Illinois Press, 1999), 298; Scott Sherman, "An Appeal to Reason," *Nation*, March 10, 1997, 15–19.

15. Jonathan Tasini, "Lost in the Margins: Labor and the Media," *EXTRA!* Summer 1990, 2–5.

16. Steve Rendall, "Media See the Poor as Aggressors in 'Class War,'" *EXTRA!* January–February 2001, 10; Tony Snow, "What the Class Warriors Don't Get About $1.6 Trillion," *Lafayette Courier Journal*, February 10, 2001, A5.

17. Peter Hart and Jim Naureckas, "Nader and the Press: Condescension Turns Nasty," *EXTRA!Update*, October 2000, 4.

18. Peter Hart, "Nader the Nightmare," *EXTRA!* January–February 2001, 11.

19. Marty Jezer, "The Missing Candidate," *Progressive Populist*, November 1, 2000, 14–15.

20. Hart, "Nader the Nightmare."

21. Robert Perrucci and Earl Wysong, *The New Class Society* (Lanham, Md.: Rowman and Littlefield, 1999), 37–40.

22. Rendall, "Media See the Poor as Aggressors in 'Class War.'"

23. Seth Ackerman, "Populist Rhetoric Unpopular With the Pundits," *EXTRA!* January–February 2001, 9.

24. Janine Jackson, "We Feel Your Pain," *EXTRA!* May–June 1996, 11–12.

25. See, for example, Daniel McGinn and Keith Naughton, "How Safe is Your Job?" *Newsweek,* February 5, 2001, 34–43; Daniel McGinn, "Weathering the Storm," *Newsweek,* March 16, 2001, 22–26; Adam Cohen, "This Time It's Different," *Time,* January 8, 2001, 18–22; Daniel Kadlec, "Zap," *Time,* March 26, 2001, 26–31.

26. Gregory Mantsios, "Class in America: Myths and Realities," in *Race, Class, and Gender in the United States,* ed. Paula S. Rothenberg (New York: St. Martin's Press, 1995).

27. Robert W. McChesney, "Journalism, Democracy, and Class Struggle," *Monthly Review,* November 2000, 1–15; Jim Naureckas, "From the Top: What Are the Politics of Network Bosses?" *EXTRA!* July–August 1998, 21–22; Jim Naureckas, "Where's the Power: Newsroom or Boardroom?" *EXTRA!* July–August 1998, 23.

28. Janine Jackson and Peter Hart, "Fear & Favor 2000: How Power Shapes the News," *EXTRA!* May–June 2001, 15–22; Gregory Mantsios, "Media Magic: Making Class Disappear," in Rothenberg, *Race, Class, and Gender in the United States.*

29. See for example, Michelle Cottle, "The Real Class War," *Washington Monthly,* July–August 1997, 12–16; Donald L. Barlett and James B. Steele, *America: Who Really Pays The Taxes?* (New York: Touchstone, 1994), 93–94; *Congressional Record, Taxpayer Relief Act of 1997,* June 26, 1997, H4810; and Rendall, "Media See the Poor as Aggressors in 'Class War.'"

30. David Croteau, "Challenging the 'Liberal Media' Claim," *EXTRA!* July–August 1998, 4–9.

31. See, for example, Hurst, *Social Inequality,* 305–12; Everett Carll Ladd and Karlyn H. Bowman, "The Nation Says No to Class Warfare," *USA Today,* May 1999, 24–26; Harold R. Kerbo, *Social Stratification and Inequality* (New York: McGraw-Hill, 2000), 258–67.

32. G. William Domhoff, *Who Rules America? Power and Politics* (Boston: McGraw-Hill, 2002), 45–68.

33. Thomas Dye, *Who's Running America? The Clinton Years* (Englewood Cliffs, N.J.: Prentice Hall, 1995), 215.

34. Hurst, *Social Inequality,* 300.

35. Richard D. Coleman and Lee Rainwater, *Social Standing in America* (New York: Basic Books, 1978).

36. Kerbo, *Social Stratification and Inequality,* 22; Hurst, *Social Inequality,* 23.

37. Randy Hodson and Teresa A. Sullivan, *The Social Organization of Work* (Belmont, Calif.: Wadsworth-Thomson 2002), 157–61.

38. George Gallup and S. F. Rae, *The Pulse of Democracy* (New York: Simon and Schuster, 1940), 169; Robert W. Hodge and Donald J. Treiman, "Class Identification in the United States," *American Journal of Sociology* 73 (March 1968): 535–47; Mary R. Jackman and Robert W. Jackman, *Class Awareness in the United States* (Berkeley: University of California Press, 1982), 18; Reeve Vanneman and Lynn Weber Cannon, *The American Perception of Class* (Philadelphia: Temple University Press, 1987).

39. Doug Henwood, "American Dream: It's Not Working," *Christianity and Crisis,* June 8, 1992, 195–97.

40. Bennett Harrison and Barry Bluestone, "The Crisis of the American Dream," in *Great Divides*, ed. Thomas A. Shapiro (Mountain View, Calif.: Mayfield, 1998), 179–91.

41. *New York Times*, *The Downsizing of America* (New York: Random House, 1996), 318.

42. Based on the authors' analysis of fifteen 2000–2001 introductory sociology texts.

43. Lawrence Mishel, Jared Bernstein, and John Schmitt, *The State of Working America 2000–2001* (Ithaca, N.Y.: Cornell University Press, 2001), 129–30.

44. Arthur MacEwan, "Ask Dr. Dollar," *Dollars and Sense*, May–June 2001, 41; Mishel, Bernstein, and Schmitt, *Working America 2000–2001*, 50, 83.

45. David Wright, "Changes in Hourly Earnings, 1947–2001," *WORK SERIES*, (Wichita, Kans.: Wichita State University), August, 2001, A19–20.

46. Economic Policy Institute, "Data Zone: Hourly Wages by Occupation, 1973–2000," on the Internet at http://www.epinet.org/datazone/dznational.html (visited July 5, 2001), 1–3.

47. Mishel, Bernstein, and Schmitt, *Working America, 2000–2001*, 45, 101, 103.

48. U.S. Bureau of the Census, "Money Income in the United States, 1999" (Washington, D.C.: U.S. Government Printing Office, 2000), xii; Economic Policy Institute, "Data Zone: Income Limits for Each Fifth and Top 5 Percent of Families, 1947–1999," 9.

49. Congressional Budget Office. *A CBO Study*, "Historical Effective Tax Rates, 1979–1997" (Preliminary Edition), Table G-1c (Washington, D.C.: Congress of the United States, May 2001), 74–75.

50. Louis Lavelle, "Special Report: Executive Pay," *Business Week*, April 16, 2001, 78.

51. Holly Sklar, "CEO Ponzi Scheme," on the Internet at http://www.inequality.org/ceopayedit2.html (visited May 11, 2001), 3.

52. Minimum-wage annual incomes were computed on the basis of 40 hours per week for 52 weeks and valued using 1999 dollars at $6.28 per hour in 1980 and $4.85 per hour in 2000. See Economic Policy Institute, "Data Zone: Historical Values of the U.S. Minimum Wage, 1960–2001," 1.

53. Sklar, "CEO Ponzi Scheme," 3.

54. Lavelle, "Special Report: Executive Pay," 77, 79.

55. John J. Macionis, "Diversity in the New Century: Changes in the Workplace," in *Sociology* (Upper Saddle River, N.J.: Prentice Hall, 2001), 424.

56. Louis Lavelle, "For Female CEOs, It's Stingy at the Top," *Business Week*, April 23, 2001, 70–71.

57. Lawrence Mishel, Jared Bernstein, and John Schmitt, *The State of Working America, 1996–1997* (Armonk, N.Y.: M. E. Sharpe, 1997), 156; Mishel, Bernstein, and Schmitt, *Working America, 2000–2001*, 139, 119.

58. Mishel, Bernstein, and Schmitt, *Working America, 2000–2001*, 142–43.

59. *Monthly Labor Review*, "Current Labor Statistics: Tables 25 and 26" (May 2001): 90–91.

60. Mishel, Bernstein, and Schmitt, *Working America, 2000–2001*, 141.

61. Ibid., 142–43.

62. Ibid., 140.

63. Ida Hellander, "A Review of Data on the Health Care Sector of the United States," *International Journal of Health Services* 31 (2001): 38.

64. *Monthly Labor Review*, "Current Labor Statistics: Table 25" (May 2001): 90.

65. See, for example, Anne E. Polivka, "Contingent and Alternative Work Arrange-

ments, Defined," *Monthly Labor Review* (October 1996): 3–9; Steve Hipple, "Contingent Work in the late-1990s," *Monthly Labor Review* (March 2001): 3–27.

66. Chuck Collins and Felice Yeskel, *Economic Apartheid in America* (New York: The New Press, 2000), 109.

67. See Mishel, Bernstein, and Schmitt, *Working America, 2000–2001*, 253. Also see Collins and Yeskel, *Economic Apartheid in America*, 109.

68. Mishel, Bernstein, and Schmitt, *Working America, 2000–2001*, 245–47, 249.

69. U.S. Department of Labor, Bureau of Labor Statistics, "Union Members Summary," press release, January 17, 2002, 1. Also see Mishel, Bernstein, and Schmitt, *Working America, 2000–2001*, 180.

70. Mishel, Bernstein, and Schmitt, *Working America, 2000–2001*, 180.

71. Ibid., 234, 232.

72. Gene Koretz, "Downsized in a Down Economy," *Business Week*, September 17, 2001, 36. Also see Martin Crutsinger, "Fresh Reports Paint Picture of Recession," *Indianapolis Star*, October 26, 2001, C1, C4.

73. Dean Baker, "Free Trade Fables," *Extra!* January–February 2000, 18.

74. Mishel, Bernstein, and Schmitt, *Working America 2000–2001*, 234.

75. Richard T. Schaefer, *Sociology* (New York: McGraw-Hill, 2001), 220.

76. Kerbo, *Social Stratification*, 337–41.

77. Greg J. Duncan and Wei-Jun J. Yeung, "Extent and Consequences of Welfare Dependence among America's Children," *Children and Youth Services Review* 17 (1995): 157–82.

78. David Dooley, JoAnn Prause, Kathleen A. Ham-Rowbottom, "Underemployment and Depression: Longitudinal Relationships," *Journal of Health and Social Behavior* 41 (December 2000): 421–36. Also see Robert A. Rothman, *Working: Sociological Perspectives, Second Edition* (Upper Saddle River, N.J.: Prentice Hall, 1998), 183–88.

79. See, for example, Aaron Bernstein, "Back on the Edge," *Business Week*, April 23, 2001, 42–43; Barry Bluestone and Bennett Harrison, *The Deindustrialization of America* (New York: Basic Books, 1982); Barbara Ehrenreich, *Fear of Falling* (New York: Harper, 1989); Katherine S. Newman, *Falling from Grace: The Experience of Downward Mobility in the American Middle Class* (New York: Free Press, 1988) and *Declining Fortunes* (New York: Basic Books, 1993); *New York Times, Downsizing of America*; Carolyn C. Perrucci, Robert Perrucci, Dena B. Targ, and Harry Targ, *Plant Closings: International Context and Social Costs* (Hawthorne, N.Y.: Aldine de Gruyter, 1988).

80. *New York Times, Downsizing of America*; Daniel McGinn and Keith Naughton, "How Safe is Your Job?" *Newsweek*, February 5, 2001, 34–43; Cohen, "This Time It's Different."

81. Stanley Aronowitz, *The Last Good Job in America* (Lanham, Md.: Rowman and Littlefield, 2001); Stanley Aronowitz and William DiFazio, "High Technology and Work Tomorrow," *Annals of the American Academy of Political and Social Science* 544 (March 1996): 52–76; Robert Perrucci and Earl Wysong, "Organizational Power, Generative Capital, and Class Closure," paper presented at the Pacific Sociological Association annual meeting, March 31, 2001, San Francisco, Calif.

82. Theoretically, downward mobility from the privileged class into the new working class could occur in our model; but we believe it is rare, and the topic would require separate attention. Therefore, we do not address it here.

83. Newman, *Falling from Grace*.

84. *New York Times, Downsizing of America,* 50.

85. Mishel, Bernstein, and Schmitt, *Working America 2000–2001,* 169.

86. Susan J. Wells, "Looking for Trouble," *HR Magazine,* January 2001, 42.

87. Mishel, Bernstein, and Schmitt, *Working America 2000–2001,* 169; John Miller, "When is the Economy in a Recession?" *Dollars and Sense,* July–August 2001, 32.

88. Koretz, "Downsized in a Down Economy."

89. Kemba J. Dunham and Greg Ip, "Weak Economy Takes Unusually Heavy Toll on White-Collar Jobs," *Wall Street Journal,* November 5, 2001, A1, A8.

90. Jeffrey R. Lustig, "The Politics of Shutdown," *Journal of Economic Issues* 19 (1985): 123–59.

91. Gene Koretz, "Downsizing's Painful Effects," *Business Week,* April 13, 1998, 23.

92. Ryan T. Helwig, "Worker Displacement in a Strong Labor Market," *Monthly Labor Review* June 2001, 13–28.

93. Charles Koeber and David W. Wright, "W/Age Bias in Worker Displacement: How Industrial Structure Shapes the Job Loss and Earnings Decline of Older American Workers," *Journal of Socio-Economics* 30 (2001): 343–52.

94. Mishel, Bernstein, and Schmitt, *Working America 2000–2001,* 120.

95. Holly Sklar, "CEO Ponzi Scheme."

96. Kurt Schrammel, "Comparing the Labor Market Success of Young Adults from Two Generations," *Monthly Labor Review* (February 1998): 3–9.

97. Geoffrey Paulin and Brian Riordon, "Making It on Their Own: The Baby Boom Meets Generation X," *Monthly Labor Review* (February 1998): 10–21.

98. Mishel, Bernstein, and Schmitt, *Working America, 2000–2001,* 157–58.

99. AFL-CIO, "Young Workers Without College Degrees Are the 'Forgotten Majority,'" *High Hopes, Little Trust: A Study of Young Workers and Their Ups and Downs in the New Economy* (Washington, D.C.: AFL-CIO, 1999), 1.

100. Michael Golay and Carl Rollyson, *Where America Stands 1996* (New York: Wiley, 1996), 167–69.

101. Ladd and Bowman, "The Nation Says No to Class Warfare," 26.

102. U.S. Department of Commerce, Bureau of the Census, *Statistical Abstract of the United States* (Washington, D.C.: U.S. Government Printing Office, 2000), 54.

103. Tom Frank, "Let Them Eat Lifestyle," *Utne Reader,* November–December 1997, 43–47.

104. See Theresa A. Martinez, "Popular Culture as Oppositional Culture: Rap as Resistance," *Sociological Perspectives* 40 (1997): 265–86; Keith Goetzman, "Righteous Babe: Interview with Ani DiFrancio," *Utne Reader,* July–August 2001, 94–96.

105. Evan Endicott, "Musical Memento," *In These Times,* July 23, 2001, 26–27.

106. Robert B. Reich, "Secession of the Successful," *New York Times Magazine,* January 20, 1991, 42.

107. Edward J. Blakely and Mary Gail Snyder, *Fortress America: Gated Communities in the United States* (Washington, D.C.: Brookings Institution Press, 1997), 180.

108. Tim Vanderpool, "Secession of the Successful," *Utne Reader,* November–December 1995, 32–34.

109. Blakely and Snyder, *Fortress America,* 7–8, 180; Collins and Yeskel, *Economic Apartheid,* 37.

110. Collins and Yeskel, *Economic Apartheid,* 37.

111. Evan McKenzie, *Privatopia* (New Haven: Yale University Press, 1994), 105, 186.

112. Charles Murray, "The Shape of Things to Come," *National Review*, July 8, 1991, 30.

113. Robert B. Reich, *The Work of Nations: Preparing Ourselves for the Twenty-first Century* (New York: Knopf, 1991), 140.

114. Jerry Adler, "The Rise of the Overclass," *Newsweek*, July 31, 1995, 45–46.

115. See, for example, Ben H. Bagdikian, *The Media Monopoly* (Boston: Beacon Press, 1997); Domhoff, *Who Rules America? Power and Politics*; Dye, *Who's Running America?*

116. U.S. Department of Commerce, *Statistical Abstract* (2000), 535; Richard B. DuBoff and Edward S. Herman, "Mergers, Concentration, and the Erosion of Democracy," *Monthly Review*, May 2001, 14–29.

117. "Inside the 500," *Fortune*, April 16, 2001, 232.

118. Manufacturing assets and profits computed from data reported in U.S. Department of Commerce, *Statistical Abstract* (2000), 558.

119. Banking assets computed from data reported in *Fortune*, "The 500 Largest U.S. Corporations" and "The *Fortune* 1000 Ranked within Industries," April 16, 2001, F-1–F-19, F-45–F-69; U.S. Department of Commerce, *Statistical Abstract* (2000), 512.

120. Insurance assets computed from data reported in *Fortune* (ibid.) and U.S. Department of Commerce, *Statistical Abstract* (2000), 532.

121. U.S. Department of Commerce, *Statistical Abstract* (2000), 561.

122. Kerry A. Dolan and Luisa Kroll, eds., "The World's Richest People," *Forbes*, July 9, 2001, 110.

123. Mishel, Bernstein, and Schmitt, *Working America 2000–2001*, 265.

124. Michael J. Mandel, "How the Super-Rich Lucked Out Twice," *Business Week*, May 14, 2001, 52.

125. Congressional Budget Office, May 2001, 125.

126. Mishel, Bernstein, and Schmitt, *Working America 2000–2001*, 58.

127. For examples, see G. William Domhoff, *State Autonomy or Class Dominance?* (New York: Aldine de Gruyter, 1996); Domhoff, *Who Rules America? Power and Politics*; Michael Useem, *The Inner Circle* (New York: Oxford University Press, 1984); and Dye, *Who's Running America?*

128. Mishel, Bernstein, and Schmitt, *Working America 2000–2001*, 85.

129. Lavelle, "Special Report: Executive Pay."

130. Donald L. Barlett and James B. Steele, *America: What Went Wrong?* (Kansas City, Mo.: Andrews and McMeel, 1992), xiii.

131. Karen Foerstel, "No Allowance, but Look at the Perks," *Congressional Quarterly Weekly*, March 17, 2001, 576.

132. Jeffrey Marshall, "The Buck$ Aren't $topping," *Financial Executive*, July–August, 2001, 40–43.

133. Dolan and Kroll, "The World's Richest People."

134. "The Top-Paid CEOs," *Forbes*, May 18, 1998, 254.

135. Alexander Cockburn and Jeffrey St. Clair, "Nike's New Wage Scam," *CounterPunch*, April 15, 1999, 1, 6; Lavelle, "Executive Pay," 80.

136. Murray L. Wiedenbaum, *Business, Government, and the Public* (Englewood Cliffs, N.J.: Prentice-Hall, 1977), 5–8.

137. Vicente Navarro, "Production and the Welfare State: The Political Context of Reforms," *International Journal of Health Services* 21 (1991): 606.

138. Robert J. Samuelson, "Great Expectations," *Newsweek*, January 8, 1996, 31; also see Mishel, Bernstein, and Schmitt, *Working America, 2000–2001*, 91.

139. John B. Judis, "The Most Powerful Lobby," *In These Times*, February 21, 1994, 22–23.

140. Navarro, "Production and the Welfare State," 606.

141. Michael Patrick Allen, "Elite Social Movement Organizations and the State: The Rise of the Conservative Policy-Planning Network," in *Research in Politics and Society*, vol. 4, *The Political Consequences of Social Networks*, ed. Gwen Moore and J. Allen Whitt (Greenwich, Conn.: JAI Press, 1992).

142. Federal Election Commission, "FEC Releases New PAC Count," press release, July 28, 1989.

143. Federal Election Commission, "PAC Activity Increases in 2000 Election Cycle: Summary of PAC Financial Activity for 1999–2000," press release, May 31, 2001, 3, Sheet 1.

144. Federal Election Commission, "FEC Reports on Congressional Financial Activity for 2000," press release, May 31, 2001, 1.

145. Center for Responsive Politics, *Influence, Inc., Summary* (Washington, D.C.: Center for Responsive Politics, 2000), pp. 1–5; Larry Makinson, *The Big Picture: Money Follows Power Shift on Capitol Hill* (Washington, D.C.: Center for Responsive Politics, 1997), 1.

146. Makinson, *The Big Picture*, 4.

147. *Hard Facts on Hard Money* (Washington, D.C.: Public Campaign, 2001), 3.

148. Center for Responsive Politics, "Business, Labor, and Ideological Donors," *Who's Paying for This Election?* (Washington, D.C.: Center for Responsive Politics, 2000), 1.

149. Quoted in Navarro, "Production and the Welfare State," 607.

150. Perrucci and Wysong, *The New Class Society*, 133–34.

151. Alexander Cockburn and Jeffrey St. Clair, "It Really Was a Coup," *CounterPunch*, December 2000, 2.

152. "Tax Cut Madness," *Nation*, June 4, 2001, 3–4.

153. Curt Anderson, "House Passes $100 Billion Stimulus Measure," *Indianapolis Star*, October 25, 2001, A5; Robert L. Borosage, "Scoundrel Time," *Nation*, November 19, 2001, 6–7, 23; Bill Moyers, "Which America Will We Be Now?" *Nation*, November 19, 2001, 12.

154. See, for example, *Newsweek* cover story June 4, 2001; the cover included a picture of a resolute Jeffords with the caption: "Mr. Jeffords Blows Up Washington."

155. Alexander Cockburn and Jeffrey St. Clair, "Real Politics and the Jeffords Jump: Was the Bush White House Truly Sorry?" *CounterPunch*, June 1–15, 2001, 2.

156. Quoted in Wesley J. Smith, "Nobody's Nader," *Mother Jones*, July–August 1996, 61.

157. Earl Wysong, *High Risk and High Stakes: Health Professionals, Politics, and Policy* (Westport, Conn.: Greenwood Press, 1992).

158. See, for example, Charles Derber, *The Wilding of America* (New York: St. Martin's Press, 1996), 40–41, 48–49; Perrucci and Wysong, *The New Class Society*, 126–35; Frederick R. Strobel and Wallace C. Peterson, *The Coming Class War and How to Avoid It* (Armonk, N.Y.: M. E. Sharpe, 1999), 55–61; David Masci, "Senate Rejects Striker Bill; More Action Unlikely," *Congressional Quarterly Weekly Report*, July 16, 1994, 1936; Deb Riechmann, "Clinton Signs Measure to Open China to U.S. Goods," *Indianapolis Star*, October 11, 2000, A3; David Moberg, "FTAA, Eh? A Bigger, Badder Trade Deal," *In These Times*, April 16, 2001, 16–19.

159. U.S. Department of Commerce, *Statistical Abstract* (2000), 561.

160. Hodson and Sullivan, *The Social Organization of Work*, 258; for projections, see Allison Thomson, "Industry Output and Employment Projections to 2008," *Monthly Labor Review* (November 1999): 34.

161. Douglas Braddock, "Occupational Employment Projections to 2008," *Monthly Labor Review* (November 1999): 73.

162. Mishel, Bernstein, and Schmitt, *Working America 2000–2001*, 245–56.

163. Collins and Yeskel, *Economic Apartheid in America*, 109–11.

164. Juliet B. Schor, "Keeping Up with the Trumps: How the Middle Class Identifies with the Rich," *Washington Monthly*, July–August 1998, 34–37. Also see Domhoff, *Who Rules America? Power and Politics*, 176–79.

165. Domhoff, *Who Rules America? Power and Politics*, 45–68; Richard L. Zweigenhaft and G. William Domhoff, *Diversity in the Power Elite: Have Women and Minorities Reached the Top?* (New Haven: Yale University Press, 1998), 192–94.

166. Seth Ackerman, "The Most Biased Name in News," *EXTRA!* July–August 2001, 10–12.

167. For a discussion of equity and liberty, see Martin N. Marger, *Social Inequality: Patterns and Processes* (Boston: McGraw-Hill, 2002), 176.

168. Derber, *Wilding of America*, 141–42.

169. Wayne Alves and Peter Rossi, "Who Should Get What? Fairness Judgments of Distribution of Earnings," *American Journal of Sociology* 84 (1978): 541–64.

3

The Global Economy and the Privileged Class

Allowing the defenders of privilege to monopolize the term "globalization" for their own vision too easily allows them to portray themselves as agents of an impersonal process and to paint advocates of global justice as narrow specialists or naïve opponents of technological progress.

—Salih Booker and William Minter, *Nation,* July 9, 2001

In 2001, record layoffs led to the worst U.S. job market since the recession of 1990–91. In the period from January to June, 2001, U.S. companies announced 652,510 layoffs. From manufacturing to high-tech, workers lost jobs at the fastest rate in years. Although the 2001 job cuts were dramatic, they were merely the latest chapter in what has been a long story for U.S. workers. Twenty years earlier we followed 850 workers through what has since become an all-too-familiar pattern for millions of workers.

On December 1, 1982, an RCA television cabinet-making factory in Monticello, Indiana closed its doors and shut down production. Monticello, a town of five thousand people in White County (population twenty-three thousand), had been the home of RCA since 1946. The closing displaced 850 workers who were members of Local 3154 of The United Brotherhood of Carpenters and Joiners. Officials at RCA cited the high manufacturing costs and foreign competition as key factors leading to the closing.

Reactions of displaced workers from RCA were varied, with most expressing either a general sense of despair or a feeling of confidence that they would survive. One worker was hopeful, stating: "Losing one's job is a serious jolt to your attitude of security, preservation, and well-being. However, I feel strongly that we must look forward to hope and faith in our country and its people. Deep inside I want to believe that tough times won't last, but tough people do. This will mean a lot of sacrifice, determination, and change in those people affected by losing one's job." Less hopeful views are revealed in the following remarks:

> We are down to rock bottom and will probably have to sell the house to live or exist until I find a job here or somewhere else. I have been everywhere looking in Cass, White, and Carroll counties. We have had no help except when the electric company was going to shut off the utilities in March and the Trustee [County Welfare] paid that $141. My sister-in-law helps us sometimes with money she's saved back or with food she canned last summer. The factories have the young. I've been to all the factories. (Personal interviews with RCA workers.)

Whether the personal response to the closing was faith, fear, or anger, the common objective experience of the displaced workers was that they had been "dumped" from the "middle class." These displaced factory workers viewed themselves as middle class because of their wages and their lifestyles (home ownership, cars, vacations). Most had worked at RCA for two decades or more. They had good wages, health care benefits, and a pension program. They owned their homes (with mortgages), cars, recreational vehicles, boats, and all the household appliances associated with middle-class membership. All the trappings of the American Dream were threatened as their seemingly stable jobs and secure incomes disappeared. In the space of a few months these workers and their families joined the growing new working class—the 80 percent of Americans without stable resources for living.

The severity of this jolt to their sense of well-being and their "downward slide" is also revealed in the bleak picture displaced workers have of their future and the futures of their children: "I'm afraid it will be years before I get up the courage to buy a car, appliance, or anything on a long-term note, regardless of how good the pay is in a new job"; "I have a National Honor Society daughter with one more year of high school. If she can't get aid there's no way she can go to college." (Personal interviews with RCA workers.)

The experiences of the 850 RCA workers from Monticello, Indiana, were part of a national wave of plant closings that swept across the land two decades ago. According to a study commissioned by the U.S. Congress, between the late 1970s and mid-1980s more than 11 million workers lost jobs because of plant shutdowns, relocation of facilities to other countries, or layoffs. Most of these displaced workers were in manufacturing. Subsequent displaced worker surveys commissioned by the Bureau of Labor Statistics estimated that between 1986 and 1991 another 12 million workers were displaced, but now they were predominantly from the service sector (about 7.9 million).[1] When these displaced workers found new jobs, it was often in industry sectors where wages were significantly lower than what they had earned and jobs were often part-time and lacked health insurance and other benefits.

Beginning in the mid-1970s and continuing to the present, the American class structure was being reshaped from the layer-cakelike "middle-class" society into the double-diamond structure described in figure 1.5. The first step in this reshaping was a privileged-class-led attack on higher-wage unionized workers, eliminating their jobs in the auto industries, steel mills, rubber plants, and textile mills. The reshaping continued through the late 1980s to the mid-1990s, when the strategy was expanded to include not only plant closings and relocations, but "restructuring and downsizing" strategies as well, often directed at eliminating white-collar jobs.

The rush to downsize in some of America's largest and most prestigious corporations became so widespread in the 1990s that a new occupation was needed to handle the casualties. The "outplacement professional" was created to put the best corporate face on a decision to downsize, that is, to terminate large numbers of employees—as many as ten thousand. The job of these new public relations types is to get the general public to accept downsizing as the normal way of life for corporations that have to survive in the competitive global economy. Their job is also to assist the downsized middle managers to manage their anger and to get on with their lives.

The *Human Resources Development Handbook* of the American Management Association provides the operating philosophy for the outplacement professional: "Unnecessary personnel must be separated from the company if the organization is to continue as a viable business entity. To do otherwise in today's globally competitive world would be totally unjustified and might well be a threat to the company's future survival."[2]

The privileged 20 percent of the population are hard at work telling the other 80 percent about the harsh realities of the changing global economy. "Lifetime employment" is out. The goal is "lifetime employability," which workers try to attain by accumulating skills and being dedicated and committed employees. Even Japan's highly touted commitment to lifetime employment (in some firms) is apparently unraveling, as reported in a prominent feature article in the *New York Times*.[3] It should be no surprise that an elite media organization like the *Times*, whose upper-level employees belong to the privileged class, should join in disseminating the myth of the global economy as the "hidden hand" behind the downsizing of America. The casualties of plant closings and downsizings are encouraged to see their plight as part of the "natural laws" of economics.

This enormous transformation of the U.S. economy over a thirty-year period has been described by political leaders and media as the inevitable and therefore normal workings of the emerging global economy. Some, like former president Reagan, even applauded the changes as a historic opportunity to revitalize the economy. In a 1985 report to Congress, he stated, "The progression of an economy such as America's from the agricultural to manufacturing to services is a natural change. The move from an industrial society toward a postindustrial service economy has been one of the greatest changes to affect the developed world since the Industrial Revolution."[4]

A contrasting view posits that the transformation of the U.S. economy is not the result of natural economic laws or the "hidden hand" of global economic markets but, rather, the result of calculated actions by multinational corporations to expand their profits and power. When corporations decide to close plants and move them overseas where they can find cheap labor and fewer government regulations, they do so to enhance profits and not simply as a response to the demands of global competition. In many cases, the U.S. multinationals themselves are the global competition that puts pressure on other U.S. workers to work harder, faster, and for lower wages and fewer benefits.

THE GLOBAL ECONOMY AND CLASS STRUCTURE

Markets, which in mainstream ideology are as natural as gravity, have frequently been created and deepened through coercive state action—ranging from enclosures (the privatization of common lands) in Britain hundreds of years ago to NAFTA's eviction of Mexican peasants from their land today.

—Doug Henwood, *In These Times,* September 30, 1996

Discussion about the new global economy by mainstream media reporters and business leaders generally focuses on three topics. First is the appearance of many new producers of quality goods in parts of the world that are normally viewed as less developed. Advances in computer-based production systems have allowed many countries in Southeast Asia and Latin America to produce goods that compete with those of more advanced industrial economics in Western Europe and North America. Second is the development of telecommunications systems that permit rapid economic transactions around the globe and the coordination of economic activities in locations separated by thousands of miles. The combination of advances in computer-based production and telecommunications makes it possible for large firms, especially multinationals, to decentralize their production and locate facilities around the globe. Third is the existence of an international division of labor that makes it possible for corporations to employ engineers, technicians, or production workers from anywhere in the world. This gives corporations great flexibility when negotiating with their domestic workforce over wages and benefits. These changes in how we produce things and who produces them have resulted in expanded imports and exports and an enlarged role for trade in the world economy. Leading this expansion has been increased foreign investments around the world by the richer nations. It is estimated that two-thirds of international financial transactions have taken place within and between Europe, the United States, and Japan.[5]

The changes just noted are often used as evidence of a "new global economy" *out there* constraining the actions of all corporations to be competitive if they hope to survive. One concrete indicator of this global economy *out there* is the rising level of international trade between the United States and other nations. In the 1960s, the United States was the dominant exporter of goods and services, while the imports of foreign products played a small part in the U.S. economy. Throughout the 1970s foreign imports claimed an increasing share, and by 1981 the United States "was importing almost 26 percent of its cars, 25 percent of its steel, 60 percent of its televisions, tape recorders, radios, and phonographs, 43 percent of its calculators, 27 percent of its metal-forming machine tools, 35 percent of its textile machinery, and 53 percent of its numerically controlled machine tools."[6] Imports from developing nations went from $3.6 billion in 1970 to $30 billion in 1980.

Throughout the 1980s, the United States became a debtor nation in terms of the balance between what we exported to the rest of the world and what we import. By 2000, the U.S. trade deficit indicated that the import of goods and services exceeded exports by $370 billion. This is the largest deficit since the previous high in 1987 of $153.4 billion. But what do these trade figures tell us? On the surface, they appear to be a function of the operation of the global economy, because the figures indicate that we have an $81.3 billion deficit with Japan, $83.8 billion with China, and $24.9 billion with Mexico.[7] It appears that Japanese, Chinese, and Mexican companies are doing a better job of producing goods than the United States and thus we import products rather than producing them ourselves. But is this the correct conclusion? The answer lies in how you count imports and exports.

Trade deficit figures are based on balance of payment statistics, which tally the dollar value of U.S. exports to other countries and the dollar value of foreign exports to the United States; if the dollar value of Chinese exports to the United States exceeds the dollar value of U.S. exports to China, the United States has a trade deficit with China. This would appear to mean that Chinese companies are producing the goods being exported to the United States. But that is not necessarily the case. According to the procedures followed in calculating trade deficits, "the U.S. balance of payments statistics are intended to capture the total amount of transactions between U.S. *residents* and *residents* of the rest of the world."[8] If "resident" simply identifies the geographical location of the source of an import, then some unknown portion of the $49.7 billion U.S. trade deficit with China could be from U.S.-owned firms that are producing goods in China and exporting them to the United States. Those U.S. firms are residents of China, and their exports are counted as Chinese exports to the United States.

Thus, the global economy that is *out there* forcing U.S. firms to keep wages low so we can be more competitive might actually be made up of U.S. firms that have located production plants in countries other than in the United States. Such actions may be of great benefit to the U.S. multinational firms that produce goods around the world and export them to the U.S. market. Such actions may also benefit U.S. consumers, who pay less for goods produced in low-wage areas. But what about the U.S. worker in a manufacturing plant whose wages have not increased in twenty years because of the need to compete with "foreign companies"? What about the worker who may never get a job in manufacturing because U.S. firms have been opening plants in other countries rather than in the United States? As the comic strip character Pogo put it: "We have met the enemy and it is us."

American multinational corporations' foreign investments have changed the emphasis in the economy from manufacturing to service. This shift has changed the occupational structure by eliminating high-wage manufacturing jobs and creating a two-tiered system of service jobs. There have been big winners and big losers in this social and economic transformation. The losers have been the three out of four Americans who work for wages—wages that have been declining since 1973; these American workers constitute the new working class (see chapter 1). The big winners have been the privileged classes, for whom jobs and incomes have expanded at the same time that everyone else was in decline. Corporate executives, managers, scientists, engineers, doctors, corporate lawyers, accountants, computer programmers, financial consultants, health care professionals, and media professionals have all registered substantial gains in income and wealth in the last thirty years. And the changes that have produced the "big losers" and "big winners" have been facilitated by the legislative actions of the federal government and elected officials of both political parties, whose incomes, pensions, health care, and associated "perks" have also grown handsomely in the past two decades.

This chapter demonstrates that the privileged classes have benefited at the expense of the working classes. The profits of corporations and stockholders have expanded because fewer workers produce more goods and services for lower wages. The profits of corporations are distributed to executives, managers, and professionals in higher salaries and benefits because they are able either to extract more work from workers while paying them less, or to justify inequality by providing distracting entertainment for the less fortunate, or control them if necessary. The privileged class is able to maintain its position of advantage because its members control the jobs and incomes of other Americans. They also control the mass media and education, which are the instruments of ideological domination. If all of this is not enough, they also control the means of violence (military, national guard, police, and the investigative and security apparatus) that are used to deal with large-scale dissent.

CREATING THE GLOBAL ECONOMY: THE
PATH TO CORPORATE PROFITS

We have entered the era of Empire, a "supranational" center consisting of networks of transnational corporations and advanced capitalist nations led by the one remaining superpower, the United States.

—Michael Hardt and Antonio Negri, *Empire*, 2000

When World War II ended in 1945, all but one of the industrial nations involved had experienced widespread destruction of their industrial system and the infrastructure that is necessary for a healthy economy to provide sufficient food, shelter, and clothing for its people. Although all nations that participated in the war suffered terrible human losses, the United States alone emerged with its economic system stronger than it was at the start of the war.

For nearly thirty years following World War II, the United States dominated the world economy through its control of three-fourths of the world's invested capital and two-thirds of its industrial capacity. At the close of the war, there was concern in the United States that the high levels of production, profits, and employment stimulated by war mobilization could not be sustained. The specter of a return to the stagnation and unemployment experienced only a decade earlier during the Great Depression led to the search for a new economic and political system that would maintain the economic, military, and political dominance of the United States.

The postwar geopolitical-economic policy of the United States was designed to provide extensive foreign assistance to stimulate the recovery of Western Europe. This policy would stimulate U.S. investment in Europe and provide the capital for countries to buy U.S. agricultural and industrial products. The policy was also designed to "fight" the creation of socialist governments and socialist policies in Western Europe, governments that might not be sympathetic to U.S. capital, trade, and influence. The foreign assistance policy known as the Marshall Plan was instituted to provide $22 billion in aid over a four-year period and to bring together European nations into a global economic system dominated by the United States.[9]

This system was the basis for U.S. growth and prosperity during the 1950s, the 1960s, and the early 1970s. By the mid-1970s, steady improvements in the war-torn economies of Western Europe and Asia had produced important shifts in the balance of economic power among industrialized nations. The U.S. gross national product was now less than twice that of the Soviet Union (in 1950 it was more than three times), less than four times that of Germany (down from nine times in 1950), and less than three times that of Japan (twelve times in 1950). With many nations joining the United States in the production of the world's goods, the U.S. rate of growth slowed. As England, France, Germany, and Japan produced goods for domestic consumption, there was less need to import agricultural and industrial products from the United States.

The profits of U.S. corporations from the domestic economy were in a steady decline through the late 1960s and into the 1970s. In the early 1960s the annual rate of return on investment was 15.5 percent. In the late 1960s it was 12.7 percent. In the early 1970s it was 10 percent, and after 1975 it slipped below 10 percent, where it remained.

The privileged classes in the United States were concerned about declining profits. This affected their accumulation of wealth from stocks, bonds, dividends, and other investments. It affected corporate, managerial, and professional salaries indirectly, through the high rate of inflation that eroded the purchasing power of consumption capital (i.e., salaries) and the real value of investment capital (i.e., value of stocks, bonds, etc.). To account for the U.S. decline, business leaders and the national media listed the usual suspects.

The leading "explanation" was that U.S. products could not compete in the global economy because of the power of organized labor. This power was reflected in the high labor costs that made products less competitive and in cost-of-living adjustments that increased wages at the rate of inflation (which was sometimes at double digits). Union control of work rules also made it difficult for management to adopt new innovations to increase productivity and reduce dependence on labor.

Next on the list was the American worker, who was claimed to have embraced a declining work ethic, resulting in products of lower quality and higher cost. U.S. workers were portrayed as too content and secure and thus unwilling to compete with the ambitious workers of the rapidly developing economies.

The third suspect was the wide array of new regulations on business that had been adopted by the federal government to protect workers and the environment. Corporate executives complained about the increased cost of doing business that came from meeting the workplace standards of the Occupational Safety and Health Administration (OSHA) or the air and water pollution standards of the Environmental Protection Agency (EPA).

The explanations business leaders put forth for declining profits, selfish unions, lazy workers, and government regulations were said to make American products less competitive in the global economy. They provided the rationale for an attack on unions and on workers' wages and helped to justify massive plant closings and capital flight to low-wage areas. They also served to put the government on the defensive for its failure to be sensitive to the "excessive" costs that federal regulations impose on business.

What was rarely discussed in the business pages of the *New York Times* or the *Wall Street Journal* was the failure of corporate management in major U.S. firms to respond to the increasing competition to the once U.S.-dominated production of autos, steel, textiles, and electronics. In the early 1960s, imports of foreign products played a small part in the American economy, but by 1980 things had changed. In the early 1960s, imports accounted for less than 10 percent of the U.S. market, but by 1980 more than 70 percent of all the goods produced in the United States were actively competing with foreign-made goods.[10]

American corporations failed to follow the well-established management approach to the loss of market share, competitive advantage, and profits. Instead of pursuing long-term solutions, like investing in more efficient technology, new plants, research and development, and new markets, corporate executives chose to follow short-term strategies that would make the bottom line of profits the primary goal. The way was open for increased foreign investment, mergers, and downsizing.

WHEN YOUR DOG BITES YOU

With industrial jobs shrinking in the United States, and so much of what we buy, from clothing to electronics to automobiles, now made abroad, a common perception is that "globalized" production is a primary cause of falling living standards for American workers.

—Richard B. DuBoff, *Dollars and Sense*, September–October 1997

While corporate profits from the domestic U.S. economy were declining steadily from the mid-1970s, investment by U.S. corporations abroad showed continued growth. The share of corporate profits from direct foreign investment increased through the 1970s, as did the amount of U.S. direct investment abroad. In 1970, direct investment by U.S. firms abroad was $75 billion, and it rose to $167 billion in 1978. In the 1980–85 period it remained below $400 billion, but thereafter increased gradually each year, reaching $716 billion in 1994. The 100 largest U.S. multinational corporations reported foreign revenue in 1994 that ranged from 30 to 70 percent of their total revenue: IBM had 62 percent of total revenue from foreign sources; Eastman Kodak 52 percent; Colgate-Palmolive 68 percent; and Johnson and Johnson, Coca Cola, Pepsi, and Procter and Gamble each 50 percent.[11]

American multinational corporations sought to maintain their profit margins by increasing investments in affiliates abroad. This strategy may have kept stockholders happy, and maintained the price of corporate stocks on Wall Street, but it would result in deindustrialization—the use of corporate capital for foreign investment, mergers, and acquisitions rather than for investment in domestic operations.[12] Instead of investing in the U.S. auto, steel, and textile industries, companies were closing plants at an unprecedented rate and using the capital to open production facilities in other countries. By 1994, U.S. companies employed 5.4 million people abroad, more than 4 million of whom worked in manufacturing.[13] Thus, millions of U.S. manufacturing workers who were displaced in the 1980s by plant closings saw their jobs shifted to foreign production facilities. Although most criticism of U.S. investment abroad is reserved for low-wage countries like Mexico and Thailand, the biggest share of manufacturing investment abroad is in Germany and Japan—hardly low-wage countries. The United States has large trade deficits with Japan and Western Europe, where the hourly wages in manufacturing are 15–25 percent higher than in the United States.[14] This fact challenges the argument made by multinational corporations that if they did not shift production abroad, they would probably lose the sale of that product.

The movement of U.S. production facilities to foreign countries in the 1980s and 1990s was not simply the result of a search for another home where they could once again be productive and competitive. It appeared as if RCA closed its plant in Monticello, Indiana, because its high-wage workers made it impossible to compete with televisions being produced in Southeast Asia. Saddened by having to leave its home in Indiana of thirty-five years, RCA would have to search for another home

Copyright © Tom Tomorrow. Reprinted with permission.

where, it was hoped, the company could stay at least another thirty-five years, if not longer. Not likely: Plants did not close in the 1980s to find other homes; the closures were the first step in the creation of the homeless and stateless multinational corporation—an entity without ties to place, or allegiances to people, communities, or nations.

Thus, the rash of plant closings in the 1970s and 1980s began as apparent responses to economic crises of declining profits and increased global competition. As such, they appeared to be rational management decisions to protect stockholder investments and the future of individual firms. Although things may have started in this way, it soon became apparent that what was being created was the *spatially decentered firm:* a company that could produce a product with components manufactured in a half-dozen different plants around the globe and then assembled at a single location for distribution and sale. Although spatially decentered, the new transnational firm was also centralized in its decision making, allowing it to coordinate decisions about international investment. The new firm and its global production system were made possible by significant advances in computer-assisted design and manufacturing that made it unnecessary to produce a product at a single location. They were also made possible by advances in telecommunications that enabled management at corporate headquarters to coordinate research, development, design, manufacturing, and sales decisions at various sites scattered around the world.

The homeless and stateless multinational firm is able to move its product as quickly as it can spot a competitive advantage associated with low wages, cheaper raw materials, advantageous monetary exchange rates, more sympathetic governments, or proximity to markets. This encourages foreign investment because it expands the options of corporations in their choice of where to locate, and it makes them less vulnerable to pressure from workers regarding wages and benefits.

The advantages of the multinational firm and foreign investments are also a product of the U.S. tax code. In addition to providing the largest firms with numerous ways to delay, defer, and avoid taxes, corporate profits made on overseas investments are taxed at a much lower rate than profits from domestic operations. Thus, as foreign investments by U.S. firms increased over the last two decades, the share of total taxes paid by corporations declined. In the 1960s, corporations in the United States paid about 25 percent of all federal income taxes, and in 1991 it was down to 9.2 percent. A 1993 study by the General Accounting Office reported that more than 40 percent of corporations with assets of more than $250 million either paid no income tax or paid less than $100,000.[15] Another study of 250 of the nation's largest corporations reported that in 1998, twenty-four of the corporations received tax rebates totaling $1.3 billion, despite reporting U.S. profits before taxes of $12.0 billion. A total of forty-one corporations paid less than zero federal income tax in at least one year from 1996 to 1998, despite reporting a total of $25.8 billion in pretax profits.[16] In testimony before the Committee on the Budget of the U.S. House of Representatives, Ralph Nader reported that in fiscal year 1999 corporations received $76 billion in tax exclusions, exemptions, deductions, credits, and so forth, and that the estimates for the years 2000–2004 will reach $394 billion in corporate tax subsidies.[17]

CREATING THE NEW WORKING CLASS

> They call this "global competitiveness," but that's globaloney. Call it by its real name: Class War.
>
> —Jim Hightower, Dollars and Sense, November–December 1997

When the large multinational firm closes its U.S. facilities and invests in other firms abroad or opens new facilities abroad, the major losers are the production workers who have been displaced and the communities with lower tax revenues and increased costs stemming from expanded efforts to attract new businesses.

But this does not mean that the firms are losers, for they are growing and expanding operations elsewhere. This growth creates the need for new employees in finance, management, computer operations, information systems, and clerical work. The total picture is one of shrinking production plants and expanding corporate headquarters; shrinking blue-collar employee rolls and two-tiered expansion of high-wage professional-managerial and low-wage clerical positions.

Having been extraordinarily successful in closing U.S. plants, shifting investment and production abroad, and cutting both labor and labor costs (both the number of production workers and their wage-benefit packages), major corporations now turned their attention to saving money by cutting white-collar employees. In the 1990s, there were no longer headlines about "plant closings," "capital flight," or "deindustrialization." The new strategy was "downsizing," "rightsizing," "reengineering," or how to get the same amount of work done with fewer middle managers and clerical workers.

When Sears, Roebuck and Company announced that it could cut 50,000 jobs in the 1990s (while still employing 300,000 people) its stock climbed 4 percent on the New York Stock Exchange. The day Xerox announced a planned cut of 10,000 employees, its stock climbed 7 percent. Eliminating jobs was suddenly linked with cutting corporate waste and increasing profits. Hardly a month could pass without an announcement by a major corporation of its downsizing plan. Tenneco Incorporated would cut 11,000 of its 29,000 employees. Delta Airlines would eliminate 18,800 jobs, Eastman Kodak would keep pace by eliminating 16,800 employees, and AT&T announced 40,000 downsized jobs, bringing its total of job cuts since 1986 to 125,000. Not to be outdone, IBM cut 180,000 jobs between 1987 and 1994. The practice continues into the new century; as reported in the *New York Times* (July 13, 2001), Motorola, Inc., announced on July 12, 2001, that it would cut 30,000 jobs in 2001. On that same day, although it reported an operating loss in the second quarter of eleven cents per share, Motorola stock rose by 16 percent.

Even the upscale, more prestigious banking industry joined in the rush to become "lean and mean." A total of ten bank mergers announced in 1995 would result in 32,400 jobs lost because of the new "efficiencies" that come with mergers. Even banks that were already successful in introducing "efficiencies" were not immune to continued pressure for more. Between 1985 and 1995, Chase Manhattan's assets grew by 38 percent (from $87.7 billion to $121.2 billion), and its workforce was reduced 28 percent, from 44,450 to 33,500 employees. Yet when Chase was "swallowed" by Chemical Banking Corporation in a merger, both banks announced further reductions totaling 12,000 people.

Job loss in the 1990s appeared to hit hardest at those who were better educated (some college or more) and better paid ($40,000 or more). Job loss aimed at production workers in the 1980s was "explained" by the pressures of global competition and the opportunities to produce in areas with lower-wage workers. The "explanation" for the 1990s downsizing was either new technology or redesign of the organization. Some middle managers and supervisors were replaced by new computer systems that provide surveillance of clerical workers and data entry jobs. These same computer systems also eliminate the need for many middle managers responsible for collecting, processing, and analyzing data used by upper-level decision makers.

Redesign of organizations was achieved by eliminating middle levels within an organization and shifting work both upward and downward. The downward shift of work is often accompanied by new corporate plans to "empower" lower-level workers with new forms of participation and opportunities for career development. All of this redesign reduced administrative costs and increased the workload for continuing employees.

Investors, who may have been tentative about the potential of profiting from the deindustrialization of the 1980s because it eroded the country's role as a manufacturing power, were apparently delighted by downsizing. During the 1990s and continuing beyond 2000, the stock market skyrocketed from below 3,000 points on the Dow Jones Industrial Average to 10,478 in mid-July 2001—an increase of almost 250 percent. The big institutional investors apparently anticipate that increasing profits would follow the broadly based actions of cutting the workforce.

Downsizing is often viewed by corporations as a rational response to the demands of competition and thereby a way to better serve their investors and ultimately their own employees. Alan Downs, in his book *Corporate Executions*, challenges four prevailing myths that justify the publicly announced layoffs of millions of workers.[18] First, downsizing firms do not necessarily wind up with a smaller workforce. Often, downsizing is followed by the hiring of new workers. Second, Downs questions the belief that downsized workers are often the least productive because their expertise is obsolete: According to his findings, increased productivity does not necessarily follow downsizing. Third, jobs lost to downsizing are not replaced with higher-skill, better-paying jobs. Fourth, the claim that companies become more profitable after downsizing, and that workers thereby benefit, is only half true—many companies that downsize do report higher corporate profits and, as discussed earlier, often achieve higher valuations of their corporate stock. But there is no evidence that these profits are being passed along to employees in the form of higher wages and benefits.

After challenging these four myths, Downs concludes that the "ugly truth" of downsizing is that it is an expression of corporate self-interest to lower wages and increase profits. This view is shared by David Gordon, who documents the growth of executive, administrative, and managerial positions and compensation during the period when "downsizing" was at its highest.[19] Gordon describes bureaucratic "bloat" as part of a corporate strategy to reduce the wages of production workers and increase and intensify the level of managerial supervision. Slow wage growth for production workers and top-heavy corporate bureaucracies reinforce each other, and the combination produces a massive shift of money out of wages and into executive compensation and profits. This "wage squeeze" occurred not only in manufacturing (because of global competition) but also in mining, construction, transportation, and retail trade.[20] Although it is to be expected that foreign competition will have an impact on wages in manufacturing, it should not affect the nontrade sector to the same extent. Thus, the "wage squeeze" since the mid-1970s that increased income and wealth inequality in the United States is probably the result of a general assault on workers' wages and benefits rather than a response to global competition.

The impact of these corporate decisions on the working class was hidden from public view by the steady growth of new jobs in the latter part of the 1990s, and by the relatively low rate of unemployment. In his second term in office, President Clinton made frequent mention of the high rate of job creation (without mentioning that they were primarily low-wage service jobs) and the historically low unemployment rate. Unfortunately, the official rate of unemployment can hide the real facts about the nation's economic health. For example, an unemployment rate of 4.2 percent in 1999 excludes part-time workers who want full-time work, and discouraged workers who have given up looking. If these workers are added to the unemployed we have an "underemployment rate" of 7.5 percent, or about 10.5 million workers. The official unemployment rate also hides the fact that unemployment for Black Americans was 8.0 percent in 1999, or that in urban areas there were pockets of unemployment that approached 25 percent.[21]

Thus, the result of more than a decade of plant closings and shifting investment abroad, and less than a decade of downsizing America's largest corporations, has been the creation of a protected privileged class and a working class with very different conditions of employment and job security. The three major segments of the working class are core workers, temporary workers, and contingent workers.

Core Workers

Core workers are employees possessing the skills, knowledge, or experience that are essential to the operation of the firm. Their income levels place them in the "comfort class" described in chapter 1. They are essential for the firm, regardless of how well it might be doing from the standpoint of profits and growth; they are simply needed for the firm's continuity. Being in the core is not the same as being in a particular occupational group. A firm may employ many engineers and scientists, only some of whom might be considered to be in the core. Skilled blue-collar workers may also be in the core. Core employees have the greatest job security with their employing organizations; they also have skills and experiences that can be "traded" in the external labor market if their firm should experience an unforeseen financial crisis. Finally, core employees enjoy their protected positions precisely because there are other employees just like them who are considered temporary.

Temporary Workers

The employment of temporary workers is linked to the economic ups and downs that a firm faces. When sales are increasing, product demand is high, and profits match those of comparable firms, the employment of temporary workers is secure. When inventories increase, or sales decline sharply, production is cut back, and temporary employees are laid off or fired. The temporary workers' relationship to the firm is a day-to-day matter. There is no tacit commitment to these employees about job security and no sense that they "belong to the family."

A good example of the role of temporary workers is revealed in the so-called transplants—the Japanese auto firms like Toyota, Nissan, and Honda that have located assembly plants in Kentucky, Ohio, Michigan, Illinois, Indiana, and Tennessee. Each of these firms employs between two thousand and three thousand American workers in their plants, and they have made explicit no-layoff commitments to workers in return for high work expectations (also as a way to discourage unionization). However, in a typical plant employing 2,000 production workers, the no-layoff commitment was made to 1,200 hires at start-up time; the other 800 hires were classified as temporary. Thus, when there is a need to cut production because of weak sales or excessive inventory, the layoffs come from the pool of temporary workers rather than from the core workers. Sometimes these temporary workers are not even directly employed by the firm but are hired through temporary help agencies like Manpower. Employment through temporary help agencies doubled between 1982 and 1989, and doubled again between 1989 and 1999.[22] These temporary workers are actually contingent workers.

Contingent Workers

Workers in nonstandard employment arrangements (part time, temporary, independent contractors) are often described as contingent workers. Some of these workers, as noted earlier, are employees of an agency that contract with a firm for their services. As we pointed out in chapter 2, about one in four persons in the labor force is a contingent worker, that is, a temporary or part-time worker.[23] These workers can be clerk-typists, secretaries, engineers, computer specialists, lawyers, or managers. They are paid by the temp agency and do not have access to a company's benefit package of retirement or insurance programs. Many of the professionals and specialists who work for large firms via temp firms are often the same persons who were downsized by those same companies. The following experience of a downsized worker is an ironic example of how the contingent workforce is created.

John Kelley, 48, had worked for Pacific Telesis for 23 years when the company fired him in a downsizing last December. Two weeks later, a company that contracts out engineers to PacTel offered him a freelance job.
"Who would I work for?" Kelley asked.
"Edna Rogers," answered the caller.
Kelley burst out laughing. Rogers was the supervisor who had just fired him. "That was my job," he explained. "You're trying to replace me with myself."[24]

These three groups of workers fit into the bottom part of the double-diamond class structure described in chapter 1, and it is only the core workers who have even the slightest chance to make it into the privileged class. Core workers with potential to move up generally have the credentials, skills, or social capital to have long-term job security, or to start their own business, and therefore the possibility of having substantial consumption capital (a good salary) and capital for investment purposes. Let us now consider how the privileged class holds on to its advantaged position in the double-diamond class structure.

CARE AND FEEDING OF
THE PRIVILEGED CLASS

The federal government of 1997 is a very different creature from that of, say, 1977—more egregiously corrupt and sycophantic toward wealth, more glaringly repressive, and even less responsive to the needs of low- and middle-income people.

—Barbara Ehrenreich, *Nation,* November 17, 1997

Most people who are in the privileged class are born there, as the sons, daughters, and relatives of highly paid executives, professionals, and business owners. Of course, they do not view their "achievements" that way. As one wag once said of former President George Bush, "He woke up on second base and thought he'd hit a double." But some members of the privileged class have earned their places, whether by means of exceptional talent, academic distinctions, or years of hard work in transforming a small business into a major corporation. Regardless of how much effort was needed to get where they are, however, members of the privileged class work very hard to stay where they are. Holding on to their wealth, power, and privilege requires an organized effort by businessmen, doctors, lawyers, engineers, scientists, and assorted political officials. This effort is often cited to convince the nonprivileged 80 percent of Americans that the privileged are deserving of their "rewards" and that, in general, what people get out of life is in direct proportion to what they put in. This effort is also used to dominate the political process so that governmental policies, and the rules for making policy, will protect and advance the interests of the privileged class.

However, before examining the organized effort of the privileged class to protect its privilege, it is first necessary to examine how members of the privileged class convince one another that they are deserving. Even sons and daughters from the wealthiest families need to develop biographical "accounts" or "stories" indicating they are deserving. This may involve accounts of how they worked their way up the ladder in the family business, starting as a clerk but quickly revealing a grasp of the complexities of the business and obtaining recognition from others of their exceptional talent.

Copyright © Lloyd Dangle. Reprinted with permission.

Even without the biographical accounts used by the privileged class to justify exceptional rewards, justification for high income is built into the structure of the organizations they join. In every organization—whether an industrial firm, bank, university, movie studio, law firm, or hospital—there are multiple and distinct "ladders" that locate one's position in the organization. New employees get on one of these ladders based on their educational credentials and work experience. There are ladders for unskilled employees, for skilled workers, and for professional and technical people with specialized knowledge. Each ladder has its own distinct "floor" and "ceiling" in terms of what can be expected regarding salary, benefits, and associated perks. In every organization, there is typically only one ladder that can put you in the privileged class, and this usually involves an advanced technical or administrative career line. This career line can start at entry levels of $70,000–80,000 annual compensation, with no upper limit beyond what the traffic will bear. These are the career ladders leading to upper executive positions providing high levels of consumption capital and opportunities for investment capital.

Claiming Turf

Many young attorneys, business school graduates, scientists, engineers, doctors, economists, and other professionals would like to get entry-level positions on these upper-level career ladders. In fact, there are probably many people who are qualified for entry positions in terms of their educational credentials and work experiences. So how are people selected from among the large number of qualified applicants for such desirable career opportunities? The answer is simple: Once credential qualifications and experience are used to define the pool of eligible applicants, the choice of who gets the job depends on the applicants' social capital. In chapter 1, we defined *social capital* as the social ties that people have with members of their college, fraternity or sorority, ethnic group, or religious group. People get jobs through their social networks, which provide them with information about job openings and with references valuable to those doing the hiring.[25] These social networks are usually composed of persons with similar social backgrounds. A recent study examined the social backgrounds of persons in the highest positions in corporations, the executive branch of the federal government, and the military. Although there is increased diversity among leaders today compared with 1950 with respect to gender, ethnicity, and race, the "core group continues to be wealthy white Christian males, most of whom are still from the upper third of the social ladder. They have been filtered through a handful of elite schools of law, business, public policy, and international relations."[26]

A good illustration of how social capital works is found in a study of 545 top position holders in powerful organizations in the United States.[27] Ten institutional sectors were studied, including *Fortune* 500 industrial corporations, *Fortune* 300 nonindustrial corporations, labor unions, political parties, voluntary organizations, mass media, Congress, political appointees in the federal government, and federal civil servants. Within each sector, fifty top position holders were interviewed—persons who may be considered "elites in the institutional sectors that have broad impact on policy making and political processes in the U.S."[28] Although we have no information on the incomes and wealth of the 545 elites, it is very likely they would fit our definition as members of the privileged class.

Table 3.1 provides some of the findings from this study, which identify the ethnic-religious composition of elites and their distribution across different institutional sectors. As can be seen from the first line of the table, 43 percent of all the elites in the study were WASPs (Protestants with ancestry from the British Isles),

Table 3.1 Ethnic Representation among Elites

	WASPs	Other Protestants	Irish Catholics	Other Catholics	Jews	Minorities	Probably WASPs
1. Overall elite	43.0	19.5	8.5	8.7	11.3	3.9	5.0
2. Men born before 1932	22.9	22.5	4.2	17.2	2.9	14.4	13.4
3. College-educated men born before 1932	31.0	19.8	6.0	15.5	8.9	5.2	10.3
4. Institutional sectors							
Business	57.3	22.1	5.3	6.1	6.9	0.0	2.3
Labor	23.9	15.2	37.0	13.0	4.3	2.2	4.3
Political parties	44.0	18.0	14.0	4.0	8.0	4.0	8.0
Voluntary organizations	32.7	13.5	1.9	7.7	17.3	19.2	7.7
Mass media	37.1	11.3	4.8	9.7	25.8	0.0	11.3
Congress	53.4	19.0	6.9	8.6	3.4	3.4	5.2
Political appointments	39.4	28.8	1.5	13.6	10.6	3.0	3.0
Civil service	35.8	22.6	9.4	9.4	15.1	3.8	3.8

Source: Alba and Moore (1982), table 1.

19.5 percent were Protestants from elsewhere in Europe, 8.5 percent were Irish Catholics, 8.7 percent were Catholics from elsewhere in Europe, 11.3 percent were Jews, and 3.9 percent were minorities (non-Whites and Hispanics). The second line indicates the percentage of the national population of men born before 1932 from different ethnic-religious backgrounds. The third line indicates the percent of the national population of college-educated men born before 1932 of each ethnic background. A comparison of line (1) with lines (2) and (3) shows the extent to which each ethnic-religious group may be overrepresented or underrepresented among the elites. Thus, WASPs and Jews are overrepresented among elites relative to their composition in the general population. The elite representation of other Protestants and Irish Catholics is comparable to their representation in the national population; and other Catholics and minorities are underrepresented among elites.

More interesting for our purposes are the overrepresentation and underrepresentation of elites in different institutional sectors. Overrepresentation would suggest the operation of social ties operating to get positions for persons with the same ethnic-religious background. White Anglo-Saxon Protestants are greatly overrepresented in business and in Congress. Irish Catholics are very overrepresented in labor and politics. Jews are sharply overrepresented in mass media, voluntary organizations, and federal civil service. This ethnic-religious overrepresentation indicates that social capital may be used to get access to career ladders leading to the privileged class. Moreover, there appears to be ethnic-religious specialization in the institutional sectors that they "colonize." People help to get jobs for relatives and friends, whether the job is for a Mexican immigrant in a Los Angeles sweat shop or a young Ivy League graduate in a Wall Street law firm. Parents invest their capital in an Ivy League education for a son or daughter, who then uses the social capital of family or school ties to enter a career path into the privileged class.

Securing Turf

After obtaining positions on career ladders that will make them members of the privileged class, our entry-level managers, attorneys, and faculty become aware of the very high incomes enjoyed by their senior colleagues. One response to these high salaries is to feel that they are unjustified and to exclaim, "Why should the President of the university make $300,000 a year when some of our professors with twenty years experience are making $60,000?" A second response is to recognize that the president's salary is used to justify the $230,000 salaries of the executive vice presidents, which in turn justify the $150,000 salaries of the deans, which in turn justify the $120,000 salaries of senior professors in selected fields. People in positions of power in organizations work together to justify their high salaries by creating beliefs about the need to be competitive in the market or to risk losing valuable people.

The second response is the typical one for people involved in career ladders that promise access to the privileged class. This response might be called symbiotic greed, where the parties are locked together in a mutually beneficial relationship. As the salary of the president rises, so do the salaries of all the others who are on the privileged-class career ladder. The rub is that only a small proportion of all the managers, attorneys, or faculty are on that career ladder, even though they may share the same educational credentials and work experience. This is a form of misguided self-interest, wherein low-level employees support the high salary of their superiors because of the belief that they may one day also have such a high salary.

Although it may seem surprising, members of the privileged class often feel that their incomes are far below what they deserve, or they feel relatively deprived in comparison to those above them in the income hierarchy. A recent story in the *New York Times* ("Well-Off but Still Pressed, Doctor Could Use Tax Cut")[29] provided thinly veiled support for President Bush's tax cut along with a sympathetic story of a surgeon earning $300,000 a year who says he does not feel rich. The good doctor, who lives in a $667,000 four-bedroom house with a pool, frets about his retirement, college tuition, and the anticipated cost of future weddings for his five daughters. Moreover, he is pained by the appearance of the new high-tech millionaires driving around in Porsches. The good doctor's wife exclaims, "We don't have the luxuries that you would think in this bracket," as she describes shopping at cheaper grocery stores and clipping coupons. The message of the article is that there are rich people and super rich people, and both would benefit from a tax cut. In short, you can never have too much money!

Now to the organized effort by businessmen, doctors, lawyers, and the like to protect the interests of the privileged class. This effort is revealed in three ways: (1) Members of the privileged class hold upper-level positions in all the major institutions of American society. These institutions control enormous resources that can be used to shape public awareness, the political process, and the nation's policy agenda. (2) The organizations to which the privileged class belong form associations in order to hire lobbyists, contribute to political campaigns, and shape legislation in their interests. (3) The members of the privileged class who are in professional occupations, like medicine and law, are represented by powerful professional associations that protect their members against any efforts by other groups to encroach on their "turf." Thus, the American Medical Association (AMA) makes sure that state legislatures continue to give doctors a monopoly over what they do by preventing nurses, or pharmacists, or chiropractors, or holistic practitioners from providing certain types of care to clients. Similarly, the American Bar Association acts to prevent paralegals from competing with lawyers in handling wills, estates, or certain types of litigation.

Not every segment of the privileged class is unified on all issues. Doctors are not pleased with the actions of attorneys when they vigorously pursue malpractice suits against doctors and hospitals. The AMA has urged Congress to pass legislation limiting the dollar amount of damages that might be awarded in malpractice claims. Lawyers resist such efforts because they make their living from obtaining 30 percent of the damage awards made to persons suing doctors or hospitals. Similarly, the banking industry and the large industrial corporations may differ on whether they would like to see the Federal Reserve Board raise or lower interest rates. Some sectors of the business community may support giving China special trade concessions, while others may be opposed.

Despite the differences and disagreements over specific policies by members of the privileged class, they are unified in their support for the rules of the game as they are currently played: The privileged class is unified in its view of how the political process should operate. Individuals and organizations should be free to lobby members of Congress on matters of interest to them. Individuals and organizations should be free to contribute money to political action committees and to political parties. And above all else, privileged-class members agree that business should be able to operate in a free and unregulated environment and that the country runs just fine with a two-party system.

Then there are the really big policy issues, where the "payoffs" are substantial to almost all segments of the privileged class. The North American Free Trade Agreement (NAFTA) and the General Agreement on Tariffs and Trade (GATT) were supported by Presidents Reagan, Bush, and Clinton and by a bipartisan majority of both houses of Congress. The new President George W. Bush took office in 2001 and proceeded to promote the so-called Free Trade Area for the Americas (FTAA), which would extend NAFTA throughout the Western Hemisphere. Taken together, NAFTA and FTAA represent the effort of the international privileged class to have countries in the Americas adopt economic policies to attract foreign investment, encourage "free trade," and restrict government efforts to protect the rights of workers. These agreements promise to advance the global economy and the continued pursuit of profits across the globe by multinational corporations.

The privileged class in the United States achieved major victories in the 1980s through their efforts to reduce government spending on a variety of social programs that benefit the working class. Using the scare tactics of budget deficits and the national debt, the privileged class supported a balanced budget agreement that required the president and Congress to reduce spending on welfare, education, Medicare, and Medicaid. In the 1990s, the privileged class turned its attention to the global economy by devising ways to protect opportunities for investment and profit around the globe. The main way to achieve this was to make it easy for large corporations to circle the globe in search of the best opportunities and thereby threaten workers everywhere so as to keep their wages and benefit demands at low levels. Facing the oft-repeated threat that there are "other" workers willing to do the same work for less money, the American working class has lived with declining earnings and disappearing health benefits and employer-provided pensions. And all this occurred during an eight-year economic recovery and a booming stock market!

During the 1990s, major U.S. and foreign corporations joined forces to lobby Washington policy makers to relax federal policies on international trade. This included granting most-favored nation trading status to China (with whom we have a high trade deficit) and passing the North American Free Trade Agreement, which eliminated trade barriers between the United States, Canada, and Mexico. Before the passage of NAFTA, the United States had a $1 billion trade surplus with Mexico, but the year following NAFTA that surplus had become a $16.2 billion deficit.[30]

To garner public support for free trade, President Clinton frequently pointed out that for every $1 billion in goods and services we export to other countries, we create 20,000 jobs at home. This may be true, but the problem is that it also works in reverse: for every $1 billion of goods that we import, we lose 20,000 jobs. And, as indicated earlier in this chapter, in 2000 the United States had a trade deficit of $370 billion with other countries.

Despite claims by officials in Canada, Mexico, and the United States that NAFTA has been a success, an analysis of the impact of NAFTA seven years after its adoption indicates that 766,000 actual and potential jobs have been eliminated in the United States "between 1994 and 2000 because of the rapid growth in the U.S. export deficit with Mexico and Canada."[31] Thus, we lose many more jobs than we create with our free-trade policies. But free trade is not about jobs; it is about profits for corporations and the privileged class.

Defending Turf

In February 1998 the *New York Times* published a two-page open letter to the Congress of the United States, entitled "A Time for American Leadership on Key Global Issues."[32] The letter expresses concern about "a dangerous drift toward disengagement from the responsibilities of global leadership." Congress is asked to approve new fast-track negotiating authority, which would extend NAFTA-like agreements to other countries in Latin America and around the globe, and to support the International Monetary Fund bailout of failed banks in Southeast Asia (although it failed to mention the benefit to U.S. banks and financial institutions that are heavily invested in those economies).

Signatories to this letter include two former presidents (Jimmy Carter and Gerald Ford), 42 former public officials (secretaries of defense, treasury, commerce, and state; CIA directors, national security advisers; U.S. senators), and eighty-eight corporate presidents and CEOs (of AT&T, Boeing, Amoco, Chase Manhattan Bank, IBM, Time Warner, Bank America, etc.). Many of the former public officials now work as lobbyists for the U.S. and foreign multinationals that "feed at the public trough" via tax loopholes and federal subsidies.

Why would these 132 members of the privileged class spend $100,000 for this two-page ad in the *Times?* Surely not to influence members of Congress. Corporations and the privileged class have more effective ways of doing that, such as the $3 million in campaign contributions by Philip Morris or the $2.5 million that Chiquita Brands CEO Carl Linder gave to both political parties from 1993 to 1996. Perhaps the ad was designed to convince the working class to support fast-track legis-lation. Probably not. The circulation of the *New York Times* is about 1.6 million, and very few of those readers are from the working class. The most likely targets of the ad were the nationally scattered members of the privileged class that the elite leaders wanted to mobilize at the grass roots. The ad was designed to get the mil-lions of privileged doctors, lawyers, journalists, managers, scientists, stock brokers, and media executives to mobilize public opinion through the hundreds of profes-sional and business associations that represent their interests. The privileged class constitutes 20 percent of the population (about 14 million families), and when mobilized, it can represent a potent political force.

Opposition to the privileged-class agenda on the global economy is fragmented, and operates with limited resources. Critics of NAFTA and the GATT, like Ralph Nader and Jesse Jackson, can hardly stand up to the National Association of Man-ufacturers or the U.S. Chambers of Commerce. The opposition to NAFTA and the GATT voiced by reactionary populists Ross Perot and Pat Buchanan, who ap-peared to be "traitors" to the interests of the privileged class, was dealt with swiftly and sharply by the major media. Perot was given the persona of a quirky, eccentric millionaire who was trying to buy the presidency because he had nothing better to do with his time and money. Buchanan was vilified as a crypto-racist, anti-Semite, and general all-around loose cannon.

The attacks on Perot and Buchanan by academics and political commentators on media talk shows should not be surprising. Elite universities and the major me-dia are controlled by the wealthy and corporate elite who are at the top of the priv-ileged class. The major networks of ABC, CBS, NBC, Fox, and Turner Broadcasting determine what the overwhelming majority of Americans will receive as news and entertainment. Two of the major networks are owned by major multinational firms, and institutional investors control substantial percentages of stock in the networks.

Is it any wonder, therefore, that efforts to attack the status quo are immediately marginalized or co-opted? An example of this process was revealed during the Re-publican presidential primary in early 1996. Pat Buchanan was making his usual bombastic attacks on immigration, NAFTA, and the GATT when he suddenly started lobbing some grenades at the corporate elite while yelling about "corporate greed." Here are a few samples, from speeches made in February of 1996: "When AT&T lops off 40,000 jobs, the executioner that does it, he's a big hero on the cover of one of these magazines, and AT&T stock soars"; "Mr. Dole put the interest of the big banks—Citibank, Chase Manhattan, Goldman Sachs—ahead of the Amer-ican People."[33]

When it appeared that Buchanan's reactionary populist attack on the corporate elite was striking a responsive chord among people on the campaign trail, the *New York Times* decided to take the extraordinary step of publishing a seven-part series, called "The Downsizing of America," which ran from March 3 through March 9, 1996. Some might call this a major public service by the *Times*, designed to inform

Americans about an important issue. Others might say it was a clever effort to take the issue out of Buchanan's hands and to shape it and frame it in ways that would deflect the criticisms and attacks on the corporate elite. The *Times* series did not point an accusing finger at corporate America for the loss of millions of jobs. If anything, the series made the reader either feel sorry for everyone, including the "guilt-ridden" managers who had to fire workers ("Guilt of the Firing Squads"), or to blame everyone, including downsized workers. In an extraordinary example of blaming the victim, consider the following "explanation" for downsizing. "The conundrum is that what companies do to make themselves secure is precisely what makes their workers feel insecure. And because workers are heavily represented among the 38 million Americans who own mutual funds, they unwittingly contribute to the very pressure from Wall Street that could take away their salaries even as it improves their investment income."[34]

The *New York Times* series did not help its readers to understand who benefits from downsizing, but it did help to defuse the issue and to take it out of the hands of those who might be critical of corporate America. It is an example of the pacification of everyday life (discussed more fully in chapter 7).

Resistance to the Global Economy

> The rules created by NAFTA are imbalanced; they encourage capital mobility by extending trinational protection to investors while protections for workers and the environment are left to national governments . . . One result has been a rise in inequality and insecurity among working people.
>
> —Jeff Faux, *Nation*, May 28, 2001

In this chapter we have tried to provide a glimpse of the meaning of the bogeyman global economy. The term has been used to threaten workers and unions and to convince everyone that they must work harder if they want to keep their jobs. The global economy is presented as if it is *out there* and beyond the control of the corporations, which must continually change corporate strategies in order to survive in the fiercely competitive global economy. It is probably more accurate to view the current global economy as an accelerated version of what U.S. financial and industrial corporations have been doing since the end of World War II—roaming the globe in search of profits. The big change is that since the 1980s, U.S. firms have found it easier to invest overseas. They have used this new opportunity to create new international agreements like NAFTA and FTAA that attack organized labor and threaten workers to keep their wage demands to a minimum. In this view, the global economy is composed primarily of U.S. companies investing abroad and exporting their products to the United States (as the largest consumer market in the world) and other countries. These multinational corporations have an interest in creating the fiction that the global economy is some abstract social development driven by "natural laws" of economics, when it is actually the product of the deliberate actions of 100 or so major corporations.

There has been growing popular opposition to the international accords that are creating the new global economy. In December of 1999 the so-called Battle in Seattle signaled the growing resistance to globalization. Tens of thousands protested against the World Trade Organization's "free trade" agenda that would threaten U.S. workers' jobs and wages, and provide little protection against environmental damage. Protesters were confronted by police using pepper spray and tear gas to prevent disruption of the WTO meeting.[35] On April 20–22, 2001, the Third Summit Meeting of the Americas took place in Quebec City, Canada. Heads of state from thirty-four countries in the Americas (Cuba was excluded) assembled for negotiations on the so-called Free Trade Agreement for the Americas. Once again, tens of thousands demonstrated against this new effort to make it easier for international finance capital and multinational corporations to control the global economy.[36]

The resistance that took place in Seattle and Quebec City (as well as in Washington, D.C., and Davos, Switzerland) reveals the operation of the Alternative Power Network described in chapter 2. Groups representing labor, environmentalists, anti-sweatshop campaigns, and human rights activists came together to challenge the international agreements that provide few protections for working people throughout the Americas. They are calling for trade agreements that protect the rights of workers to a living wage, regulations on the behavior of multinational corporations and international finance capital, and consideration of environmental protections consistent with economic and social development.

The problem posed by the global economy is that it has increased the influence of large corporations over the daily lives of most Americans. This influence is revealed in corporate control over job growth and job loss, media control of information, and the role of big money in the world of national politics. At the same time that this growing influence is revealed on a daily basis, it has become increasingly clear that the major corporations have abandoned any sense of allegiance to, or special responsibilities toward, American workers and their communities.

This volatile mix of increasing influence and decreasing responsibility has produced the double-diamond class structure, where one in five Americans is doing very well indeed, enjoying the protection that comes with high income, wealth, and social contacts. Meanwhile, the remaining four out of five Americans are exploited and excluded.

NOTES

1. Office of Technology Assessment, *Technology and Structural Unemployment* (Washington, D.C.: Congress of the United States, 1986); Thomas S. Moore, *The Disposable Work Force* (New York: Aldine de Gruyter, 1996).

2. Joel Bleifuss, "The Terminators," *In These Times*, March 4, 1996, 12–13.

3. Sheryl Wu Dunn, "When Lifetime Jobs Die Prematurely: Downsizing Comes to Japan, Fraying Old Workplace Ties," *New York Times*, June 12, 1996.

4. John Miller and Ramon Castellblanch, "Does Manufacturing Matter?" *Dollars and Sense*, October 1988.

5. Noam Chomsky, *The Common Good* (Monroe, Me.: Common Courage Press, 2000).

6. Robert B. Reich, *The Next American Frontier* (New York: Times Books, 1983).

7. U.S. Bureau of the Census, Foreign Trade Division, Washington, D.C. 20233, 2000.

8. John Pomery, "Running Deficits with the Rest of the World—Part I," *Focus on Economic Issues*, Purdue University (Fall 1987). (Emphasis added.)

9. For an extended discussion, see Michael Stohl and Harry R. Targ, *Global Political Economy in the 1980s* (Cambridge, Mass.: Schenkman, 1982).

10. Reich, *Next American Frontier.*

11. "The 100 Largest U.S. Multinationals," *Forbes*, July 17, 1995, 274–76.

12. Barry Bluestone and Bennett Harrison, *The Deindustrialization of America* (New York: Basic Books, 1982).

13. Louis Uchitelle, "U.S. Corporations Expanding Abroad at a Quicker Pace." *New York Times*, July 25, 1998.

14. David M. Gordon, *Fat and Mean: The Corporate Squeeze of Working Americans and the Myth of Managerial Downsizing* (New York: Free Press, 1996).

15. Richard J. Barnet and John Cavanagh, *Global Dreams: Imperial Corporations and the New World Order* (New York: Simon and Schuster, 1994).

16. Robert S. McIntyre, "Testimony on Corporate Welfare," U.S. House of Representatives Committee on the Budget, June 30, 1999. On the Internet at http://www.ctj.org/html/corpwelf.htm (visited June 25, 2001).

17. Ralph Nader, Testimony on Corporate Welfare," U.S. House of Representatives Committee on the Budget, June 30, 1999. On the Internet at www.nader.org/releases/63099.html (visited June 25, 2001).

18. Alan Downs, *Corporate Executions* (New York: AMACOM, 1995).

19. See Gordon, *Fat and Mean*, chap. 2.

20. Ibid., 191.

21. Lawrence Mishel, Jared Bernstein, and John Schmitt, *The State of Working America 2000–2001* (Ithaca, N.Y.: Cornell University Press, 2001), 220; Marc Breslow, "Job Stats: Too Good to Be True," *Dollars and Sense*, September–October 1996, 51.

22. Mishel et al., op cit., 252.

23. Chris Tilly, *Half a Job: Bad and Good Part-Time Jobs in a Changing Labor Market* (Philadelphia: Temple University Press, 1996); Kevin D. Henson, *Just a Temp* (Philadelphia: Temple University Press, 1996).

24. Ann Monroe, "Getting Rid of the Gray," *Mother Jones*, July–August 1996, 29.

25. Mark Granovetter, *Getting a Job: A Study of Contacts and Careers* (Cambridge: Harvard University Press, 1974).

26. Richard L. Zweigenhaft and G. William Domhoff, *Diversity in the Power Elite: Have Women and Minorities Reached the Top?* (New Haven: Yale University Press, 1998), 6.

27. Richard D. Alba and Gwen Moore, "Ethnicity in the American Elite," *American Sociological Review* 47 (June 1982): 373–83.

28. Ibid., 374.

29. Jim Yardley, "Well-Off but Still Pressed, Doctor Could Use Tax Cut," *New York Times,* April 7, 2001: 1, A8.

30. Richard W. Stevenson, "U.S. to Report to Congress NAFTA Benefits Are Modest," *New York Times,* July 11, 1997.

31. Robert E. Scott, "NAFTA'S Hidden Costs," *Economic Policy Institute,* Washington, D.C., May 21, 2001.

32. *New York Times,* February 11, 1998.

33. Francis X. Clines, "Fueled by Success, Buchanan Revels in Rapid-Fire Oratory," *New York Times,* February 15, 1996.

34. Louis Uchitelle and N. R. Kleinfield, "On Battlefield of Business, Millions of Casualties," *New York Times,* March 3, 1996.

35. Jim Phillips, "What Happens After Seattle?" *Dollars and Sense,* January–February 2000, 15–16, 31–32.

36. David Moberg, "Tear Down the Walls: The Movement Is Becoming More Global," *In These Times,* May 28, 2000, 11–14.

4

The Invisible Class Empire

The way our ruling class keeps out of sight is one of the greatest stunts in the political history of any country.

—Gore Vidal, *Progressive*, September 1986

"The truth is out there." This cryptic tagline from the long-running *X-Files* television series reflects the elusive nature of evidence sought by FBI agents Mulder, Scully, and Doggett. Everyone knows something real is going on, but powerful force fields—emanating sometimes from paranormal phenomena and sometimes from shadowy and sinister human organizations—keep the truth just out of reach.

Like X-Filers, we also believe an elusive truth is out there, but not of a paranormal sort. Our concern is with superclass political power and evidence that reveals the "truth" about this highly charged issue. As Gore Vidal suggests, ruling-class political dominance is a long-standing but typically unacknowledged and unexplored feature of American society. Occasionally it has been candidly recognized—sometimes by writers of elite origins such as Vidal as well as by players at the top of the political game. President Woodrow Wilson once observed that "the masters of the government of the United States are the combined capitalists and manufacturers of the U.S."[1] However, such public candor is rare and may entail negative personal and professional consequences. Vidal, for example, maintains that his public musings on ruling-class political power have earned him undying elite enmity as a class traitor and that as a result, both he and his work have been marginalized and demonized by the privileged-class-controlled mass media.[2]

Superclass elites have long recognized that publicly acknowledged, front-page robber-baron plutocracy is inconsistent with American cultural ideals of democracy and political equality—and dangerous to their interests. Up-front publicity revealing the nature and extent of superclass political dominance would magnify

119

the tensions between democratic ideals and concentrated class-power realities by calling into question the institutional legitimacy of American politics and public policy. For these reasons, superclass leaders prefer to keep the existence of and details about the extent of their class-based power out of sight.

THE INVISIBLE EMPIRE
AND THE GOLDEN TRIANGLE

The first issue we face in claiming the upper class is a ruling—or governing—class is that many of its members do not seem to be involved in ruling.

—G. William Domhoff, *State Autonomy or Class Dominance?* 1996

We believe the superclass preference is for Americans to know less, not more, about "the truth that is out there" concerning the invisible class empire that dominates our national political system. The term *invisible class empire* refers to the hidden structures and processes through which superclass leaders, along with their credentialed-class allies, penetrate and dominate the American political system. It also refers to the processes used to disguise this reality and the concealed political, economic, and cultural dimensions of superclass power.

It is an empire in the sense that the privileged-class leadership has crafted a far-flung and widely dispersed collection of resources, organizations, and processes into a coherent political force that ensures the perpetuation of its interests. It is invisible in the sense that the class-based dimensions of the resources and control processes that undergird the empire are largely excluded from American public attention. In the political arena, the silence of incumbents, wannabes, and pundits promotes public inattention. In the cultural arena, public inattention grows out of an almost total mass-media blackout of reporting on the empire combined with a nearly total neglect of the subject by the U.S. educational system—at all levels.

As noted in chapter 2, the privileged-class leaders who guide and direct this empire are sometimes referred to as the power elite.[3] At the top, this group consists of superclass members who are active in organizational governance (corporate and political). It shades downward to include a second tier (with respect to class) of semi-autonomous managers and assistants. This junior partner portion of the power elite includes upwardly mobile corporate officers, attorneys, major political office holders, national lobbyists, and other specialists drawn largely from the credentialed class. These groups directly assist the superclass elite or indirectly serve their interests. All of these groups together—with superclass leadership at the center—form a kind of directorate that charts and oversees general economic and political policies as well as routine institutional practices necessary to maintain the class empire.

This chapter begins the process of peeling back the cloak of invisibility that shields the empire by exposing the organizational foundations of what we call the

Figure 4.1 The Golden Triangle of Class Power

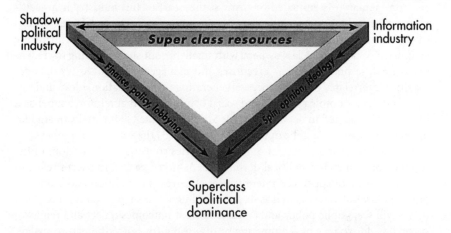

golden triangle of class power. As figure 4.1 illustrates, superclass resources, grounded in the investment capital that members of this class personally hold or control as corporate officers, serve as the basis for financing and controlling two major "industries." The shadow political industry (explored in this chapter) and the information industry (examined in chapter 5) both drive and conceal super-class power. The convergence of these twin structures leads to superclass political dominance. This term refers to the ways in which the routine operation of the two industries promotes superclass domination over major class-relevant public pol-icy outcomes concerning economic and political issues. And it reflects the reality that superclass media ownership provides this class with substantial cultural influ-ence (e.g., shaping popular cultural content), which also has important political and class power implications and consequences.

The shadow political industry extends downward as the left flank of the trian-gle. It consists of several real-life organizations that provide the political muscle underlying the class empire. This industry parallels—or shadows—the national political- and public-policy-making processes. Created, funded, and dominated by the superclass, this industry consists of three specialized, interrelated organiza-tional groups devoted to (1) political finance—corporate-based individual wealth and political action committees (PACs); (2) policy planning—think tanks, re-search institutes, policy discussion groups, and foundations; and (3) classwide lobbying—peak corporate groups and corporate-professional group coalitions. Control of politics and government are the primary "products" of this industry. Its goal is to monitor and intervene in the political arena in ways that protect and pro-mote superclass economic and political interests.

The information industry anchors the right flank of the triangle. Grounded in the largest mass media corporations, this industry serves privileged-class leaders' political and economic interests in two ways. First, much of the "news" and editorial commentary disseminated by firms at the heart of this industry help legitimate or conceal the nature and extent of superclass power. Second, large portions of the megaprofits generated through the operations of large media firms are channeled back to superclass owners, with smaller profit shares flowing to credentialed-class, second-tier media executives and managers.[4] This industry operates via three interrelated control processes generating the information, ideas, and images, and the economic political, and social commentary that reinforce superclass interests. Considered in detail in chapter 5, these include (1) the mainstream ideology process, (2) the public opinion process, and (3) the spin-control process.

The structures and processes of both industries converge at the bottom of the triangle into superclass political dominance. As noted earlier, this term refers to the domination of superclass interests over class-relevant political and economic public policy outcomes as well as its potent influence in shaping cultural content. As we will see, public policy and cultural content outcomes reflect and reinforce superclass dominance by legitimating or disguising (or both) the nature, extent, and consequences of privileged-class power generally. In the political and economic arenas, superclass leaders, along with their credentialed-class allies, are viewed as directing and controlling most major class-relevant national public policy outcomes. Examples of superclass-dominated policy outcomes are considered later in this chapter—especially as the results of classwide lobbying. The concept of superclass political dominance also includes the idea that privileged-class leaders, especially through the information industry, influence the dissemination of news and commentary as well as the entertainment content of popular culture in ways that reinforce superclass interests. These topics are considered at length in chapters 5 and 7.

The triangle model develops selected features of the more general class-power-network model introduced in chapter 2. It does not attempt to address all dimensions or features of superclass power. Even so, it provides a powerful tool for conceptualizing the core of privileged-class economic, political, and cultural power in the United States. By locating superclass power and dominance in organizationally based resources, structures, and processes driven by class interests and unified by a class-based ideology, this concept avoids conspiracy-based theories as the basis for understanding superclass cohesion and power.

Superclass holders of wealth, power, and privilege, as well as their credentialed-class allies, have individual and collective interests in maintaining their advantaged positions. The triangle model (fig. 4.1) zeroes in on the two "industries" that support and sustain privileged-class-based advantages. It also calls attention to the reality that superclass leaders frequently know and interact with one another because they occupy interlocked top positions in large organizations; they control high levels of investment capital; and they participate in overlapping corporate, political, and social arenas. These circumstances, combined with high levels of social, consumption, and skill capital held by superclass members and their credentialed-class allies, serve as the foundation for a widely shared superclass worldview, or political-economy ideology. This idea system blends assumptions grounded in privileged-class interests concerning how the political and economic systems should be organized and function together. In general, it tends to view the economic and political status quo as reasonable, legitimate, and just.[5] The model views the common bonds of economic resources, interests, social identity, and ideology as foundations upon which superclass leaders create, maintain, and justify the linked structures and processes that drive the triangle.

Acting on the basis of a shared worldview and through routine organizational structures and processes, superclass leaders and their credentialed-class allies orchestrate political strategies and media policies aimed at preserving and extending their wealth, power, and privilege. The model views those at the top as holding a strong, shared sense that the "system" works and pursuing concerted, but nonconspiratorial, strategies and tactics that preserve it. Their mantra is, "Why change what works for us?"

THE SHADOW POLITICAL INDUSTRY

> Politicians. We Love to hate them. And they make it so easy for us. But should they be the true objects of our scorn? . . . The real power, the men and women who really call the shots, are nowhere to be found on the ballot.
>
> —Michael Moore, *DownSize This!* 1996

Although the shadow political industry is not a totally new development, in the new class society this flank of the triangle has expanded to unprecedented levels of size, complexity, and sophistication. Compared with the recent past, this industry has also become a much more widely shared, class-collaborative project linking superclass leaders with growing numbers of credentialed-class professionals who work—either directly or indirectly—on behalf of superclass interests. These political, legal, and policy-oriented professionals possess specialized legal, lobbying, research, communication skills and political contacts that are critical to the maintenance of superclass interests and power.

Class collaboration in the shadow industry is particularly evident in the growing numbers of credentialed-class professionals—especially those located in the Washington, D.C., area—who work for superclass-controlled organizations concerned with political finance, policy, and lobbying. For example, attorneys figure prominently in the Washington lobbying community. In 2001, more than 73,000 attorneys were members of the District of Columbia Bar (compared with 10,925 in 1972).[6] Based on data reported per the federal Lobbying Disclosure Act (LDA) of 1995, the number of active lobbyists in Washington totaled 12,113 in 1999, up from 11,043 in 1998. Although this group is large, the LDA definition of a lobbyist is very narrow and does not cover many professionals involved in lobbying activities such as "'strategic advisors' and consultants who devise lobbying strate-gies" (e.g., former members of Congress).[7] Using more expansive definitions of lobbyists, some political analysts estimate the total Washington-area lobbying community to include at least 80,000 and perhaps more than 100,000 employees.[8]

Focusing only on the conservative LDA reporting requirements, we can see that lobbying is a big business within the shadow industry. For example, "on average, there were more than 22 active lobbyists and $2.7 million in lobbying expendi-tures for each member of Congress in 1999." According to LDA reports, total lob-bying expenditures reached $1.45 billion in 1999, up from $1.26 billion in 1997. Lobbying firms reporting incomes of over $1 million numbered 130 in 1999, up from 117 in 1998.[9] The web of superclass corporate influence is evident in this area as illustrated by the fact that several Washington lobbying firms are subsidiaries of huge public relations and advertising corporations. For example, the lobbying firm BKSH & Associates is part of Burson-Marsteller, the largest public relations firm in the United States, which in the late 1990s was owned by the giant Young & Rubicam advertising company.[10] In October 2000, a corporate merger expanded the BKSH lobbying and corporate parent connection into the international area: "Young & Rubicam, the former parent company of Burson-Marsteller, joined the WPP Group of Companies. . . . WPP Group plc is the world's most comprehensive communications services group. . . . The client base of WPP includes more than 300 of the *Fortune* Global 500 and over one-third of the NASDAQ 100."[11]

Most Washington, D.C., members of the growing credentialed-class profes-sional community—including attorneys and lobbyists—are employed (directly or indirectly) by large corporate clients or trade associations representing corporate interests because these groups have the most money to spend.[12] This is especially evident when we consider that the one thousand largest industrial, financial, and service firms control 75 percent of the sales, assets, and profits in these areas.[13] The links tying D.C.-area credentialed-class professionals—and many others—to su-perclass-controlled corporate clients form a dense, reciprocal web, weaving to-gether superclass corporate interests, credentialed-class professional skills, and political contacts. These links are cemented by steep-green contracts and salaries ranging from $100,000 to $250,000—and much more.[14] Such bonding occurs in part because superclass-controlled organizations represent the main market for the highly paid, specialized legal, lobbying, research, and communication skills possessed by political, legal, and policy-oriented professionals. By their sheer size—corporate-based trade associations and other research and lobbying groups funded by the superclass make up 72 percent of the Washington lobby commu-nity[15]—these organizations are the major employers of high-paid professional tal-ent.

The group that generally supervises and controls the shadow industry and drives the market for credentialed-class professionals' services consists of the top 25,000 officers and directors located in the one thousand largest U.S. industrial, fi-nancial, and service firms.[16] These top corporate office holders form the privileged-class heart of the institutional power elite, and their firms represent the core of the superclass organizational power base. This group exercises control over enormous levels of investment capital and tends to intersect or overlap with the wealthiest 1 percent of all Americans.[17] The members of this group also either possess or are hardwired into the highest levels of social capital and command extremely high levels of consumption capital. Many members of this group—a third or more—occupy their positions because of inherited wealth from family fortunes.[18]

Approximately 60 percent of superclass leaders come from families in the top 20 percent income group (the privileged class by our definition), and only about 3 percent come from families located in the bottom 80 percent income group (the new working class). Some superclass leaders, such as Steve Case (AOL-Time Warner) and Bill Gates (Microsoft), are "newly rich" as a result of entrepreneurial ventures. While often described in the media as "middle-class," many superclass entrepreneurs such as Case and Gates actually come from wealthy family backgrounds.[19] Some current superclass leaders have in fact "moved up" in major corporate hierarchies to elite positions, but in almost every case these rising executives are from credentialed-class family origins.[20] This route typically involves assistance from superclass "sponsors." Such individuals act as gatekeepers in identifying and grooming a few rising executives and political operatives from non-superclass backgrounds for membership in the power elite—typically, first as junior members and later as full partners. Nonelites who are sponsored in this fashion are usually selected and assisted on the basis of their acquisition of critical social capital (e.g., elite educational credentials) and relevant personal qualities such as allegiance to superclass ideology, organizational effectiveness, talent, and charm.[21]

Despite commanding huge resources, great power, and high status, the superclass is still a relatively small group. Its leadership base is too small to attend to the detailed activities necessary to translate general superclass policy preferences into specific public policy outcomes favoring its interests and perpetuating its political dominance. Superclass leaders need junior partners to help ensure that their interests are protected and served in the political and economic arenas. Thus, through their presence on policy-making boards of corporate, cultural, civic, and other organizations, the most organizationally active superclass leaders (the senior power elite) recruit, cultivate, utilize, and generously reward the expertise and assistance of a wide range of professionals who serve superclass interests in the shadow industry. These are the individuals who direct the industry's daily activities. They include high-profile political operatives like Karl Rove (President Bush's chief political advisor) along with thousands of lesser-known professionals located in the various superclass-funded political finance, policy-planning, and lobbying organizations that are at the core of the shadow industry.[22]

Largely faceless and unknown to the American public, the shadow industry's professional cadre, along with the staff members they supervise, have an increasingly routine presence in the political life of our society. Their careers are closely linked to the success of the superclass project of controlling U.S. politics and the state. They are the shock troops for and key political allies of the class empire, and they are active participants in the political finance, policy-planning, and classwide lobbying organizations that are central to superclass power and dominance in the United States.

POLITICAL FINANCE:
IT'S MONEY THAT MATTERS

Underwriting campaigns has become part of the cost of doing business, an investment that pays dividends in access to policymakers with the power to reduce taxes, ward off regulations, award contracts, and dole out subsidies.

—Eric Bates, *Mother Jones*, March–April 2001

The story of superclass domination of politics and the state through the shadow industry begins with political finance: the relationship between politics and money. Money has always been an important factor in politics, but the increasing use of expensive, high-tech production, communication, and marketing technologies in political campaigns has shifted it to center stage. The effects of these changes on the costs of political campaigns have been dramatic. In 2000, the cash required to mount *winning* political campaigns complete with paid staff, computers, polling, consultants, phone banks, direct mailing, and media advertising topped out at $193 million for the presidency (not counting indirect party funding), $7.2 million for a Senate seat, and $837,083 for a House seat.[23] By comparison, Bill Clinton's 1996 presidential campaign cost $113 million and winning Senate and House candidates in 1996 spent an average of $4.7 million and $673,000 on their campaigns.[24] As the dollar figures rise higher for each new election cycle, it is important to recall that campaign expenditures are not one-time costs. Each new campaign requires new money. To pay for future campaigns, representatives (in 2002) and senators (in 2006) need to raise at least $8,000 and $23,000 respectively, *every week* of their current terms in office. Being a serious candidate today requires serious money.

The nature of the American winner-take-all political system also helps to drive up the cost of campaigns. Politicians clearly understand the sentiment expressed in Vince Lombardi's well-known sports aphorism: "Winning isn't everything. It's the only thing." In American elections, second place means losing—which is possibly a political ELE (extinction-level event). Although large sums of money do not guarantee political victories, they come close. In the 2000 congressional elections, the candidates who raised the most money won 94 percent "of the 469 seats up for grabs in the Congress."[25] In a winner-take-all system, increasing the odds of winning requires mountains of money. In 2000 the mountain was $3 billion high—the total amount candidates for federal office raised for political campaigns that year ($700 million more than 1996).[26]

So where does the cash come from? The answer is the same for both Democrats and Republicans: primarily from wealthy individuals and from PACs (especially corporate and trade PACs). In the 2000 House campaigns, contributions of more than $200 from individuals and donations from business PACs made up 64 percent of Republican candidates' revenues and 53 percent of Democrats' revenues.[27] In the 2000 Senate races, candidates from both major parties raised a total of $250.3 million from individual contributors, with 69 percent of that amount coming from individuals donating more than $200.[28] Congressional candidates from both parties raised a total of $563 million in the 2000 elections from individual contributors (up 25 percent from 1997–98).[29] Of that total, 70 percent came from individuals donating more than $200.[30]

Both major political parties and most candidates they field today are primarily financed—in one form or another—by funds from the superclass. Large contributions by wealthy individuals and PACs (typically corporate PACs), often in amounts of $100,000 or more, are legally given to both major political parties in the form of "soft money." Only loosely regulated by federal law, soft money is used by state and national parties to finance party-building activities that assist individual candidates in many ways.[31] In the 2000 elections both major parties together raised a total of $495 million in soft money (up 90 percent from the $262 million they raised in the 1995–96 election cycle).[32]

Soft money donations received extensive political and media attention in 2001 as Congress debated, but failed to pass, the McCain-Feingold campaign finance reform bill.[33] Even so, it is "hard money" that drives the political process. Wealthy individuals and PACs contribute hard money both to parties (which is mostly passed along to individual candidates) and directly to candidates. Contributions through these channels are somewhat constrained by federal law establishing maximum amounts of hard money that individuals and PACs may donate to parties and to candidates. "Individuals are allowed to give $20,000 and PACs $15,000 to political parties per calendar year (hence, double the limit per election cycle)."[34] Regarding direct contributions to candidates, individuals are not allowed to donate more than $1,000 per candidate per election and are limited to a $25,000 total for individual donations in a given two-year election cycle. But individuals may also contribute up to $5,000 per year to a PAC. PACs are allowed to contribute $5,000 per candidate per election, which means $5,000 each for the primary and general elections—or a total of $10,000 per candidate. But there are no limits on how many candidates PACs may support—and thus no limits on the amount of money PACs may contribute in any election.[35]

Despite hard-money regulations, the amounts raised are staggering. In 2000, of the $3 billion raised by federal candidates for the 2000 elections, "three-fourths—$2.2 billion—was hard money."[36] Candidates from both major parties running for the House in 2000 received 73 percent of their hard-dollar campaign funds from individuals contributing more than $200 and from PACs. Of course, these are two groups that typically have vested interests in public policy decisions. By contrast, only about 19 percent of hard-dollar contributions for House candidates came from small donors (i.e., contributors of less than $200).[37]

Individual Contributions: Top of the Class

Although PACs receive the most media attention, the primary sources of campaign funding for candidates in the 2000 House and Senate elections were individual contributions—most often in amounts of more than $200.[38] Contributions from individuals to congressional candidates totaled $567.7 million in 2000. Senate candidates received a total of $252 million from individuals, of which $234 million was in amounts of $200 or more and $48.3 million was from donations of $750 or more. House candidates received $315.6 million from individuals, of which $274.2 million was in amounts of more than $200.[39]

Individual contributions of more than $200 made up the single largest source of funding for Republican and Democratic candidates in the 2000 congressional races, averaging 38 percent of all contributions.[40] Sometimes the candidates and the wealthy contributors were the same people, because in several congressional races, wealthy candidates legally financed their own campaigns. In 2000, congressional candidates contributed or loaned $175.9 million to their campaigns, "up 61 percent from the $107.2 million reported in 1997–98. Senate candidates used $107.7 million of their own funds, while House candidates used $53.6 million in candidate funds."[41]

Aside from personally wealthy politicians, who are the people making large political donations? The short answer is, a tiny minority of Americans—mainly privileged-class members, and especially those in the superclass. Few people make political contributions, and the ones who do, especially those who contribute more than $200, are almost entirely upper-income members of the privileged class. Of the donors who contribute over $200 to political campaigns or parties, 80 percent make more than $100,000 per year, but only 6 percent of the overall population have incomes at this level.[42] During the 1999–2000 election cycle, only about one-quarter of 1 percent of the U.S. population gave direct contributions of $200 or more to federal candidates, totaling $595 million (not counting party contributions). This tiny group donated "three-fourths of hard money contributions to [federal] candidates [in 2000]." Business executives dominate the individual donor group and "out-contributed labor leaders and staff by a factor of 1000:1."[43]

People with family incomes above $75,000 are more than one hundred times likely to contribute to candidates than those with family incomes below $15,000.[44] But even $75,000 incomes are far below the amounts earned by the 265,000 Americans who, in amounts of $1,000 or more, gave $380 million to federal candidates in 1999–2000. This group, representing one-eighth of 1 percent of the U.S. population, contributed 44 percent of all individual political donations to federal candidates in the last election cycle.[45] These donors reside almost exclusively in large cities: contributors in three urban areas—the Washington, D.C., metro area; New York City; and the Los Angeles–Long Beach area—donated a combined total of $334.6 million to federal campaigns in 1999–2000.[46]

A recent study of the four hundred top individual political contributors found that this group donated nearly $123 million to federal candidates in the 1999–2000 election cycle. Most of the top 400 contributors (257) were corporate executives in three industries: (1) finance, insurance, and real estate (169); (2) communications (51); and (3) high-tech (37). The top-ranked individual donated $1.5 million (S. Daniel Abraham, former Chairman of Slim-Fast Foods, Palm Beach, Fla.), while the bottom-ranked donor (#400) contributed $152,340 (Barry Wigmore, former partner, Goldman, Sachs & Co., New York). Of the total contributed, $66 million went to Democrats, $54.4 million went to Republicans, and a smaller amount went to the Natural Law Party.[47]

An earlier study of the same group found that half of the donors were either corporate heads or lawyers, and many appeared on the *Forbes* magazine list of America's wealthiest individuals. "The majority are bankers, lawyers, investors, or other businessmen with a big financial stake in the outcome of [federal] legislation."[48] In short, the top four hundred are superclass members, superclass wannabes, or credentialed-class agents representing superclass clients. In each case the strategy is the same—the top four hundred invest in politics to protect privileged-class interests.

Corporate PACs: Another Class Act

In the 2000 congressional races for the general election, PACs donated $125.3 million to Republicans and $114.5 million to Democrats; this made PACs the third largest source of congressional candidate funding, averaging 26 percent of all contributions (after individual contributions and candidate contributions and loans).[49] However, the overall average masks the relative importance of PAC funding in House and Senate races. In 2000, PAC contributions accounted for just 13 percent of the funds raised by winning Senate candidates; but among winning House candidates, PAC contributions made up 40 percent of their total receipts.[50]

Corporate PACs combined with corporate-dominated trade, membership associations, and health PACs are of special importance to reinforcing superclass political dominance—for four reasons. First, these PACs collect, control, and disburse a majority of all PAC money. Second, they are almost exclusively organized and administered by committees of upper-level corporate managers from large corporations who share a common business-based worldview that reflects superclass interests. Third, corporate PACs consistently reflect classwide business unity growing out of shared interests and the effects of federal limits on PAC donations. Fourth, although PAC funding accounts for only about one-fourth of all

congressional campaign receipts, business PAC dollars tend to follow the contribution patterns and political preferences of large individual donors from the privileged class. As the authors of a recent PAC study observed, "[PAC] money may be given to legislators who have the support of the members and patrons of the PAC-affiliated organization in their district."[51] These four factors lead to contribution patterns whereby most corporate PAC contributions flow to politicians who endorse policies that protect and extend the wealth and power of large corporations and the superclass elites who control them.

In the 1999–2000 election cycle, a total of 4,499 PACs disbursed $579.4 million; but the 1,846 corporate PACs plus the 900 trade, membership association, health PACs (most with close corporate links) accounted for $307.6 million—53 percent of that total.[52] Despite the huge sums they control today, corporate PACs as campaign-funding vehicles are relatively new. Following the Watergate-related revelations of secret corporate political donations to the Nixon campaign, it first appeared that corporate campaign contributions would be severely limited. However, in 1975 the Federal Election Commission (FEC, established by federal law in 1971) ruled, by a vote of four to three, that the Sun Oil Corporation PAC could solicit funds from both stockholders and employees. After the so-called SUN-PAC decision, the number of corporate PACs increased from 89 in 1974 to 433 in 1976 and has continued to increase since that time.[53]

The political power of the 2,746 corporate and corporate-dominated PACs (in 2000) rests in the hands of corporate PAC committees that are almost exclusively composed of privileged-class corporate managers and officers.[54] These committees bring together superclass members and upwardly mobile credentialed-class corporate professionals. The two groups are closely linked through their shared involvement with and concern for shaping corporate policies that favor superclass and corporate interests and through a shared political worldview. The political unity, consensus, and cohesion typically found among corporate PAC managers is based on "a set of underlying material relations—loans from the same banks, sales and purchases from each other, interlocking boards of directors, common interests in accumulating capital and avoiding government regulations that might restrict their power."[55] These material and social relations reinforce PAC managers' interpretations of, and decisions and actions on, both politics and business—in favor of superclass interests. Thus, the millions of dollars that corporate PACs raise, control, and disburse tend to be directed by PAC committees to those candidates most favorable to shared, superclass-based business interests.

Although corporate PAC contributions are sometimes disbursed in ways that appear to reflect efforts by competing firms or economic sectors to promote their narrow interests at the expense of other firms or sectors, such patterns are not the norm. More often, corporate PAC contributions tend to be mutually supportive. Convergent patterns of corporate PAC giving indicate classwide business unity on a wide range of regulatory and labor policy issues—rather than hardball competition. Superclass unity is especially evident in cases of policies affecting corporate control over labor markets—including issues such as working conditions and unionization campaigns.[56]

Corporate PAC contribution patterns of classwide unity also reflect the influence of federal law, which limits PAC donations to $5,000 per candidate per election. Under this rule, superclass leaders recognize that only by acting together can the corporate community have a major impact on the political process in ways that protect and serve their common class interests. The $5,000 PAC limit means that individual competing PACs would have very limited power because several small, cross-purpose PAC contributions would cancel out one another's influence. By contrast, a classwide strategy of mutually supportive, convergent patterns of campaign funding magnifies corporate PAC power over the political process. This strategy serves the interests of the superclass power elite who occupy and control the top positions in corporate America. Thus, the legal incentives for PAC collaboration combined with corporate PAC officers' experiences with their peers results in a shared network of contacts, information, and reciprocal patterns of gift giving to those candidates most supportive of shared superclass and corporate interests.[57]

Studies of corporate PAC contributions consistently document the pattern of classwide business unity rather than competition or conflict in the political arena as the dominant reality. Although a few examples of competing business PACs can be found, "Opposed to this [behavior] are literally dozens of examples of companies that 'hate each other,' are 'suing each other all of the time,' and are each other's major competitors but that nonetheless work well together in Washington. They cooperate in promoting the same policies, sponsoring joint fundraisers [for candidates], and in general behaving as a unified bloc." One study of corporate PAC donations found business to be unified in three out of four political races, giving, on average, nine times more money to one candidate than to the other. Moreover, "PAC officers may disagree with their counterparts at other corporations, but the unstated rules forbid public disputes, and only reluctantly will one business directly oppose another."[58] The superclass leadership of the corporate community recognizes that only by acting together can business PACs use their combined resources to exert substantial sustained power over the campaign-funding dimension of the political process.

Connecting the Dots

As we have seen, corporate PACs are not the only players in the campaign funding game, but compared with their most obvious competitors such as organized labor and public citizen groups, they are by far the largest and best-funded PACs. The importance of corporate PACs in funding the political process, the superclass bias of PACs, and corporate PAC links to both major parties are key features of the political finance process. Consider the following "dots":

- Corporate, Trade, Membership, Health PACs, 2,746; Labor PACs, 350. In 2000, corporate-linked PACs outnumbered labor PACs by nearly eight to one.[59]

- Business contributions, 15; Labor contributions, 1. Combining PAC and large individual contributions for the 2000 elections, business contributed fifteen times more than labor to federal candidates. (For soft-money donations, the ratio was nearly 17-to-1).[60]

- PAC contributions (1999–2000) to Democratic candidates for federal offices, $123 million; PAC contributions to Republican candidates for federal offices, $130 million.[61]

- PAC contributions (1999–2000) to incumbent candidates for federal offices, $195.4; PAC contributions to challenger candidates, $27.5 million.[62]

If we connect the corporate PAC and wealthy individual-funding "dots," we begin to see a pattern. Superclass-driven campaign funding represents more than just the pooled resources of another interest group. Corporate PAC dollars combine with wealthy donor contributions to create a powerful political force field dominating both major political parties and the entire political process. Although the Republican Party has long been perceived as the party of superclass and business interests in American politics, these same groups also have a long record of channeling substantial funds to the Democratic Party and Democratic candidates.

Over the past two decades, superclass support for the Democratic Party and Democratic candidates generally—especially for national offices—has increased dramatically. In the 1990s it became increasingly clear that both major parties were receiving similar levels of superclass-based funding. For example, from 1991 through 1994, the Republican Party raised $95 million in soft money, with more than 90 percent of the large donations, more than $20,000 each, coming from business interests including corporations, executives, trade associations, and lobbying firms. During the same period, the Democratic Party raised $75 million in soft money with more than 70 percent coming from corporate donors.[63] In the 1999–2000 election cycle, 76 percent of PAC, soft, and individual donations to federal candidates and to the Democratic and Republican Parties came from business interests.[64]

Since the late 1970s, the traditional superclass dominance of the Republican Party has been complemented by its increasing "colonization" of the Democratic Party. This process was facilitated by the takeover of the Democratic Party by the corporate-linked Democratic Leadership Council (DLC). Founded in the mid-1980s, the DLC is directly and indirectly linked (via the New Democrat Network—NDN) with dozens of corporate contributors from the *Fortune* 500 such as Bank One, Dow, DuPont, Merrill Lynch, Microsoft, Morgan Stanley, and Raytheon.[65] One researcher summarized the effects of the increasing penetration of the Democratic Party by superclass interests through its political funding practices in these terms: "Fifteen years ago when the Democrats became more adept in attracting corporate money, a *Wall Street Journal* article stated that 'Business already owns one party and now has a lease, with an option to buy, on the other.' The disregard for labor by centrist Democrats has less to do with ideology, analysis, or changing demographics. It's simply a reflection of Democrat dependence on corporate money."[66]

The combination of wealthy contributors and corporate PAC money tilts the political playing field into a perpendicular configuration with the high end accessible only to elite players with steep-green chips. Preliminary information on the 2002 congressional elections indicates a continuation of this pattern. In the first six months of 2001, the National Republican Senatorial Committee raised more than $24.6 million (double the 1999 rate). In the same period, the Democratic Senatorial Campaign Committee raised $20 million.[67] Virtually all of the money raised by these two committees for both parties came from wealthy individuals, corporations, and trade associations.[68] At mid-year 2001, House and Senate candidates on average had raised $201,718 and $543,799 respectively for the 2002 campaign—well ahead of comparable amounts raised in mid-1999.[69] Thus, it appears the 2002 elections will set a new record for campaign spending.

As we have shown, the political campaign dimension of the class empire rests on a dense web of financial connections whereby funds donated and controlled by the superclass become the dominant financial resource that underwrites the political process—for both major political parties. Moreover, wealthy campaign donors are not disinterested citizens acting on the basis of some civic obligation to fund the democratic process. In fact, "a survey of donors in the 1996 presidential elections revealed that 76 percent said 'influencing policy/government' was a 'very important' reason why they gave money."[70] The evidence supporting our contention that the magic mountain of superclass-controlled, politically targeted cash affords this class an iron grip over U.S. politics is more than circumstantial. "Judge for yourself. The evidence . . . [is] enough to convict our political system of serving the interests of the wealthy. Whether the subject is health care reform, environmental regulation, farm subsidies, weapons production, or trade policy, it is difficult to even get a hearing in Washington without spreading around a lot of dough."[71]

POLICY PLANNING: THE BIG PICTURE

The policy-planning network is . . . the programmatic political party for the upper class and the corporate community.

—G. William Domhoff, *State Autonomy or Class Dominance?* 1996

Is big government the source of our most pressing national problems today? Are vampire-like "greedy geezers" sucking the financial lifeblood of the younger generation—pushing Social Security and Medicare toward bankruptcy? Do we need to slash and burn the funding of social programs to reduce taxes and promote economic growth? Are welfare, drugs, and crime eroding America's moral fabric? The short answer to these questions is yes—at least according to many organizations that are part of the superclass-funded national policy-planning network.[72]

The Policy-Planning Network

The policy-planning network consists of several superclass-dominated organizations, including think tanks, research institutes, policy discussion groups, and foundations.[73] Grounded in superclass resources and institutions, this network is dedicated to setting the national policy agenda, establishing policy priorities, and shaping public policy outcomes. It is based on a superclass worldview—shared by credentialed-class professionals who implement routine network functions—that sees the existing economic and political reward, opportunity, and power structures as the most legitimate and the preferred national organizational arrangement (especially compared with more egalitarian alternatives).[74] The network functions through a variety of organizations and processes that collectively promote superclass interests by sustaining the economic and political status quo—or slight variations thereof.

The links between this network and superclass political dominance are tied to the reality that "policy planning in the United States takes place largely outside of government, in private policy-planning organizations funded by private corporations and foundations."[75] This means that the organizations in the superclass-funded policy-planning network generate most of the research, ideas, and policy discussions that dominate and shape the national policy agenda, priorities, debates, and most legislative or regulatory "solutions." The multifaceted input from this network to the national government is clearly tilted in favor of policies that support and extend existing class-based wealth, income, and power inequalities and thereby reinforce superclass economic and political interests. Although it may be argued that divisions exist within the superclass on some policies and issues, there is also a clear consensus in favor of policies that support "economic growth, a stable business cycle, incentives for investment, economy and efficiency in government, a stable two-party system, and maintaining popular support for political institutions."[76]

Network Members: Naming Names

Think tanks and research institutes are typically nonprofit organizations that provide settings where experts from academic disciplines and former public officeholders discuss a wide range of contemporary social problems and consider alternative policies for dealing with them.[77] Although the classification of specific organizations as think tanks or research institutes is contested terrain in the social sciences, researchers generally agree that the policy-planning network core consists of a very short list of five superclass-connected and politically influential "centrist" organizations. The Business Roundtable, the Brookings Institution, and the RAND Corporation are key players in the formation of U.S. domestic policies, and the Council on Foreign Relations (CFR) and the Trilateral Commission play similar, central roles in the establishment of American foreign policies.[78] In addition to the five core players, five other major centrist groups also play important roles in the policy-planning network: the Business Council, the U.S. Chamber of Commerce, the Committee for Economic Development (CED), the Conference Board, and the National Association of Manufacturers (NAM).[79]

Parallel with the major centrist organizations is an increasingly influential cluster of conservative think tanks. Prominent organizations in this group include the Hoover Institution, American Enterprise Institute, Heritage Foundation, the Center for Strategic and International Studies, the Manhattan Institute, and the Institute for Research on the Economics of Taxation.[80] Over the past thirty years these organizations have emerged as important contributors to the policy formation process. "In the mid-to late 1970s, business began its own [political] countermobilization. . . . Money was shifted out of liberal and moderate think tanks and policy organizations (the Brookings Institution, Council on Foreign Relations, and Committee for Economic Development) to newly founded or reinvigorated conservative equivalents (the American Enterprise Institute, Hoover Institution, and Heritage Foundation). . . . [By] 1980 the conservative organizations spent substantially more than the moderate ones."[81] A study by the National Committee for Responsive Philanthropy found that in the 1990s "center-right and far-right think tanks [continued] to grow rapidly suggesting the 1990s [extended the process of] continued institution building by political conservatives." Over the 1990–2000 period, the Committee estimated that spending by the top twenty conservative think tanks exceeded $1 billion.[82]

Policy-discussion groups are often affiliated with think tanks and research institutes, but these groups have somewhat different goals and function in ways that are distinct from think tanks. They serve as important meeting grounds where superclass corporate elites and their professional allies from various venues come together. The purpose of these informal weekly or monthly meetings is partly to share ideas but also to allow superclass leaders opportunities to identify, recruit, and groom talented individuals from the professional ranks for top leadership positions within government and other key organizations in the policy-planning network. The meetings also help to legitimate the organizations and their activities by portraying both in altruistic terms and by emphasizing the nonprofit, "independent" status of the organizations. The key organizations that serve as policy-discussion groups (or facilitate such activities) often overlap with think-tank organizations and include the NAM, the U.S. Chambers of Commerce, the Conference Board, the CFR, the CED, the American Assembly, and the Brookings Institution.[83]

Foundations and Board Interlocks

As we saw earlier, campaign funding is a central feature of superclass influence over the political process. The same basic principle also applies to policy planning, but instead of wealthy individual donors and corporate PACs, superclass-dominated foundations serve as the major financial engines providing much of the funding for the policy-planning network.[84] These tax-exempt, nonprofit organizations are often the creations of corporate entrepreneurs and wealthy families who founded them in part to reduce their own taxes as well as to use them as vehicles for encouraging policies favorable to their class interests.[85]

The resources controlled by foundations are staggering. The 2001 *Foundation Directory* lists the 10,000 largest grant-making foundations in the United States (out of more than 40,000). This group's combined assets totaled over $403 billion (90.5 percent of all foundation assets) and awarded grants totaling more than $21.1 billion (92 percent of all foundation giving) in the most recent year of record. The one hundred largest foundations (by assets) held more than $198 billion in assets, accounting for more than 57 percent of all assets held by the top 10,000 foundations. This elite group includes many well-known corporate names with asset levels placing them in the top ranks of the top one hundred, including the Bill & Melinda Gates Foundation (Microsoft, no. 1, $15.5 billion), the David and Lucile Packard Foundation (Hewlett-Packard, no. 2, $13.1 billion), the Ford Foundation (no. 3, $11.9 billion), and Lilly (pharmaceuticals, no. 4, $10.4 billion).[86]

Foundations are managed by boards of directors or trustees composed primarily of members from the superclass and closely allied members of the credentialed class. One study of large foundations found that over 34 percent of the top foundation leaders were members of exclusive upper-class social clubs. The top fifty foundation boards include a total of 402 director positions that are filled mainly by men (85 percent) who attended Ivy League or other prestigious universities. Moreover, many Rockefellers, Mellons, Lillys, Danforths, and members of other wealthy families (such as the Waltons of Wal-Mart fame) sit on the boards of directors of their family foundations and also often serve on corporate boards of several other firms.[87] For example, recent Rockefeller foundation trustees have included John D. Rockefeller III; Richard H. Jenrette, chairman of Equitable Life Insurance; Arthur Levitt, chairman of the American Stock Exchange; Frank G. Wells, former CEO of Walt Disney; and Harold Brown, a director of AMAX, CBS, and IBM and former U.S. secretary of defense.[88]

Foundation budgets come mainly from dividends received through their ownership of large blocks of corporate stock. These organizations spend their annual budgets on a variety of activities, but support of policy-planning network organizations is a consistent funding priority. For example, the Brookings Institution—a mainstream, centrist think tank with a staff of 250 and an annual budget of $20 million[89]—received a total of $5,661,475 in foundation grants during 1993–94.[90] Over the years Brookings has also benefited from both foundation and corporate funding, attracting, for example, 24 foundation and 150 corporate sponsors during the mid-1980s.[91]

Top foundations have historically provided substantial support to a variety of large, mainstream, politically centrist policy-planning organizations like the Brookings Institution. The Ford Foundation, for example, has been one of its most important financial supporters.[92] Another example of a mainstream policy-planning group benefiting from financial support by top foundations is the Council on Foreign Relations. Over the years it has received substantial funding from the Ford, Lilly, Mellon, and Rockefeller foundations.[93]

Conservative policy-planning think tanks have also benefited substantially from foundation support. Between 1977 and 1986, twelve foundations (including Pew Memorial, Coors, Lilly, and nine other smaller foundations) provided more than $63 million of the $88 million in grant funds received by the top ten conservative think tanks.[94] More recently, conservative foundations have increased their involvement in funding conservative think tanks, university programs, media groups, and other organizations linked to the policy-planning network. Their goal is to promote a more conservative policy agenda extolling the virtues of the free market and the dangers of government regulations.

A 1997 study by the National Committee for Responsive Philanthropy found that from 1992 to 1994, twelve core conservative foundations (including Lynde and Harry Bradley, Sarah Scaife, Carthage, Philip McKenna, John M. Olin, and seven others) donated $210 million to promote conservative activities. More than $80 million went to conservative think tanks and other organizations that explicitly advocated unregulated free markets, such as the Heritage Foundation ($8.9 million), the American Enterprise Institute ($6.9 million), the Cato Institute ($3.9 million), the Hudson Institution ($3.3 million), and the Manhattan Institute ($2.1 million). Large portions of the remaining $130 million went to academic centers, legal groups, and media outlets that promote the free-market cause. Examples include support for conservative scholarships, endowed chairs, and research centers, such as the $3 million donated to the Institute for Humane Studies and $2.1 million for the Center for the Study of Marketing Processes. Both promote free-market principles and are located at George Mason University in Fairfax, Virginia.[95]

In a follow-up report to the 1997 study, the National Committee for Responsive Philanthropy found that conservative foundations continued to serve as important sources of support for conservative think tanks. Over a third of the estimated $1 billion spent by the top twenty conservative think tanks over the 1990–2000 period came from conservative foundations. Contributions from scores of large corporations and several wealthy individuals accounted for most of the rest of conservative think-tank funds expended over the past decade.[96]

In addition to foundation funding, superclass members influence policy planning by serving as directors on think-tank boards. Mainstream policy-planning organizations' boards of directors are especially likely to reflect close ties with the superclass. For example, the Business Roundtable has 220 corporate members including some of the largest banks and industrial firms in the United States, such as Citicorp, General Motors, and Exxon.[97] The organization is led by 79 directors who are extensively interlocked with the corporate community. In 1997 the Roundtable directors held 207 directorships with 134 corporations, including 32 that were in the top 50 in size. Many Roundtable directors have also served as directors or trustees for policy-planning organizations such as the Business Council, the Council on Foreign Relations, and the Brookings Institution.[98] The trustees of the Brookings Institution and the CFR average four corporate directorships each, and only 6 percent of the trustees for these two organizations were not members of corporate boards. Moreover, more than two-thirds of the directors of the CFR, the Business Roundtable, and the Brookings Institution graduated from just twelve prestigious universities.[99]

CLASSWIDE LOBBYING:
INVESTING IN PRIVILEGE

On Capitol Hill, it is the lobbyists who have the clout. They speak for the vested interests. . . . And they have been extraordinarily successful in blocking . . . law[s] that would be detrimental to the privileged as well as in preserving [laws] that benefit the few at the expense of the many.

—Donald L. Barlett and James B. Steele, *America: What Went Wrong?* 1992

In American politics, lobbying has two faces: special-interest competition and classwide practices. The former is familiar and widely reported, but the latter, consistent with the class taboo, is seldom the topic of media attention or public discussion. Lobbying's special-interest face has been the subject of increased media attention following the passage of the Lobbying Disclosure Act (LDA) of 1995, which took effect January 1, 1996.[100] As noted earlier, LDA records reveal special-interest lobbying groups (primarily large corporations) spent $1.45 billion in 1999 on efforts to influence federal laws and policies (up from $1.26 billion in 1997).[101] This means that publicly disclosed lobby expenditures—through registered agents at the national level—now average about $120 million per month. But even this staggering sum is only part of the lobby story. An earlier study of all forms of lobbying estimated that "$8.4 billion is spent each year in Washington to lobby the federal government."[102]

Mainstream media reports on lobbying typically emphasize that although lobbying is a big business, it is also a highly competitive enterprise involving intense rivalries among powerful forces and organizations contending with one another to promote their own narrow agendas and interests. A study by the Center for Responsive Politics in the late 1990s illustrates this storyline. The study identified the American Medical Association (AMA) and Philip Morris as among the top-spending lobbyists in the first half of 1997, reporting expenditures of $8.5 and $5.9 million respectively.[103] A related report distributed via the Associated Press (AP) to many mainstream newspapers identified Philip Morris as a firm that "wants to limit its legal liability on cigarettes," and the AMA was said to be interested in health care issues such as "urging caution on reform of the Food and Drug Administration."[104] It is easy to infer from the context of the report that Philip Morris is lobbying to *prevent* tighter controls on tobacco products and the AMA is working, in part, to *promote* the strength of a federal agency (the FDA) that is likely to play a major role if tobacco is regulated as a drug.

Mainstream media accounts of lobbying tend to leave readers and viewers with the impression that although lobbying is not necessarily fair to poorly funded groups, the high-stakes, special-interest competition among "heavy hitters" leads to a rough balance of power. In fact, such stories often imply that competition among the "big boys" combined with the spotlight of media attention act as a kind of checks-and-balances system limiting the most egregious excesses of undue government influence among well-heeled lobby groups. Although we would agree that special-interest competitive lobbying is an important feature of our political system, we contend it is of secondary importance compared with the political-influence dealing and policy-shaping power of lobbying's other face.

Classwide lobbying is very different from the competitive, special-interest face of political lobbying most often presented in the media. It is supported by a wide array of superclass-dominated organizations acting in concert to promote legislative and regulatory policies supportive of superclass interests. The next five sections describe and illustrate classwide lobbying. First, we provide a brief overview of the classwide lobbying community. Second, we illustrate how classwide coalitions have produced policy outcomes favoring superclass interests in the areas of worker health and safety, free trade, health care "reform," and ergonomic regulations. Third, we examine recent policy contests involving NAFTA expansion and labor funding of political campaigns to illustrate that classwide political domination does not equal total control of policy making. In the final two sections we summarize how privileged-class-crafted national taxation and spending policies benefit this class at the expense of the working class.

We could have chosen many examples to illustrate the nature, extent, and consequences of classwide lobbying, but we believe our choices exemplify how superclass unity and political dominance are reflected in classwide lobbying campaigns and policies. The examples illustrate that classwide campaigns organized and funded by the superclass typically dominate public policy making and produce policy outcomes that serve the economic and political interests of this class (at the expense of the working class). Even so, groups within the alternative power networks do challenge and contest superclass dominance—and sometimes they win.

The Classwide Lobby Community

The classwide lobby community comprises a core of peak business groups, which are mainly nonprofit trade associations consisting of several individual corporate members with shared views and policy objectives. Depending on the issues, peak groups can and do participate in both classwide and special-interest lobbying, and some also serve as members of the policy-planning network. Peak groups tend to be organized around groups of top corporate leaders from large firms (e.g.,

CEOs) and specific industries (e.g., oil, electronics) as well as general, shared business interests (e.g., commerce and trade). Historically, peak groups have formed the organizational core of classwide lobbying efforts. On several issues that have reached Congressional legislative or regulatory reform policy contests, a small number of peak groups have consistently been at the center of lobbying activities representing the interests of the business community as a whole as well as the class interests of wealthy elites.

Among the most influential classwide lobbying groups are the CEO-dominated organizations, including the Business Roundtable, the Committee for Economic Development, and the Conference Board.[105] Specific, industrywide peak groups that frequently play leadership roles in promoting, coordinating, and supporting classwide lobbying campaigns include the National Association of Manufacturers (NAM), the Chemical Manufacturers' Association (CMA), the American Petroleum Institute (API), the American Mining Congress (AMC), the Health Insurance Association of America (HIAA), the Pharmaceutical Manufacturers' Association (PMA), and many others. More general shared business interests are represented by peak groups such as the U.S. Chambers of Commerce and, for smaller firms, the National Federation of Independent Business (NFIB).

Classwide Coalitions and Policy Outcomes

Industrywide and CEO-headed peak groups have historically taken the lead in creating ad hoc coalitions to promote classwide business unity and to spearhead lobbying campaigns aimed at influencing legislative outcomes on policies where superclass and corporate interests are at stake. In the mid-1980s, NAM created and led the Coalition on Occupational Disease Notification that helped defeat the labor-supported High-Risk Occupational Disease Notification Act.[106] In 1993, the Business Roundtable organized the USA*NAFTA business coalition that helped secure passage of the North American Free Trade Agreement.[107] The Business Roundtable also led the fight against health care reform in 1993–94 with help from the insurance industry including the Alliance for Managed Competition (created by the "Big Five": Aetna, Prudential, Travelers, CIGNA, Metropolitan Life, and the HIAA).[108] In early 2001, NAM served as the nerve center for a coalition of business groups known as the "National Coalition on Ergonomics," which opposed workplace rules to prevent repetitive motion injuries issued in the closing days of the Clinton administration. With NAM at the point, joined by the U.S. Chamber of Commerce, NFIB, and other groups, the Coalition orchestrated an intense lobbying campaign that led to votes in both houses of Congress in favor of legislation repealing the rules (March 6–7, 2001).[109]

Classwide lobbying campaigns draw upon resources provided by a variety of corporate-oriented, law, lobbying, and public relations firms. In the political battle over NAFTA, for example, the USA*NAFTA coalition hired the Wexler Group, a Washington lobbying firm headed by Anne Wexler—a former Carter White

House aide with strong ties to the Clinton administration—to promote the bill.[110] USA*NAFTA, with donations from firms such as Exxon, DuPont, General Electric, and Dow Chemical, spent more than $4 million to promote NAFTA's passage, with money flowing to lobbyists as well as to public relations firms that crafted numerous pro-NAFTA ads that ran in newspapers, magazines, and on television.[111]

In addition to utilizing high-dollar, professional "hired guns" in the legal, lobbying, and public relations communities, classwide lobbying campaigns also rely on the resources of corporate-dominated professional associations. Many of these organizations can be counted on as dependable class allies and lend their scientific expertise in support of classwide lobbying efforts. The American Industrial Hygiene Association and the American Occupational Medical Association worked on behalf of corporate interests in the classwide campaign to defeat the High-Risk legislation in the mid-1980s.[112] Professional groups are valuable allies because they lend legitimacy to classwide lobby efforts. They provide a patina of scientific respectability to what might otherwise appear to be purely superclass, "wealth- and privilege-protection" lobbying campaigns. Together with law and public relations firms, the expertise of professional associations helps to maximize the effectiveness of superclass-driven policy-intervention lobbying campaigns.

The recent classwide campaign to repeal the ergonomics rules was somewhat unique in that it was conducted and concluded in a very compressed time period (about four months). Moreover, it relied almost exclusively on forceful, unified business lobbying rather than clever public relations advertising or scientific testimony. The campaign began with closed-door meetings, such as one held on February 6, 2001, that was organized by NAM and involved nearly 100 out-of-town business executives, Washington lobbyists, and aides of Senator Don Nickles (R–OK) and Representative Michael B. Enzi (R–WY). (Nickles and Enzi cosponsored the legislation that would overturn the ergonomic rules.) Next, the NAM-led National Coalition on Ergonomics mounted a massive lobbying effort coordinating telephone calls, e-mails, and business owner visits to members of Congress during the President's Day recess. "On Feb. 27, NAM flew in nearly 500 executives [to Washington] to coax lawmakers to rescind the regulation." On that same day, President Bush agreed to support efforts to rescind the rules. Senator Nickles then "invited about 50 executives to his office to finalize an endgame strategy."[113]

The campaign was a complete superclass success. Then Senate Minority Leader Tom Daschle (D–SD) acknowledged that business groups "were willing to invest much of their political capital in the issue." "Corporate America . . . [put] intense pressure on Democrats to . . . kill the ergonomics policy that President Bill Clinton had issued in November. Business interests made it clear that rejection . . . would carry political consequences." "'No contest,' said Senator Max Baucus, D–Mont. 'The lobbying was 20–1 against the reg.'" Bill Samuel, a top AFL-CIO lobbyist, said that the business community "spared no expense in promoting their position."[114]

Challenging Classwide Lobbying and Superclass Dominance

In the late 1990s, two classwide lobbying campaigns organized and funded by superclass sponsorship were defeated by labor-led alternative power network coalitions. The first issue involved superclass efforts to win fast-track status for a trade agreement to expand NAFTA to Chile, Brazil, and other Central and South American nations. "Fast track" was the media label for a legislative device that would increase the U.S. president's power to negotiate terms of foreign trade pacts and then allow him to submit such agreements to Congress for up or down votes—no amendments allowed. The second issue involved superclass support for federal and state legislation that would have required labor unions to "obtain written permission from union members every year before spending money on politics."[115] In part, this effort was a superclass response to the relative success of the AFL-CIO's Labor '96 campaign, which supported prolabor candidates through a $35 million union-provided election fund.[116]

In August 1997, President Clinton used his national radio address to press the case for fast track. At about the same time, the Business Roundtable sent a letter to hundreds of corporate heads asking for donations to support "a multi-pronged fast-track lobbying campaign." The letter said, "We believe we need to raise a minimum of $3 million in order to insure that the voice of the business community is heard." It was signed by the CEOs from Boeing, Caterpillar, Chrysler, TRW, General Motors, and Procter and Gamble—and each of these firms had already agreed to donate $100,000 to the cause. The letter also outlined a strategy involving a "grassroots campaign" that included "aggressive use of [a] 1–800 number to generate congressional communications from company employees, suppliers, and constituents." And it promised the "distribution of fast-track lobbying kits to companies for congressional visits." These efforts would be supported by a "Washington campaign relying on use of corporate offices of Roundtable companies and CEO communication with legislators."[117]

Despite this well-funded superclass effort, the fast-track campaign failed to win public support and failed in Congress. The labor-led, anti-fast-track coalition won the public opinion battle as polls showed 56 percent of Americans opposed the fast-track effort.[118] In October 1997 the legislation barely passed the Republican-controlled House Ways and Means Committee—but only four of sixteen Democrats on the committee supported it.[119] On November 10, 1997, President Clinton and Republican congressional leaders withdrew the bill after it failed "to get the votes needed to pass it."[120]

In 1998 a major classwide superclass-funded lobbying campaign was aimed at members of Congress as well as state voters (especially in California) as part of an effort to reduce union funding of prolabor political candidates and policies. In Congress, Republicans introduced the deceptively titled Worker Paycheck Protection Act, and in California (and in other states) superclass-funded organizations placed propositions on ballots for statewide votes.[121] In both cases the goal was the same: to pass federal and state legislation that would force unions to "obtain advance, written, annual permission from members to use dues money for 'political purposes.'"[122]

Superclass supporters of these efforts included the "usual suspects" and raised a huge war chest estimated at $149 million. The Business Roundtable raised $20 million to support federal and state efforts to legislate "paycheck protection" laws. This amount was augmented by an $18.75 million pledge from NAM to support the legislative campaigns and by the support of the U.S. Chambers of Commerce. These core groups' efforts were reinforced by Americans for Tax Reform (who contributed $10 million and field coordination responsibility), the National Right to Work Committee ($10.5 million), and the American Legislative Exchange Council (which provided model legislation).[123]

The federal "paycheck protection" legislation was stopped by a filibuster led by prolabor senators in early 1998 which also had the effect of shifting the battle to California.[124] There, the AFL-CIO and California-based unions mounted a major campaign to defeat Proposition 226 (the title of the proposed law on the June 2, 1998 California ballot). Through the efforts of three hundred union field organizers, thousands of volunteers, and a budget of some $20 million, Proposition 226 was defeated by a 53- to 47-percent margin.[125]

These two campaigns illustrate that superclass political dominance does not equal absolute control over all class-relevant policy contests. Even so, these were not stake-through-the-heart losses for the superclass. Despite setbacks in these two battles, the superclass war against workers continues on many issues, including free trade and the political balance of class power. The historical record reveals that when superclass economic and political interests are at stake, the organizations representing this class are persistent, resourceful, and often victorious—even after sustaining initial defeats.[126]

As noted earlier, a recent example of superclass policy resilience occurred when the business-led campaign against the ergonomic rules issued by President Clinton were overturned by the U.S. Congress in 2001. Also, superclass efforts to suppress the political clout of unions via paycheck protection legislation continues. Following the labor-led defeat of Proposition 226 in California, the business community continued the fight in other states. Labor succeeded in defeating subsequent paycheck protection schemes in North Dakota, Oregon, Mississippi, and South Dakota, but lost in Utah and remains on the defensive in Montana.[127] As the struggle continues, unions are forced to devote portions of their resources to these campaigns, thus limiting their abilities to engage in other prolabor activities—such as growing labor's political clout.[128]

The fast-track expansion of NAFTA is yet another example of superclass policy resilience. Although defeated by opponents in 1997, the issue returned in 2001. President Bush sought "presidential trade promotion authority" (the new name for fast track) from Congress so he could negotiate an expanded version of NAFTA that would cover all of Latin America through a new proposed trade policy known as the Free Trade Area of the Americas (FTAA) agreement.[129] (Called "NAFTA on steroids" by some opponents.) At the time of this writing, the outcome of Bush's request for "fast-track authority" on the FTAA was uncertain. After the September 11 attacks, Robert Zoellick, Bush's U.S. Trade Representative, crafted a "Countering Terror with Trade" campaign to build support for trade promotion authority. It remained to be seen if such an effort could take advantage of the Congressional bipartisanship created by the attacks and the U.S. "war on terrorism," or if it might create a Congressional and public opinion backlash against what appeared to be blatant political opportunism—using a national tragedy to support a narrow, politically motivated trade policy.[130]

The historical record makes it clear that superclass policy losses almost never equal capitulation—especially where classwide superclass and corporate interests are at stake. The earlier paycheck protection and fast-track defeats are likely to represent only temporary setbacks for superclass interests. The policy-making process is still in motion on these issues, and the jury of history is still out. Superclass policy preferences on core economic issues such as labor law, trade, and taxes are akin to the qualities of characters in classic science fiction films such as *Dawn of the Dead* and *The Terminator*. Like undead zombies, superclass-promoted policies are continually reanimated, and like futuristic cyborgs, *they never stop!*

Classwide Lobbying: Federal Taxation and Spending Policies

The jury is not out on the issue of superclass dominance over federal tax and spending policies. However, these are two areas where classwide and special-interest lobbying sometimes intersect and overlap—thereby at times obscuring classwide campaigns and superclass dominance. Journalists often focus on special-interest lobbying and point out that the political contributions of individual firms or industry PACs often appear to lead to specialized tax breaks or federal subsidies for specific firms or industries. Although such policy outcomes are often both obvious and outrageous, they are actually of secondary importance to classwide lobbying. The cumulative effects of classwide campaigns dating from the 1960s aimed at shaping federal (as well as state and local) tax and spending policies to further advantage privileged-class interests are evident in current federal, state, and local laws. Classwide tax campaigns in 1985–86, 1996–97, and 2001 provide three examples of efforts that produced major changes in tax rates benefiting the wealthy and corporations.

Classwide Campaigns and Tax Reform: 1986

The list of companies and trade associations that lobbied Congress as key committees considered and crafted the Tax Reform Act of 1986, the 1997 Budget Reconciliation Act, and the 2001 Tax Relief Act included the "usual suspects" involved in classwide lobbying campaigns—plus a few new groups. The record of the 1985

House tax reform hearings fills nine volumes and more than nine thousand pages, and the vast majority of the nearly one thousand witnesses who appeared represented corporate interests. Although many corporate representatives were seeking specialized benefits for individual firms or industries, some of the most potent corporate players advocated preserving and extending corporate tax breaks that would promote the classwide advantages and interests of wealthy corporate owners and officers. This message was evident in testimony from witnesses representing the Business Roundtable, NAM, the U.S. Chambers of Commerce, NFIB, and many others.[131]

Even coalitions that appeared to represent specialized corporate interests secured results that on closer inspection had classwide implications. The 1985 coalition known as the Alliance for Capital Access, formed with contributions from 120 financial companies, illustrates this point. The alliance, with close connections to Michael Milken (the "junk-bond king" of the 1980s) and Carl Lindner (CEO of Chiquita Brands International), spent $4.9 million from 1985 through 1990 to help preserve the tax deduction for interest paid on corporate debt—an effort in which they succeeded. The Tax Reform Act of 1986 left the deduction intact.[132] This provision benefited not only the "junk-bond" industry but the entire corporate community as well, and since the bill's passage corporations have increasingly turned to debt rather than issuing more stock as a preferred means of financing corporate operations and expansion.

House hearings held in 1990 on the impact, effectiveness, and fairness of the Tax Reform Act of 1986 generated seventy-six statements for the record. Of this number, forty-nine came from corporations or trade associations, with most praising various features of the 1986 act. Many of these statements were submitted by the same classwide organizational advocates that had supported the legislation in 1985. The few critics submitting statements in 1990, such as the AFL-CIO and the American Federation of State, County, and Municipal Employees (AFSCME), pointed to problems that the 1986 tax law had created as a result of reducing tax rates for corporations and very wealthy individuals. The critical testimony of these witnesses called attention to the classwide benefits and costs embedded in the 1986 act—extensive financial benefits for superclass and many credentialed-class members—and to the substantial costs that were passed along to the entire working class.[133]

Classwide Campaigns and Tax Reform: 1997

In the spring of 1997 the "same old gang" came forward to lobby for further reductions in corporate taxes, federal capital gains taxes, and federal inheritance taxes. In the context of an expanding economy, political pressures to balance the budget, Republican control of the Congress, and a compliant president, the issue was not whether taxes would be cut—that was a foregone conclusion. The real issues involved which taxes would be cut and how the cuts would be distributed.

During the 1997 budget negotiations, Deputy Treasury Secretary Lawrence H. Summers remarked that "the interests pushing for a cut in estate taxes were motivated by 'selfishness.'" He emphasized that "the overall tax package has to have as its thrust helping middle-class America." Summers was immediately attacked by congressional Republican leaders and by a variety of conservative groups and pundits for "promoting class warfare" and favoring "socialism." Two days after his remarks, he was "forced to issue a public apology." Summers had violated an important dimension of the class taboo: "[He] acknowledged that all tax cuts do not benefit all Americans equally and that class is very much the defining issue."[134]

The tax cuts mandated by the Budget Reconciliation Act of 1997 primarily benefited privileged-class members and their wealth-producing machines called corporations. As the details of the tax bill were being crafted, members of Congress again—as in 1986—listened closely to lobbyists from NAM, the U.S. Chambers of Commerce, and NFIB, who coordinated their efforts to win business tax cuts—ostensibly to improve fairness, investment, and productivity (and not just to juice profits).[135] This corporate-focused lobbying effort to reduce taxes was reinforced by classwide coalitions seeking cuts in the capital gains and estate taxes. In all three instances the lobbying campaigns were aimed at tax cuts that would primarily produce classwide benefits for wealthy Americans.

The lobbying effort to reduce the capital gains tax was led by a coalition of conservative groups that publicly focused attention on the need for Congress to use "tax revenue windfalls" created by a rapidly growing economy "for tax cuts for all Americans." The precise kinds of tax cuts favored by these groups were not always publicly specified. But the coalition included several groups fronted by well-known conservative political and business leaders that have long favored cuts in capital gains taxes: Jack Kemp, of Empower America; Lewis K. Uhler, of the National Tax Limitation Committee; David Keating, of the National Taxpayers Union; Steve Forbes, of Americans for Hope, Growth, and Opportunity; Matt Kibbe, of Citizens for a Sound Economy; and Harrison Fox, of Citizens for Budget Reform.[136]

The estate-tax-reduction campaign was led by a coalition of 105 lobbying groups backed by privileged-class members with financial interests in passing family fortunes intact (tax free) to the next generation.[137] And federal estate tax rates are not a trivial issue for the rich. Prior to the 1997 tax law, estates were taxed at federal rates of 18 percent on the first $10,000, 37 percent for assets of more than $500,000, and 55 percent for estates valued in excess of $3 million. Although the estate-tax cut was claimed by its supporters to benefit all Americans, few parents amassed estates above the pre-1997 $600,000 federal exemption ($1.2 million for married couples) to pass along to their heirs. In 1996, a total of 69,772 estates with assets in excess of $600,000 filed forms with the Internal Revenue Service, but after allowable deductions and exemptions, only 31,918 estates paid federal estate taxes—just 1.2 percent of all estates.[138]

The 1997 classwide tax-reduction campaigns paid off for the privileged class.

Copyright © Lloyd Dangle. Reprinted with permission.

The Budget Reconciliation Act of 1997 cut capital gains taxes from 28 to 20 percent. The minimum corporate tax was eliminated, and the federal estate (inheritance) tax exemption was raised from $600,000 to $1 million ($1.3 million for family farms and businesses).[139] The 1997 tax act distributed three-fourths of individual tax cuts to people with annual incomes of more than $100,000. Over one-third of all tax breaks went to the wealthiest 1 percent, who ended up with more tax relief than the bottom 80 percent. At the same time, "changes in the Alternative Minimum Tax (AMT) . . . lowered the tax burden for corporations by $18.3 billion over 10 years."[140]

The tax act did not come close to the high priority Deputy Treasury Secretary Summers placed on restructuring the tax code so as to help "middle-class America." Instead, the richest 5 percent of American families got 83 percent of the benefits from cuts in the capital gains tax, the elimination of the minimum corporate tax, and the near doubling of the estate-tax exemption. Families in the top 20 percent income group scored annual tax breaks of more than $1,000, but those in the top 1 percent received tax breaks averaging "$16,157 per year." This amount included average tax cuts of $7,939 in capital gains, $6,313 in estate taxes, and $2,353 in corporate taxes, minus small increases ($451 on average) in excise taxes. Families in the middle 20 percent income group received a tax break of only $153 per year, and families in the lowest and second-lowest income groups saw either no tax cuts or slight tax increases.[141] Final tax-savings score: privileged class, billions of dollars; new working class, chump change.

Classwide Campaigns and Tax Reform: 2001

During the 2000 presidential campaign, candidate Bush proposed a tax-cut plan to be phased in over ten years at a total cost in lost revenue to the U.S. Treasury variously estimated at between $1.3 and $2.1 trillion.[142] After Bush won the election, on February 8, 2001, Treasury Secretary Paul O'Neill presented the Bush plan, known then as the "Agenda for Tax Relief" to Congress.[143] The Bush plan was marketed to the public and Congress on the grounds of fairness and as a recession-fighting measure.[144] Four months later on June 7, President Bush signed the "Economic Growth and Tax Relief Reconciliation Act of 2001" (PL 107–16) into law at an estimated cost to the Treasury of $1.35 trillion in lost revenue over the next ten years.[145] (The law included a "sunset provision" that will cause it to expire after December 31, 2010.)[146]

Nearly 71 percent of the tax law's benefits goes to individuals in the top 20 percent income group; but some features, such as the repeal of the federal estate tax (in 2010), primarily benefit only the richest 1 percent.[147] By contrast, the law leaves marginal tax rates unchanged for Americans with taxable incomes of less than $27,050 (singles) or $45,200 (married couples).[148] Most of the law's benefits for wealthy taxpayers will be phased in gradually, as illustrated by stepwise declines in tax rates for the top income groups over the next several years.[149] Also, tax cuts implemented in 2001 for the top 1 percent groups represent just 6 percent of the benefits for this group. The rest (94 percent) are yet to come. Taxpayers in next highest 4 percent income group will receive 70 percent of the law's benefits in future years.[150]

The most pernicious effects of the 2001 tax law will be to "starve" federal programs that benefit working-class Americans in the future. According to the UAW, "the new law will effectively crowd out the ability of the federal government to provide funds to strengthen Social Security and Medicare. . . . In addition, it will preclude the federal government from making major investments in education, health care, and many other important areas."[151] Some political observers view such long-term effects as part of a deliberate strategy by the privileged class.[152] As

writer Ruth Conniff observed, "Make no mistake. We are being set up for the repeal of the last of the hard-earned New Deal antipoverty and health care programs
for the elderly and poor Americans."[153]

So why did the lopsided tax law loaded with benefits for the highest income
groups and laden with many long-term negatives for working-class Americans
pass so quickly? We know it wasn't because of a grassroots clamor by average-
income Americans. Polls showed little public support. Although a majority of
Americans in a national survey favored the *concept* of reducing federal income tax
rates "across the board," only 16 percent thought the Bush plan would "do 'a lot' to
improve their own financial situation."[154] In one poll of registered voters, only 7
percent of respondents ranked taxes as the "most important issue facing the country."[155] Moreover, a substantial coalition of groups representing middle-income
workers' interests, known as "Fair Taxes for All," opposed the Bush plan and the PL
107–16 version of it (e.g., AFL-CIO, AFSCME, NAACP, National Women's Law
Center, People for the American Way).[156]

The real reason the tax-cut legislation moved so expeditiously through Congress
was because of unified, active support provided by a group of several powerful organizations representing the material and ideological interests of the privileged
class. This group, known as the Tax Relief Coalition, was organized in February; its
founding members included the U.S. Chamber of Commerce, NAM, the National
Association of Wholesalers-Distributors, and NFIB. Another 250 business and taxpayer groups were invited to join the Coalition and were asked to pay $5,000 each
in dues, primarily to pay for advertising "in Capitol Hill publications."[157]

The Coalition members set aside individual organizational interests for specialized forms of tax cuts in favor of a unified, classwide approach in support of Bush's
plan. Jerry Jasinowski, president of NAM, pointed out that "loading up the bill
with too many [special] provisions could doom it." He emphasized the need for
business unity and said, "We need to be very judicious and forego trying to add a
lot of things to this bill because it will just be seen as a corporate Christmas tree."[158]
The Coalition's objective was simply to get the Bush plan through Congress. As
Dirk Van Dongen, president of the Wholesalers-Distributors, said, "our goal is to
mobilize grass roots on behalf of the package. We welcome into membership in
the coalition any organization or corporation that will take the pledge [to support
Bush's package]." Other corporate trade groups that were considering lobbying efforts to add specialized tax cuts to the bill—which might have complicated Congressional support for it—were waved off by the Coalition.[159] Based on the end
results and the final form of the law, it is clear the Coalition was a major political
force behind the successful classwide campaign in favor of PL 107–16.

Taxploitation and Spendsploitation

As we noted earlier, the new working class comprises some 80 percent of Americans with limited capital resources and with a share of total economic output that

is small and declining. As the history of federal tax and spending policies illustrates, not only does this group have little influence in the shaping of national policies, it is increasingly exploited by policies governing how taxes are collected on individuals and corporations and by the ways in which government spends tax revenues.

Of course, the policies directing how government taxes and spends do not have to be exploitative. For example, tax rates could be used to remedy the high levels of income and wealth inequalities in the United States today by levying higher tax rates on corporations and wealthy individuals. The money raised by such policies could be spent on public goods that improve opportunities for, and the economic well-being of, the nonprivileged. Better schools, national health insurance, government-financed higher education, reconstruction of public infrastructure facilities, and job creation, training, and placement are all examples of public goods that could be financed by funds raised through higher taxes on the privileged class. As it now stands, goods that potentially could be publicly funded, such as health care and higher education, must be purchased by most Americans from their earnings; but most of the nonprivileged can barely afford these goods. Thus, tax and spending policies in the United States do not function to redistribute wealth and income but rather extend their maldistribution and concentration.

In the United States today, national (as well as state and local) tax laws and spending policies are dictated by the wealthy and powerful through both classwide and interest-group lobbying. As we have seen, these lobbying efforts are very effective, because they are driven by the same groups that are centrally involved in the financing of most political campaigns. Thus, the ways that tax dollars are collected and distributed are not only not redistributive, but they collect an increasing share of taxes from the nonprivileged and spend the money in ways that disproportionately benefit the privileged. We should think of superclass-dominated national tax and spending policies as examples of *taxploitation* and *spend-sploitation*—two types of exploitation that compound the more general levels of wealth and income inequality.

We illustrate these forms of exploitation with three figures depicting "American pies." The basic idea of the "Wealth pie" shown in figure 4.2 was introduced in our chapter 1 discussion of wealth inequalities in the United States. It shows that the richest 20 percent of Americans control 96 percent of the financial wealth of the country, meaning ownership of stocks, bonds, and commercial real estate. The other 80 percent of Americans hold the remaining 4 percent of total wealth.[160] This means that about 112 million workers (80 percent of the total U.S. labor force in 2001) work every day throughout their entire adult lives producing wealth that goes largely to others, while they receive a few "crumbs" from the pie themselves. The extraordinary extent of wealth inequality in the United States could be reduced if the wealthy were required to pay higher tax rates on their incomes and assets and if they were prevented from transferring their wealth to their children. But as we have seen, that is not the way U.S. tax and inheritance laws have been written.

Figure 4.2   The Wealth Pie, 2002

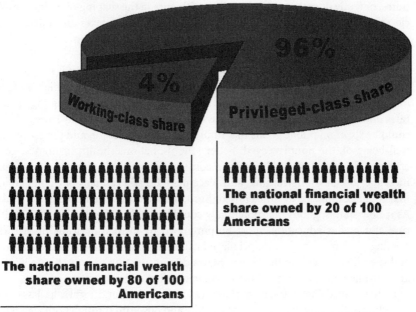

The national financial wealth
share owned by 80 of 100
Americans

The national financial wealth
share owned by 20 of 100
Americans

Source: Mishel, et al., 2001: p. 259, 265.

The "tax pie" (figure 4.3) illustrates the share of total taxes paid by individuals
and corporations. In 2002 the share of federal tax revenues paid by corporations
was estimated at 10 percent. This figure is down sharply from the 27 percent share
corporations paid in 1950. By contrast, in 2002 taxes paid by individuals (individual income taxes plus Social Security and Medicare taxes) made up an estimated
82 percent of federal tax revenues. This figure is up sharply from the 51 percent
share paid by individuals in 1950.[161]

But as we have already noted, not all individual taxpayers get the same breaks
from federal tax policies. Take the case of Social Security. In 2001 all American
workers paid about 7.7 percent of the first $80,400 in annual earnings to the Social
Security fund (increasing to $84,900 in 2002).[162] However, in 2001 more than 90
percent of American workers earned less than $80,400 annually, so they paid So-
cial Security taxes on 100 percent of their earned incomes.[163] In contrast, privileged-class Americans who earned $200,000 or $2 million in 2001 also paid Social
Security taxes, but only on $80,400 of their income. So the nonprivileged pay taxes
on all of their income, and the privileged pay taxes on a small percentage of their
income. But at payout time, the rich still collect their full Social Security checks,
even though they are likely to still have incomes in the range of hundreds of thousands of dollars.

The U.S. Tax Code is filled with ways for rich individuals and corporations to

Figure 4.3 The Tax Pie, 2002

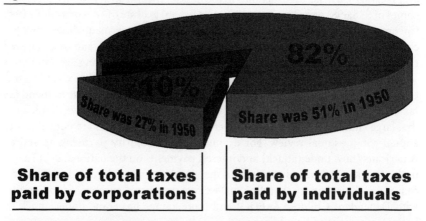

| Share of total taxes paid by corporations | Share of total taxes paid by individuals |

Source: Office of Management and Budget, 2001.
Note: The amounts shown in the diagram do not total 100% because other forms of taxes were collected. However, these other forms include taxes (such as excise) that are typically paid by individuals. Thus, the individual share shown in the diagram is lower than the actual share paid by individuals.

reduce their taxes (often to less than zero), while working-class Americans make up for these lost taxes. The reason for this is simple: the tax code is written by the privileged class and for the privileged class, who justify their advantaged status with the widely shared ideological aphorism, "when the rich do well, everyone does well." Why would this be the case? Because, as the rest of the story goes, the rich invest their money, which in turn creates more jobs and more wealth shared by all Americans. This fairy tale—akin to the former Divine Right of kings myth— was invented by the superclass, seconded by the credentialed class, widely believed by the working class, and turned into law by Congress. Congress is receptive to this tale because most of its members are either already among the rich or are on the make, and they are provided with huge contributions to influence their votes on taxes.

The crash-and-burn reality of this fairy tale propagated by the privileged class is evident every year at tax time, when thousands of corporations and wealthy individuals escape taxes. For 1999 (the most recent year available), of the 2,429,802 income tax returns with adjusted gross income (AGI) of $200,000 or more, 2,429 returns showed no "total income tax liability." In 1998, 70,777 tax returns in the highest income brackets (more than $200,000) were taxed at only a 10 percent rate. Although most taxpayers with AGIs over $200,000 paid tax rates between 24.1 and 28.9 percent in 1999, these levels were not much above the rates paid by average wage earners.[164] Households in the middle-income fifth (average pretax incomes of $38,698) were taxed at an effective federal tax rate of 18.9 percent in 1999 (income taxes, Medicare, and Social Security).[165] Such tax inequalities exist because the rich enjoy a variety of special exemptions, deductions, and other favored rules written into the tax code by our generous and understanding legislators.

The final figure presents two "redistribution pies," which provide vivid illustrations of how the largely privileged-class members of Congress choose to spend the tax dollars that are collected. However, before we look at figure 4.4, we should note that large chunks of federal spending are legally mandated and are not subject to annual congressional review. For example, Social Security payments to retired Americans (now under attack) and interest payments on the national debt (never under attack) are forms of entitlement spending that cannot be avoided. But in recent years, discretionary spending on "welfare programs" such as Aid to Families with Dependent Children (AFDC) and food stamps has come under attack by both Democrats and Republicans.

In 1996 a majority of both parties in both houses of Congress voted to "end welfare as we know it." This effort culminated in President Clinton's signing of the Personal Responsibility and Work Opportunity Act in August 1996. The new law ended the AFDC program and replaced it with the Temporary Assistance to Needy Families (TANF) program. Among other things, the 1996 law ended the federal guarantee of cash assistance to poor families, set time limits on how long families can receive assistance from TANF funds (sixty months), mandated 22 percent cuts in foodstamps and Supplemental Security Income (SSI) over six years, and instituted penalties to states that do not force substantial portions of their adult TANF recipients into narrowly defined work programs.[166]

Although AFDC was the primary federal "welfare program" of last resort providing cash assistance to the poorest of poor American families, it accounted for less than 1 percent of annual federal expenditures. The TANF program that replaced AFDC will cost taxpayers about $16.5 billion in 2002—which also amounts to less than 1 percent of the total $1.9 trillion federal budget. It is instructive to compare the political attacks on and the media attention devoted to "welfare dependency" to almost exact opposite reactions where the U.S. defense budget of $319 billion is concerned.[167] In fact, following the September 11 terrorist attacks, U.S. military spending increased sharply and "could hit $375 billion" for fiscal year 2002.[168] Moreover, "analysts are predicting that the defense budget will increase 66 percent to $500 billion by 2005."[169]

Figure 4.4 illustrates the relative size of federal "wealthfare" spending (the pre–September 11 defense budget) versus federal welfare (TANF) appropriations for 2002. Of course, some portion of defense spending is legitimate on the grounds of protecting U.S. national security (though how much is open to debate). But large chunks of defense spending exist primarily to juice the profits of military contractor firms and to feed the hundreds of thousands of high-paid scientists, engineers, and civilian employees who work in government, industry, and

Figure 4.4   The Redistribution Pie, 2002

On Defense

On TANF

Note: TANF: (Temporary Assistance to Needy Families) is the current federal program providing cash assistance to poor families. In 1997 it replaced the previous Aid to Families with Dependent Children (AFDC) federal program.

university research and administration units throughout the "national security state."[170] In short, the superclass and their credentialed-class allies are the principal beneficiaries of much of the defense spending. Consequently, we do not see political attacks or hear media complaints about the "dependency" induced by defense spending.

There is no national debate over the defense "wealthfare" for the privileged class (or other forms of wealthfare), because this group has strong lobbies in Washington and its members control the major media and educational institutions. But no one lobbies for the poor. As Bob Dole (Republican candidate for president in 1996) once said, "poor people don't have a PAC." All they do is irritate the rich by their presence—and sometimes serve as a convenient scapegoat to blame for the fading fortunes of the working class. But poor people do not vote and they have no political clout, so their programs are cut while defense spending continues to grow—even in a post–Cold War world.

It is clear that classwide lobbying helps juice federal spending in ways that ensure the privileged class gets large shares of the American pie. True, as Ringo Starr once sang, "You know it don't come easy." Keeping the federal cash spigot open requires that the superclass funnel millions of dollars to prime the congressional pump. Classwide political-campaign-financing and classwide lobbying practices are expensive. But for the superclass and its credentialed-class allies, the tax and spending payoffs are huge.

SUPERCLASS INTERESTS, POLITICAL POWER, AND LEGITIMACY

The power elite has the economic and political resources to continue its domination of the federal government . . . and most people are likely to accept the current arrangements as long as they can make their lives work.

—G. William Domhoff, *Who Rules America?* 1998

The superclass has always had critical interests in controlling politics and government. These political interests are logical extensions of its economic interests. Superclass control over great wealth has historically provided this group with a critical resource for influencing the selection and election of political candidates, the electoral process, and policy formation, implementation, and enforcement. As we have seen, superclass funding of candidates leads to powerful influence over elected lawmakers and helps ensure superclass dominance over the formation and implementation of laws and public policies as well as major appointments to the state bureaucratic apparatus. Under this system, the state becomes a vehicle for legitimating existing class-power relationships and the production and distribution of wealth. Laws governing incorporation, corporate rights, taxes, and the regulation of labor markets ensure the dominance and legitimacy of large corporate enterprises in the economy. The stamp of state legitimacy combined with ancillary laws and regulations affords corporations effective control over workers' terms of employment and control over the production and distribution of wealth for elite owners. Completing the circle of power, corporate-generated wealth provides superclass members with the economic resources they need to access and dominate the political process and the state.

Although economic wealth and the shadow political industry provide the superclass with the structural foundation facilitating its domination of politics and government, this arrangement is inconsistent with American democratic ideals. Superclass domination of the political and economic arenas is contradicted by widely shared democratic values and equal opportunity ideals. Left unaddressed, these contradictions could lead working-class members to call into question the legitimacy of the U.S. political and economic systems. However, superclass-owned organizations that make up the information industry have developed control processes that help obscure—and thereby reduce—the tensions generated by the clash between economic and political realities and cultural ideals. These control processes help minimize the prospects of a "crisis of legitimacy" for superclass-controlled economic and political institutions. The next chapter explores the role played by the information industry in maintaining the legitimacy of superclass power.

NOTES

1. Quoted in Vicente Navarro, "Medical History as Justification Rather Than Explanation: A Critique of Starr's *The Social Transformation of American Medicine,*" *International Journal of Health Services* 14 (1984): 516.

2. Gore Vidal, "The End of History," *Nation*, September 30, 1996, 11–18.

3. G. William Domhoff, *State Autonomy or Class Dominance?* (New York: Aldine de Gruyter, 1996), 25; G. William Domhoff, *Who Rules America? Power and Politics* (Boston: McGraw-Hill, 2002), 95–98.

4. Ben H. Bagdikian, *The Media Monopoly* (Boston: Beacon Press, 1997), 13; Doug Donovan and Peter Kafka, "Hosts with the Most," *Forbes*, March 19, 2001, 164–66; Robert W. McChesney, *Rich Media, Poor Democracy* (Chicago: University of Illinois Press, 1999), 48–62; Robert W. McChesney, "Journalism, Democracy, and Class Struggle," *Monthly Review*, November 2000, 1–15.

5. Val Burris, "The Myth of Old Money Liberalism: The Politics of the *Forbes* 400 Richest Americans," *Social Problems* 47 (2000): 360–78; Domhoff, *Who Rules America? Power and Politics*, 45–68; Michael C. Dreiling, "The Class Embeddedness of Corporate Political Action: Leadership in Defense of the NAFTA," *Social Problems* 47 (2000): 21–48; Alan Neustadtl and Dan Clawson, "Corporate Political Groupings: Does Ideology Unify Business Political Behavior?" *American Sociological Review* 53 (1988): 172–90; Maynard S. Seider, "American Big Business Ideology: A Content Analysis of Executive Speeches," *American Sociological Review* 39 (1974): 802–15; Richard L. Zweigenhaft and G. William Domhoff, *Diversity in the Power Elite: Have Women and Minorities Reached the Top?* (New Haven: Yale University Press, 1998), 192–94.

6. District of Columbia Bar, "Attorney Resources," on the Internet at http://www.dcbar.org/attorney_resources/index.html (visited July 8, 2001).

7. *Influence, Inc.* "Summary" (Washington, D.C.: Center for Responsive Politics, 2000), 1, 3.

8. Jeffrey H. Birnbaum, *The Lobbyists* (New York: Times Books, 1992); Kevin Phillips, "Fat City," *Time*, September 26, 1994, 51.

9. *Influence, Inc.* "Summary," 1.

10. Domhoff, *Who Rules America? Power and Politics*, 104, 159.

11. "Burson-Marsteller: Overview: Family of Companies" and "BKSH Government Relations Worldwide" on the Internet at http://www.bm.com/overview/family2.html and www.bksh.com/company.htm (visited August 12, 2001).

12. Allan Shuldiner and Tony Raymond, *Who's in the Lobby? A Profile of Washington's Influence Industry* (Washington, D.C.: Center for Responsive Politics, 1998), 7–19.

13. Dan Clawson, Alan Neustadtl, and Denise Scott, *Money Talks* (New York: Basic Books, 1992), 182; "Fortune 1000 Industry Totals," *Fortune*, April 16, 2001, F-69.

14. Domhoff, *Who Rules America? Power and Politics*, 140–41, 154–61; Phillips, "Fat City," 52.

15. Kay L. Schlozman and John T. Tierney, *Organized Interests and American Democracy* (New York: Harper and Row, 1986), 77.

16. Clawson, Neustadtl, and Scott, *Money Talks*, 182; Domhoff, *Who Rules America? Power and Politics*, 18–30.

17. Domhoff, *Who Rules America? Power and Politics*, 57–68.

18. Chuck Collins, "Horatio Alger Where Are You?" *Dollars and Sense*, January–February 1997, 9; S. M. Miller, "Born on Third Base: The Sources of Wealth of the 1996 *Forbes* 400," *United for a Fair Economy*, February 1997, 5–6.

19. Domhoff, *Who Rules America? Power and Politics*, 27, 58, 63.

20. Thomas Dye, *Who's Running America? The Clinton Years* (Englewood Cliffs, N.J.: Prentice-Hall, 1995), 175; Domhoff, *Who Rules America? Power and Politics*, 63–64.

21. Domhoff, *State Autonomy or Class Dominance*, 1996, 25; Domhoff, *Who Rules America? Power and Politics*, 63–65; Harold R. Kerbo, *Social Stratification and Inequality* (New York: McGraw-Hill, 2000), 356.

22. David Corn, "Rove-r and Out?" *Nation*, July 16, 2001, 5–6; Louis Dubose, "Bush's Hitman," *Nation*, March 5, 2001, 11–15.

23. Center for Responsive Politics, "2000 Election Overview, Stats at a Glance: Congressional Races," "2000 Presidential Race: Total Raised and Spent," on the Internet at http://www.opensecrets.org/2000elect/index/AllCands.htm (visited July 29, 2001).

24. Larry Makinson, *The Big Picture: Money Follows Power Shift on Capitol Hill* (Washington, D.C.: Center for Responsive Politics, 1997), 5–6.

25. Eric Bates, "Campaign Inflation," *Mother Jones*, March–April 2001, 48.

26. Ibid., 47; Larry Makinson, *The Big Picture*, 1.

27. Federal Election Commission (FEC), *FEC Reports on Congressional Financial Activity for 2000*, Tables: "Contributions from Individuals by Size of the Contribution, 1999–2000" and "1999–2000 Financial Activity of Senate and House General Election Campaigns," press release, May 15, 2001.

28. FEC, "Contributions from Individuals by Size of the Contribution, 1999–2000."

29. FEC, *FEC Reports on Congressional Financial Activity for 2000*, Tables: "Contributions from Individuals by Size of the Contribution, 1999–2000," "Financial Activity of All U.S. House of Representative Candidates—1988–2000," "Financial Activity of All U.S. Senate Candidates—1988–2000," press release, May 15, 2001.

30. FEC, "Contributions from Individuals by Size of the Contribution, 1999–2000."

31. Clawson, Neustadtl, and Scott, *Money Talks*, 11; *Hard Facts on Hard Money* (Washington, D.C.: Public Campaign, 2001), 4.

32. FEC, *FEC Reports Increase in Party Fundraising for 2000*, press release, May 15, 2001, 1–2.

33. Steve Weissman, "Discharge Petition May Force Hastert's Hand," *Public Citizen News*, September–October 2001, 6; Derek Willis, "Debating McCain-Feingold," *Congressional Quarterly Weekly*, March 10, 2001, 524–27.

34. Marty Jezer, "Soft Money, Hard Choices," *Dollars and Sense*, July–August 1996, 30.

35. Clawson, Neustadtl, and Scott, *Money Talks*, 11.

36. *Hard Facts on Hard Money* (Washington, D.C.: Public Campaign, 2001), 1.

37. FEC, *FEC Reports on Congressional Financial Activity for 2000*, Tables: "Contributions from Individuals by Size of the Contribution, 1999–2000" and "1999–2000 Financial Activity of Senate and House General Election Campaigns," press release, May 15, 2001.

38. Ibid.

39. FEC, "Contributions from Individuals by Size of the Contribution, 1999–2000."

40. FEC, "Contributions from Individuals by Size of the Contribution, 1999–2000" and "1999–2000 Financial Activity of Senate and House General Election Campaigns."

41. FEC, *FEC Reports on Congressional Financial Activity for 2000*, 2.

42. Micah L. Sifry, "How Money in Politics Hurts You," *Dollars and Sense*, July–August 2001, 17.

43. *Hard Facts on Hard Money*, Public Campaign, 9, 12.

44. Ellen Miller and Randy Kehler, "Mischievous Myths about Money in Politics," *Dollars and Sense*, July–August 1996, 23.

45. *Hard Facts on Hard Money*, Public Campaign, 9.

46. Center for Responsive Politics, "2000 Election Overview: Top Metro Areas," on the Internet at http://www.opensecrets.org/2000elect/storysofar/ topmetro.asp (visited July 29, 2001).

47. *Mother Jones*, "Wall Street Leads Top Campaign Contributors on *Mother Jones* 400," on the Internet at http://www.motherjones.com/about_us/pressroom/ 030501_2.html (visited July 21, 2001).

48. Ted Gup, "The *Mother Jones* 400," *Mother Jones*, March–April, 1996, 43.

49. FEC, "1999–2000 Financial Activity of Senate and House General Election Campaigns."

50. FEC, *FEC Reports on Congressional Financial Activity for 2000*, 2.

51. Marie Hojnacki and David C. Kimball, "PAC Contributions and Lobbying Contacts in Congressional Committees," *Political Research Quarterly* 54 (March 2000): 177.

52. FEC, *PAC Activity Increases in 2000 Election Cycle*, Table: "PAC Financial Activity 1999–2000," press release, May 31, 2001.

53. Clawson, Neustadtl, and Scott, *Money Talks*, 32–33.

54. FEC, "PAC Financial Activity 1999–2000."

55. Clawson, Neustadtl, and Scott, *Money Talks*, 161.

56. Ibid., 140–41.

57. Ibid., 181.

58. Ibid., 176, 160.

59. FEC, "PAC Financial Activity 1999–2000."

60. Larry Makinson, "Business, Labor, and Ideological Donors," *Who's Paying for this Election?* (Washington, D.C.: Center for Responsive Politics, 2000), 1.

61. FEC, "PAC Financial Activity 1999–2000."

62. Ibid.

63. Charles Lewis, "The Buying of the President," *Dollars and Sense*, July–August 1996, 28, 41.

64. Makinson, "Business, Labor, and Ideological Donors."

65. John Nichols, "Behind the DLC Takeover," *Progressive*, October 2000, 29.

66. Jezer, "Soft Money, Hard Choices," 30.

67. Hank Kalet, "We Need Electoral Reform Now," *Progressive Populist*, August 1–15, 2001, 19.

68. Center for Responsive Politics, "No Recess: How the Divided Senate has Bolstered

Campaign Fund-Raising," on the Internet at http://www.opensecrets.org/alerts/v6/alertv6_18asp (visited July 29, 2001).

69. Center for Responsive Politics, "2002 Election Overview: Fundraising by Members of Congress," on the Internet at http://www.opensecrets.org/2002elect/storysofar (visited September 17, 2001).

70. *Hard Facts on Hard Money,* Public Campaign, 9.

71. Marc Breslow, "Government of, by, and for the Wealthy," *Dollars and Sense,* July–August 1996, 23–24.

72. Seth Ackerman, "The Most Biased Name in News," *EXTRA!* July–August 2001, 10–18; Dean Baker, "Generation Excess," *EXTRA!* March–April 1996, 12–13; Doug Henwood, "TV on Social Security: It's Broke, Fix It," *EXTRA!* May–June 1999, 8–12; Mike Males, "The Myth of the Grade-School Murderer," *EXTRA!* May–June 2001, 30.

73. Domhoff, *Who Rules America? Power and Politics,* 69–98.

74. Dye, *Who's Running America?* 215; Also see Michael Dolny, "What's in a Label?" *EXTRA!* May–June 1998, 9–10; David Croteau, "Challenging the 'Liberal Media' Claim," *EXTRA!* July–August 1998, 4–9.

75. Thomas R. Dye, "Organizing Power for Policy-Planning: The View from the Brookings Institution," in *Power Elites and Organizations,* ed. G. William Domhoff and Thomas R. Dye (Newbury Park, Calif.: Sage, 1987), 185–86.

76. Ibid., 188.

77. Domhoff, *Who Rules America? Power and Politics,* 78–80.

78. Dye, *Who's Running America?* 222–27.

79. Val Burris, "Elite Policy-Planning Networks in the United States," in *Research in Politics and Society,* vol. 4, *The Political Consequences of Social Networks,* ed. Gwen Moore and J. Allen Whitt (Greenwich, Conn.: JAI Press, 1992), 115–20.

80. Michael Patrick Allen, "Elite Social Movement Organizations and the State: The Rise of the Conservative Policy-Planning Network," in Moore and Whitt, *Research in Politics and Society,* vol. 4, 95.

81. Clawson, Neustadtl, and Scott, *Money Talks,* 139.

82. National Committee for Responsive Philanthropy, "$1 Billion for Ideas: Conservative Think Tanks in the 1990s," press release, March 12, 1999, (Washington, D.C.: 2001 S Street NW), 2.

83. Domhoff, *State Autonomy or Class Dominance?* 34, 38.

84. Ibid., 29–32.

85. Harold R. Kerbo, *Social Stratification and Inequality* (New York: McGraw-Hill, 1996), 180–81; also see Domhoff, *Who Rules America? Power and Politics,* 73–78.

86. David G. Jacobs, ed., *The Foundation Directory, 2001 Edition* (New York: Foundation Center, 2001), vii–xi, xi.

87. Dye, *Who's Running America?* 11, 135, 171, 192.

88. Kerbo, *Social Stratification and Inequality* (1996), 180; also see Dye, *Who's Running America?* 135.

89. Sandra Jaszczak, ed., *Encyclopedia of Associations* 31st ed., vol. 1 (Detroit: Gale Research, 1996), 2265.

90. Linda G. Tobiasen, ed., *The Foundation Grants Index, 1996* (New York: Foundation Center, 1995).

91. Dye, "Organizing Power for Policy-Planning," 183.

92. Ibid.

93. Dye, *Who's Running America?* 225.

94. Allen, "Elite Social Movement Organizations and the State," 96–97.

95. Robert Parry, "Who Buys the Right?" *Nation,* November 18, 1996, 5–6.

96. National Committee for Responsive Philanthropy, "$1 Billion for Ideas," 1–2. Also see Sam Husseini, "Checkbook Analysis," *EXTRA!* May–June 2000, 23–24.

97. John B. Judis, "The Most Powerful Lobby," *In These Times,* February 21, 1994, 22–23.

98. Domhoff, *Who Rules America? Power and Politics,* 92–94.

99. Dye, *Who's Running America?* 236–37.

100. Peter Nye, "Lobbying and Gift Reform Shines Sunlight on Influence Peddling," *Public Citizen,* January–February 1996, 1, 3.

101. Center for Responsive Politics, *Influence, Inc.* "Summary" (Washington, D.C.: Center for Responsive Politics, 2000), 1.

102. Office of Congressman Dick Armey, "Washington's Lobbying Industry: A Case for Tax Reform—Executive Summary," June 19, 1996, 1–4, 1.

103. Shuldiner and Raymond, *Who's in the Lobby?* 7.

104. Jim Drinkard, "Lobbying Costs Hit $100 Million a Month," *Indianapolis Star,* March 7, 1998, A1–2.

105. Domhoff, *Who Rules America? Power and Politics,* 84–94. Also see Clawson, Neustadtl, and Scott, *Money Talks,* 180.

106. Earl Wysong, *High Risk and High Stakes: Health Professionals, Politics, and Policy* (Westport, Conn.: Greenwood Press, 1992), 59.

107. Dreiling, "Class Embeddedness of Corporate Political Action." Also see Judis, "The Most Powerful Lobby," 22–23.

108. Joel Bleifuss, "Money Talks, Democracy Walks," *In These Times,* May 16, 1994, 12–13.

109. Rebecca Adams, "GOP-Business Alliance Yields Swift Reversal of Ergonomics Rule," *Congressional Quarterly Weekly,* March 10, 2001, 535–39.

110. Gabriella Boyer, "Corporate America Stacks the NAFTA Debate," *Public Citizen,* July–August 1993, 26.

111. Joan Claybrook, "Why It's Their NAFTA, Not Ours, Not Yours," *Public Citizen,* November–December 1993, 2, 15.

112. Wysong, *High Risk and High Stakes,* 102–10.

113. Adams, "GOP-Business Alliance Yields Swift Reversal of Ergonomics Rule," 536.

114. Ibid., 535, 536, 538.

115. "Phony Paycheck Protection: It'll Cost You More Than You Think," *UAW Solidarity,* March–April 1998, 10–11.

116. Russ Davis, "AFL-CIO Unveils Program to Revitalize Labor Movement," *Labor Notes,* March 1997, 1, 14; George Melloan, "Whatever Happened to the Labor Movement?" *Wall Street Journal,* September 4, 2001, A23; John Nichols, "Real Paycheck Protection," *Nation,* March 26, 2001, 8.

117. Ken Silverstein and Alexander Cockburn, "Our Little Secret: Life on the Fast Track," *CounterPunch,* September 1–15, 1997, 2–3.

118. "Fast Track Media Misperceptions," *Extra!Update,* February 1998, 1.

119. "Fast Track Falters in Major House Vote; UAW Steps UP Drive," *UAW Solidarity,* October 1997, 9.

120. "Fast Track Sidetracked," *UAW Solidarity,* November 1997, 7.

121. "Paycheck Deception Act: Don't Let Them Fool You," *AFSCME Public Employee,* March–April 1998, 7–19.

122. "What Is the 'Paycheck Deception Act'?" *AFSCME Public Employee,* March–April 1998, 10–11.

123. "Paycheck Deception Act," 7.

124. "Phony Paycheck Protection," 10–11.

125. Marc Cooper, "Labor-Latino Beat in CA," *Nation,* June 29, 1998, 5–6.

126. Domhoff, *Who Rules America? Power and Politics,* 175; G. William Domhoff, *Who Rules America? Power and Politics in the Year 2000* (Mountain View, Calif.: Mayfield Press, 1998), 266–81.

127. Nichols, "Real Paycheck Protection," 8.

128. Linda Chavez, "Union Workers Deserve Choice in Use of Dues," *Indianapolis Star,* September 17, 2001, A12. Also see Melloan, "Whatever Happened to the Labor Movement?"

129. Jane English, "Bush Eyes 'Fast Track' Authority," *Public Citizen News,* July–August 2001, 1, 7; Laurie McClure, "Free Trade Ache of the Americas," *Labor Party Press,* July 2001, 1, 4; David Moberg, "Fast Track is Back," *In These Times,* July 23, 2001, 17–18; David Moberg, "FTAA, Eh?" *In These Times,* April 16, 2001, 16–19.

130. Robert L. Borosage, "Scoundrel Time," *Nation,* November 19, 2001, 6–7, 23; David Broder, "Expanded Trade Authority Faces Political Realities," *Indianapolis Star,* November 7, 2001, A16; Naomi Klein, "Trading on Terrorism," *In These Times,* November 12, 2001, 9; David Moberg, "Going Down: Congress is Only Going to Make It Worse," *In These Times,* November 12, 2001, 20–21; John Nichols, "Policy Profiteers," *Nation,* October 22, 2001, 4–5.

131. U.S. Congress, House of Representatives, *Comprehensive Tax Reform,* Committee on Ways and Means, 99th Congress, 1st sess., serial 99–41, 1985, Washington, D.C.: U.S. Government Printing Office.

132. Donald L. Barlett and James B. Steele, *America: What Went Wrong?* (Kansas City, Mo.: Andrews and McMeel, 1992), 207.

133. U.S. House Committee on Ways and Means, *Impact, Effectiveness, and Fairness of the Tax Reform Act of 1986,* 101st Cong., 2d sess., 1990, serial 101–92.

134. Michelle Cottle, "The Real Class War," *Washington Monthly,* July–August 1997, 12, 13. Summers later left the treasury. On July 1, 2001 he became president of Harvard University. See Matt Bivens, "Harvard's 'Fitting Choice,'" *Nation,* June 25, 2001, 6–7.

135. *Congressional Record, Alternative Minimum Tax Reform Act: Chamber of Commerce of the United States of America,* and *Alternative Minimum Tax Reform Act: Statement of National Association of Manufacturers,* May 8, 1997, S4236–38; *Congressional Record, The Small Business Capital Gains Enhancement Act of 1997,* May 15, 1997, S4588–91; *Congressional Record, Amendment no. 519,* June 26, 1997, S6449–51.

136. *Congressional Record, Pro-Taxpayer Groups Urge Congress to Act Now on Future Tax Cuts,* June 27, 1997, S6678–79.

137. Cottle, "The Real Class War," 15.

138. John Miller, "More Wealth for the Wealthy: The Estate Tax Giveaway and What to Do about It," *Dollars and Sense,* November–December 1997, 26–27.

139. John Miller, "Tax Cuts: Clinton and Congress Feed the Wealthy," *Dollars and Sense,* November–December 1997, 43; Miller, "More Wealth for the Wealthy," 26.

140. "The Rich Get a Good Return on Their Campaign Investments," *Sanders Scoop,* Winter 1998, 1.

141. Miller, "Clinton and Congress Feed the Wealthy," 43.

142. Daniel J. Parks, "Bush May Test Capitol Hill Clout Early with Expedited Tax-Cut Proposal," *Congressional Quarterly Weekly*, January 6, 2001, 42.

143. Lori Nitschke, "Tax Plan Destined for Revision," *Congressional Quarterly Weekly*, February 10, 2001, 318–21.

144. Howard Fineman and Rich Thomas, "Snip! Snip! Snip!" *Newsweek*, February 19, 2001, 18–22.

145. Daniel J. Parks, "Under Tight Spending Ceilings, Democrats Lower Their Sights," *Congressional Quarterly Weekly*, June 9, 2001, 1364.

146. Lori Nitschke and Wendy Boudreau, "Provisions of the Tax Law," *Congressional Quarterly Weekly*, June 9, 2001, 1394 (1390–94).

147. Citizens for Tax Justice, "Final Version of Bush Tax Plan Keeps High-End Tax Cuts, Adds to Long-Term Cost," on the Internet at http://www.inequality.org/bushtaxplan2.html (visited August 8, 2001). Also see John Miller, "Getting Back More than They Give," *Dollars and Sense*, September–October 2001, 60–62.

148. Jane Bryant Quinn, "Tax Cuts: Who Will Get What," *Newsweek*, June 11, 2001, 30.

149. Nitschke and Boudreau, "Provisions of the Tax Law," 1390.

150. Citizens for Tax Justice, "Post-2001 Tax Cuts Offer Little to Most Americans," on the Internet at http://www.ctj.org/html/gwblater.htm (visited August 12, 2001).

151. "Bush Tax Plan Will Squeeze Medicare, Education," *UAW Solidarity*, July–August 2001, 4.

152. William Greider, "Stockman Returneth," *Nation*, April 2, 2001, 4–6.

153. Ruth Conniff, "The Budget Surrender," *Progressive*, June 2001, 13.

154. Fineman and Thomas, "Snip! Snip! Snip!" 20.

155. Lori Nitschke, "Tax-Cut Bipartisanship Down to One Chamber," *Congressional Quarterly Weekly*, March 10, 2001, 532 (529–32).

156. Lori Nitschke, "Coalitions Make a Comeback," *Congressional Quarterly Weekly*, March, 3, 2001, 474.

157. Ibid., 470, 474.

158. Nitschke, "Tax Plan Destined for Revision," 321.

159. Nitschke, "Coalitions Make a Comeback," 474.

160. Lawrence Mishel, Jared Bernstein, and John Schmitt, *The State of Working America 2000–2001* (Ithaca, N.Y.: Cornell University Press, 2001), 259, 265.

161. Office of Management and Budget, "Historical Tables," *Budget of the United States Government: Fiscal Year 2002* (Washington, D.C.: U.S. Government Printing Office, 2001).

162. U.S. Department of Commerce, Bureau of the Census, *Statistical Abstract of the United States* (Washington, D.C.: U.S. Government Printing Office, 2000), 383; Social Security Administration, "2001 Social Security Changes," on the Internet at http://www.ssa.gov/cola/cola2001.htm (visited August 17, 2001); Tom Herman, "Tax Report," *Wall Street Journal*, October 24, 2001, A1.

163. U.S. Department of Commerce, Bureau of the Census, *Statistical Abstract of the United States*, 473.

164. U.S. Department of the Treasury, Internal Revenue Service, *The Statistics of Income (SOI) Bulletin*, Spring 2001, 32, 276–77.

165. Mishel, Bernstein, and Schmitt, *The State of Working America 2000–2001*, 58.

166. Randy Albelda, "Farewell to Welfare but Not to Poverty," *Dollars and Sense*, November–December 1996, 17; Hank Hoffman, "Time is Tight," *In These Times*, November

12, 2001, 7–8.
    167. Office of Management and Budget, *Budget of the United States Government: Fiscal Year 2002* (Washington, D.C.: U.S. Government Printing Office, 2001), 19; Office of Management and Budget, "Appendix," *Budget of the United States Government: Fiscal Year 2002* (Washington, D.C.: U.S. Government Printing Office, 2001), 464.
    168. William D. Hartung, "New War, Old Weapons," *Nation,* October 29, 2001, 4–5.
    169. Keith Naughton, "Lock and Download," *Newsweek,* October 22, 2001, 61.
    170. Joel Bleifuss, "Warfare or Welfare," *In These Times,* December 9, 1996, 12–14.

5

The Information Industry

In media, we see the core contradiction of our age, where the democratic interests of the many are undermined by the private selfish interests of the powerful few.

—Robert W. McChesney, *Monthly Review*, November 2000

"All the news that's fit to print." This quote published daily as part of the *New York Times* masthead suggests the ideal of news reporting in the U.S. media: diverse, impartial, balanced, and complete. But this ideal is far from reality. As we will see, there is substantial evidence that subtle and insidious forms of censorship are pervasive throughout virtually all print and electronic news media outlets owned and operated by large corporations in the United States (the mainstream media). Media censorship in the United States doesn't involve overt, heavy-handed, formal rules of reporting or the killing of new stories by government censors. "Instead, it comes stealthily under the heading of Missed Opportunities. . . . [It is] a subtle system of information suppression in the name of corporate profit and self interest."[1]

For the past twenty-five years Project Censored, a nonprofit media watchdog group, has been "identifying and researching important news stories that are underreported, ignored, misrepresented, or censored in the United States." The organization's publications make it clear that such forms of censorship in the United States today grow largely out of the routine structures and operations of the mega-merged corporations that own and control the U.S. news media. "The Top 25 Censored Stories of 2000" covered a wide range of topics from reports on multinational corporations seeking to privatize water supplies (#1) to a 552-day campaign by community activists to stop the construction of a McDonald's restaurant in Hinchley Wood, England (#25). The common thread binding all twenty-five stories together is their neglect or marginalization by the mainstream media. As the authors noted, "the top 25 censored stories for 2000 are the news that the corporate media refused to cover."[2]

Project Censored's annual list of censored news stories reveals two important features of the relationship between superclass-based corporate power and the media. First, contrary to what some conservatives imagine to be the case, mass media reports that are somehow critical of superclass corporate power or policies are extremely rare.[3] Mainstream media accounts of corporate activities rarely include the kind of in-depth, critical investigative reporting found in the censored stories. Second, the censored stories illustrate that media reports critical of corporate power, corporate policies, or instances of corporate-government collusion against public or workers' interests are almost always "broken" by small, alternative media sources. For the past twenty-five years, virtually all of the reports in Project Censored's "top 25 censored stories" list were first published by alternative news magazines such as the *Nation, In These Times,* the *Progressive,* and *Mother Jones.*

An important aspect of corporate media censorship not explicitly addressed by Project Censored is the use by well-heeled corporations and trade associations of "strategic action lawsuits against public participation" (SLAPP suits). Such lawsuits provide deep-pocket corporations with a potent weapon for suppressing media reports and activities by citizens' groups, which corporate owners and managers may view as unflattering, embarrassing, or threatening to their interests. "Libel suits, such as the meat industry's [1998] case against talk show host Oprah Winfrey that are basically frivolous . . . can bankrupt citizen organizations that criticize corporate behavior."[4] Small media outlets can also be targets. For example, in the 1990s the Briggs and Stratton corporation filed a $30 million libel and invasion-of-privacy lawsuit against the *National Catholic Reporter* (*NCR*) in response to a story critical of the company's plans to downsize its Milwaukee area operations.[5]

SLAPP suits make it clear that when the agents of superclass power are stung by media critiques, they have enormous resources at their disposal to punish offenders. These suits serve as chilling reminders to all potential critics of the risks they face if they challenge superclass corporate power or policies. While the exact number of SLAPP suits filed each year in the United States is difficult to know, the California Anti-SLAPP Project estimates that thousands of such cases occur annually.[6]

Even if SLAPP suits are ultimately decided in favor of critics, they are expensive, time-consuming, and energy-draining challenges to organizations with typically limited resources. The threat of SLAPP suits is likely to induce caution and even self-censorship as citizens' group activists or writers and editors for small media outlets consider whether to publish actions or story lines critical of powerful corporations. Consider the Briggs and Stratton suit. Although the case was eventually dismissed by a federal judge in 1998, the *NCR* editorial announcing the decision noted that: "Such suits have lately grown more common and are designed to make individuals or seemingly more vulnerable media think twice before criticizing big corporations or interests. It is, in other words, a bullying tactic rather than a search for justice, never mind a search for truth."[7]

This chapter explores how organizationally based structures and processes produce what Project Censored describes as "information suppression." It focuses on the links between class interests, mega-media firms, and powerful media-driven processes that shape public views on economic, political, and cultural issues. In short, we consider how the mainstream media shape, censor, manage, and disseminate ideas, information, and news in ways that protect and promote privileged-class interests while ignoring or marginalizing working-class interests. As we will see, information industry owners and managers have a preference for media content that will maximize profits. Their message is keep it light, keep it bright, and keep it moving.

THE MAINSTREAM CORPORATE MEDIA

A specter now haunts the world: a global commercial media system dominated by a small number of super-powerful . . . transnational media corporations.

—Robert W. McChesney, *EXTRA!* November–December 1997

The information industry consists of giant interlocked electronic and print-media corporations that are largely owned by superclass members and managed by a small number of superclass leaders in conjunction with credentialed-class junior partners.[8] These firms disseminate information, ideas, and images about, and interpretations of, national and global economic, political, and social news and issues to national and international audiences. The industry can be viewed as part of an even larger enterprise that some critics have termed the "culture industry" or the "national entertainment state."[9] Such labels suggest that in addition to generating news and commentary largely consonant with superclass interests, the industry also serves as a major conduit for disseminating most forms of mass entertainment, corporate public relations propaganda, product ads, promotional campaigns, and paid political advertising.

The content of the news and information delivered by the electronic and print-media arms of the information industry is not neutral in terms of viewpoints conveyed or class interests served. But the news media are also not liberal in the sense of being critical of mainstream economic and political institutions or policies—as many conservative pundits, such as Rush Limbaugh and best-selling author Bernard Goldberg, claim. Studies of media content do reveal consistent biases—but of a pro-business, pro-privileged-class sort. News story lines and accompanying images typically begin with pro-business sources, such as superclass-funded think tanks.[10] And the commercial media most often "favor style and substance that [are] consonant with their corporate [economic] interests."[11] The information industry consistently delivers news and information that effectively reinforce superclass and corporate interests—at the expense of working-class interests in an informed citizenry and participatory democracy. "It is a disaster for anything but the most superficial notion of democracy—a democracy where, to paraphrase John Jay's maxim, those who own the world ought to govern it."[12]

Polls suggest deep public skepticism exists concerning news media credibility.[13] Even so, the information industry dominates national attention regarding current affairs, with most Americans getting most of their news about such events from mass media outlets. According to national surveys, 61 percent of Americans report they get most of their news from television. Newspapers are a distant second news source (24 percent) followed by radio (8 percent), internet or online services (2 percent), and magazines (1 percent).[14] These findings indicate that TV and newspapers are the major news sources for 85 percent of the public. This means the five major television news networks (ABC, CBS, CNN, FOX, NBC) are the primary sources of information in the United States today. It also means the 1,483 daily U.S. newspapers rank as the second most important source of news for Americans.[15] However, it should be noted that "ninety-eight percent of all cities have only one daily newspaper and these are increasingly controlled by huge chains like Gannett and Knight-Ridder."[16] To illustrate, in 2000, Gannett and Knight-Ridder reported annual revenues of $6.2 and $3.2 billion (respectively) and ranked 288 and 499 on the *Fortune* 500 list.[17]

In the early 2000s, the core of the information industry consists of several large, interlocked news media firms that often include both electronic and print divisions. However, large news firms are themselves typically owned by even larger corporate conglomerates. In 2001, General Electric (GE), AOL-Time Warner (AOL-TW), Disney, Viacom, and the News Corporation (NC) owned, as subsidiaries, the largest electronic media firms that run major television news operations in the United States. Four are U.S. firms. The News Corporation, headed by CEO Rupert Murdoch, has its corporate headquarters in Australia. These five giant parent firms also own or control several other media and entertainment corporations including cable television networks, radio stations, newspapers, magazines, book publishing companies, and film studios. The following listing of the five firms includes (1) the total 2000 corporate revenues for each firm, (2) the major television networks and news operations owned by each firm, (3) the 2000 revenues generated by television networks and cable operations for each firm, (4) a partial listing of other media companies owned or jointly operated by each parent firm through various subsidiaries.

- *General Electric.* In 2000, GE's total corporate revenues were $129.9 billion. GE owns NBC and NBC News and in 2000, its TV network revenues totaled $6.8 billion. GE, mainly through NBC, also owns 13 television stations and has interests in several TV cable operations including CNBC, MSNBC, the A&E Network, the History Channel, National Geographic International Channels, AMC, Bravo, the Independent Film Channel, and the Madison Square Garden Network. The company also has interests in Rainbow Media Holdings, TiVo, and DirecTV.

- *AOL-Time Warner.* In 2000, AOL-TW's total corporate revenues were $36.2 billion. AOL-TW owns Turner Broadcasting and CNN News and in 2000, its TV network and cable revenues totaled $12.9 billion. AOL-TW TV ownership and joint cable ventures include TBS, TNN, Home Box Office, the WB Network, the Cartoon Network, Court TV, and Time Warner Cable. Other holdings include Time, Inc., which publishes over 64 magazines including *Time, Sports Illustrated, People,* and *Fortune.* Time Warner Trade Publishing includes several imprints including Little, Brown and Warner Books. Warner Brothers produces movies for theaters (e.g., *The Matrix*) and for television and owns diverse properties such as DC Comics and *Mad Magazine.*

- *The Walt Disney Company.* In 2000, Disney's total corporate revenues were $25.4 billion. Disney owns ABC and ABC News and in 2000, its media network revenues totaled $5.9 billion. Disney owns 10 television stations, 44 radio stations, plus TV network and cable operations including ESPN, the Disney Channel, Toon Disney, and Soap Net. Disney has joint ventures with the History Channel, A&E Entertainment, Lifetime Entertainment, and E! Entertainment Television. Disney produces films under five studio titles including Miramax, Walt Disney, Touchstone, Hollywood, and Dimensions. The firm also distributes videotapes through Buena Vista Home Entertainment. Disney publications include *ESPN* and *Discover* magazines and Hyperion books. The Disney-owned Buena Vista Music Group includes Walt Disney and Mammoth Records.

- *Viacom Incorporated.* In 2000, Viacom's total corporate revenues were $20 billion. Viacom owns CBS and CBS News and in 2000, its TV network and cable revenues totaled $9.3 billion. Viacom owns 34 television stations and operates over 180 radio stations through Infinity Broadcasting. The firm also owns or jointly operates MTV Networks, Black Entertainment Television (BET), Paramount Television (including King World, which produces syndicated programming such as *Wheel of Fortune, Jeopardy,* and *The Oprah Winfrey Show*), United Paramount Network (UPN), Showtime Networks, and Comedy Central. Other Viacom media holdings or joint ventures include movies (Paramount Pictures, United International Pictures, and Paramount Home Entertainment), theaters (United Cinemas International), music (Famous Music Publishing), video (Blockbuster rental stores), publishing (Simon & Schuster), and Internet operations (MTVi Group, CBS.com, CBS.MarketWatch.com, and Nickelodeon Online). (Viacom also owns the theme park company, Paramount Parks.)

- *The News Corporation.* In 2000, NC's total corporate revenues were $11.5 billion (U.S. dollars). NC owns Fox Entertainment Group and Fox News, and in 2000 its TV network and cable revenues totaled $8.6 billion (U.S. dollars). The News Corporation, primarily through the Fox Entertainment Group, operates four major business segments in the United States: (1) filmed entertainment (Twentieth Century Fox and Fox Searchlight Pictures—films such as *Titanic* and *Star Wars*), (2) television stations (23 owned by Fox), (3) television broadcast network (broadcasts network programming to Fox-owned and affiliated TV stations), (4) cable network programming (11 cable channels/programs including the Fox News Channel, National Geographic Channel [U.S.], Fox Sports Networks, Los Angeles Dodgers, FX, and Fox Family). Other News Corporation media holdings in the United States include book publishing (HarperCollins, William Morrow, Avon), magazines (*TV Guide*), and newspapers (*New York Post*).[18]

Corporate interlocks linking the boards of directors of the largest media firms to nonmedia companies illustrate how the web of superclass owners and employers cuts across the top levels of corporate America. In the late 1990s, the six largest electronic media firms (Time Warner, Disney, Viacom, NC, CBS, GE) had eighty-one directors on their boards. This group held "104 additional directorships on the boards of *Fortune* 1000 corporations."[19] The top 11 electronic and print media firms in the late 1990s had "thirty-six *direct* [corporate] links, meaning two people who served on different media firm boards of directors and also served on the same board for another *Fortune* 1000 corporation."[20]

In the early 2000s, we find increasing numbers of interlocks between large media and nonmedia firms. In 2001, the five giant electronic media firms listed earlier plus the six largest newspaper corporations—New York Times Co., Washington Post Co., Tribune Co. *(Chicago Tribune/L.A. Times)*, Dow Jones *(Wall Street Journal)*, Gannett *(USA Today)*, and Knight-Ridder—combined for a total of 154 directors. The members of these 11 boards "interlocked with 272 corporations with a total of 321 links."[21] Recent trends in corporate interlocks between media and nonmedia firms illustrate the growth of such interlocks. In 1997 "the 14-member board of the New York Times Co. had interlocks with eight *Fortune* 1000 companies. In 2001, the number of ties has grown to 21 companies. Knight-Ridder's 11-member board linked to 14 *Fortune* 1000 boards in 1997; by 2001, the number grew to 26."[22] The growing numbers of media-nonmedia interlocks underscore the reality that "the media in the United States effectively represent the interests of corporate America."[23]

The complex and extensive web of media and nonmedia corporate interlocks illustrates how the parent firms of the major U.S. TV news networks, and most of the other large media firms outside of the current five corporate giants, are integrated into a tightly woven superclass-based corporate structure. Through interlocks and joint ventures, the media segment of this corporate structure is largely owned or controlled by the same 25,000 officers and directors of the one thousand largest firms that also supervise and control the shadow political industry.[24] This means that the mainstream electronic and print media are almost exclusively composed of large corporate firms whose policies, personnel, and reporting practices reflect superclass and corporate interests.[25]

Many of the fortunes of the wealthiest Americans are directly tied to media holdings. About 17 percent of the *Forbes* list of the richest 400 Americans "derived their wealth from media, entertainment, or software. Exactly 20 percent of the fifty largest family fortunes were derived therefrom."[26] But this outcome should not be surprising, since "the truth about the news industry has always been that rich businessmen (and a few rich women) own it."[27] And although news media ownership today more often takes a corporate rather than patriarchal form, the top news media CEOs are structurally bound to policies that advance privileged-class interests.[28] Today, the combined influence of superclass-based ownership and credentialed-class management practices where the news media are concerned have produced a kind of "corporate ministry of information." As one media critic put it, "It is normal for all large businesses to make serious efforts to influence the news, to avoid embarrassing publicity, and to maximize sympathetic public opinion and government policies. Now they own most of the news media that they wish to influence."[29]

Corporate interlocks that tie media firms' news operations with superclass interests of political control and profits lead to interesting contradictions. As a cultural ideal, news is supposedly delivered by "objective" media sources free from biases. In practice, as we have glimpsed and as we will see in more detail later, this is never the case. The stakes are too high. For superclass members and their credentialed-class allies to maintain their positions of wealth, power, and privilege, the working class must be persuaded that the economic and political status quo and the institutions that comprise and sustain them are legitimate. This means the news media must provide those who are not members of the privileged class with ideas, information, and interpretations that support a superclass worldview while ignoring or discrediting alternative views. Thus, news and editorial content trend heavily in the direction of reports and interpretations of events that legitimate the status quo, thereby protecting the interests of superclass members at the top of the class structure.

Of course the existence of dominant, pro-superclass media reporting trends does not mean oppositional trends, views, or interpretations are totally absent from the media. They do exist—mainly as fragmented and minority positions—but our focus here is on superclass dominance of the mainstream mass media. The following sections explore three major control processes that operate through the information industry. The mainstream ideology, opinion-shaping, and spin-control processes function in ways that not only promote superclass domination of economic and political thinking in the United States but also help conceal the operation and effects of both the shadow political and information industries.

THE MAINSTREAM IDEOLOGY PROCESS

The ideology process consists of the numerous methods through which members of the power elite attempt to shape the beliefs, attitudes and opinions of the underlying population.

—G. William Domhoff, *The Powers That Be*, 1979

The mainstream ideology process is the most general of the three control practices operating as part of the information industry. But before we discuss this process, the term *ideology* needs a bit of clarification. This concept may seem like a remote, abstract reference. In fact, ideology is quite simple. It refers to idea systems that organize our thinking on various subjects. If we think sex is pleasurable—or disgusting, or that sports are fun—or boring—it is because of the idea systems we have learned that surround those topics and color our experiences with them. Our sex and sports ideologies include assumptions and conclusions about these subjects as well as selected "facts" (gleaned from personal experiences or conveyed to us by credible sources) that "prove" that our views are right and those held by others are wrong.

In the economic and political arenas, idea systems exist that have the same basic features as our sex and sports idea systems. Political-economy ideologies consist of assumptions about how power and wealth are (or should be) organized and distributed along with selected "facts" that "prove" that the views people hold on these topics are "correct." Political-economy ideologies are most often referred to as ranging from "left" to "center" (or middle of the road) to "right." These labels can take on many meanings, but leftist ideologies are basically grounded in the view that democratic government can and should serve as an agent promoting political, economic, and social justice for all citizens. By contrast, ideologies on the right today tend to publicly portray "big government" as an enemy "of the people." However, rightist views typically endorse government subsidies to businesses and favor powerful, government-funded and -controlled police and military agencies. Right-wing views also tend to see nothing wrong with the development of powerful *private* concentrations of wealth and power—as in the case of large corporations.

Whether we know it or not, most Americans have little experience with leftist ideologies but lots of experience with centrist and rightist ideologies. This situation reflects the ongoing socialization of the working class to economic and political ideas and views that promote and reinforce superclass economic and political interests. Such training occurs through several social institutions, including schools and the mass media, with the latter serving, in part, as a major conduit for the ideology process.

The *mainstream ideology process* refers to the powerful, indirect influence that the superclass has, especially through the mass media, upon the political-economy ideological views held by most Americans—including those in the new working class. It refers to the numerous ways that superclass-supported pro-corporate, free-market, individual-choice, "government is bad" (or at best inefficient) ideas get woven into and subtly dominate the content of mass-media-disseminated news and commentary. As a result of this process, public debates and discussions on political and economic issues and policies tend to reflect superclass ideological views, preferences, and interests.

Credible evidence exists to support our view that the superclass shares a rather uniform political-economy ideology that in turn dominates public thought via the mainstream ideology process. We also believe that the operation of the process whereby superclass ideological views dominate news and information content delivered to working-class members via the mass-media-based information industry can be illustrated by an examination of four key topics. These are (1) the corporate media-management structure, (2) the influence of corporate interests and advertising on media content, (3) the deep structural ideological foundation of the media, and (4) classroom penetration by media-produced materials.

Superclass Political-Economy Ideology

The mainstream ideology process is grounded in superclass leaders' ownership of and control over the mainstream media and their shared economic and political ideas, which comprise a dominant "ideological umbrella" ranging across a short, neoliberal-centrist-conservative spectrum. Of course, it would be an oversimplification to argue that all superclass members share the same political-economy ideology. But the apparent emerging consensus among superclass leaders favoring domestic austerity policies in the United States, Europe, and elsewhere in the world, as well as corporate-mediated international trade, suggests widespread superclass support for the "neo-liberal agenda of privatization, deregulation, and 'free trade.'"[30] Differences in superclass leaders' ideological views appear to be matters of nuance, emphasis, and degree across the dominant ideological umbrella rather than fundamental differences in values and policy directions.[31] Thus, the core values underlying the superclass ideological spectrum emphasize free enterprise, competition, equal opportunity, individualism, and minimal government involvement in business activities.[32] These values and principles reinforce what is claimed by privileged-class leaders to be a superior (compared to the alternatives) and preferred (for all citizens) political and economic status quo.

With the information industry owned and controlled by the same core of superclass leaders who direct the shadow political industry, it is hardly surprising that the political-economy ideological preferences of this group cover a short spectrum. Research on this topic reveals that mass media CEOs are typically economic conservatives interested in profits and markets and that they use the media to promote corporate values consistent with their interests.[33] As one researcher put it, "Media moguls—from Rupert Murdoch ... to Laurence Tisch to the executives of General Electric—may not exactly be 'movement' conservatives. But neither are they 'liberals.'"[34]

A recent study of CEOs who headed parent firms controlling the major TV networks characterized their political views as conservative. Moreover, three of the four at the time of the study—Jack Welch (GE/NBC), Michael Jordan (CBS), and Rupert Murdoch (News Corporation/Fox)—were described as taking actions aimed at influencing news and commentary content in their media divisions in support of conservative political causes or neoliberal-conservative corporate economic policies (e.g., aggressive downsizing and opposition to government regulation). Michael Eisner (Disney/ABC), characterized as a Democratic Party centrist, was described as holding views that were not much different from those of the first three.[35]

The Corporate Media-Management Structure

Although conservative superclass corporate leaders control enormous media resources, as a group they are too few in number to supervise the details necessary for the translation of their shared ideological views into routine media policies and content. Dependable corporate media managers who hold compatible views are recruited by superclass-dominated corporate boards to handle those tasks. These upper-tier, credentialed-class professionals operate under a supervision and reward structure that ensures pro-corporation content standards are met—along with high profits and bonuses for superclass owners and upper-level media management.[36] At the top, media CEOs are handsomely compensated. In 2000, Stephen Case (AOL-Time Warner) received $73.4 million in total compensation ($2.2 million in salary plus $73.4 in long-term compensation). Michael Eisner (Disney/ABC) received a $72.8 million total compensation package.[37] In the same year, the CEOs at 12 publicly held newspaper companies averaged $3.6 million in compensation. Apparently, media firms find it easier than some industries to justify high salaries for top executives since profit margins are routinely in the 20 percent plus range. For example, Knight-Ridder posted a profit of "18.5 percent in the first quarter of 2001. . . . That is double the profitability of the average *Fortune* 500 company."[38]

Unfortunately, lower-level media staffers seldom benefit from the high profits, nor do they share in the largess found among top management and the elite reporting staff. In fact, several media firms recently announced sweeping layoffs—claiming such actions were necessary due to declining ad revenues. But media critics are skeptical, arguing that "The more proximate and problematic cause . . . is media companies' insistence on ever-higher profits." Whatever the reasons, many media staffers lost their jobs. In the February–August 2001 period, nine of the largest media firms (electronic and print) announced more than nine thousand job cuts. Media companies announcing job cuts during this period included Knight-Ridder (2,100), Tribune Co. (1,400), Reuters (1,340), CNN (420), NBC (385), and ABC (260).[39]

Job cuts at the bottom notwithstanding, top corporate media managers extend the superclass ideological "food chain" downward. They recruit and richly reward their immediate subordinates and top media professionals such as network TV-news anchors, producers, reporters, writers, and commentators for performing three important tasks: (1) structuring media content that will for the most part reflect superclass ideological views and principles, (2) attracting the largest possible audience (with the right demographics—usually young, affluent adults), and (3) not offending corporate advertisers. The third issue is not inconsequential, because most media profits come from advertising revenues. In 1999 corporations spent an estimated $215 billion on advertising.[40] If all forms of corporate marketing are considered, the total could easily exceed $1 trillion.[41]

Corporate Interests, Advertising, and Media Content

Because the news divisions of media firms have emerged as major profit generators in recent years, media managers, producers, and reporters are under increasing pressure to produce media content that conforms to pro-corporate views. For members of this group, the result is a collection of news media policies, practices, traditions, and personal experiences that favor bland, noninvestigative news reporting and toothless commentary. This style of news frequently lapses into corporate cheerleading ensuring that media ad revenues are not interrupted by negative news stories or controversial, critical commentary concerning high-spending corporate advertising clients.[42]

Soft news-reporting practices are shaped sometimes by covert links between corporate interlocks and media reporting practices and sometimes by direct corporate pressure on the media. Both types of influence result in corporate censorship of the news—in one form or another. The covert influence source is illustrated by an *EXTRA!* (a media-watch publication) reporter's observation concerning the power of subtle internal corporate pressures on news reporting: "Most people who work for large corporations understand without being told that there are things you should and should not do."[43] A recent example involved a producer at *20/20* (an ABC TV news program) who was considering doing a report on executive compensation. "Two people familiar with the deliberations say the idea was dropped because no one wanted to draw attention to the extraordinarily rich pay package of Disney's chairman, Michael Eisner."[44]

Direct corporate pressure to change or kill news stories is also placed on media firms, but obviously the most successful attempts are those the public never hears about. One recent case illustrating this practice began in 1997 and continued through 2001. It involved television reporters Jane Akre and Steve Wilson, Fox TV station WTVT in Tampa, Florida, and an investigative news series. The reports focused on Posilac, a drug based on the genetically engineered recombinant bovine growth hormone (rBGH) and sold by the Monsanto Corporation. Questions were raised about how the drug was tested for safety, possible negative health effects of the drug on cows, and possible health hazards people might face by consuming milk from cows injected with the drug (which increases milk production by up to 30 percent).[45]

As a result of legal pressures brought by Monsanto against Fox News, the investigative series was never broadcast. An attorney representing Monsanto in a February 21, 1997, letter to Fox News CEO Roger Ailes warned that "enormous damage can be done by the reckless presentation of unsupported speculation as fact." The letter was forwarded to the WTVT station and promoted a series of internal discussions and reviews of the series. The reporters stood by their story, but the station management decided not to run it. As the station manager told the reporters, "We paid three billion dollars for these television stations. We'll tell you what the news is."[46]

The reporters said Fox News tried to buy their silence, offering them a settlement "which amounted to nearly $200,000."[47] But in return they would have to sign a gag order "promising never to discuss the rBGH story, Monsanto's involvement, and how Fox responded." They refused and were fired in December 1997. Both reporters sued, "charging that they were fired because they refused to put inaccurate information on the air and threatened to report WTVT to the federal communications commission."[48] In August 2000, a six-person Florida jury agreed with the charges brought by the reporters and "awarded $425,000 in damages to Akre." While the jury did not find for Wilson, he is appealing the decision "based on his claim of an erronous jury instruction."[49] Meanwhile, "Fox News is also appealing the verdict on several grounds."[50]

Perhaps not surprisingly, the Akre and Wilson lawsuit and trial received very little media coverage. Using their website, the reporters "had to resort to covering their own trial for lack of coverage not only by the mainstream media, but by the liberal/progressive alternative media as well."[51] When Wilson and Akre prepared their original story, it included comments from Dr. Samuel Epstein at the University of Illinois School of Public Health concerning the possible human health risks posed by the use of rBHG. Dr. Epstein also suggested a possible explanation for the dearth of media coverage of the lawsuit and trial in a quote that was included in the reporters' version of the rBHG story. "We are living in the greatest democracy in the world in many ways, but in other ways we are living in a corporate dictatorship in which big government and big industry decide what information the consumer can and should have."[52]

This case and others, such as the widely reported "mad cow" lawsuit brought against TV talk show host Oprah Winfrey, illustrate that corporate efforts to directly influence (or silence) news media content are both real and powerful. Oprah's case was somewhat different from the Akre and Wilson episode because she was sued for civil damages by the National Cattlemen's Beef Association (NCBA). The NCBA claimed that Howard Lyman, a guest on Oprah's TV show, made comments "disparaging" beef (while discussing "mad cow disease") that were in violation of a Texas "food disparagement" statute, but a Texas jury disagreed and in 1998 ruled in favor of Oprah.[53]

Although these cases illustrate direct corporate actions aimed at shaping media content, such efforts are probably less important than more routine business-media connections. A more common route of corporate influence over media content occurs through the informal clout businesses have as a result of their massive expenditures for mass media advertising. Some sense of the extent of this clout is evident in surveys of reporters and media executives. In a 2000 Pew Research Center–*Columbia Journalism Review* survey, 37 percent of 300 journalists and news executives reported they avoided stories that might damage advertisers' interests.[54] The results of an earlier survey of 241 members of the group Investigative Reporters and Editors, working at commercial television stations, were even more telling. "Nearly three-quarters of the respondents reported that advertisers had 'tried to influence the content' of news at their stations." A majority also reported that advertisers had tried to kill stories. Forty percent said their stations had caved in to advertiser pressures, 43 percent said they had not, and 59 percent said there was pressure from within their stations "*not* to produce stories that advertisers might find objectionable."[55]

In the print media, the *Wall Street Journal* has reported that large corporate advertisers demand to know magazine content in advance to ensure that their ads do not appear in publications with "offensive content." As an illustration, "Colgate-Palmolive Co. sends its agencies guidelines forbidding them from running ads in magazine issues with 'offensive' sexual content or material the company 'considers antisocial or in bad taste.' Michael Samet, media director at Colgate's lead agency, Young & Rubicam Advertising, says the agency has a 'protocol' . . . to make sure every magazine carrying Colgate's ads honors its rules."[56]

According to the *Journal*, the practice of corporate advertisers demanding control over magazine content is widespread and involves large firms and entire industries. This would appear to be the case with *Time* magazine's Spring 2000 issue, which concluded the magazine's "Heroes for the Planet" series. Started in 1998, the series "profiled individuals around the globe who are working to protect the natural world."[57] However, the series was sponsored by Ford Motor Company, which apparently meant that not all environmental issues would be considered and not all heroes recognized. The international editor for *Time* "admitted to the *Wall Street Journal* that . . . the series wasn't likely to profile environmentalists battling the polluting auto industry."[58]

Industrywide involvement by advertisers insisting on control over media content is further evidenced by the long-standing policy of tobacco and alcohol advertisers, who demand advance warnings from publications about any articles dealing with people who abuse or who have been harmed by their products. As the *Wall Street Journal* noted, "Big advertisers have always tried to influence the contents of magazines, and every other medium." Such practices are not new, not illegal, and not even unethical: "The American Society of Magazine Editors . . . [does not have] any policy to prevent magazines from giving advertisers advance warnings about stories."[59]

Deep Structure

Conscious corporate efforts influencing media content to ensure a favorable advertising climate are paralleled by a deeper and more pervasive penetration of media organizations by superclass and corporate ideological views and values.

Deep structure refers to the institutionalization of superclass-based political-economy views and values in the training and reward structures of, and working conditions experienced by, most mass media professionals. In part, this concept is similar to what media critic Ben Bagdikian has termed "internalized bias"—the unstated and taken-for-granted understanding that journalists working for mainstream media develop concerning what constitutes "acceptable" (to corporate interests) reporting topics, practices, and news content.[60]

Deep structure acts as a kind of hidden context. It is the vehicle through which superclass-favored values and beliefs are woven into the organizational hierarchies, management policies, print and programming decisions, and daily reporting practices of the mainstream media. And these are the firms that generate most of the electronic and printed news and commentary in the United States. Like a transparent fishbowl shaping and bounding the water world of fish, deep structure imposes constraints and patterns on media policies and practices that are nearly invisible—unless its configurations are consciously perceived.

The deep structure of superclass ideological influence in the electronic media is reflected in many ways, but it is especially evident in how resources are granted or withheld in programming decisions. Corporate-media managers routinely select, showcase, and lavishly support conservative, "free-market" corporate cheerleaders. Commercial media examples include John Stossel (ABC TV *20/20* correspondent), *Wolf Blitzer Reports* (CNN), *Special Report with Brit Hume* (Fox TV), and Rush Limbaugh (Premier Radio Networks). Examples on Public Broadcasting Service (PBS) television include Louis Rukeyser (former host of *Wall $treet Week*) and John McLaughlin (host of *The McLaughlin Group*, sponsored by GE).[61] By contrast, the same media managers closely scrutinize and often quickly ax the few corporate critics or progressive commentators that typically find short-lived mass media exposure.

Examples of popular progressive reporters and commentators fired for their views are infrequent, in part because the deep structure filtering process prevents people with such views from accessing highly visible media positions. Also, when such events do occur, media managers routinely deny that such firings are related to the views of those who lose their jobs. Consider the firings in 2000 of popular and progressive radio talk-show hosts Pat Thurston (KSRO, Santa Rosa, California) and Mike Malloy (WLS, Chicago). Both shows had high ratings in their respective markets, but were axed by corporate management anyway. A report on the firings pointed out that "Thurston didn't shy away from criticizing powerful business interests," and that Malloy tackled "issues involving the environment, foreign policy, and corporate irresponsibility that other hosts rarely touch." However, in both cases station managers deny that the reporters' progressive views had anything to do with the decisions to fire them.[62]

Five years earlier a similar story occurred as popular corporate critic Jim Hightower had his program, *Hightower Radio*, dropped by ABC (in 1995). Company officials denied that the decision was related to the critical content of his show.[63]

On television, Michael Moore has had recurring difficulties in getting and keeping his sometimes corporate-biting television programs on the air. His first show, *TV Nation*, ran briefly in the summer of 1994 on NBC but was quickly dropped by the network. It was picked up in 1995 by the Fox Network, only to be quickly dropped again.[64] His second show, *The Awful Truth*, financed by the British Broadcasting Company, aired in the United States on the Bravo satellite/cable channel in 1999 and 2000, but has not returned. Coincidence? Or cause and effect? (Despite his current absence from television, in 2002 Moore published the best-selling book, *Stupid White Men*.)

Radio and television shows that are sometimes critical of corporate power clearly have problems simply staying on the air. This fact illustrates that the combination of corporate sponsorship and informal censorship leads to a very narrow range of neoliberal-centrist-conservative, pro-business news, information, and commentary disseminated by virtually all mass media outlets.[65] Such a reality is in sharp contrast to the frequently repeated charge (most often by conservative pundits) that a "liberal bias" exists in mass media news reporting.[66]

Classroom Penetration

The information industry disseminates superclass ideological views not only to the public but also to schools. Classroom programs and educational discounts made available to schools and colleges by the major newsmagazines *(Time, Newsweek, U.S. News and World Report)* ensure that superclass-compatible views and interpretations of national and world events reach high school and college age groups in the guise of "educational materials." Where schools are concerned, the information industry frequently works hand in glove with the public relations industry (examined in more detail in the section on spin control). Together, these industries create and promote "educational materials" for the U.S. Chambers of Commerce, NAM, and other corporate-sponsored groups that disseminate free, pro-corporate teaching materials to teachers and professors.

The National Council on Economic Education (NCEE) serves as a centralized source of materials and training in support of superclass efforts to shape students' views on economic issues. Founded in 1949 by members of the Committee for Economic Development, the NCEE is governed by a 29-member board that includes a number of corporate officials (e.g., from AT&T, General Mills, Ameritech) and it is primarily funded by large corporations and corporate foundations. The NCEE has produced an "Economics America" program that is provided to students through a network of state councils and 260 university training centers. The NCEE claims that each year its network trains 120,000 teachers serving 8 million students and helps provide economic education programs to over 2,600 school districts involving 40 percent of U.S. students.[67] The scope of business involvement in schools was underscored by a recent study in *Business Week* magazine, which concluded that "Corporations are flooding schools with teaching aids—and propaganda."[68]

Media critic Ben Bagdikian has pointed out that:

> Free classroom materials are produced by 64 percent of the 500 largest American industrial corporations, 90 percent of industrial trade associations, and 90 percent of utility companies. . . . The publication *Media Decisions* estimated that as much as $3 billion in corporate money goes into all methods of promoting the corporation as hero and into "explanations of the capitalistic system," including massive use of corporate books and teaching materials in the schools, almost all tax deductible.[69]

These information and public relations industry products are always represented as educational aids and tools. The content is never described for what it is: mainstream-ideology corporate propaganda promoting the interests of the superclass.

Mainstream Ideology Results

The results of an information industry dominated by superclass ownership, political-economy ideological values, pro-corporate managers, and co-opted journalistic professionals are threefold. First, the superclass-approved "pluralistic" model of political power is promoted at several levels and in a variety of forms through the major media firms that make up the information industry. Second, political-economy views that differ from superclass views—and the groups that promote them—are ignored, marginalized, or demonized by the information industry. Third, working-class members are encouraged to embrace superclass values and views as their own and to accept the economic and political status quo as the most desirable institutional arrangement.

"Pluralism" Promoted

The extensive promotion of a "pluralism model" of politics and government by the information industry is evident by the ideas and imagery used by nearly all mass media where political reporting is concerned. This model rests on an interest-group interpretation of politics in America. A wide range of interest groups is claimed to exist, but the model argues that no one group is dominant in the political process. Such a view of the nature of politics in America is a constant refrain in media reports and commentary throughout the information industry and effectively neutralizes or excludes alternative perspectives on the nature of U.S. politics and political power.[70]

Media accounts of corporate PAC money and political influence typically reflect—at an implicit level—pluralist interpretations. Political reporters typically point out that a wide array of "special-interest" PACs exist and then go on to explain that this situation actually promotes democracy. Such a reporting focus reinforces the view that American politics consists of competing, interest-based "veto groups" that check one another's power. From this viewpoint, politics and public policies are seen as a kaleidoscopic swirl of pluralistic confusion with a multitude of PACs and individual donors competing for political influence in a kind of rotating king-of-the-hill game of governance. According to pluralist imagery, corporate PACs are simply one of many PAC types, and they are typically presented in media reports as fragmented interest groups more often competing than cooperating with one another for narrow gains in the political process. This comforting view reinforces the notion that the U.S. political system ensures no single interest group can corrupt or capture the democratic process.

Corporate PAC donations receive extensive media coverage as potential sources of political influence, but reporters typically look only at specific PAC donations to specific candidates. The idea is to detect evidence connecting the policy-interest "fingerprints" of specific PAC contributors with the actions of specific elected officials. When such connections are found, they are used by reporters as evidence that the media is an effective watchdog providing the public with tough investigative reporting.

Of course, the problem with "pluralist-based" reporting on corporate PAC money as a source of political influence is that the focus on divided interest-group power—rather than upon unified superclass power—in effect calls attention to the trees while ignoring the forest. Pluralist-based reporting leads readers to the conclusion that no single group dominates the political process—and thereby disguises the nature of superclass political power and the operation of the shadow political industry.

Marginalization of Alternatives

In addition to promoting pluralist-based reporting, the mainstream ideology process also encourages media marginalization and demonization of economic and political views or groups disfavored by the superclass. For example, mass media reports on unions are rarely framed in favorable or positive terms.[71] Also, trade union political contributions or PACs are routinely subjected to media attacks as efforts by "union bosses" to manipulate and control the political process.[72] In fact, virtually all organizations, ideas, and public policies or programs promoting working-class interests are often subject to negative mass media reporting.[73] The negation of alternative worldviews is a necessary part of superclass efforts to control the terms of economic and political discourse in the United States. The reality of conflicting class interests means that the experiences, policy priorities, and legislative preferences of the working class are not the same as those of the superclass (or their credentialed-class allies). The consequences for the superclass of allowing the working class to translate its shared interests and experiences into legitimate political discussion, debate, and coherent policy alternatives without the benefit of "ideological coaching" from the information industry would be to risk the growth of class consciousness and class politics. The mainstream ideology process is part of superclass efforts to prevent these prospects from becoming reality.

Embracing Superclass Values?

Superclass ideology legitimates centrist-conservative politics, predatory corporate business practices, and the existing class system—including the wide array of advantages and privileges it provides for the superclass and its credentialed-class allies combined with extensive inequalities for the working class. As a result of our exposure to the mainstream ideology process, most of us tend to take the way the world is organized politically and economically—including the whole catalog of extensive class inequities—for granted. We assume that it is sort of natural and that there is not much we can do about it, so we tend to accept it—perhaps with some grousing and complaining—and go on. In fact, what this attitude reflects is our familiarity with only one ideological perspective: the superclass view. This is the case because it is the one that is subtly and powerfully woven into much of what we see, hear, and read in mass-media-provided news and commentary via the mainstream ideology process.

Unfortunately for superclass leaders, their political-economy ideological foundations are problematic because the public principles they espouse are often at odds with the routine business practices pursued by the large firms they control. For example, superclass leaders claim to favor the ideals of free enterprise, competition, and equal opportunity. But in practice, the large firms, owned largely by the superclass, clearly prefer to dominate markets and maximize profits through monopolistic or oligopolistic practices that exclude the existence of competitive free enterprise or equal opportunity. Also, although corporate executives pay lip service to individualism, they clearly prefer a labor force tightly regimented by unchallenged corporate rule and a consuming public manipulated and dominated by mass advertising. Finally, whereas large firms oppose government regulation of business as well as government policies that would expand the "social wage" (economic programs that would increase the income and economic security of working-class Americans), they typically support the existence and expansion of government programs that channel tax dollars into business revenues and profits. As we will see later in this chapter, reducing the tensions between publicly promoted superclass ideological values and contradictory corporate practices is a major concern of the information industry—often pursued via the opinion-shaping and spin-control processes.

THE OPINION-SHAPING PROCESS

> Most mainstream news outlets share an ideology that can best be described as corporate centrism, a belief in the worthiness of the establishment and the necessity of the status quo.
>
> —Jim Naureckas, *EXTRA!* July–August 2001

The mainstream ideology process morphs seamlessly into the opinion-shaping process. The two processes overlap in many ways, but the key difference is that whereas the former promotes general neoliberal-centrist- conservative ideological values and principles, the latter involves their detailed infusion into the specifics of news programming, content, and commentary. The opinion-shaping process is most evident through the information industry's consistently favorable treatment—through images, reports, and interpretations—of superclass-dominated ideas, organizations, and policies. Two widespread media practices help create and reinforce public opinion favorable to superclass interests: deck stacking and selective reporting.

Deck Stacking

"Deck stacking" refers to the overwhelming preponderance of pro-superclass and pro-corporate media managers, editors, commentators, and reporters within the information industry. One way for superclass media owners and their credentialed-class top-level media managers to subtly achieve this result is through staffing and pay practices that distance upper-tier media professionals from average workers' experiences and pay levels and link them more closely to the interests (and views) of elite owners and managers. In fact, as average workers today struggle with declining real wages and as the labor force becomes increasingly diverse, recent studies reveal that media professionals remain a relatively uniform and well-paid group of mainly white males from middle- and upper-middle-class backgrounds.[74] A 1998 survey of 444 journalists based in Washington, D.C., listed in the *News Media Yellow Book* found that 52 percent of the 141 respondents reported annual household incomes of more than $100,000 and 14 percent reported incomes of more than $200,000 per year.[75]

At the highest reaches of the media hierarchy are elite professionals earning millions who can be counted on to express views consistent with their superclass owner-employer bosses. Examples from the early 2000s include multimillion-dollar news and commentary media stars such as news anchors Tom Brokaw (NBC), Peter Jennings (ABC), and Dan Rather (CBS)—who each reportedly earn more than NBC's *Today Show* coanchor Katie Couric, who signed a four-year contract in 1998 worth $7 million per year.[76] In 2001 *Forbes* magazine reported that Fox News anchor Bill O'Reilly was being paid *only* $1 million a year, putting him far below Larry King ($7 million, CNN), Barbara Walters ($10 million, ABC), and Jane Pauley ($5.5 million, NBC). (The *Boston Globe* reported in early 2001 that O'Reilly's upcoming contract would be worth $20 million.) On radio, Rush Limbaugh was reported to earn $31 million per year (Premier Radio Network) while Paul Harvey was not far behind at $29 million. However, in the world of infotainment, nobody tops talk show host Oprah Winfrey, at $130 million per year.[77]

The uniform staffing of information industry management and reporting personnel leads to an ideological filtering and opinion-shaping system generating news content and commentary that consistently parallels and reflects but virtually never challenges superclass ideological views. This situation begins with built-in structural biases grounded in corporate ownership of the media, leading to owners' hiring and rewarding of managers and editors who reflect pro-superclass and pro-corporate values and views. Acting as gatekeepers, these groups in turn hire and reward reporters who share their views—or who are willing to self-censor their work to conform with the ideological boundaries imposed by the corporate structure and enforced by editorial oversight.[78]

Informal social events promoted by top media management linking editors and reporters with superclass leaders in congenial settings help reinforce a shared worldview and promote cordial media-business ties. For example, in the 1990s, *Time* magazine spent $3 million to "fly dozens of corporate chiefs around the world for nine days . . . [escorted] by *Time*'s top managers and editors." The firms represented included Lockheed Martin, General Motors, Rockwell, Philip Morris, and Mitsubishi, and the executives met with heads of state from India, Hong Kong, Vietnam, Russia, and Cuba. Commenting on the event, the media magazine

EXTRA! asked, "How eager will *Time's* . . . reporters be to scrutinize the firms their bosses have wined and dined across the globe?"[79]

Poll results regarding media professionals' views on labor and their ideological orientations illustrate the nature and extent of deck stacking in the press. A *Los Angeles Times* poll found 54 percent of editors side with business in labor disputes, and only 7 percent side with labor. A survey sponsored by the United Auto Workers (UAW) of the one hundred largest daily newspapers found that 60 percent opposed union positions on minimum-wage increases, trade regulations, and plant-closing laws.[80] A Brookings Institution study of Washington, D.C., journalists found that 58 percent identified themselves as either conservative or middle of the road.[81] A recent survey of Washington-area journalists found that 66 percent characterized their political orientation as center or right on social issues, but on economic issues 83 percent characterized their political orientation as center or right.[82]

Deck stacking extends across all media formats and is especially evident in the lopsided spectrum of viewpoints presented by television news programming and by nearly all nationally syndicated electronic and print commentators. In the early 2000s, all of the leading political-opinion talk shows on national commercial or public television had centrist or conservative hosts and moderators: *Face the Nation, Meet the Press, The McLaughlin Group, Crossfire, Firing Line, One-on-One, Tony Brown's Journal,* and *Damn Right!*[83]

Findings from a recent 18-month study of four major Sunday morning television talk shows (*Meet the Press, The McLaughlin Group, Face the Nation, This Week*) illustrate the nature of deck stacking in television "news" programming. All four programs supposedly encourage national dialogue on major current events and policy issues. While these shows "help set the agenda for debate in Washington," the study found that they consistently failed to address important issues related to corporate power. Less than 4 percent of the show's discussion topics over the 18-month study period focused on corporate power issues such as "the environment, corporate crime, labor, mergers, consumer rights, corporate welfare, national health care, free trade agreements, redlining, blockbusting, multinational capital flight, tort reform, renewable energy, [and] the commercialization of children." The study also found that "an overwhelming majority of invited guests on the shows are lawmakers, government officials, and politicians—a skew that tends to reinforce narrow parameters of discussion and exclude issues of corporate power."[84]

Studies of ABC's *Nightline* and CNN's *Crossfire* news programs yielded findings similar to those from the Sunday talk show study. As the media-watch group Fairness and Accuracy in Reporting (FAIR) points out, such results are predictable. "True advocates for the left—people who actually push for progressive social change and identify with left-of-center activists—are almost invisible on TV."[85]

Syndicated columnists writing for the print media reflect a pattern of centrist-conservative thought similar to television news and commentary programming.

Two recent surveys of the most widely distributed syndicated newspaper political columnists document a pattern of dominance by conservative and centrist writers such as James Dobson, Cal Thomas, Robert Novak, David Broder, and George Will.[86] This reality has even been acknowledged by the conservative American Enterprise Institute: "Despite the image of a media dominated by liberals, the reality is much different. The most widely syndicated columnists are conservatives."[87]

Selective Reporting

"Selective reporting" refers to unstated but routine news-reporting policies and practices that produce a preponderance of flattering (virtue-exaggerating) news media coverage of superclass-favored and superclass-sponsored issues, organizations, activities, policies, or people and ignore or play down the merits or significance of topics that threaten superclass interests. Selective reporting is especially evident in news media treatment of business and labor issues.

Business Good, Unions Bad

Selective reporting begins with much greater chunks of media time and space devoted to covering business topics as against labor and union issues. A study of national news television broadcasts found that business and economic reporting receives double the amount of time devoted to workers' issues. Moreover, workers are virtually never interviewed or portrayed as "experts"; and no worker has ever been selected as "Person of the Week" by *ABC World News Tonight*—although many corporate executives are often chosen for this feature.[88] A study of local television news broadcasts found that stations devote fewer than 2 percent of news time to labor issues.[89] In addition to imbalanced television news coverage, there are also many specialty business television programs (e.g., *Wall $treet Week, The Nightly Business Report*) and mass-circulation national business publications (e.g., *Wall Street Journal, Business Week, Forbes*) that have no parallels among worker or labor union audiences.

The largely positive media portrayal of business interests, corporate actions, and company executives—including the corporation-as-hero theme—is another feature of selective reporting. This tendency stands in sharp contrast to complaints by some corporate officials that the media often treat businesses harshly. However, the evidence overwhelmingly supports the conclusion that "the standard media— mainstream newspapers, magazines, and broadcasters—have always been reliable promoters of the corporate ethic."[90] This is illustrated by a survey of CEOs from the one thousand largest industries in the United States, which revealed that two-thirds believe media treatment of their companies is good or excellent and only 6 percent feel it is poor.[91]

When the mainstream media do present what appear to be negative accounts of corporate actions, a closer look at such stories typically reveals a different truth:

Copyright © Tom Tomorrow. Reprinted with permission.

"When news shows like *60 Minutes* or *20/20* do segments on 'big business versus the little people,' they usually define the problem in terms of the greed of one group of executives or the excesses of a single company. They never seriously address the nature of capitalism and the structural factors that often lead companies to harm the 'little people.'"[92]

In contrast with how the media treat corporations, when unions are the subject of media reporting, they are most often depicted in negative terms: as outdated, confrontational, out of touch with global economic realities, selfish, and corruption riddled.[93] A UAW study identified six negative myths about unions repeatedly cited in the mass media, including these especially damning notions: "Unions have been slowly strangling American business. Workers and unions demand the moon and make consumers pay for it. Unions can't do anything to reverse the falling fortunes of workers. Unions might have once been valuable, but now have too much power and need to be weakened or eliminated."[94] Despite the reality that these myths are easily refuted by accurate information, the study found such information is seldom reported in the mainstream media.

A university study entitled "Media Portrayals of Organized Labor" also reported a pattern of negative media depictions of unions. This study found unions were frequently portrayed by reporters according to eight negative stereotypes that paralleled the myths identified by the UAW study.[95] These findings are consistent with media critic Ben Bagdikian's observations regarding corporate power and media reporting on corporations and unions: "The result of the overwhelming power of relatively narrow corporate ideologies has been the creation of widely established political and economic illusions in the United States. . . . [One is] that labor-union-induced wages are a damaging drag on national productivity and thus on the economy. [It is] false but [it has] been perpetuated by corporate-controlled media for decades."[96] (The lessons here? Unions are bad! Silence criticism!)

Greedy Geezers

Selective reporting also applies to specific issues and results in one-sided media presentations that attempt to sway public opinion in the direction of superclass interests and public policies that would serve those interests. Illustrating this prac- tice is the media trend of depicting senior citizens as "greedy geezers" endangering the federal budget. "Geezer bashing," the portrayal of the aged as "greedy or spoiled, and unwilling to sacrifice," emerged as a growth industry in the main- stream media.[97] These depictions are part of a superclass-based attack on federal entitlement programs, particularly Social Security and Medicare, which are claimed by many politicians (in both parties) and much of the mass media to be on the verge of "bankruptcy."[98]

The superclass interests involved with these issues are twofold. First is money. If just 2 percentage points of "the 12.4% Social Security payroll tax were channeled to workers' private accounts in 2002, the savings would generate $86 billion for in- vestment."[99] Management fees and administrative charges on privatized, individ- ual retirement accounts would juice Wall Street profits to the tune of millions of dollars. Similar results would occur with the privatization of Medicare. The sec- ond issue is political. Reductions in the "social wage"—material benefits provided through the state to citizens as a "right"—increase the economic insecurity of the working class and thus strengthen the political and economic power of the super- class. If workers are confronted with a future that does not include state-funded programs to secure health care and pensions for them in old age, they are rendered even more vulnerable to whatever wage levels and working conditions superclass- controlled employer organizations impose on them.[100]

Social Security and Medicare have long been opposed by conservative elites, who would prefer to privatize parts or all of them as a way of diverting funds to profit-making insurance and investment firms and to reduce the social wage. However, in recent years what was once the conservative position on Social Secu- rity and Medicare has moved increasingly to the political center. In the early 2000s President Bush, his Republican allies, and many Democrats in Congress agreed on the "need" to restructure both programs. The media, owned and controlled by the superclass, have been active partners in making the case for cutting so-called budget-busting programs benefiting "greedy geezers."

One media practice encouraging attacks on seniors has been selective reporting on "generational accounting." This term refers to the idea that people born in re- cent years will pay enormous tax rates to finance federal funding of entitlement programs for the aged and also to service the growing national debt incurred to support these programs. High-profile media reports on this topic appeared in the 1990s and early 2000s in the *New York Times* and the *Washington Post*, on ABC's *Nightline*, and in many other national media outlets.[101] At the same time, schemes for privatizing Social Security and controlling Medicare costs through "private-sector efficiencies" also received increasing media attention. Media attacks on Social Security were paralleled by similar stories and commentary on the need to "reform" Medicare. As one media critic observed, "By focusing narrowly on the conflict . . . over the depth of cuts, most reporting has obscured the elite consensus on the need to cut Medicare spending and accelerate the privatization of the program."[102]

As the early 2000s unfolded, superclass pressures to privatize Social Security and reform Medicare continued. Organizations promoting the privatization of Social Security continued to pour substantial resources into campaigns that started in the 1990s. The Cato Institute pushed "its donors to contribute to a $100 million ad campaign boosting privatization."[103] In 2001, "The Coalition for American Financial Security" (formed in 2000 by financial service companies including Brinson Partners and Mellon Financial Group) was reportedly developing a major ad campaign for privatization. At the same time, the "Alliance for Worker Retirement Security" (formed in 1998 by NAM, the U.S. Chambers of Commerce, NFIB, and the Securities Industry Association), was "supplying key staff for the Bush administration."[104] In 2001, "all told, pro-privatization groups [hoped] to raise as much as $20 million."[105]

The mainstream media were reliable allies in the campaigns to privatize Social Security and reform Medicare. After President Bush's "Commission to Strengthen Social Security" issued a preliminary report on problems with the Social Security trust fund, *Newsweek* published a ringing endorsement of the report in a full-page essay by financial reporter Allan Sloan.[106] As the economy continued its slide into recession in the fall of 2001, the *Wall Street Journal* and the *New York Times* published editorials and op-ed pieces arguing for more tax cuts and for using funds supposedly reserved for Social Security and Medicare to stimulate an economic recovery. Both pieces essentially argued that Social Security and Medicare are already bankrupt and that economic growth is the only sure way to sustain those programs.[107] The logic of these assessments suggested that only "the market" could "save" Social Security and Medicare, and the unstated implication was clear: Privatization would be the most effective salvation.

By mid-2001, the campaign to privatize Social Security appeared to be bearing fruit. A *Business Week*/Harris Poll, taken July 20–25, 2001, found 56 percent of Americans favored a partial privatization of Social Security and 39 percent were opposed. Even so, the results were highly age dependent. Only 40 percent of American over age 65 supported partial privatization, while 70 percent under age 25 favored it.[108] These results were encouraging to the privatization forces, but they also indicated the public was sharply divided. Also worrisome to privatizers were the findings from polls and focus groups conducted in August by the Democratic Party, which found very strong support among "baby boomers" (those born between 1946 and 1964) for dedicating the federal surplus to Social Security. As one reporter observed, "Expect them to insist on full benefits, now and forever."[109] Moreover, public support for privatization could fade quickly in response to economic uncertainty. This prospect was enhanced as the September 11 terrorist attacks on the World Trade Center towers and the Pentagon were followed by sharp increases in unemployment and a slumping U.S. economy headed for recession.[110]

Some mainstream media reports have called attention to the economic motives of the privatizers and to practical problems associated with creating private Social Security accounts.[111] However, virtually all mainstream media reports on privatizing Social Security or reforming Medicare have ignored the class-based interests of organizations supporting such policies. But given the class taboo noted in chapters 1 and 2, such a media blackout is not surprising. By contrast, media associated with the alternative power network have published numerous investigative reports, articles, and editorials calling attention to the class-based interests, resources, and ideological motivations of groups and political figures promoting privatization schemes for Social Security and Medicare. In the the 1990s and early 2000s, alternative media outlets documented how superclass-controlled organizations orchestrated the campaign to privatize Social Security and undermine public confidence in it.[112] Such reports stand in stark contrast to most mainstream media storylines, which favor superclass interests where Social Security, Medicare, and other entitlement programs for the aged and the poor are concerned. But the limited resources of the alternative media make it difficult for reports on social programs grounded in analyses of class-based interests to counter mass media accounts grounded in superclass-generated propaganda.

Think Tanks (Again!)

Selective reporting on a wide range of topics is reinforced through extensive media reliance on information derived from superclass-funded "official sources" such as think tanks. A 2002 study of media references to major think tanks according to their ideological orientations found an overwhelming reliance on conservative and centrist organizations. Using a Nexis database search of major newspapers and radio and TV transcripts for 2001, the study found a total of 25,853 media citations involving think-tank sources. There were 12,390 references (48 percent) to conservative or right-leaning think tanks such as the Heritage Foundation and 9,319 references (36 percent) to centrist organizations such as the Brookings Institution. By contrast, the study found only 4,114 references (16 percent) to progressive think tanks such as the Economic Policy Institute (829 references).[113]

Given extensive superclass funding of and media firm links to conservative-centrist think tanks, the study results should not be surprising. For example, the

Cato Institute, the conservative think tank most widely cited by the U.S. media in 2001 (2,364 citations), received contributions totaling $26 million in 1997–98.[114] Cato receives major contributions from "drug, medical device, biotechnology, and tobacco manufacturers and their corporate foundations." Also, Cato's board of directors includes two major media CEOs. News Corporation owner Rupert Murdoch (who also sits on the Philip Morris board of directors) joined the Cato board in 1997, and John C. Malone (CEO of Tele-Communications Inc., the largest U.S. cable operator) has been a Cato board member since 1995.[115] The conservative Heritage Foundation (1,770 citations in 2000) collected $43 million in contributions in 1998, with much of the money coming from wealthy conservatives such as "right wing beer tycoon Joe Coors, a longtime Heritage benfactor."[116]

THE SPIN-CONTROL PROCESS

The role of public relations is to so muddle the public sphere as to take the risk out of democracy for the wealthy and corporations.

—Robert W. McChesney, *Monthly Review*, November 2000

The "spin-control process" refers to a wide array of propaganda-driven media practices. It involves media owners, managers, reporters, pundits, and commercial and political advertisers using the information industry as a platform for disseminating news, commentary, images, and advertising with a pro-superclass and pro-corporate slant. The objectives of spin control include ideological justifications of the economic and political status quo and the commercial marketing of products, services, and corporate images as well as media-based marketing of political candidates, public officials, and public policies. Spin control involves a symbiotic linkage between the information industry and the public relations (PR) industry, a $10 billion corporate enterprise based on the twin goals of manipulation and deception. Using the information industry as a platform, the public relations industry provides a wide array of services—mainly to superclass, corporate, and political clients—ranging from conventional press releases to commercial and political advertising campaigns to "the hiring of spies, the suppression of free speech, and even the manufacture of 'grass roots' movements."[117] "Surveys show that PR accounts for anywhere from 40 to 70 percent of what appears as news."[118]

The spin-control process operates at two levels. The first involves interpretation: it consists of information-industry-channeled news reporting and commentary that is "shaded"—through media professionals' choices of value-laden terms, images, references, context, and illustrations—in directions that reflect positively on superclass-favored ideas, policies, organizations, and interests and negatively on topics disfavored by elites. The second level involves propaganda, deception, and calculated manipulation. It consists of all forms of advertising and public relations strategies and tactics aimed at manipulating target populations' opinions, attitudes, tastes, and behaviors (mainly those of the working class) on behalf of goals established most often by superclass-controlled corporate and political clients.

Spin control is a complex process with many facets extending beyond the scope of this book. The purpose of this section is simply to highlight, through illustrative examples, how each spin-control level furthers superclass interests, often in ways that conceal the nature and extent of these interests and of superclass power as well.

Spin Control: Interpretation

As noted earlier in this chapter, tensions between superclass ideological assertions that the U.S. economic and political systems are the best in the world and routine corporate practices producing a variety of negative economic and political consequences for the working class are problematic for elites. Efforts to reduce or reconcile these tensions are a routine focus of the spin-control process. Mainstream media reporters and pundits typically address these tensions with interpretive news reports and commentary that represent U.S. economic, political, and social problems as resulting from a host of non-class-based causes. Most often these "causes" are represented as various individual-level flaws (often psychological or biological), subcultural pathologies, governmental meddling, and temporary, unavoidable, but good-for-everyone-in-the-long-term consequences of large-scale "natural laws." These latter forces often include the wonderful and mysterious "free market" or the equally magical "global economy." One important effect of media interpretations of these factors as causal forces driving social problems is that it distracts audiences from the problematic effects of superclass domination and control of the media and indeed of most other institutions in the society.

Superclass to Media: Downsize, but Don't Kill the Dream!

Some of these themes were evident in the mid-1990s as the mainstream media focused briefly on economic changes negatively affecting nonelite workers and their families: downsizing, job losses, global trade, and declining real income. In 1996 two major U.S. newspapers ran reports on the trend of growing economic inequalities. The *New York Times* series, "The Downsizing of America," explored some of the human costs of downsizing and was later expanded and published as a book-length report.[119] The *Philadelphia Inquirer* series, "Who Stole the Dream," was more starkly descriptive of growing class inequalities than the *Times* series and focused more directly on how government policies had contributed to growing economic polarization.[120]

Although there was a total absence of any real critique of superclass or corporate power in either series, big spin-control guns were quickly rolled out to blunt even implied criticism of the American economic system. The *Inquirer* series was too much for the *Seattle Times*. The paper first decided to reprint the series, "but canceled it after just one installment—and apologized to readers for running that one."[121] Both series were critiqued by Robert J. Samuelson, economic columnist for the *Washington Post* and *Newsweek*. Using labels such as "junk" and "shoddy journalism," Samuelson dismissed both series as products of ignorance on the part of the journalists and their editors. He also took care to praise a more balanced series (in his view) from the *Los Angeles Times* that profiled "the gains that economic change creates as well as the trauma it inflicts."[122]

In the early 2000s, as the gap between the haves and the have-nots (and the "have-littles") continued to grow and became harder to ignore than in the 1990s, mainstream media pundits responded with a spirited spin-control defense of the American economic and class systems. Mortimer B. Zuckerman, editor of *U.S. News and World Report*, celebrated the millennial Fourth of July with an essay claiming that upward economic mobility was rising and that Americans were materially better off than ever. He acknowledged that while some inequalities exist, the presence of abundant opportunities trumps such concerns. And he argued, "if today's abundance feels inadequate, it is only because Americans today view as essential many things that used to be considered luxuries."[123]

The next year, in a *Newsweek* essay, economist Robert J. Samuelson echoed Zuckerman's ideas. Samuelson maintained that "Americans don't get so upset by rising inequality because they don't feel it dooms them." Like Zuckerman, he argues that "Americans care less about inequality . . . than about opportunity and achievement." Samuelson went on to claim that the recent "obsession" with rising inequality is irresponsible and "it implies that the rich are somehow responsible for the plight of the poor. . . . This is an illusion." He concluded his essay by asking readers to consider a hypothetical example: "Suppose a market decline reduces the wealth of the very rich . . . more than that of the middle-class or poor. There would be less economic inequality. Would anyone be better off? Would any one feel better? Not Likely."[124] The moral of the story? Quit whining about inequality!

Demonizing Critics

Switching from positive to negative spin-control modes is routine in the information industry when it comes to individuals and groups viewed as critics of the economy—or of the superclass-credentialed-class power elite that runs it. One example occurred in early 1996 when Labor Secretary Robert Reich, commenting on corporate policies and decisions negatively affecting workers, their families, and communities, called for "a new corporate citizenship" and encouraged business leaders to "do some soul searching" and "size up their responsibilities to America." In reporting on his comments, the *Washington Post* spin referred to the "strident tone" of Reich's "barrage" and sarcastically described his efforts as a "crusade" for corporate responsibility. As FAIR pointed out, "When the *Post*'s news reporters refer to such measured comments as 'strident,' it's evidence that there's a need for more *journalistic* responsibility."[125]

Labor unions have a history of criticizing class-based corporate policies that undermine worker's interests; and as we noted earlier in this chapter, the information industry often portrays unions in negative terms. Thus, we should not be surprised to find unions demonized by the information industry. This practice is evident in the superclass campaign to "defund" union political contribution sources (discussed in chapter 4). A recent *Wall Street Journal* op-ed essay on the U.S. labor movement praised union contributions in the *past*, but demonized unions today. The essay asserts that "today's AFL-CIO . . . has engaged in anti-globalization demonstrations side-by-side with socialists, Naderites, anarchists, and environmental radicals." Even worse, unions were able "to introduce labor and environmental standards into international trade negotiations, which had the effect of bogging down chances for further trade liberalization." The essay concluded with a rousing cheer for Linda Chavez's campaign called "Stop Union Political Abuse"—which would "stop the use of union dues for political purposes without the consent of dues payers."[126] The demonization efforts continued in other forums as essays by Chavez "explaining" her campaign and further vilifying unions appeared in newspapers around the United States in 2001.[127] (Chavez was Bush's choice for secretary of labor, but her candidacy was defeated by Democrats—and unionists.)

Spin Control: Propaganda

The public relations industry is the major force driving explicit, calculated spin control through the use of advertising, propaganda of all sorts, and newer techniques such as the creation of "grassroots" movements to support any given client's interests, as well as the conscious manipulation of journalists. The industry is led by large firms, such as Burson-Marsteller, Hill and Knowlton, and Ketchum PR; it employs "150,000 people (20,000 more than all the reporters in the U.S.)" and influences "an estimated 40 percent of what Americans now see and read."[128] Propaganda-based spin control comes in many forms, but three are especially important to protecting and concealing superclass and corporate interests and power: corporate-image advertising, "astroturf" campaigns, and journalistic manipulation.

Corporate Image Advertising

Corporate advertising to promote the ideology and image of corporations represents at least a half-billion-dollar-a-year enterprise today.[129] Ads attesting to the altruism and benevolent good works of corporations such as Dow, DuPont, Mobil Oil, Phillips, and others are routinely published in national magazines and aired on network television. Meanwhile, "on so-called 'public TV,' a dozen big corporate polluters—including BASF, Goodyear and Mobil—polish their images by underwriting nature shows."[130] The head of a large advertising agency described the purpose of corporate advertising thus: "It presents the corporation as hero, a responsible citizen, a force for good, presenting information on the work the company is doing in community relations, assisting the less fortunate, minimizing pollution, controlling drugs, ameliorating poverty."[131]

The point of corporate advertising is to create favorable public opinion regarding corporate ideas, motives, and actions. This helps maintain the legitimacy of corporations—and by extension helps protect not only their business interests but also the economic and political interests and power of superclass corporate owners.

Astroturf Campaigns

Corporations may be able to count on the built-in pro-corporate biases of commercial journalism, but these leanings do not necessarily guarantee favorable media coverage for any specific firm or industry—especially where sensitive health, safety, or environmental issues are concerned. However, corporations have discovered that "astroturf campaigns" organized by the public relations industry can be very useful in generating positive press coverage, public opinion, and favorable treatment by policy makers and the courts. Indeed, this form of lobbying, whereby citizens are used as pawns in pseudograssroots, corporate-sponsored public relations offensives, is now a billion-dollar PR sub-specialty.[132] It typically involves the use of "industry-generated 'citizens' groups who can be relied upon to lobby government and speak eloquently to [the] media."[133]

The most successful examples of astroturf campaigns—from a corporate perspective—are not publicly known because they are the ones whose true nature and purposes were never discovered or revealed. However, recent examples that have come to light illustrate how such campaigns serve corporate interests via the spin-control propaganda process.

Some of the best-known illustrations of astroturf campaigns have involved "smokers' rights" groups. For example, in the 1990s, Burson-Marsteller (the PR firm mentioned in chapter 4) helped create (with funding from Philip Morris) a "grassroots" group known as the National Smokers Alliance to promote smokers' rights.[134] The Alliance was one of many artificial grassroots groups created by U.S. tobacco firms in the 1990s to help protect their economic interests in the $45 billion industry. Another example involved RJR Nabisco, which helped create and then hired the Ramhurst Corporation, a PR company, in 1993. This firm "combines 'grassroots lobbying' with inside-the-Beltway influence peddling."[135] As these "grassroots" campaigns have been exposed in the media, the tobacco industry has shifted its tactics: "Smokers' rights groups have given way to more effective—and more covert—coalitions with anti-tax groups."[136] Even so, as one investigative reporter put it, "'Grassroots' coalitions have become a vital tool for tobacco's survival because of the industry's increasingly negative public image."[137]

More recently, Burson-Marsteller, the PR firm for the chemical giant Monsanto, was involved in paying for a "pro-genetic modification demonstration at a recent Food and Drug Administration hearing." The PR firm reportedly gave "some of the 100 participants cash . . . free food, and transportation." Once the story broke, "even Monsanto admitted that the practice of paying people to demonstrate was 'abhorrent.'" In reporting the story, the *New York Times* ran the headline: "Monsanto Campaign Tries to Gain Support for Gene-Altered Food." *EXTRA!* described this innocuous wording as a "prime example of the 'please don't read this story genre.'" The magazine also noted: "Is it a surprise to learn that in addition to representing Monsanto, Burson-Marsteller is the PR agency for the *New York Times*?"[138]

The examples cited above represent only the tip of a giant corporate iceberg involving phony "grassroots" campaigns. The public relations industry's expanding use of these campaigns on behalf of corporate clients is well documented in books, scholarly articles, alternative media reports and websites.[139] Astroturf campaigns traffic in calculated deception, but translate into favorable media coverage, political influence, and economic gains for corporate clients, public relations firms, and their superclass owners.

The net effects of such campaigns extend beyond single-corporation or industry gains. Astroturf campaigns can be (and are) used on behalf of entire clusters of firms and industries to promote classwide policy outcomes favorable to superclass interests. The fact that such campaigns strike at the heart of representative democracy is irrelevant to corporate clients. Superclass astroturf campaign clients understand that it is possible to combine the sentiments of National Football League coach Vince Lombardi's well-known cliche and singer-songwriter Randy Newman's song title into a single line: "It's Winning and Money That Matters in the U.S.A."

Journalistic Manipulation

Since the public relations industry's mission essentially involves serving the interests of wealthy clients, it has an ongoing concern with developing practices that will generate media spin control in directions desired by its clients. To maximize media influence and control on behalf of wealthy clients, some PR firms now specialize in "compiling dossiers on [reporters] so . . . corporate clients will know how to manipulate individual members of the media." One such firm, called TJFR Products and Services and founded by former *Wall Street Journal* reporter Dean Rotbart, had six thousand reporters' biographies in its computerized files in 1993. These files are for sale to corporate clients. As Rotbart says, "If at any point you get a call from a journalist and don't know who it is, call us up and we will fax you that bio within an hour."[140]

Other public relations firms track specific issues and prepare reports on the journalists who cover them. For example, Rowan and Blewitt, headquartered in Washington, D.C., was retained by the dairy industry to analyze media coverage of the recombinant bovine growth hormone (rBGH) issue. The CARMA International public relations firm was also hired to track this issue and "ranked individual reporters based on whether their stories were 'favorable' or 'unfavorable' to rBGH."[141]

Public relations firms also provide media manipulation spin skills to corporate public relations representatives by hiring real journalists to take part in training exercises. For example, Robert J. Meyers and Associates of Houston hired three journalists to help ARCO Petroleum "practice its PR plan for handling the news media following environmental disasters." According to one of the journalists involved, the reporters were assigned to play the role of the "predatory press" while professional actors were hired to play the part of environmentalists. For the Meyers firm this was not an isolated event. In the past six years the company has conducted more than 400 similar training drills.[142]

These examples of journalistic manipulation illustrate some of the many ways the public relations industry can "spin" so much of what Americans read, see, and hear in the media in pro-superclass and pro-corporate terms. They also underscore the point that these kinds of services are provided mainly on behalf of wealthy corporate clients to further their economic and political interests—and those of their superclass owners. Finally, they call attention to the lamentable dearth of "counterspin" agents and practices working on behalf of working-class interests and power.

THE INFORMATION INDUSTRY:
CONCLUSIONS

Consider . . . what a different country we would be if we had a Citizens Channel with a mandate to cover real social problems.

—Bill Moyers, *Nation*, November 19, 2001

The mainstream ideology, opinion-shaping, and spin-control processes are driven not by a superclass conspiracy, but rather by superclass media ownership, a shared ideology that views the economic and political status quo as the best possible world, in accordance with common classwide interests and routine business practices. These factors thread superclass preferences and ideological biases into the fabric of virtually all news reporting, commentary, and advertising generated by the information industry. The industry consistently tilts reporting and commentary on events, institutions, personalities, and policies relevant to superclass interests in directions consistent with those interests. Of course, the three processes operating through the information industry may not always lead to a uniform, superclass-blessed "corporate ministry of information party line" on all issues and topics. But they clearly produce a lopsided presentation of ideologically infused news and commentary that trends in the direction of privileged-class interests on most issues, most of the time.

Root, Root, Root for the Home Team?

Media-based "ideological coaching" may not always lead the working class to share the views and policy preferences of superclass-sponsored opinion shapers. However, such efforts *appear* to predispose public opinion among working-class members in those directions—at least on some critical class-based issues such as legitimating the accumulation of private wealth and the importance of reducing the federal deficit. For example, as the United States was emerging from the Great Depression in 1939, a Roper poll found only a minority—24 percent—agreeing that there should be a law limiting the amount of money a person could earn in a year. By 1992, with economic inequality accelerating, that number had shrunk to a tiny 9 percent.[143] A national survey in 2000 found that despite growing economic polarization, 85 percent of Americans surveyed agreed with the statement: "I believe it is possible in America to pretty much be who you want to be."[144] Such findings appear to suggest that large numbers of Americans continue to accept the legitimacy of the current distribution of income and wealth in the United States— a view that favors superclass interests.

On the second issue, many U.S. progressives view the "balanced budget" movement as a superclass-driven smoke screen for dismantling more social programs.[145] But unlike progressives, sizable numbers of Americans appear to be convinced of the need for the government to "balance its checkbook"—just like average folks. In the mid-1990s, a Gallup poll reported 82 percent of Americans said "significant" deficit reduction should be the top or a high priority for Congress.[146] In 1997, most Americans surveyed "favored an amendment to the constitution to balance the federal budget."[147] These poll findings and those cited earlier concerning the distribution of income and wealth *appear* to illustrate superclass successes in shaping public opinion on critical economic issues.

A further effect of the control processes operating via the information industry relates to the political awareness of and choices made by the working class. By restricting the expression of alternative perspectives, superclass-based media control leads to confusion among working-class members over how the shadow political industry is both driven by and serves superclass resources and interests. It also leads to circumscribed, sterile politics and fatalistic or de facto support among workers for the economic and political status quo. The lopsided ideological spectrum and stunted political debate presented in the media "leaves most citizens without a coherent view of politics . . . [and] a population unable to select alternative patterns of power sustains the status quo."[148]

The Persistence of Resistance?

The preceding section suggests working-class members frequently share superclass-favored views, but other evidence indicates that significant divisions also exist on some issues. The divergent nature of privileged-class and working-class experiences, interests, and views is evident in results from recent surveys. A poll conducted by the *Nation* magazine and the Institute for America's Future compared the views of average Americans with those of wealthy donors who contributed $5,000 or more to federal political candidates in the 1993–96 period. The findings revealed that while average Americans were concerned with growing economic insecurity and corporate power, elite donors were not. For example, 83 percent of average Americans agreed (almost three-fifths strongly agreed) that "average working families have less economic security today, because corporations have become too greedy and care more about their profits than about being fair and loyal to their employees." By contrast, most large donors disagreed with the statement.[149]

Some recent polls have found that substantial numbers of Americans hold views that are hostile to superclass interests and control. In a 1999 Gallup poll, 63 percent of Americans agreed that "money and wealth should be more evenly distributed."[150] A 1999 Pew Research Center national survey found that while 63 percent of Americans in families earning over $75,000 annually viewed globalization as positive, that percentage fell to 48 percent among those in families with incomes of $50,000 to $75,000 and to 38 percent for those in families earning less than $50,000 (one-half of all families in 1999).[151] A 1996 poll sponsored by the Preamble Center for Public Policy found 70 percent of the respondents believed corporate greed, not the global economy, is behind corporate downsizing. Moreover, 46 percent saw corporate greed as the biggest obstacle to middle-class living standards, compared with 28 percent who saw government waste and inefficiency as the main problem. Also, 76 percent supported "living-wage laws" and 82 percent favored congressional action for "setting standards for responsible corporate behavior" and lowering taxes on companies that comply.[152] More recently, a 2001 Pew Research Center poll found 44 percent of Americans agree with the view that the United States is now a "have/have-not society." The proportion agreeing with this view is up substantially from 26 percent in 1988 and 39 percent in 1999.[153]

The results of such polls illustrate that despite the superclass biases inherent in the information industry, working-class members are not simply passive vessels filled with superclass-generated information and propaganda. Instead, such results indicate resistance among nonelites to the massive dissemination through the information industry of information and commentary that preponderately supports the status quo. It is apparent that increasing experiences with and knowledge about class-based inequalities among the nonprivileged is fostering a growing awareness of and concerns about the nature and extent of superclass interests, motives, and power in the economic and political arenas.

The Stealth Industries

Despite the size, power, and record of success in promoting superclass interests, most features of the information industry—including details concerning superclass funding and control of its operations—are seldom reported by the mainstream media.[154] The scant media and public attention paid to superclass control of this industry as well as its control of the shadow political industry reveals their stealthy qualities: They're there, but they do not register on media radar screens or generate much public attention. Why not? We believe the answer has three parts.

First, these industries are cloaked in the same powerful political force field that drives the class taboo: the mass media's avoidance of reporting on class issues—based in and funded by the superclass and its corporate domain—including the absence of serious inquiries into the organizational foundations of class inequities.[155] Second, the information and shadow industries consist of numerous legitimate organizations with extensive resources and payrolls. Their links to major corporations, the mainstream mass media, and the national government make them a routine part of society—a nonstory, by mainstream media standards. Third, when either industry does become the focus of media reports or books, the "pluralist-special-interest group" model typically organizes and drives these accounts.[156] Viewers and readers are left with the impression that both industries consist of a diverse collection of competing organizations and sectors. No mention is made of the existence or importance of the superclass to funding, organizing, and coordinating the activities of these industries.

These factors help ensure that for each industry, the superclass-based political control structures and processes as well as the class consequences of their actions are largely shielded from media reporting and public attention. The result is the "stunt" Gore Vidal described in the opening of chapter 4: Superclass political dominance vanishes behind the unreported, widespread business-as-usual routines and legitimacy accorded to most features of the information and shadow political industries. In effect, the organizational foundations of the class empire and the results of its activities are hidden—in plain sight.

NOTES

1. Peter Phillips and Project Censored, *Censored 2001: 25th Anniversary Edition* (New York: Seven Stories Press, 2001), 38.

2. Ibid., 36, 38.

3. Peter Hart and Steve Rendall, "Meet the Myth Makers," *EXTRA!* July–August 1998, 26–27.

4. Joan Claybrook, "Corporate Accountability," *Public Citizen News: Special Anniversary Edition* 21(1), 2001, 20–21, 29.

5. Timothy D. Schellhardt, "Are Layoffs Moral? One Firm's Answer: You Ask, We'll Sue," *Wall Street Journal*, August 1, 1996. Also see Robert A. Sirico, "The Capitalist Ethic: True Morality," *Forbes*, December 2, 1996, 85; "Soundbites," *EXTRA!* September–October 1996, 5.

6. California Anti-SLAPP Project, "What are SLAPPs?" on the Internet at http://www.sirius.com/-casp/survival.html (visited September 15, 2001).

7. Editorial, "$30 Million Can Make Media Shy of Truth," *National Catholic Reporter,* April 24, 1998, 1.

8. Robert W. McChesney, *Rich Media, Poor Democracy* (Chicago: University of Illinois Press, 1999), 16–29. Also see Jim Naureckas, "From the Top: What Are the Politics of the Network Bosses?" *EXTRA!* July–August 1998, 21–22.

9. Mark C. Miller, "Free the Media," *Nation,* June 3, 1996, 9–15.

10. Michael Dolny, "Think Tanks Y2K," *EXTRA!* July–August 2001, 6–7.

11. David Croteau, "Challenging the 'Liberal Media' Claim," *EXTRA!* July–August 1998, 9.

12. Robert W. McChesney, "The Global Media Giants," *EXTRA!* November–December 1997, 11.

13. U.S. Department of Commerce, *Statistical Abstract of the United States* (Washington, D.C.: U.S. Government Printing Office, 2000), 289.

14. Evan Thomas and Gregory L. Vistica, "Fallout from a Media Fiasco," *Newsweek,* July 20, 1998, 25.

15. John W. Wright, ed., *The New York Times 2001 Almanac* (New York: Penguin Group, 2000), 384.

16. Phillips and Project Censored, *Censored 2001,* 37.

17. "Fortune 1000 Ranked within Industries," *Fortune,* April 16, 2001, F-60.

18. The summary profiles presented for each of the five media firms, including the revenue figures, are based on information from the 2000 annual corporate reports for each company and from additional information provided on each of the five corporate websites available on the Internet. See the Bibliography for complete citations for each company website.

19. McChesney, *Rich Media, Poor Democracy,* 29.

20. Ibid.

21. Matt Carlson, "Boardroom Brothers," *EXTRA!* September–October 2001, 18.

22. Ibid.

23. Peter Phillips, "Self Censorship and the Homogeneity of the Media Elite," in *Censored 1998,* ed. Peter Phillips (New York: Seven Stories Press, 1998), 152.

24. Carlson, "Boardroom Brothers," 18–19. Also see Phillips, "Self Censorship and the Homogeneity of the Media Elite," 141–52.

25. Ben H. Bagdikian, *The Media Monopoly* (Boston, Mass.: Beacon Press, 1997), 6–8, 15–16.

26. McChesney, *Rich Media, Poor Democracy,* 29.

27. Robert Parry, "The Right-Wing Media Machine," *Extra!* March–April 1995, 7.

28. Naureckas, "From the Top," 21–22. Also see Jim Naureckas, "Where's the Power: Newsroom or Boardroom?" *EXTRA!* July–August 1998, 23.

29. Bagdikian, *The Media Monopoly,* 26.

30. Janine Jackson, "Let Them Eat Baguettes," *EXTRA!* March–April 1996, 14–15.

31. Thomas R. Dye, *Who's Running America? The Clinton Years* (Englewood Cliffs, N.J.: Prentice-Hall, 1995), 196.

32. G. William Domhoff, *Who Rules America? Power and Politics* (New York: McGraw-Hill, 2002), 103, 141–44.

33. Bagdikian, *The Media Monopoly,* 6.

34. Parry, "The Right-Wing Media Machine," 7.

35. Naureckas, "From the Top," 21–22.

36. Bagdikian, *The Media Monopoly*, 85–86.

37. Louis Lavelle, "Special Report: Executive Pay," *Business Week*, April 16, 2001, 77.

38. Janine Jackson, "Wall Street's Gain Is Journalism's Loss," *EXTRA!* September–October 2001, 20.

39. Ibid.

40. U.S. Department of Commerce, *Statistical Abstract of the United States*, 579.

41. Eyal Press, "Spin Cities," *Nation*, November 18, 1996, 30.

42. Bagdikian, *The Media Monopoly*, 159–61.

43. Jim Naureckas, "Corporate Censorship Matters: The Case of NBC," *EXTRA!* November–December 1995, 13.

44. Janine Jackson and Peter Hart, "Fear & Favor 2000," *EXTRA!* May–June 2001, 21.

45. Sheldon Rampton and John Stauber, "This Report Brought to You by Monsanto," *Progressive*, July 1998, 22–25.

46. Jane Akre, "We Report, They Decide: Fox TV Censors Series on Milk Hazards," *National News Reporter*, June 1998, 13.

47. Rampton and Stauber, "This Report Brought to You by Monsanto," 24.

48. Jim Gordon, "Mystery Milk, Journalistic Debate," *EXTRA!* January–February 2001, 29.

49. A. V. Krebs, "Court Upholds Award in Suppressed TV Report," *Progressive Populist*, January 1–15, 2001, 7.

50. Gordon, "Mystery Milk, Journalistic Debate," 30.

51. Krebs, "Court Upholds Award in Suppressed TV Report," 7. Also see the Akre and Wilson website on the Internet at http://www.foxBGHsuit.com.

52. Gordon, "Mystery Milk, Journalistic Debate," 30.

53. Sheldon Rampton and John Stauber, "Oprah's Free—Are We?" *EXTRA!* May–June 1998, 11–12. Also see Ralph Nader, "Product Libel," *Public Citizen News*, May–June 1998, 4.

54. The Pew Research Center for the People and the Press, "Journalists Avoiding the News, Self Censorship: How Often and Why?" on the Internet at http://www.people-press.org/jour00rpt.htm (visited June 8, 2001).

55. Lawrence Soley, "The Power of the Press Has a Price," *EXTRA!* July–August 1997, 11–13.

56. Bruce G. Knecht, "Hard Copy: Magazine Advertisers Demand Prior Notice of 'Offensive' Articles," *Wall Street Journal*, April 30, 1997, A1.

57. Charles P. Alexander, "To Our Readers," *Time*, April–May 2000, 4.

58. Jackson and Hart, "Fear & Favor 2000," 16.

59. Knecht, "Hard Copy," A1.

60. Bagdikian, *The Media Monopoly*, 218. Also see Norman Solomon, "The Media Oligarchy: Undermining Journalism, Obstructing Democracy," in *Censored 2001*, ed. Peter Phillips (New York: Seven Stories Press, 2001), 277–90; and Lawrence Soley, "Corporate Censorship and the Limits of Free Speech," *EXTRA!* March–April 1999, 19–21.

61. Seth Ackerman, "Has ABC News Given Up on Accuracy?" *EXTRA!* November–December 1999, 18–19. Also see Seth Ackerman, "The Most Biased Name in News," *EXTRA!* July–August 2001, 10–12, 14–18; and William Hoynes, "The Cost of Survival," *EXTRA!* September–October 1999, 11–19.

62. Kimberly Pohlman, "Solid Ratings Don't Protect Progressive Radio Voices," *EXTRA!* July–August 2000, 22.

63. Edward S. Herman, "The Media Mega-Mergers," *Dollars and Sense*, May–June 1996, 8–13. Also see "Action Alert," *EXTRA!* December 1995, 4.

64. Chris Lehmann, "Michael & Me," *In These Times*, October 14, 1996, 39–40.

65. Jackson and Hart, "Fear & Favor 2000," 15–22. Also see "Field Guide to TV's Lukewarm Liberals," *EXTRA!* July–August 1998, 14–17.

66. Ackerman, "The Most Biased Name in News," 10; Hart and Rendall, "Meet the Myth Makers," 26–27; Joseph Perkins, "Caught in the News Media's Liberal Bias," *Indianapolis Star*, July 18, 1998; "The 89 Percent Liberal Media," *EXTRA!* July–August 1998, 10; Parry, "The Right-Wing Media Machine," 6–19.

67. Domhoff, *Who Rules America? Power and Politics*, 111–12.

68. Pat Wechsler, "This Lesson is Brought to You By," *Business Week*, June 30, 1997, 68–69.

69. Bagdikian, *The Media Monopoly*, 51, 58.

70. Domhoff, *Who Rules America? Power and Politics*, 183–85. Also see Kevin Phillips, "Fat City," *Time*, September 26, 1994, 49–56.

71. Terry Thurman, "Political Action is a Year-Round Process," *UAW Solidarity*, "Region 3 Moving Forward" insert, November 2001, 1–2.

72. For examples, see Linda Chavez, "Union Workers Deserve Choice in Use of Dues," *Indianapolis Star*, September 17, 2001, A12; George Melloan, "Whatever Happened to the Labor Movement?" *Wall Street Journal*, September 4, 2001, A23. Also see Janine Jackson, "Major Player or Big Bully?" *EXTRA!* January–February 1997, 9–10; "Don't Let Them Fool You!" *AFSCME Public Employee*, March–April 1998, 6–11.

73. Croteau, "Challenging the 'Liberal Media' Claim," 4–9. Also see Gail Dines, "Capitalism's Pitchmen," *Dollars and Sense*, May 1992, 18–20.

74. Jennifer L. Pozner, "Power Shortage for Media Women," *EXTRA!* July–August 2001, 8–9. Also see "The Whitening Newsroom," *EXTRA!Update*, June 2001, 2; Jennifer L. Pozner, "Women Have *Not* Taken over the News," *EXTRA!* January–February 2000, 9–10.

75. Croteau, "Challenging the 'Liberal Media' Claim," 8.

76. Rick Marin and Yahlin Chang, "The Katie Factor," *Newsweek*, July 6, 1998, 53.

77. Doug Donovan and Peter Kafka, "Hosts with the Most," *Forbes*, March 19, 2001, 164–65. Also see Peter Hart and Seth Ackerman, "Bill O'Reilly's Sheer O'Reillyness," *EXTRA!* July–August 2001, 19–20; and Robert J. Samuelson, "Down with the Media Elite!?" *Newsweek*, July 13, 1998, 47.

78. George Seldes, "Is the Entire Press Corrupt?" *EXTRA!* November–December 1994, 26–27.

79. "CEOs Play Reporter," *EXTRA!Update*, February 1996, 2.

80. David Elsila, Michael Funke, and Sam Kirkland, "Blaming the Victim: The Propaganda War against Workers," *UAW Solidarity*, April 1992, 11–17.

81. Martin A. Lee and Norman Solomon, "Does the News Media Have a Liberal Bias?" in *Taking Sides*, ed. Kurt Finsterbusch and George McKenna (Guilford, Conn.: Duskin, 1996), 28.

82. Croteau, "Challenging the 'Liberal Media' Claim," 4.

83. Jerold M. Starr, *Air Wars: The Fight to Reclaim Public Broadcasting* (Boston, Mass.: Beacon Press, 2000), 49. Also see "Field Guide to TV's Lukewarm Liberals," 14–17.

84. George Farah and Justin Elga, "Sunday Morning Political Talk Shows Ignore Corporate Power Issues," *Essential Information*, on the Internet at http://www.essential action.org/spotlight/report/index.html (visited September 15, 2001). Also see George Farah and Justin Elga, "What's *Not* Talked about on Sunday Morning?" *EXTRA!* September–October 2001, 14–17.

85. "From the Left: More than a Figure of Speech?" *EXTRA!Update,* February 1996, 1. Also see Dines, "Capitalism's Pitchmen," 20.

86. Steve Rendall, "Nation's Top Columnists Still Lean Right," *EXTRA!* January–February 2000, 11–12.

87. Elsila, Funke, and Kirkland, "Blaming the Victim," 12.

88. Jonathan Tasini, "Lost in the Margins: Labor and the Media," *EXTRA!* Summer 1990, 2–6.

89. Jennifer Gonnerman, "Media Watch," *In These Times,* December 25, 1995, 9.

90. Bagdikian, *The Media Monopoly,* 52.

91. Ibid., 57.

92. Dines, "Capitalism's Pitchmen," 18.

93. Janine Jackson, "Moribund Militants: Corporate Media on (Re)Organized Labor," *EXTRA!* January–February 1996, 6–7.

94. "Media Myths & Facts," *UAW Solidarity,* April 1992, 17.

95. Jonathan Tasini, "Media Stereotypes about Unions," *EXTRA!* Summer 1990, 4.

96. Bagdikian, *The Media Monopoly,* 44.

97. "Ageism on the Agenda: Special Issue," *EXTRA!* March–April 1997. Also see Jeff Cohen and Norman Solomon, *Adventures in MediaLand* (Monroe, Me.: Common Courage Press, 1993), 28.

98. Dean Baker, "Misleading Options on Social Security," *EXTRA!* May–June 1999, 15; Walt Duka, "Panel Hypes Social Security Problems, Experts Caution," *AARP Bulletin,* September 2001, 3, 30–31; Laura McClure, "Social Security Sneak Attack," *Labor Party Press,* September 2001, 8; "Ageism on the Agenda: Special Issue," *EXTRA!* March–April 1997; Diana Zukerman, "The Derailing of Social Security," *EXTRA!* May–June 1999, 13–14.

99. John D. McKinnon and John Harwood, "Wall Street Ponies Up to Back Bush's Social Security Plan," *Wall Street Journal,* June 12, 2001, A24. Also see Trudy Lieberman, "Social Insecurity: The Campaign to Take the System Private," *Nation,* January 27, 1997, 12.

100. Marc Breslow, "Death by Devolution," *Dollars and Sense,* January–February 1996, 20–22, 38; Domhoff, *Who Rules America? Power and Politics,* 164–69.

101. Seth Ackerman, "Surplus Shell Games," *EXTRA!* November–December 2000, 8–10; Seth Ackerman, "Populist Rhetoric Unpopular with the Pundits," *EXTRA!* January–February 2001, 9; Dean Baker, "Generation Excess," *EXTRA!* March–April 1996, 12–13; Richard B. DuBoff, "Social Security: Hardly Secure at the *New York Times*," *EXTRA!* March–April 1997, 10–11; Catherine Hill, "Privatizing Social Security Is Bad, Particularly for Women," *Dollars and Sense,* November–December 2000, 17–19, 35.

102. John Canham-Clyne, "When Elites Say 'Cut Medicare,' Press Debates 'How Much?'" *EXTRA!* January–February 1996, 12. Also see Doug Henwood, "TV on Social Security: It's Broke, Fix It," *EXTRA!* May–June 1999, 8–12.

103. AFL-CIO, "Social Security: Who's Behind the Private Accounts Scheme?" on the Internet at http://www.aflcio.org/socialsecurity/private.htm (visited September 17, 2001).

104. McClure, "Social Security Sneak Attack," 8. Also see Center for Responsive Politics, "The Calm Before the Storm: Wall Street and Social Security Reform," on the Internet at http://www.opensecrets.org/alerts/v6/alertv6_25.asp (visited July 23, 2001).

105. McKinnon and Harwood, "Wall Street Ponies Up to Back Bush's Social Security Plan."

106. Allan Sloan, "A Lot of Trust, but No Funds," *Newsweek,* July 30, 2001, 34.

107. William Safire, "Jimmy That 'Lockbox'," *New York Times,* September 10, 2001, A29; "Yes, We Have No Bananas," *Wall Street Journal,* September 4, 2001, A22.

108. Richard S. Dunham, "Privatizing Social Security: Despite the Slump, Support Is Solid," *Business Week,* August 13, 2001, 41.

109. Howard Fineman, "Move Over, Gray Panthers," *Newsweek,* September 10, 2001, 29.

110. Leigh Strope, "Job Cuts Hit 21-Year High," *Indianapolis Star,* November 3, 2001, A1, A10.

111. McKinnon and Harwood, "Wall Street Ponies Up to Back Bush's Social Security Plan." Jane Bryant Quinn, "Private Accounts Won't Work," *Indianapolis Star,* September 17, 2001, C1.

112. "Bush Stacks His Social Security Commission," *UAW Solidarity,* July–August 2001, 5; Center for Responsive Politics, "The Calm before the Storm"; Ruth Conniff, "Will Democrats Abandon Social Security?" *Progressive,* March 1999, 19–23; David D. Kallick, "Saving Social Security (from its saviors)," *In These Times,* March 7, 1999, 10–13; McClure, "Social Security Sneak Attack," 8; "Social Security Heist," *Nation,* July 9, 2001, 3; Fred J. Solowey, "Selling Social Insecurity," *EXTRA!* March–April 1998, 22–23; Christian Weller, "The Commission Straw Man: Social Security Well Prepared for Retirement of Baby Boomers in 2016," *Economic Policy Institute, Issue Brief #159,* July 19, 2001, 1–3.

113. Michael Dolny, "Think Tanks in a Time of Crisis," *EXTRA!* March–April 2002, 28–29.

114. Sam Husseini, "Checkbook Analysis," *EXTRA!* May–June 2000, 23–24.

115. Norman Solomon, "Media Moguls on Board," *EXTRA!* January–February 1998, 19–22.

116. Husseini, "Checkbook Analysis," 24.

117. Press, "Spin Cities," 32.

118. Robert W. McChesney, "Journalism, Democracy, and Class Struggle," *Monthly Review,* November 2000, 5.

119. *New York Times, Downsizing of America* (New York: Random House, 1996).

120. Donald L. Barlett and James B. Steele, "America: Who Stole the Dream?" *Indianapolis Star,* September 22–29, 1996.

121. Janine Jackson, "Economic Pack Journalism," *EXTRA!* November–December 1996, 12.

122. Robert J. Samuelson, "Confederacy of Dunces," *Newsweek,* September 23, 1996, 65.

123. Mortimer B. Zuckerman, "A Time to Celebrate," *U.S. News and World Report,* July 17, 2000, 120.

124. Robert J. Samuelson, "Indifferent to Inequality?" *Newsweek,* May 7, 2001, 45.

125. "Soundbites," *EXTRA!* May–June 1996, 5.

126. Melloan, "Whatever Happened to the Labor Movement?" A23.

127. Chavez, "Union Workers Deserve Choice in Use of Dues," A12.

128. Press, "Spin Cities," 30.

129. Bagdikian, *The Media Monopoly,* 58.

130. Cohen and Solomon, *Adventures in MediaLand,* 45.

131. Bagdikian, *The Media Monopoly,* 58.

132. Sharon Beder, "Public Relations' Role in Manufacturing Artificial Grass Roots Coalitions," *Public Relations Quarterly* 43 (1998):21–30.

133. Laura Flanders, "Is It Real . . . Or Is It Astroturf?" *EXTRA!* July–August 1996, 6.

134. Ken Silverstein, "Manufactured News," *EXTRA!* January–February 1997, 23–24.

135. Peter H. Stone, "The Nicotine Network," *Mother Jones,* May–June 1996, 50.

136. Ted Gup, "Fakin' It," *Mother Jones,* May–June 1996, 54.

137. Stone, "The Nicotine Network," 50.

138. "Don't Read This Soundbite," *EXTRA!* January–February 2000, 5.

139. Sharon Beder, *The Corporate Assault on Environmentalism* (White River Junction, Vt.: Chelsea Green Publishing, 1998). Also see Beder, "Public Relations' Role in Manufacturing Artificial Grass Roots Coalitions"; John Stauber and Sheldon Rampton, *Toxic Sludge Is Good for You: Lies, Damn Lies, and the Public Relations Industry* (Monroe, Me.: Common Courage Press, 1996); Shawn Zeller, "Thriving in a Crisis," *National Journal*, October 14, 2000, 3262; for websites and articles on the Internet search under "astroturf."

140. John Stauber and Sheldon Rampton, "Watching the Watchdogs: How Corporate PR Keeps Tabs on Reporters," *EXTRA!* May–June 1996, 22.

141. Ibid.

142. Ibid.

143. Todd Gitlin, "Unum Versus Pluribus," *Nation*, May 6, 1996, 32.

144. Richard Powers, "American Dreaming," *New York Times Magazine*, May 7, 2000, 66–67.

145. "Balance This," *In These Times*, May 13, 1996, 4–5.

146. Michael Golay and Carl Rollyson, *Where America Stands, 1996* (New York: Wiley, 1996), 16.

147. Domhoff, *Who Rules America? Power and Politics*, 118.

148. Bagdikian, *The Media Monopoly*, 206.

149. Robert L. Borosage and Ruy Teixeira, "The Politics of Money," *Nation*, October 21, 1996, 21–22.

150. "Working to Tell the Untold Story," *Too Much*, Winter 2000, 8.

151. Andrew Kohut, "Globalization and the Wage Gap," *New York Times*, December 3, 1999, A29.

152. "In Fact," *Nation*, August 26–September 2, 1996, 5.

153. The Pew Research Center for the People and the Press, "Economic Inequality Rising, Boom Bypasses Poor," on the Internet at: http://www.people-press.org/june01mor.htm (visited August 12, 2001).

154. Michael Dolny, "What's in a Label?" *EXTRA!* July–August 1998, 9–10; McChesney, *Rich Media, Poor Democracy*, 63–77; McChesney, "Journalism, Democracy, and Class Struggle"; Parry, "Right-Wing Media Machine," 6–10.

155. McChesney, "Journalism, Democracy, and Class Struggle," 1–15. Also see Solomon, "The Media Oligarchy: Undermining Journalism, Obstructing Democracy," 277–90; and Domhoff, *Who Rules America? Power and Politics*, 1–13.

156. Martin N. Marger, *Social Inequality* (Boston: McGraw-Hill, 2002), 247–53, 354–56. Also see Dines, "Capitalism's Pitchmen," 18–20; and Phillips, "Fat City," 49–56.

6

Educating for Privilege: Dreaming, Streaming, and Creaming

> The educational system is an integral element of the reproduction of the prevailing class structure of society.
>
> —Samuel Bowles and Herbert Gintis, *Schooling in Capitalist America,* 1976

Nick Caradona and Arnie Seebol were an unlikely pair to become good friends in high school. They were from different parts of the city and from widely different ethnic and religious traditions—one Italian and a nominal Catholic, the other from a Jewish family with practicing parents and recalcitrant kids. Nick's and Arnie's paths would never have crossed if they had not both passed a citywide exam to get into an "elite" science-oriented high school. Most of the kids in the high school were college bound, but the idea of college had never occurred to Nick or Arnie, or to their parents for that matter.

Nick's and Arnie's parents had a tough time making ends meet, because of their unstable low-income jobs. Only one of the four parents claimed a high school diploma. Nick's parents were separated. When Nick was five years old, his father went to Washington, D.C., to look for work; he drove a cab in D.C. for the rest of his working years, but he never returned to his family. Nick's mother worked as a domestic until he was twelve years old and then took a job as a clerk in a laundry. Arnie's father drove a truck for the *New York Daily News,* and his mother did "home work" for shops in the garment district. Nick and Arnie were both urged by their junior high teachers to take the exam for admission to the select high school, and after being admitted they both enrolled.

At first, the bond between Nick and Arnie was based on the extremity of their shared differences, focusing on the "dirty secrets" of their elders and their ethnic cultures, namely, the disparaging terms and put-downs they had heard used against members of the in-group and the out-group. Arnie taught Nick the fine points of distinction between a *putz* and a *schmuck*. Nick also learned to smack himself in the head and exclaim "goyisha kopf" whenever he did something stupid. Arnie told him that Jews would use this routine whenever they did something foolish, exclaiming with the phrase that they were acting like Gentiles. It reminded Nick of his grandfather's frequent practice of referring to someone as an American in broken English ("you must be 'Merican"), pronounced in such a way that it sounded very much like "merde de cane," which Italians would understand literally as "shit of the dog." It was an unschooled double entendre, which Nick taught Arnie to use against other kids in school.

Arnie and Nick soon discovered other bonds. They both liked baseball (Nick a Yankee fan, Arnie a Dodger fan), and both had a flair for "hustling," as they were both always short of money. They took bets in school from other students, who would choose three baseball players whom they expected would get a total of six hits in that day's ball games. The odds on each bet were three to one. Thus a kid would bet a nickel that his three favorite players would get a total of six hits that day. If the three players scored the six hits, the bettor won fifteen cents; if not, Nick and Arnie won the nickel. The odds were always with the "bookmaker" as long as there were a sufficient number of bettors. Many kids had favorite ball players who rarely got more than one hit a game, but they bet on them nonetheless. Nick and Arnie would also "pitch pennies" and play cards during the lunch hour. Their high school was huge (five thousand students), so there was always plenty of "action" for Nick and Arnie.

Late in their senior year, Nick started to have problems, academically and otherwise. He went "on the hook" too many times and faked letters of excuse from his mother. In the midst of these problems, he quit high school a month before the end of term, failing to take any final exams. He went to work as a "runner" for a bookmaker and was soon "promoted" to a "writer" in a betting room where men assembled to talk about horse racing and to make bets on races at a number of tracks in New York, New Jersey, and the New England area. Off-track betting was illegal, but it was carried out openly with the paid-for cooperation of local police.

Arnie graduated on schedule and went to work for his uncle in his dry cleaning store. Arnie would learn all about the business, and he hoped one day to own his own store or several stores.

The preceding vignette calls attention to how the intersection of students' social class backgrounds and educational opportunities for upward mobility can sometimes be both serendipitous and problematic. Nick and Arnie were kids who showed some talent in elementary school. Their teachers had a "dream" that they were worthy of moving into an educational tracking system that gave talented kids a chance to "make it" in the opportunity contest—meaning a chance to go to college. But Nick and Arnie themselves did not have the dream, and they never gave any thought to the track that could lead to a college education and beyond. It was partly because the cost of college-going was beyond the means of Nick and Arnie's parents. But it also required Nick and Arnie to forgo the income they would earn from working and the claim to adult status that comes with the end of schooling. Many of Nick and Arnie's classmates were middle class and college bound from years of anticipatory socialization. They were "hot-house" kids who had been cultivated for years in an environment of controlled feeding and sunlight. They did not yearn for the freedom of adult status, for their sense of self was fused with the wishes held for them by their parent cultivators.

Nick and Arnie were working-class kids from low-income, working-class families, and their parents were working too hard to be involved in the school activities of their children. The opportunity provided by their admission to an elite high school does not exist in a vacuum. In Nick and Arnie's case it existed within the working-class culture that was their everyday reality. Thus, if all the poor kids in East St. Louis were suddenly enrolled in a school with good teachers, facilities, and programs, it would be great for the kids; but only so much can be expected to follow from an enriched educational experience. The kids will still be poor, as will their parents and friends. Their educational system and experience is contained within a context, a class structure that shapes events that extend far beyond the classroom.

The American Dream of equality of opportunity is contradicted daily in primary and secondary schools throughout the country. A substantial body of research indicates that when students come to the "starting line" in first grade, they do not come as equals. They are advantaged and disadvantaged by their class situation, their race or ethnicity, and their gender, which shapes school experiences and educational outcomes.[1]

AMERICAN EDUCATION SYSTEM

A fundamental premise of the so-called "American Dream" is that the postponement of personal gratification, especially in the pursuit of educational goals, will result in social rewards attached to a prestigious occupational position. . . . In the end, the American Dream is a barrier in public education. . . .

—Adalberto Aguirre Jr. and David V. Baker, *Structured Inequality in the United States*, 2000

In effect, if not by design, the American education system functions primarily to transmit advantage and disadvantage across generations. This assertion flies in the face of a powerful and dominant ideology that permeates all levels of society, namely that education is the great equalizer. Education is what brought Abe Lincoln from a log cabin to the highest office in the land. Education is what gave millions of poor but aspiring immigrants in the United States the chance to be whatever they were willing to work for. This is the ideology of the American Dream. The dream is so powerful that parents will fight "tooth and claw" to control local schools, so that their programs, teachers, and curriculum will serve the interests of their children. In the dream, education is the passport to a future that exceeds (if you are poor) or matches (if you are privileged) the economic situation of your parents.

For the Dream to become a reality, schools have to be organized to meet the aspirations of the dreamers. In schools in which all the kids are from professional families, only one kind of education is needed—a college preparatory program. But when the kids in school come from diverse economic backgrounds, a system must be devised to provide not only the best education to the college-bound children from professional families and to some of the poor kids—who, based on probabilities alone, would be able to compete with the college bound—but also a quality educational experience for those who are not heading to college. The idea behind this system is that the educational experience should be designed to meet the "needs of the child."[2] The system is called *tracking*.

Tracking seems to be a very progressive idea, permitting teachers "to tailor instruction to the ability level of their students. A good fit between a student's ability and the level of instruction is believed to maximize the effectiveness and efficiency of the instructional process."[3] Does it not make sense to identify students who are headed to college, white-collar employment, or mechanical trades and provide them with the particular knowledge and skills that will be most useful—vocational and shop courses for the young men and women going to work in factories, keyboarding and word processing for those who would be clerks and secretaries in corporate bureaucracies, and literature, languages, mathematics, and the sciences for those headed toward colleges and universities? The problem with this theory of education is that students' vocations need to be identified fairly early in their young lives to make use of this system. Of course, this is no easy task, but the ideology of the American Dream states that with the help of "objective" testing, student's strengths can be identified and tracked to make the best use of their abilities.

Tracking was needed when schools were heterogeneous in terms of the economic backgrounds of their students. If a school had the children of professionals, white-collar clerks, and unskilled workers, tracking was necessary to meet the needs of the child. But today, many schools are much more homogeneous in terms of the backgrounds of students and their educational plans. Children from the corporate and managerial classes are generally either in private schools or in suburban schools limited to members of their social class. Virtually all of these students are college bound; so what would be the point of tracking? At the other end of the class-structure spectrum we have poor rural schools or inner-city schools filled with children from the bottom one-third to one-half of the economic system. The closest thing you might have to tracking in these schools is the effort of dedicated teachers to reach out and identify those with the greatest potential and to groom them for college, hoping that they might have a chance to attend.

These homogeneous schools, which today largely serve the children of the affluent and privileged class, are involved in *streaming*, not tracking. *Tracking* is a competitive metaphor, implying a contest among entrants in a race where all the "runners" have an equal chance to win. *Streaming* is a noncompetitive metaphor, implying that participants are "carried along" to their destination without any substantial competition with their peers. If you go to the right private schools or the better suburban schools, college attendance is the assumed outcome for all involved.

An excellent example of the streaming metaphor is revealed in the following remarks made by the Dean of the Harvard Law School when greeting a new class of students at the orientation session.

> The fact is that you are not competing with each other. Your life at the school and your life as a lawyer will be happier and more satisfying if you recognize that your goal is to become the best possible lawyer so that you can serve your clients and society with maximum skills. Although you will experience frustrations from time to time, I think that rather than the *Paper Chase* you will see the school as much closer to the image involved in a letter we received some years ago from a Japanese lawyer who had just been admitted: "Dear Sir: I have just seen the movie *Love Story* with Ryan O'Neal and Ali McGraw and I am looking forward to a very romantic time at the Harvard Law School."[4]

Compare this "laid-back" welcoming speech with the prototype competitive welcome offered by the dean or professor at a less "prestigious" program: "Look at the person on your right and the person on your left. At the end of the first year, only one of you will still be in the program." Those in the privileged classes attempt to create an elementary and high school educational structure that is characterized by streaming, so that their children are "guaranteed" good grades, high test scores, an enriched curriculum, extracurricular activities, and advising that will get them admitted to the country's most elite schools. Privileged-class parents also frequently supplement the school's programs by providing their children with special prep classes for taking college SAT tests. Such prep classes may cost close to $1,000, but as parents know: "It isn't a matter of just getting into college, but of making it into UC-Berkeley or UCLA or MIT."[5] Privileged classes work to develop these "guarantees" at the same time they support the myth of the dream, extolling the virtues of equality of opportunity as the hallmark of American society.

THE POWER OF THE DREAM

> If kids go to college because high school jobs are so terrible, they may wind up with these jobs anyway. We won't slow our rising inequality just by jamming more and more kids into college.

> —Thomas Geoghagen, *New York Times*, 1997

The myth of the American Dream is a powerful force in American life, and it is based on two distinct beliefs: First, that everyone can aspire to levels of success that exceed their starting points in life, because where a person starts life is an accident that can be remedied; and second, that there is equality of opportunity to reach one's goals, and that the game has a set of rules that are fair and capable of producing the desired success goals.

The dream can be a source of inspiration for the young and a source of hope for parents who push their children to better themselves. It also serves to legitimate the great inequality in society in wealth, power, and privilege. It leads to the belief that those who receive high rewards are deserving because they have contributed more in terms of effort and hard work. The dream is a comfort to the privileged and a heavy burden for the less fortunate.

The dream is so pervasive in our culture, so embedded in our family rituals and significant celebrations, that we often follow its logic without examination. It is a kind of cultural reflex leading us to continually search for evidence of the dream in action, and to urge it on others as a guide for living. Consider the following obituary, which the writer, with little or no evidence, chooses to frame within the myth of the dream. The headline reads, "B. Gerald Cantor, Philanthropist and Owner of Rodin Collection, Is Dead at 79."

This headline, in half-inch type, is accompanied by an almost full-page story reporting the achievements of the deceased. The story begins,

> B. Gerald Cantor, who started out as a boy selling hot dogs at Yankee Stadium, became a wealthy financier and philanthropist, amassed the world's most comprehensive collection of Rodin sculpture in private hands, and gave much of it away to dozens of cultural institutions, died on Wednesday in Los Angeles after a long illness. . . .
>
> Mr. Cantor, who was raised in modest circumstances in the Bronx, and his wife Iris, who grew up three blocks from the Brooklyn Museum, came to be widely known in New York for their generosity to the Metropolitan Museum of Art, the Brooklyn Museum, and to medical institutions in the city. . . .
>
> Before he was 15, Bernie Cantor became a vendor at Yankee Stadium. "I only worked during Sunday double headers," he recalled, because "you could sell more things" in the delay between the two games. . . .
>
> He graduated from DeWitt Clinton High School and went on to study law and finance at New York University from 1935 to 1937. He originally planned to become a lawyer, but he changed his mind when he spotted a lawyer friend who had had to take a job working with a pickax on a construction project of the Works Project Administration.[6]

This fifty-five paragraph story about a well-known philanthropist manages to create, for the casual reader, the clear impression in its opening sentence, and in the first few paragraphs, that we are dealing with yet another personification of the "rags to riches" American Dream.[7] Poor boy works hard—selling hot dogs, no less, at Yankee Stadium (a double dose of the dream being played out in the playground of dreams)—achieves phenomenal success, and gives all his money back to the "people" (actually to museums, hospitals, and at least a half-dozen universities).

But before we can make sense of Cantor's life, we need to know what it means to be raised in modest circumstances. We also need to know how these "modest circumstances" carried him to New York University during the height of the depression. The point of these questions is neither to ignore Cantor's achievements nor to diminish his generosity. The point is to show the ease with which the cultural production industry of newspapers, TV, films, and so forth creates the powerful myth of the American Dream. Even this straightforward story of one person's life and achievements was "torqued" to feed into the myth. The story not only pumps up the dream, but it also legitimates the wealth of multimillionaires by first saying they "did it themselves, with hard work and dedication," and by then dwelling on how many millions they "gave back."

It is precisely because of such obituaries, *Forrest Gump*-genre films, and other rags-to-riches cultural products that most Americans appear to accept the myth of the American Dream. Figure 6.1 reports the results of a national survey in which Americans were asked to rate the importance of various factors in "getting ahead in life." Almost nine out of ten Americans report that a good education and hard work are the keys to "getting ahead," whereas only six out of ten say the same about natural ability. In contrast, only two out of ten surveyed say that being from a wealthy family and having political connections are very important. The other factors involving social capital (knowing the right people or having well-educated parents) are considered very important by four out of ten Americans.

Figure 6.1   Factors of Success

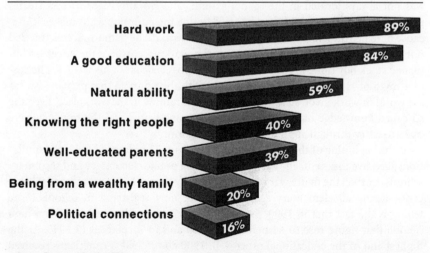

Source: Davis and Smith, 1989.
Note: Figures given are percentages of respondents who rated various factors as very important in "getting ahead in life."

Americans put their faith in education and hard work as the keys to success. In answering the survey questions, respondents did not have to make a choice between a wealthy family and a good education. They could have chosen both as being very important. The power of the American Dream is not only that it defines the paths to success (education and hard work); it also defines what is not related. The dream cannot tolerate a simultaneous belief in the value of education—which makes great sense in a credentialing society—and the advantage that comes from wealth. The myth creates facts that do not exist (you can be whatever you want to be) and denies facts that do exist (the chances for a poor child to rise to the privileged class are very slim).

The power of the dream among minorities is revealed by findings of a recent study of low-income African American high school students. Students were asked to provide a personal perspective on the importance of their race, class, or gender in limiting or enhancing opportunities for upward mobility ("What can prevent students from doing well in school?" "What is the best way of getting ahead in American society?"). Almost all students accept the "dominant narrative" of how one makes it in America: "When they were asked the best way of getting ahead in American society, without hesitation they discussed the importance of hard work, individual effort, and education."[8] However, they also provided alternative narratives of how race, class, or gender can limit an individual's efforts to improve his or her life chances.

The dream is manufactured in the popular culture, and the main vehicle for achieving it is the school system. Equality of opportunity for all, regardless of accidents of birth, is the official ideology of American education. Education is the great equalizer, providing skills and knowledge, attitudes and values. The dream was not always located in the school system. The Horatio Alger success stories popular around the turn of the century describe the poor boy who "makes it" because of his virtues of thrift, honesty, and hard work.[9] The path to success traveled not through the classroom but through the workplace, where the street urchin turned stock boy came to the attention of the boss because of his virtues. The secular myth of Horatio Alger was consistent with the times, in that preparation for the world of work involved acquiring skills and training in the workplace. Even the so-called knowledge-based professions of law, medicine, and the ministry were open to entry through apprenticeship preparation.

At the beginning of the twentieth century, about 72 percent of the U.S. population, aged five to seventeen years, was attending public elementary and secondary schools. In 1960 the figure was 82 percent, and by the mid-1990s it reached 92 percent—nearly all elementary-age children are now registered in school. More telling is the fact that in 1900, 6.4 percent of 17-year-olds graduated from high school; that figure rose to 68 percent in 1960 and to 71 percent in 1995. At the highest end of the educational process, in 1900 about 29,000 Americans received college degrees (bachelors, masters, doctors, and first professional degree); this figure climbed to 485,600 in 1960 and to 1,706,000 in 1999–2000.[10]

This virtual explosion in America's enrollment at different levels in the educational system probably does not owe simply to love of learning. Increasingly in the twentieth century, and especially after World War II, good jobs have been linked to educational credentials. First, it was the high school diploma, then the bachelor's degree, and finally the specialized professional degree. Some analysts believe that the strong connection between education and jobs is the result of major technological advances that have changed the skill requirements of jobs. As the proportion of jobs requiring high levels of skill have increased, there has been increased reliance on the formal educational system to provide the required knowledge and skills. However, it is also possible that the increase in educational requirements for jobs is a way that privileged groups protect their access to those jobs that provide the greatest rewards.[11]

As more people enrolled in elementary schools, the high school diploma became the credential for many jobs that were formerly held by people with an eighth-grade education. Then, as enrollments in high school increased, the bachelor's degree became necessary for many jobs formerly held by people with a high school diploma. And so it goes. With expansion of higher education and 1.7 million graduates a year from four-year schools, the new credential derives from *where* you get your bachelor's degree. The privileged classes that control the major corporations and universities keep moving the goalpost whenever too many of the nonprivileged class start to get access to the valued educational credential.

Once schools became established as the place where peoples' futures were determined, their programs, activities, and curricula took on a larger significance. Schools became the models of a "small society" where the things that were learned formally and informally were relevant for the larger society. Schooling is carried out on a very rigid schedule, starting and ending at a predetermined time. Weekends are free, and there is an established schedule of vacations. Tardiness and absences must be explained, and if they are excessive they will be punished. The school has established authority figures who must be followed without question. The Pledge of Allegiance, acceptance of God and country all serve to reaffirm the legitimacy of the established order. The daily activities and classes are built around respect for rules, self-discipline, grades, and performance according to externally imposed standards.

Within this "small society" framework, there is variation among schools, usually reflecting the class composition of its students. Schools for the privileged typically provide students with more opportunities for creativity, autonomy, and self-directed activities, whereas schools for the nonprivileged are more concerned with discipline, obedience, and job-related skills. Pressure for these different emphases often comes from parents. Parents who know their children are going to college emphasize enrichment in the arts, music, and cultural activities; those who know their children are headed for jobs emphasize the need for job-related activities.

In addition to the social and technical skills learned at school, students are also prepared for their futures as citizens of a political and economic system. Does schooling have a "liberating" effect on students, calling upon them to question the political-economic order and to play an active role in promoting change or reform? Or does schooling lead students to accept things as they are, believing that they are living in the best of all possible worlds? A number of studies of the schooling experience indicate that schooling has a conservative effect on students and that there are important class differences in this experience.[12]

Students in elementary and high school are encouraged to think about themselves as members of society primarily in courses on government and civic education. A content analysis of civics textbooks in "working-class" and "middle-class" schools indicates that students learn very different things about their government and economy and about their responsibilities as citizens. Moreover, interviews with school administrators, teachers, PTA officials, and leaders of community civic groups indicate that they have very different views of how the political process should be presented in the school's civic education program. The main findings from this research follow.

1. Civics textbooks in the working-class school (compared with those in lower-middle and upper-middle-class schools) are particularly bland, containing more descriptive material about the political process and less atten-

tion to power, influence, and intergroup conflict. Textbooks in the upper-middle-class school give the most attention to the use of power as the main ingredient resolving political struggles.

2. Parents in the upper-middle-class school endorse the inclusion of "realistic" political themes in the civics programs. These parents view politics "as a process involving the resources of politicians and power, and the conflict-alleviating goal of politics." These views tend to reinforce the content found in the upper-middle-class civics textbooks. Parents from the lower-middle- and working-class communities tend to ignore or avoid "realistic" themes, thereby reinforcing the bland content found in civic textbooks in their schools.

3. Measures of the political attitudes of students taken before and after they had taken civic education classes indicate that only the attitudes of upper-middle-class students change in the direction of supporting greater awareness of power and conflict in the political process. Students from lower-middle- and working-class schools show little change, suggesting that in their schools and communities "politics is treated and learned as a formal, mechanistic set of governmental institutions with emphasis on its harmonious and legitimate nature, rather than as a vehicle for group struggle and change."[13]

These findings indicate that students at these three socioeconomic levels are being socialized to play different roles in the political system, and this is done in a way that legitimates the existing system of economic and political inequality. Children from working-class and lower-middle-class communities are being prepared to continue the low levels of political participation exhibited by their elders. Moreover, they are prepared for a passive role in the political process because they have been taught that the institutions of government work for the benefit of all citizens. Students from the privileged upper-middle-class community are clearly being prepared to participate in and influence the political agenda. The privileged are made aware of the role of power, influence, and conflict in public affairs, whereas nonprivileged are encouraged to work together in harmony.

Other research on the effects of schooling indicates that students' early socialization leads them to develop positive and trusting orientations toward the symbols and institutions of political authority.[14] Moreover, schools transmit the idea that government is the main center of power in society, thereby neglecting the role of large corporations and the conflict that exists among competing political and economic interests.[15] This shaping of students' attitudes toward the economic and political order tends to bring them into conformity with the dominant ideology that serves the interests of the privileged class. The longer students are in school the greater is their exposure to the dominant ideology. In a study of elementary and secondary students from urban schools in the southwestern United States, two-thirds of third-graders supported government intervention in the economy through assistance for those out of work and for the poor. The same level of support was found among sixth-graders; but less than one-third of the ninth- and twelfth-graders supported an active role for government. Student attitudes toward private ownership of major industries became increasingly positive across the four grade levels, with 16 percent of third-graders being positive compared to 63 percent of twelfth-graders. Finally, attitudes toward trade unionism became increasingly negative as they progressed across grade levels. Third-graders were least negative toward unionism (17 percent) and twelfth-graders were most negative (59 percent).[16]

There may be naiveté and poorly formed attitudes among students (especially third-graders), but it is clear from this research that the ideology that benefits the privileged gains greater strength in the minds of students as they move from the third to sixth to ninth to twelfth grade. Students do not necessarily start school supporting the ideas of private property, government restraint, or antiunionism, but that is clearly where most of them wind up at high school graduation. Schools function to affirm the legitimacy of the dominant political and economic order and perpetuate the myth of equality of opportunity. In so doing, they serve the interests of the privileged class.

TRACKING AND STREAMING

> The objective of primary and secondary education, as enunciated by the legislators, educators, and community leaders who control it, is to propagate a devotion to the dominant values of the American system.
>
> —Michael Parenti, *Power and the Powerless*, 1978

One of the main concerns of the privileged class is to protect their advantage and to transmit it to their children. In a society where educational credentials are used by the privileged to justify their rewards, it is critical that the rules of the game are designed to give advantage to the children of the privileged class. Of course, others can also play by these rules if they choose, but it may be comparable to poker players who try to draw to an inside straight—a risky bet.

Tracking and streaming are two ways in which the rules of the game are used to give advantage to children of the privileged class. In order to understand how these strategies work, it is important to remind ourselves how precollege public education is financed in the United States. Funds for public education are drawn primarily from local property taxes (state and federal governments also provide funds). The amount of money raised through property taxes depends on the tax rate applied to the assessed value of homes and businesses. Communities with newer and more expensive homes and a strong business community will be able to generate more tax revenue for use in paying salaries of teachers and providing educational resources for students. They can often do this with a lower tax rate than that of poorer communities, because the aggregate value of their homes and businesses is larger. Because property taxes and mortgage interest are deductible from federal income tax, the privileged classes receive a larger indirect subsidy for the education of their children than that received in poorer communities.

Evidence from recent research on the effects of school expenditures indicates that higher per-pupil expenditures for instruction are associated with higher levels of student achievement.[17] Higher student achievement comes from smaller class size and a higher ratio of teachers to students. The more money a school can spend on instruction, the more teachers they can hire and the more money they have to pay experienced teachers. The presence of more teachers and better-paid teachers also improves the social environment of the school, as lighter workloads both improve teacher morale and enable teachers to get to know students better. This research also reports the interesting finding that some types of school spending are a "dead end" for student achievement: Capital outlays for building improvements and school-level administration had no impact on student achievement. Spending additional money on more and better teachers is the way to improve education, but such money is often not available in poor school districts.

In heterogeneous school districts, where children of the privileged and nonprivileged are in the same school, there is a single pool of money to fund that school. That money is used to get the best teachers, the most up-to-date books, the best laboratory equipment, films, computers, and other educational resources. In order to give an advantage to the privileged children, it is necessary for the school to develop programs that allocate the best teachers, the most computers, and the best resources to programs that are most likely to be taken by the privileged class. The money is not given to the children of the privileged class, but to programs in which they are more likely to enroll. Thus, tracking is invented—a system that allocates resources to programs that are tied to distinct outcomes—a college preparation or a vocational preparation. Tracking is a form of inequality within schools.

In homogeneous school districts, where almost all the children are from the privileged classes or almost all are from lower classes, there is no need for tracking. In the rich schools, at least nine out of ten children are headed for college; but in poor schools, one out of ten children is going to college. When the percentage attending college in poor schools exceeds one in ten, it is usually because of special circumstances like a local state college or a community college enabling poor students to work or live at home while attending school. However, the rich schools will have more money to spend on schooling because of the higher value of assessed property in their school districts. With more money, these schools hire better teachers, purchase better equipment, provide more extracurricular activities, better guidance and counseling, and thereby provide a better all-around education. In poor schools with less money to spend, the quality of education suffers in all areas of the schooling experience. Streaming is a form of inequality between schools.

Tracking, despite its official noble intentions, is a process that segregates students by ability groupings, curriculum choices, race, and socioeconomic status. It is a process that separates winners from losers in the contest for good jobs and high income. It is estimated that about 85 percent of public schools use a system of tracking[18] to provide different and unequal education for those believed to be college bound and those believed to be heading directly to the labor market. Some tracking programs provide maximum separation, as students remain in the same track for all their courses, and some provide minimum separation with all students taking at least some courses together. Placing students in tracks based upon beliefs about their futures can be a powerful self-fulfilling prophecy. Track placement is directly and indirectly related to the class and racial background of students. The direct effects are a result of the expectations that teachers and administrators have of children from higher-class backgrounds.[19] The indirect effect occurs because less-privileged children may express less interest in college, receive less parental and peer encouragement to go to college, and lack the achievement scores to be selected for placement in the college track. There is substantial agreement among analysts of tracking, based on strong research evidence, that tracking has negative consequences for low-income and non-White students.

However, there are sharply different views on whether tracking should be retained or eliminated.[20] Some see it as a way of providing opportunities for students who might otherwise be ignored; others see it as a way of reproducing social inequality. Although many factors influence how schools choose students for track placement, there is substantial evidence that class and racial background are important.[21] This choice, however, is crucial to a student's future in terms of academic achievement, high school graduation, and college attendance.[22]

Inequality between schools (i.e., streaming) is revealed most sharply in the differences between school districts in the amount of money they spend to educate their students. Per-pupil expenditures are the best single indicator used to compare schools on the quality of their teachers, programs, and facilities. The national average of per-pupil expenditures was $6,584 in the 1999–2000 school year, with some states spending as much as $8,904 per student (Connecticut), and some as low as $3,969 (Utah). Within states, comparisons between rich and poor school districts (based on land values and family income) provide the most revealing evidence of class-based inequality. Urban school districts in larger cities spend far less money than suburban districts. Per-pupil expenditures in 1988–89 in the Chicago area ranged from a high of $9,371 in the suburbs to $5,265 in the inner city. In Camden, New Jersey, suburban spending was $7,725 per pupil, compared with $3,538 in the city. A comparison of six districts in the New York City area revealed a high of $15,084 in the suburbs and a low of $7,299 in the central city. In 1989–90, the wealthiest school district in New York spent $19,238 per pupil, while the poorest district spent $3,127.[23] National data for 1994 indicate that urban school districts spent $4,500 per pupil, compared with $5,066 in nonurban districts. The spending gap between urban and nonurban districts in major cities like New York was about $4,300 per student. Rural areas, which in general are predominantly White, spend far less money on schooling than either the urban or suburban school districts.[24] Wealthy suburban schools that spend nearly twice as much per pupil are able to have better teachers, better facilities, smaller classes, and a variety of enriching activities and programs. Such advantages will never find their way into inner-city schools as long as school funding is based on property taxes.[25]

The one large consequence of tracking and streaming is their effect on college enrollment. Students who are in vocational tracks or in high schools composed primarily of students from low-income families are at a great disadvantage. Their educational aspirations are reduced because they receive little encouragement from peers and parents in their social milieu. Even students with high academic achievement and potential are less likely to think about college as a goal.[26] In contrast, students whose friends are the children of doctors, lawyers, and other professionals are likely to receive sustained social encouragement from parents, friends, and teachers to view college attendance as a "natural destination" in their educational careers.

Ample research evidence indicates that even students with high academic achievement and high measured intelligence are not likely to enter college if they are from lower economic groups. One study reports that 91 percent of students with high intelligence and high-social-class backgrounds attend college, compared to 40 percent of students with high intelligence but low-social-class backgrounds.[27] The combination of money to pay for college and the encouragement of peers and parents results in 84 percent of all students from higher-class backgrounds attending college, compared with only 21 percent of all students from lower-class backgrounds.

The advantages of going to college include better chances for higher-prestige jobs and higher incomes. In 1979, a male college graduate received almost 50 percent more income than a high school graduate. In 1999, the advantage of the college graduate increased to 80 percent more income.[28] In short, access to high positions and high income are more closely related to educational credentials today than was the case several decades ago.

Evidence from the past thirty years indicating how education is linked to better jobs and higher earnings has led many to jump on the education bandwagon and to propose more and better education as the solution to many of society's problems. Workers displaced by new technology or plant closings are told that they must improve their skills to find work in the high-tech economy. Young men and women from the poorest groups are encouraged to get a high school degree and to think about going to college, even if only a community college. Politicians love to talk about legislation to increase financial aid to students. In 1999, President Clinton proposed a $1,500 tax credit for college to help pay for the first two years of college. He also proposed a $5,000 tax deduction for college education or job training.[29] The education bill proposed by President George W. Bush in 2001 also contains a number of tuition-related tax credits.

It is hard to argue with the call for more education, for it has certainly worked for those members of the privileged class who have converted their credentialed skills into high-paying positions in business, finance, and the professions. In 1975, about 40 percent of the young men and women from the richest one-quarter of the population earned college degrees. This was about seven times greater than the 6 percent of high schoolers from the poorest one-quarter who went to college. By 1994, eight out of ten sons and daughters from the richest quarter of the population earned a college degree, doubling the rate from twenty years earlier. In contrast, college attendance for the poor increased to a meager 8 percent from the 6 percent of twenty years earlier.[30]

Clearly, the privileged class got the message about the changing global economy in the mid-1970s and the increased importance of credentialed skills in that economy. The privileged class has, in recent years, sent almost all its children to college, as did many families of better-paid blue-collar workers and middle-income groups. But they did not all go to the same type of college, they did not major in the same fields, and they did not enjoy the same rewards in later years.

PRINCETON VS. PODUNK: GETTING "CREAMED"?

It is often asserted that new technologies will equalize learning opportunities for the rich and poor. It is devoutly to be wished for, but I doubt it will happen.

—Neil Postman, *Nation*, October 9, 1995

Up to this point, we have demonstrated the strong influence schooling has on the reproduction of class inequality. Contrary to the beliefs contained in the American Dream, education is not the means for providing equality of opportunity to all Americans regardless of their social position at birth. Schooling serves to reproduce inequality through the power of the myth of the American Dream and through the effects of tracking and streaming as the way to deny equal access to the means for upward mobility. We now continue our analysis of schooling by examining the question of who goes to college and where they go.

As noted earlier in this chapter, rates of college attendance have increased dramatically in the past fifty years. In 1940, 216,000 degrees were awarded by American colleges and universities. By 1999–2000, some 1.7 million degrees were being awarded by accredited institutions offering degrees at the associate, baccalaureate, masters, and professional and doctoral levels. A total of 15,135,000 students were enrolled in 4,070 higher education institutions in 1999–2000. These institutions consist of 2,343 four-year colleges and universities, and 1,727 two-year institu-

tions.[31] The expansion in college enrollments has had the effect of introducing greater diversity into the college environment.

It is probably safe to assume that in the era of small enrollments, the college population was composed of persons with similar social and economic backgrounds. Only the sons and daughters of the most privileged classes attended college. But what are we to say about a time when 15 million young people are in college? Although they do not represent all of those persons from lower economic backgrounds who would go to college but cannot afford to, it must surely contain some of them. Perhaps what we have is a modified form of the American Dream, where at least some persons from the nonprivileged classes do get access to equality of opportunity. Perhaps.

The main argument of this section is that although the expansion of enroll-ments at the college level has resulted in larger proportions of nonprivileged youth attending colleges and universities, there has been at the same time movement to-ward a more rigidly class-based system of inequality within the framework of higher education. This more subtle and less visible form of inequality is reflected in the schools that privileged and nonprivileged students attend and in the areas in which they choose to specialize. Students from homes with modest finances may be more likely to select two-year, or four-year programs with immediate em-ployment opportunities, rather than advanced degree or professional degree pro-grams. In addition to class-based choices of academic majors, there is some evidence that female and non-White students also make career choices that result in lower incomes.[32]

The consequences of class, race-, and gender-based systems of inequality within higher education are as serious in terms of wasted human resources as the class- or race-based systems of tracking and streaming that determine who goes to college. Let us begin with the approximately four thousand institutions of higher education that are available to serve the needs of America's aspiring youth. Approximately 42 percent of those institutions are two-year colleges that students typically attend ei-ther because they lack the academic credentials to be admitted to a four-year insti-tution or because they lack the money to pay for tuition, room, and board. Some enrollees at two-year colleges are nontraditional students who are already em-ployed and are trying to improve their credentials and career opportunities.

The remaining 58 percent, the twenty-three hundred four-year institutions, are also highly differentiated. About two hundred of these institutions are the larger and more prestigious research universities that award almost all the professional and advanced degrees in the United States. These institutions graduate the doc-tors, lawyers, engineers, scientists, economists, and managers that populate the privileged class. These two-hundred "top" universities can be further subdivided into the Ivy League (Brown, Columbia, Cornell, Dartmouth, Harvard, Pennsylva-nia, Princeton, and Yale), the so-called Big Ten (Illinois, Indiana, Iowa, Michigan, Michigan State, Minnesota, Northwestern, Ohio State, Penn State, Purdue, and Wisconsin), and other state universities. And then there are the small "elite" liberal arts colleges that provide high-quality education, strong social ties (the basis of so-cial capital), and very high tuition (Amherst, Bates, Bowdoin, Clark, Colby, Franklin and Marshall, Hamilton, Haverford, Hobart, Oberlin, Reed, William Smith, Swarthmore, and Tufts among others).

The point of this little exercise (aside from the fact that we have probably mis-classified many schools) is to indicate that higher education is highly differenti-ated, with a small number of schools that are very selective about their admissions and consistently rated by many sources as among the elite colleges and universi-ties. The number of elite schools in the United States that confer great advantages on their graduates probably numbers about thirty, or less than 1 percent of all the colleges and universities in the country. If you are admitted to one of these thirty elite schools, after graduation the odds are dramatically increased that you will also be admitted to one of the elite graduate or professional schools if you apply. And when schooling is completed, the graduates of elite schools will assume high-level positions in the major institutions of American society and join the privileged class. Students admitted to the "elite 1 percent" are getting "creamed," which is the positive meaning of this term used at the beginning of this section. Those who rise to the top in this system will enjoy the "good life" with all of its material and psychological benefits.

Students who are enrolled at the 1,388 community colleges, and at most of the 2,100 nonelite schools, are getting creamed in the negative meaning of the term— that is, they are getting "clobbered." Most of these students are caught between a rock and a hard place. They choose to go to college because it is their only hope for getting a decent job. The absence of good jobs for people with only a high school diploma drives most into college. Their parents cannot really afford to cover the costs of college, and so students work and take out loans in the hope that all the debt and sacrifice will pay off in the end. They forgo income for four years and incur debt, yet when they graduate, all they may find is a job paying $10–15 an hour, or $21,000–31,000 a year. The median starting salary for 1993 college graduates was $22,968 (about $27,000 in 2000 dollars), with education majors receiving about $19,000 and computer science and engineering majors receiving $31,000. About 40 percent of these graduates reported that the job they held did not require a college degree (only 17 percent of engineering graduates said this, but about 50 percent of graduates in humanities and social sciences said a college degree was not required for their current job).[33] To be sure, at the 2,100 nonelite schools there is a small minority of graduates who do better. They are usually graduates in engineering or business or those with teaching certificates who have the skill capital and credentials to command better incomes. But they will not be joining the privileged class.

This two-tiered system of schooling for privilege is summarized in figure 6.2. In the top panel of the figure is the secondary school system that was described in the section on tracking and streaming. The children of the wealthiest members of the privileged class enter the stream in the elite prep schools that prepare students primarily for Harvard, Princeton, and Yale. The remaining children of the privileged class are being educated in the resource-rich suburban high schools that are homogeneous in terms of the economic class of their students and are well funded from their property taxes. These students from the privileged class compete among themselves for admission to a small number (about fifty) of elite universities and liberal arts colleges. They are elite because they are well endowed by financial contributions from wealthy alumni and because their admissions procedures are highly selective (i.e., they get applications from many more students than they can ever admit). Some of the graduates of these elite schools go on to the elite schools of law, medicine, business, and engineering, and most of the rest go into entry-level positions in America's major corporations.

Figure 6.2   Two-Tiered System of Schooling for Privilege

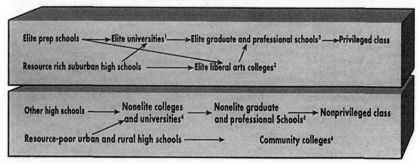

Notes:
¹Elite universities: Approximately 20, including Harvard, Yale, Princeton, Chicago, Stanford, Northwestern, California-Berkeley, Michigan, Wisconsin, UCLA, North Carolina, Columbia, Duke, Pennsylvania.
²Elite graduate and professional schools: Approximately 15, including Harvard, California-Berkeley, Yale, Chicago, Wisconsin-Madison, Michigan, Columbia, Stanford, Princeton, Cornell, Illinois-Urbana, Pennsylvania.
³Elite liberal arts colleges: Approximately 30, including Amherst, Bates, Bowdoin, Brown, Bryn Mawr, Reed, Swarthmore, Tufts, Colgate, Smith, Wellesley, Williams, Oberlin, Hamilton, Franklin and Marshall, Wesleyan of Connecticut, Barnard, Brandeis, Mount Holyoke, Haverford, Hobart, Skidmore, Union.
⁴Nonelite colleges and universities: There are approximately 2,100 schools in this group.
⁵Nonelite graduate and professional schools: There are approximately 200 schools in this group.
⁶Community colleges: There are 1,388 schools in this group.

The lower panel of figure 6.2 indicates where most students are located. In 2000, 2.8 million students graduated from high school; of that number, about 294,000 graduated from private schools. Enrollments in the fifty elite colleges and universities make up a small fraction of the millions enrolled in higher education, with the overwhelming proportion of students enrolled in the 2,300 nonelite colleges and universities and the 1,727 community colleges. A very small percentage of these students "escape" their nonprivileged paths and are admitted to elite schools, usually owing to their academic achievements and their performance on the Scholastic Aptitude Tests (SAT) that are used with all applications for college.³⁴ A study of Harvard's admission process indicates that the school does attempt to admit a small number of "working-class" students and "students of color" who have academic merit based on scores on the SAT and other achievement tests.³⁵ This possibility of "moving up" describes the small amount of creaming from the bottom tier of figure 6.2 into the schooling streams of the privileged class.

The interesting thing about this two-tiered system of schooling for privilege is that the way it works has not changed very much in the past forty years. Graduates of the elite colleges and universities have always obtained better jobs (in terms of prestige, opportunities, and income) than graduates of the nonelite schools, and this is true independent of merit. The prestige of the degree-granting institution has an effect on postcollege jobs and incomes over and above the ability of their individual graduates.

In the 1950s, research compared the incomes of graduates from Ivy League schools, prestigious "technical" schools (e.g., Cal Tech, Carnegie, MIT), elite private colleges, the Big Ten, other midwestern colleges, and other eastern colleges. The findings indicated that the median incomes of male graduates are directly related to the prestige ranking of the schools, and this pattern was found across different fields of study. The following summary from the researchers is important for its historic value, given that this was a period before higher education became as differentiated by prestige as it is today.

> Although we have noted that good grades may at least sometimes lead to good incomes, it develops that even the poorest students from the Ivy League share in the general prosperity—and do better than the best students from other schools. Of the Ivy Leaguers who just got by—the C and D students—42 percent had reached the [highest income] level. Of the A students from the Big Ten, only 37 percent had hit that mark, and only 23 percent of the A students from "all other Midwest" colleges. Even the great financial disadvantage of a general education, rather than a specific one, does not seem to hold back the Ivy Leaguers. Of the Ivy League humanities majors, 46 percent had reached the [highest income] bracket, and of the social scientists 50 percent. But even among the Big Ten's engineering graduates, with their highly specific training and all the advantages that go with it, only 23 percent had reached the [highest income] level. [At the time of this study, the "highest income" was about three times the median income for all U.S. men. A comparable "highest income" figure in 2001 would be $118,000].
>
> What all this amounts to is that the differences in earning power between graduates of rich and famous schools and those from small, obscure schools are so great that they override everything else. Earning power rises steadily with each increase in wealth and prestige of the school. At the extremes, the Ivy League graduates do best of all financially—even when they make poor grades and take a general rather than specific course, both of which are ordinarily handicaps—while the graduates of the smallest schools do not get up to the averages even when they make fine grades and take the type of specific courses that ordinarily produce the biggest incomes.[36]

The pattern of advantage for graduates of elite schools observed more than forty years ago is still in operation today. Students from privileged-class backgrounds are more likely to enroll in the most prestigious schools, and they choose programs of study that have the greatest potential for high income.[37] In fact, the effects of privilege on who goes where to college may be greater today then they were forty years ago. Sons and daughters of the privileged class go to better high schools (if not private schools) and are provided with an educational experience that is geared to satisfy entrance requirements at the most selective elite colleges. And as if that is not enough, privileged-class families have the money to help their children prepare for college entrance exams.

The final barrier for even the brightest working-class high school graduate is the cost of attending an elite college. How can a family earning the median family income of $48,816 a year (2000) afford to pay $30,000 a year for tuition, room, and board? Lacking funds, such students go to state colleges with lower costs, and they obtain financial aid and work to cover expenses. Choosing a major is often driven by practical considerations, such as the need to get a job after graduation. This can lead to vocationally oriented programs such as education, nursing, and technology degree programs, which assure jobs after the baccalaureate degree but allow limited opportunities for achieving high income or for accumulating wealth.

Findings such as those just reported indicate a clear lack of correspondence between the expectations derived from the American Dream and the actual experiences of college graduates. Ability and merit are important for a person's success after college, but where one goes to school is also important.

In the 1960s there was growing interest in the science-based professions, such as engineering, as examples of a profession that was open to talented people, regardless of their social and economic origins. In the professions of medicine and law it is possible that a graduate's family background could influence postcollege success by providing the money to start a practice or the social contacts for attracting wealthy clients. But engineers work in large corporations where their scientific and technical expertise is often thought by many to determine their movement up the corporate ladder. One might assume that an engineer's social and economic background should have less significance for his or her success than might be the case in medicine or law.

Once again, contrary to the myth of equality of opportunity and the belief that engineering is a career open to talent, engineering graduates from higher social origins (based on their father's occupation) were more likely to hold engineering positions that provided greater prestige, power, and income.[38] This finding was based on a study of the graduates from a single university of moderate prestige, not part of the elite schools. When the research was expanded to a national sample of engineering graduates, it was found that engineers with upper social origins earned more money and held more responsible positions than engineers from lower social origins. Moreover, this class difference was found to be true even among engineers who had the highest grades in college and had attended the most selective engineering schools.[39] Thus, even when working-class high school graduates are creamed (i.e., are recruited to elite universities), their final rewards of income and position may not put them in the privileged class.

The American Dream puts great emphasis on a college education as the one true path to upward mobility (along with hard work, of course). Traveling down the "yellow brick road" paved with academic tracks, good grades, and high SAT scores should result in a college degree and entrance into the Emerald City. However, one of the details missing from the official version of the American Dream is that it is not just a college degree that gets you into the privileged class, but one from an elite school. Another detail missing from the American Dream is that it fails to prepare working-class or Black students, who are often first-generation college entrants, with a glimpse of the nonacademic obstacles and pressures they will face in college. The Dream seems to assume that poor but talented adolescents are all prepared to be college students because they are upwardly mobile achievers waiting for a break to come their way (a version of the Horatio Alger stories). It is further assumed that they have the "right stuff" (the values and aspirations) that have been instilled by parents who value education, like-minded college-oriented peers, and teachers who have worked hard to help them with their dream of attending college. In short, the poor but talented Black and White students who "make it" have made *socialized choices* to attend college. These choices reveal a temporal sequence whereby the values and aspirations for college come first, and mobility opportunities follow. However, it is also possible that some low-income students wind up in college because of *situational choices* that are unplanned, and do not reflect any real preparation for college life. Let us consider this possibility by returning to the story of Nick Caradona, whom we met at the beginning of this chapter.

When we left Nick, he had dropped out of high school and was working as a runner and writer for a "bookmaker." He did this work for several years and aspired to start his own "handbook" as soon as he accumulated enough money and found a good spot (the right neighborhood/ethnic niche). Unfortunately, the Korean War intervened and Nick was drafted into the Marines. After two years of service he returned to his old neighborhood with two goals—to buy a car with money he had accumulated in the service, and to take advantage of all his GI benefits while avoiding going to work. After he bought a car, the next thing he did was go to the Veterans Administration (VA) and sign up for the 20/20 club—collect $20 a week for 20 weeks while allegedly looking for a job ($20 then was equal to $125 today). Nick collected $20 for 20 weeks and returned to the VA to see what was next. The clerk advised that since he didn't graduate from high school he should consider getting his high school diploma in a night school program. While enrolled, he would get $90 a month. So Nick went to night school, took an English course and a history course, and received a high school diploma. Back to the VA with the "what's next" question.

This time the VA clerk said, "Why not go to college?" The idea had never crossed Nick's mind. The clerk told Nick that his weak academic record would prevent him from getting into a "good" college, and suggested that he apply for admission to one of the state teacher's colleges. The most attractive part of this idea to Nick was that he would continue to get $90 per month while going to school. A "no-brainer" for Nick!

Nick enrolled in the teacher's college and found it to be a very alien environment. He checked into a motel for his very first night at the college, in preparation for the next day's orientation for freshman. That night he took some records with him to the student union in search of a record player. On the way, he bought a bottle of wine to drink while he was listening to his favorite records (he was into sax players, and he had selections from Benny Carter, Vido Musso, and Coleman Hawkins, among others). Nick set up his records and wine and settled into an easy chair to sip and listen. It didn't take long before he was told, politely, that he would have to leave because alcohol was not permitted on campus. Nick was astounded. You could drink at age 18 in the state, but you couldn't drink on campus.

Remaining at college was a struggle for Nick, not academically but socially. But for a fortuitous event, Nick would probably not have lasted beyond the first semester. During his first month at school he ran into a neighborhood buddy he hadn't seen since before the war. Tony Lembo was a neighborhood kid who had played softball with Nick when they were about fifteen. Tony's father had a hot-dog pushcart that he set up every day near the subway. Tony had been in the Army in Korea, and he was using his benefits to become a phys-ed teacher. Tony and Nick decided to room together, and soon they met several other ex-GIs and formed a drinking and card-playing circle that sustained them while facing the ambiance of academe.

Nick was following the American Dream, but not quite according to the script linked to the conventional version of the Dream. Nick never quite became a part of the college scene, but sustained and protected himself by hanging out with other working-class guys who found themselves in the same place facing similar problems of adjustment. Nick's situation was similar to that facing many working-class African Americans and Hispanics who are the first in their families to attend college. People of color who attend predominantly White colleges face significant hurdles in trying to become a part of academic life.[40] Hopefully, their lives will be better because of having attended college. But using the college degree to get into the Emerald City is another matter!

THE FUTURE: CONTINUING INEQUALITY AND CORPORATIONS IN THE CLASSROOM

Corporations and their foundations have become sacred cows to university administrators. Few professors are willing to jeopardize their standing in universities by publishing research articles critical of these donors.

—Lawrence C. Soley, *Leasing the Ivory Tower*, 1995

The main argument of this chapter is that the American educational system operates in a way that reproduces the existing structures of inequality in the larger society, especially those grounded in class and racial distinction. It achieves this end, first of all, by promoting an ideology that proclaims schooling to be the great equalizer and the main avenue for upward mobility. Second, inequality is perpetuated through a multitiered system of education made up of elite schools, average schools, and horrible schools. The different quality of these schools is directly linked to class and racial categories of their students. The quality of the educational experience in primary and secondary schools helps to determine a student's chances for attending college.

The inequalities in primary and secondary schools linked to students' social class membership and/or their racial/ethnic identities are likely to be reinforced and extended in the years ahead. A recent study by Harvard University's Civil Rights project reports an increasing trend toward segregation in K-to-12 grades, especially in Northern states like New York, Michigan, Illinois, and California.[41] The study found that 70 percent of Black children attended predominantly minority schools in 1998–99, an increase from 66 percent in 1991–92 and from 63 percent in 1980–81. Similar patterns of segregation are reported for Latino students. The study also reports that the pattern of segregated schools closely matches the pattern of high-poverty schools. This is a situation where class and race-based segregation are used to relegate millions of children to a second-class education.

Projections of demographic trends suggest that primary and secondary schools will have increasing proportions of students of color in highly segregated settings. This should result in increased demands from parents for improvements in the quality of education provided for their children. Privileged-class parents may respond by moving their children from public to private educational settings. This would be consistent with trends that we described as "class secession" in chapter 2, namely, the expansion of private, class-segregated communities and the erosion of privileged-class support for public institutions. Working-class parents may also be attracted to opportunities to move their children out of failing schools into so-called charter schools or other alternatives that appear to offer some benefits as conventional public school budgets decline.

Concern about public education has been part of the basis for some innovations that are currently on the public agenda, namely, the voucher system and the charter school. The voucher system provides families each school year with a voucher ($2,000 to $4,000) that can be used to enroll their children in nonreligious, private schools. There have been attempts to extend the use of vouchers to religious schools, but such efforts have been blocked by lawsuits. Charter schools enable groups of parents, teachers, and community members to propose a new way of providing education for their children. For example, they might wish to emphasize self-paced learning, cross-disciplinary education, or traditional back-to-basics programs. Such groups apply for a charter from the local school board or state board of education to create the new school, and if approved, they receive public funding on a per-pupil basis similar to funding for public schools.

Vouchers and charter schools are attractive ideas because they appear to empower parents who have become frustrated with the public school system's failure to educate their children. Many parents in low-income inner cities have come to view these new ideas as the only way to provide their children with a better education. Unfortunately, only a fraction of inner-city families will be able to take advantage of vouchers or charter schools. Charter schools are not obligated to take all students who apply, and the ability to use a voucher may be dependent on the availability of transportation and other resources to get children to schools outside of their neighborhood. The main impact of vouchers and charter schools will be to siphon money away from public schools, leaving those left behind with even poorer facilities. The more affluent will take advantage of vouchers to move to private schools, leading to greater segregation in schools.

Students from resource-rich schools receive the kind of preparation that enables them to compete for admission to elite colleges and universities. Students from resource-poor schools are more likely to drop out or to terminate their education with the high school diploma. Those who do go to college attend community colleges and a wide variety of average-to-good state colleges and universities.

Based on everything we know today about the U.S. economy and the actions of corporations (as discussed in chapter 3), the educational inequalities just described will not only continue; in all likelihood, they will get worse. Students from families in the bottom of the double-diamond class structure will find it increasingly difficult to pay the costs of attending college. Moreover, it is likely to become increasingly apparent that large numbers of college graduates will be unable to find any but the lowest-level jobs available in the service sector. Such a trend will highlight the growing reality that there is a significant mismatch between the kinds of jobs that most colleges prepare most students to enter and the kinds of jobs that are actually available to most nonprivileged-class college graduates.

In addition to continuing inequality in schooling, we expect greater involvement of private sector corporations in the educational system at all levels. At the primary and secondary levels, there will be continuing interest in alternative ways of "delivering" education to the young. The current antiunion, antibureaucracy, antigovernment climate will stimulate proposals to "privatize" education. Edison Schools Inc., a private sector firm, enrolls over 50,000 students in over 100 schools that they run on a for-profit basis. The privatization movement will probably grow because of the ideology of school choice and a potential multibillion-dollar market.[42] The CEOs from *Fortune* 500 firms have become involved in school reform efforts at the state and national levels.[43] Since these business leaders are used to thinking in terms of the "bottom line," productivity, and efficiency, their involvement gives one pause as to the kind of educational "reforms" that may appear on the nation's agenda. In addition to "for-profit" private schools, we should expect great attention to new educational technology that will reduce the need for teachers and increase dependence on telecommunications-based instruction.

Corporations have already recognized the potential for advertising commercial products to the millions of school children who are today's consumers as well as consumers of the future.[44] Classroom films, television, and weekly papers are owned by large corporations, and the products developed for schoolroom use are accompanied by corporate logos and advertising material.[45]

Many of the proposals to bring corporate expertise and technology into the classroom are based on the assertion that the telecommunications revolution increasingly is available to and will equally benefit rich and poor alike. Schooling will therefore be able to deliver on its promise as the "equalizer," as all students will have access to the same educational resources, the same information, and the same master teachers, on the information superhighway. Once again, a technological fix appears ready to solve the problem of class inequality. Such promises are reminiscent of the claims made by the educational system that embraced Nick and Arnie, whom we met at the beginning of this chapter. These youngsters were brought by a progressive program into the best schools in the city and exposed to other talented kids who were college bound. But the imagined equalizing force of this experience did not "take." The boys lived in another world outside of the school that superceded and blunted the best intentions of a progressive educational model a generation ago. Like Nick and Arnie, the life experiences of class inequality today will not disappear simply because educational opportunities today are extended to working-class kids through the information superhighway.

Finally, we need to consider corporate penetration of higher education.[46] Private firms are no strangers to higher education. Corporate CEOs are prominent as trustees of most major universities but especially the elite schools. Such representation helps to encourage corporate-university relations that result in corporate funding of research and a variety of university programs. In return, corporations get access to the latest knowledge that can be converted into patents on products and processes that benefit the corporations providing the funding. Often, corporations that provide funds for research by faculty or graduate students are able to obtain agreements guaranteeing that the results of the funded research will remain secret for an agreed-upon period of time. The doctoral dissertation in biomedical engineering or pharmacology of a student whose research has had corporate funding can be kept from public disclosure until such time as the corporation that funded the research can realize its expected benefits. Students and professors may not be able to publish the results of such research until given permission to do so by the corporation. This practice of secret or confidential research may have started during the Cold War era, when the Department of Defense funded research involving national security interests. Today, the private corporations can prevent publication because of private financial interests.

Many faculty at major research universities are active participants in corporate-university relations. Those whose work may have commercial possibilities are actively pursued by corporations with substantial research grants or consulting fees. Some faculty are able to double their incomes through their consulting agreements, especially in several fields in engineering, science, and the business schools. Those faculty with a more entrepreneurial bent often start their own firms in a research park near the university while retaining their academic positions and salary.

Faculty at large research universities may receive e-mail messages from their research offices with titles such as "Leveraging Your Research by Starting a Business." This "call-out" to faculty, staff, and students is an attempt to stimulate interest in starting a business by offering information on university guidelines for faculty-owned businesses and discussions of where to find capital. These cyberspace messages are supplemented with hard-copy slick brochures with announcements like the following:

The climate for starting technology based businesses has never been better. Owing to steady or dwindling budgets, coupled with increasing demand of and competition for funds, government support for university research projects is harder to secure. University research programs are seeking alternative funding sources, such as funneling research ideas with commercial potential into start-up businesses. The bottom line: becoming an entrepreneur is not only 'in' but is encouraged.[47]

University administrators and boards of trustees generally sidestep evidence of active corporate pursuit of faculty. Universities usually have regulations stipulating that faculty may be involved in "outside activities" for one or more days per week or month, depending on the university. There is no stipulation as to how much they may earn as consultants, and no requirement that the university must be reimbursed for the time taken away from university responsibilities. Universities encourage these relationships in part because administrators hope to increase the flow of dollars from the private sector into the university's budget. Also, as noted in chapter 1, university administrators themselves are often actively involved in corporate roles.

In recent years there has been a decline in federal money coming to universities for their research programs. This money often comes with agreements to cover overhead costs that allow universities to support other activities. In addition to the decline of federal dollars, many public universities have not been able to obtain more state funds or raise tuition. The only source for new money has been the private sector, which has been only too willing to help—but at a price. The price might be confidential research (as noted earlier). Private sector funding might give the corporation the right to select researchers for projects and define the research topics to be pursued. It might even give corporations a voice on matters of promotions and tenure of faculty who work on corporate projects.

And it is also possible that corporate penetration of academe will have a chilling effect on those faculty members in the liberal arts whose inclinations or disciplines tend to raise questions about the role of corporations in American society. Consideration by faculty of issues such as the relative merits of capitalism versus socialism, the impact of unrestrained technology on the environment and our communities, and the political power of corporations in a democracy may be muted by a strong corporate presence within the university. Just as downsizing and plant closings serve to depress wages and discourage unionization, corporate penetration of academe could serve to create a climate of "corporate correctness" that will dominate the minds of students and faculty alike.

NOTES

1. Roslyn Arlin Mickelson, "The Attitude-Achievement Paradox among Black Adolescents," *Sociology of Education* 63 (1990): 44–61; Patricia A. Adler, Steven J. Kless, and Peter

Adler, "Socialization to Gender Roles: Popularity among Elementary School Boys and Girls," *Sociology of Education* 65 (1992): 169–87; Karl S. Alexander, Doris R. Entwisle, and Carrie S. Horsey, "From First Grade Forward: Early Foundations of High School Dropout," *Sociology of Education* 70 (1997): 87–107; Vincent J. Roscigno and James W. Ainsworth-Darnell, "Race, Cultural Capital, and Educational Resources: Persistent Inequalities and Achievement Returns," *Sociology of Education* 72 (1999): 158–78; Samuel R. Lucas and Aaron D. Good, "Race, Class, and Tournament Track Mobility," *Sociology of Education* 74 (2001): 139–56.

2. Michael B. Katz, *The Irony of Early School Reform* (Cambridge: Harvard University Press, 1968).

3. Maureen T. Hallinan, "Tracking: From Theory to Practice," *Sociology of Education* 67 (April 1994): 79.

4. Robert Granfield and Thomas Koenig, "Pathways into Elite Law Firms: Professional Stratification and Social Networks," in *Research in Politics and Society,* vol. 4, *The Political Consequences of Social Networks,* ed. Gwen Moore and J. Allen Whitt (Greenwich, Conn.: JAI Press, 1992), 325–51.

5. Brian Doherty, "Those Who Can't, Test," *Mother Jones,* November–December, 1998: 71.

6. Eric Pace, "B. Gerald Cantor, Philanthropist and Owner of Rodin Collection, Is Dead at 79," *New York Times,* July 6, 1996.

7. The *Chicago Tribune* published a much abbreviated eight-paragraph story about Cantor obtained from the *New York Times* News Service. The *Tribune* story started with the same lead sentence used in the fifty-five paragraph *Times* story, revealing the extraordinary appeal of the rags-to-riches story, even when it may not be true in its substance.

8. Carla O'Connor, "Race, Class, and Gender in America: Narratives of Opportunity among Low-Income African American Youths," *Sociology of Education* 72 (1999): 137–57.

9. Richard Wohl, "The 'Rags to Riches Story': An Episode of Secular Idealism," in *Class, Status, and Power,* ed. Reinhard Bendix and Seymour M. Lipset (New York: Free Press, 1966), 501–26.

10. U.S. Department of Education, National Center for Educational Statistics, *Digest of Educational Statistics,* NCES 2001–034, by Thomas D. Snyder, Charlene M. Hoffman, and Clair M. Geddes (Washington, D.C.: Government Printing Office, 2000).

11. For a discussion of these two different views of why educational requirements for many jobs have increased, see Randall Collins, *The Credential Society* (New York: Academic Press, 1979); and Randall Collins, "Functional and Conflict Theories of Educational Stratification," *American Sociological Review* 36 (1971): 1002–19.

12. Edgar Litt, "Civic Education, Community Norms, and Political Indoctrination," *American Sociological Review* 28 (February 1963): 69–75.

13. Ibid., 72, 73.

14. Dean Jaros, *Socialization to Politics* (New York: Praeger, 1973); Edward S. Greenberg, *Political Socialization* (New York: Atherton, 1970).

15. Alan Wolfe, *The Seamy Side of Democracy* (New York: David McKay, 1973); Ira Katznelson and Mark Kesselman, *The Politics of Power* (New York: Harcourt Brace Jovanovich, 1975).

16. Scott Cummings and Del Taebel, "The Economic Socialization of Children: A Neo-Marxist Analysis," *Social Problems* 26 (December 1978): 198–210.

17. Harold Wenglinsky, "How Money Matters: The Effect of School District Spending

on Academic Achievement," *Sociology of Education* 70 (July 1997): 221–37.

18. Christopher Jencks, Marshall Smith, Henry Acland, Mary Jo Bane, David Cohen, Herbert Gintis, Barbara Heyns, and Stephan Michelson, *Inequality: Reassessment of the Effect of Family and Schooling in America* (New York: Harper and Row, 1972).

19. Robert Rosenthal and Lenore Jacobson, *Pygmalion in the Classroom* (New York: Holt, Rinehart and Winston, 1968).

20. Hallinan, "Tracking: From Theory to Practice," and Jennie Oakes, "More than Misapplied Technology: A Normative and Political Response to Hallinan on Tracking," *Sociology of Education* 67 (1994): 79–91.

21. Sally Kilgore, "The Organizational Context of Tracking in Schools," *American Sociological Review* 56 (1991): 189–203.

22. Karl Alexander, Martha Cook, and Edward McDill, "Curriculum Tracking and Educational Stratification," *American Sociological Review* 43 (1982): 47–66.

23. Jonathan Kozol, *Savage Inequalities* (New York: Harper, 1991); Ron Renchler, *Financial Equity in Schools*, ERIC Digest No. 76. Eugene, Ore.: ERIC Clearinghouse in Educational Management, 1994; U.S. Department of Education, *Digest of Educational Statistics, 2000*, Washington, D.C.: U.S. Government Printing Office, 2001.

24. Noreen Connell, "Underfunded Schools: Why Money Matters," *Dollars and Sense*, March–April 1998, 14–17, 39.

25. Ibid.

26. William A. Sewell, A. O. Haller, and G. W. Ohlandorf, "The Educational and Early Occupational Status Attainment Process," *American Sociological Review* 35 (1970): 1014–27.

27. William A. Sewell and Vimal Shah, "Parents' Education and Children's Educational Aspirations and Achievements," *American Sociological Review* 33 (1968): 191–209.

28. Robert Kominski and Rebecca Sutterlin, *What's It Worth? Educational Background and Economic Status*, U.S. Bureau of the Census, Household Economic Studies, P70–32 (Washington, D.C.: U.S. Government Printing Office, 1992); U.S. Bureau of the Census, 2000.

29. Thomas Geoghegan, "Overeducated and Underpaid," *New York Times*, June 3, 1997.

30. Thomas Mortenson, of the National Council of Educational Opportunity Associations, Washington, D.C., reported in Karen W. Arenson, "Cuts in Tuition Assistance Put College beyond Reach of Poorest Students," *New York Times*, January 27, 1997.

31. U.S. Department of Education, *Digest of Educational Statistics, 2000*.

32. Jerry A. Jacobs, "Gender and Academic Specialties: Trends among Recipients of College Degrees in the 1980s," *Sociology of Education* 68 (1995): 81–98.

33. U.S. Department of Education, National Center for Education Statistics, *The Condition of Education 1996*, NCES 96–304, ed. by Thomas Smith (Washington, D.C.: U.S. Government Printing Office, 1996).

34. James Hearn, "Academic and Nonacademic Influences on the College Destinations of 1980 High School Graduates," *Sociology of Education* 64 (July 1991): 158–71.

35. David Karen, "Toward a Political-Organizational Model of Gatekeeping: The Case of Elite Colleges," *Sociology of Education* 63 (1990): 227–40.

36. Ernest Haveman and Patricia Salter West, *They Went to College* (New York: Harcourt, Brace, 1952), 180.

37. Scott Davies and Neil Guppy, "Fields of Study, College Selectivity, and Student Inequalities in Higher Education," *Social Forces* 75 (1997): 1417–38.

38. Robert Perrucci, "The Significance of Intra-Occupational Mobility," *American Sociological Review* 26 (1961): 874–83.

39. Carolyn C. Perrucci and Robert Perrucci, "Social Origins, Educational Contexts, and Career Mobility," *American Sociological Review* 35 (1970): 451–63.

40. Robert Perrucci (and ten coauthors), "The Two Faces of Racialized Space in a Predominantly White University," *International Journal of Contemporary Sociology* 37 (2000): 230–44.

41. Diana J. Schemo, "U.S. Schools Turn More Segregated," *New York Times*, July 20, 2001: A12.

42. Peter Schrag, "Edison's Red Ink Schoolhouse," *Nation*, June 25, 2001, 20–24.

43. Douglas D. Noble, "Schools as 'Instructional Delivery Systems,'" *In These Times*, November 30, 1992, 28–29.

44. Marianne Manilov, "Channel One, Joe Camel, Potato Chips, and ABC," *EXTRA!* July–August, 1966, 18–19.

45. Luke Mines, "Globalization in the Classroom," *Nation*, June 1, 1998, 22–24; William Hoynes, "News for a Captive Audience: An Analysis of Channel One," *Extra!* May–June 1997, 11–17.

46. For an expanded discussion, see Lawrence C. Soley, *Leasing the Ivory Tower: The Corporate Takeover of Academia* (Boston: South End Press, 1996).

47. Purdue Research Foundation, *Home for High-Tech Business.* W. Lafayette, Ind.: Purdue Research Park, 1998.

7

The Pacification of Everyday Life

> The strongest is never strong enough to be master, unless he transforms his
> strength into right, and obedience into duty.
>
> —Jean-Jacques Rousseau, *The Social Contract*, 1782

As the twenty-first century opened, U. S. public opinion polls revealed a surge of
interest in paranormal phenomena—including psychics, ghosts, UFOs, and space
aliens.[1] American popular culture reflected and reinforced this trend as media
firms expanded their offerings in paranormal and science-fiction-oriented television programs, movies, video games, and internet websites. The Sci-Fi cable channel hit, *Crossing Over with John Edward*, Fox's *Freakylinks*, and UPN's *Enterprise* (a
Star Trek prequel) fed growing public interest in paranormal and science fiction
themes. Recent hit movies also resonated with the zoroaster-zoned zeitgeist as indicated by the popularity of trailers, ticket sales, and follow-up video rentals for
films such as *The Sixth Sense* (1999), *The Others, Lord of the Rings, Harry Potter
and the Sorcerer's Stone* (2001), *Star Wars Episode I: The Phantom Menace* (1999),
Planet of the Apes (2001), and *Star Wars Episode II: Attack of the Clones* (2002). As
we move deeper into the new century, the culture industry continues to produce,
at warp speed, a steady stream of media offerings that both fill and magnify public interest in a wide range of paranormal and science fiction phenomena.

American fascination with paranormal phenomena and space aliens is not a new
trend in popular culture. Many earlier films, TV series, books, and magazines have
plowed this same ground. But as the window of the new century opens wider, the intensity of public interest in such topics appears to be reaching higher and more sustained levels than in the past. Of course, this cultural trend does not erase public
unease over growing economic inequalities and insecurities. And it has not displaced
popular enthusiasm for the optimistic sentimentalism of *Forrest Gump* or for the ro-
mantic tragedy of *Titanic*. But it does underscore the culture industry's tendency to

channel mass entertainment in directions that distract public attention from class-based issues. It reminds us that the culture industry is more about distraction and pacification than it is about inspiration or instruction—especially where class inequalities are concerned. But sometimes even the culture industry can surprise us.

From the perspective of social-class analysis, one of the more interesting sci-fi movies dates not from the early 2000s, but from the late 1980s. *They Live!* is a 1988 John Carpenter film that explicitly links extraterrestrial aliens with social-class inequalities and superclass dominance. The movie portrays creepy reptilian aliens—who mingle with the general population in human form—as forming a secret alliance with an elite group of ruling-class humans. In league together, these two groups dominate the nonelite human population through hedonistic consumerism, subliminal mass media-based manipulation and thought control, and—as needed—coercive force.

The secrets of this dark alliance are revealed to the audience through an unemployed laborer who accidentally finds a special pair of sunglasses produced by a growing human resistance movement. Wearing these "shades," the actor walks the streets of an ordinary community—but he views the people and events from a totally new perspective. The audience sees through the eyes of the actor and his special sunglasses. We see aliens who have assumed human forms and the "real" text of disguised messages embedded in mass media content reinforcing alien and ruling-class control of nonelite humans: Submit, Conform, Consume, Inform, Reproduce, and above all, Do Not Question Authority!

They Live! was not a huge box-office success. It barely made a blip on the radar screen of popular culture and quickly dropped from sight. Its theme of an alliance between aliens and the human ruling class was not repeated in the story lines of popular science-fiction films or TV programs running through the early 2000s. Certainly the film could be critiqued on many grounds—including its tendency to reinforce a conspiratorial view of rich and powerful elites dominating nonelites. Despite its weaknesses, the unusual (by movie standards) class-based features of the film help call attention to how the routine and seemingly "invisible" practices of mainstream social institutions perpetuate privileged-class dominance and at the same time legitimate and reproduce social-class inequalities—especially at the level of everyday life. *They Live!* illustrates that the culture industry sometimes produces films with class themes woven into story lines that call attention to and help illuminate the nature of the process that is the central focus of this chapter—the pacification of everyday life.

PACIFICATION: THE HOMETOWN FILES

How do you prevent people who are fed up with the way they are being treated from doing anything about it? It's simple: deprive them of any sense that people have ever fought back.

—David Reynolds, *Democracy Unbound*, 1997

Pacification refers to the transformation of potentially disruptive social situations or restive populations into serenity: passive, peaceful, and calm—as dramatically illustrated in *They Live!* In the context of conflicting class interests, pacification also implies the manipulation and control of subordinate classes by dominant classes (but not necessarily in a conspiratorial sense). By linking pacification with everyday life, the title of this chapter is meant to call attention to how the class-related consciousness of average people going about their day-to-day routines is shaped.

In this chapter we consider how the power and advantages of the privileged class are exercised, reinforced, and legitimated at the level of everyday life. To bring this complex process down to earth, we focus first on two case studies, involving community development and drug education. These cases link national trends with local activities and illustrate how privileged-class-dominated organizations promote control of consciousness, ideological domination, and the legitimation of class inequalities among the nonprivileged class. These cases also illustrate how privileged-class power and ideas are embedded in taken-for-granted institutional routines and practices through which the pacification of everyday life occurs. Following the two cases, we consider the relationship between politics and pacification as illustrated by recent congressional debate over legislation popularly known as the "patient's bill of rights." We then shift our attention to the culture industry. Following up on themes introduced in the opening of this chapter, we consider how this industry—especially through television programming and the movies directed at hometown consumers—reinforces the pacification process.

Our first case study considers the story of how Japanese automobile assembly plants came to be located in several midwestern communities. It calls attention to the way the privileged class creates local crises, demands local sacrifices, legitimates these sacrifices, and benefits from "solutions" to the problems it created. It shows how citizens' awareness of local class-related issues is shaped by the interests of the privileged class (often called "community leaders") through local media in the form of local decisions on taxes, bond issues, and financial incentives for business. Average citizens are typically provided by community newspapers with only one way to think about important local decisions—unless they happen to belong to groups with alternative points of view (e.g., taxpayer associations, labor unions, environmental groups).

The second case focuses on the Drug Abuse Resistance Education (DARE) program as a form of symbolic politics. The DARE story calls attention to how, despite its record of ineffectiveness in preventing youth drug use, this school-based drug prevention program, which came out of the "War on Drugs," has expanded into a cultural and political force serving the economic, political, and ideological interests of the privileged class. We show how DARE grew and how it boosts the careers of its supporters, serves the public relations and political interests of corporate sponsors, and encourages unquestioned acceptance of privileged-class-controlled authority structures. In each instance our focus is on showing how

DARE contributes to public distraction from class issues and to the legitimation of class inequalities.

The two concluding sections of the chapter illustrate how the pacification and legitimation processes introduced in the case studies operate at the level of everyday life in the national political and cultural arenas. The "Politics and Pacification" section considers how the class-based structure of the U. S. Congress influences its deliberations and actions on health care issues in ways that reinforce privileged class interests while *appearing* to address working-class concerns. In the "Culture Industry and Pacification" section, we focus on the electronic media dimension of the culture industry—especially television and the movies—to illustrate how this industry helps distract attention away from class issues and legitimate the new class society. We document the massive size, scope, and largely class-free content of the electronic media arm of the culture industry to show how it effectively dominates public consciousness and discourages critical thought and reflection. Using this informational and conceptual framework, we illustrate how the routine operation of the industry marginalizes class issues, distracts public attention from class inequalities, and generally contributes to the pacification of everyday life.

GROW OR DIE: THE PRIVILEGED-CLASS
THREAT TO SMALL-TOWN AMERICA

> A move by a major corporation can have a devastating impact on a local growth coalition. . . . The net result is often a "race to the bottom" as [rival] cities offer tax breaks, less environmental regulation, and other benefits to corporations in order to tempt them to relocate.
>
> —G. William Domhoff, *Who Rules America?* 2002

As we have seen, the privileged class has been very successful in keeping the largest shares of income and wealth for itself. We have also seen that this outcome does not come easy—or cheap. It requires the constant care and feeding of the shadow political and information industries by the superclass. Moreover, shaping and delivering politics and policies favorable to privileged-class interests does not stop at the national level. It continues in states, cities, and towns throughout the United States.

We have to recall that the privileged class consists of some 20 million families, and they do not all live in New York, Washington, or Los Angeles. Although members of the superclass are more likely to live in exclusive urban gated enclaves, the more numerous credentialed class of highly paid professionals is scattered across the country in small communities with names not usually associated with wealth and power. Consider, for example, obscure small towns like Marysville, Ohio; Smyrna, Tennessee; Lafayette, Indiana; Normal, Illinois; Flat Rock, Michigan; and Georgetown, Kentucky. With populations ranging from 6,500 to 85,000, these small towns shared the experience in the 1980s of becoming the "hometown" of a large Japanese automobile assembly plant. Each city and state was the "winner" in a multistate competition to attract foreign investment. The story behind these winners reveals how the privileged class in America creates crises and then benefits from solutions to the problems they created.

Picture a small town with about 20,000 to 30,000 people. The city has a couple of large companies employing about a thousand workers each, a dozen mid-size firms each with two hundred or so employees, and hundreds of small retail and service businesses in the downtown area and on the outer edges of town. One day, out of the blue, one of the large companies announces that it plans to shut down and move to another location. The company "spin" is often that the plant is rather old, and, based on a cost-benefit analysis, it would cost too much to upgrade its production line and improve other parts of its support system.

The mayor of the city immediately begins talks with corporate executives about what it would take to make them reconsider. The union representing the workers starts to talk with management about a new contract with wage concessions, productivity-linked benefits, and greater flexibility concerning plant work rules. The threat of eliminating a thousand jobs in a small community sends ripples of anxiety throughout the community. The loss of one thousand workers each earning, on average, $25,000 annually would take a lot of buying power out of the community. And the loss of payroll taxes and property taxes on plant and equipment would significantly reduce the city's revenue. The plant and its employees also have traditionally made sizable annual contributions to the United Way and to local churches, to say nothing of volunteer work performed by workers and their families in a variety of community organizations.

Before the city can begin to digest this unanticipated crisis, the local business community starts to pressure the mayor and the city and county councils to spend more money on community development activities. Maybe they need to hire a development professional and print some special brochures outlining the attractive qualities the town has for new corporations. Of course, all this will cost money, at a time when revenue is declining. To make matters worse, some of the other businesses start to remind the city and county about their own increased costs of doing business. Several would like to expand and employ more people but question the wisdom of such a move at this time. Perhaps, they suggest, a waiver of taxes on new expansion might be helpful. The city has given tax abatements before, but doing so now would mean fewer dollars for schools, fire and police protection, city services, and, of course, the new push for a professional community development office.

Some of what is described in this story about a hypothetical small town sounds a bit like extortion, blackmail, and bribery—although these activities are not called by those terms in political and business circles. And it is not just a hypothetical story. This story line reflects the basic outline of what has happened—and is still happening—in hundreds of small communities across the United States over the past thirty years.

From the mid-1970s through the late 1990s, millions of high-wage jobs in the manufacturing industries were lost as a result of waves of plant closings in the auto, steel, rubber, electronics, and textile industries. As we saw in chapter 3, thousands of U.S. plants closed down and moved their operations to lower-wage foreign production centers. The waves of plant closings and resulting high levels of unemployment had devastating effects on many states and communities faced with the sudden loss of revenue from payroll taxes and corporate property taxes. These losses were magnified by increased demands for public services to assist the unemployed as well as development expenditures aimed at trying to strengthen local economies. The intersection of structural change in the U.S. economy, plant closings, and increased unemployment resulted in heavy pressure on national and state governments to cut spending. As the federal government tried to save money by cutting assistance programs to states, state and local problems were compounded even further.

Rust Belt states like Michigan, Illinois, and Ohio were hard hit by plant closings involving major corporations and were drawn into "regional wars" of competition for new businesses.[2] And how do communities attract new industries? The short answer is by providing attractive "incentives." In 1991 the fifty states gave $16 billion to businesses to relocate plants in their states. By the early 2000s, such expenditures were estimated at $26.4 billion annually.[3] Sometimes the money would lure a corporation to close a plant in one state and move to another state—as in the case of Mack Truck, which moved its production plant from Pennsylvania to Winnsboro, South Carolina, in the late 1980s.[4] And sometimes the money was used to attract foreign corporations to come to the United States.

State "incentive packages" for large foreign industrial firms typically highlight a powerful "language hook": FREE! (translation: taxpayer subsidized). The list of freebies often begins with land and also usually includes site preparation (roads, water, sewer lines), worker training, and property tax waivers—with the total incentive package value often reaching $200 million or more. In 1985 the state of Kentucky gave Toyota $12.5 million for land, $20 million to prepare the land for construction, $47 million for road improvements, $65 million for worker training, and $5.2 million to meet the special educational needs of Japanese managers' children. These breaks were all part of the incentive package to attract the firm to Kentucky. When the cost of bond interest payments is added to the "up-front" incentives, the total cost to Kentucky taxpayers reaches $350 million.[5] And the beat goes on. When Toyota decided to expand its production to include more light trucks, Indiana landed the new truck plant in 1996 by providing an incentive package of $75 million.[6]

Other nations have also gotten in on the incentive package action. In the 1990s two German firms, BMW and Mercedes, announced plans to open assembly plants in the United States. When the dust from the state bidding wars settled, South Carolina landed the BMW plant (opened in 1994 in Spartanburg) and Alabama was awarded the Mercedes plant (opened in 1997 in Vance). South Carolina taxpayers kicked in $150 million in direct and indirect subsidies to BMW, and Alabama taxpayers provided Mercedes with a $250 million incentive package.[7]

Of course, the purpose of the incentives is to attract a company that would bring new jobs to the state and stimulate fading local economies. But the cost in incentives represents an increasingly high price tag for economic growth. In the 1980s the incentive packages amounted to $50,000 for each job in the Japanese transplants and continued to climb in the 1990s to $79,000 per direct job at the BMW plant and then to a staggering "sticker-shock" level of $167,000 per direct job at the Mercedes plant.[8] These price tags are typically covered by increased state taxes—most often levied on nonprivileged-class members—in the form of more sales, property, and income taxes.

The Privileged Class Comes Calling: Pacification in the Heartland

Narrowing our focus to just the decade of the 1980s, we find the states of Michigan, Tennessee, Ohio, Illinois, Kentucky, and Indiana chipping in a total of more than one billion "incentive package" dollars to land Japanese auto assembly plants. Honda built a plant in Ohio; Nissan located in Tennessee; Mazda went to Michigan; Mitsubishi set up shop in Illinois; Toyota chose Kentucky; and Indiana got Subaru-Isuzu. For the one thousand to two thousand workers who would get jobs in the new plants, the money for the incentives would be seen as well spent. And it would certainly be seen as a good idea by the business community that benefits from growth—especially the banks, lawyers, and realtors who would facilitate the new growth-related business transactions. But most residents in the cities and counties where the plants were located (probably 90 percent) would not join in the benefits. Instead, they got to pay higher taxes to cover the multimillion-dollar incentive packages. They also "won" increased traffic congestion, higher housing costs (for rental units and new homes), and more municipal spending to cover school costs for children who would accompany their parents to the jobs created by the "growth boom."

Obviously there are economic benefits associated with growth, but benefits for whom? The costs are real, both in terms of dollars in taxes and in the more intangible "quality of life" changes that occur when a town grows quickly. But perhaps more important is the fact that nobody asked people in the towns whether or not they thought it was a "good deal" to spend more than $50,000 of taxpayers' money for each new job that would be created. No one asked local citizens if they would prefer to spend the tax money in different ways, such as helping local small businesses expand in the city or providing new educational and recreational facilities for existing families. There were no public referendums on the question of growth or of growth at what cost. The deals were made between the managers of incoming corporations and state and local members of the privileged class (political, business, and professional leaders), and the deals were then sold to the people in the affected communities.

The privileged class typically develops economic projects that it wants and that will serve its interests and then presents the projects to the nonprivileged class as if they will serve the general good. This happens all the time at the national level. It is often so transparent that virtually anyone can recognize how privileged-class interests drive such deals and also generate a "common-good" justification incorporated into the media "spin" on stories about these deals.

A high-profile case in point was the 1997 "balanced-budget agreement" negotiated by President Clinton and Republican congressional leaders. As part of the deal, both sides agreed to changes in federal tax laws that would reduce the tax on capital gains. This meant that investors would pay lower taxes on the "paper-profit" gains they make when stocks, bonds, commercial real estate, and other investments go up in value compared with what they paid for them. The cut in the capital gains tax primarily benefited members of the privileged class, who are the principal owners of most investments affected by the tax changes. But the justification presented by politicians who supported the tax cut, and the one reported almost without critical examination in the media, was that people who get to keep more of their capital gains will invest or spend the money in ways that stimulate the economy. And when the economy grows, there is a need for more workers to produce the goods and services being purchased by the new dollars available to the privileged from the capital gains tax cut.[9] In short, the capital gains deal was justified by a recycled version of "trickle-down" economic theory—a familiar fairy tale left over from the Reagan era. For average Americans, it was "deja vu all over again," but the privileged-class-controlled media treated the deal like a great creative leap forward for the good of all mankind.[10]

A similar story line is used at the local level. The taxpayer-provided incentives for the industry transplants are presented as spending packages that will benefit all residents of the communities. That is the "spin" at the heart of the transplant stories, and it is used to justify the millions of dollars in incentives given to foreign corporations. This story is told locally by the electronic and print media. Local newspapers are especially important in telling this story because they are institutions with long-standing reputations of journalistic objectivity and civic responsibility. Although local newspapers are known to have political biases (to be conservative or liberal, to support Republicans or Democrats), they are often seen as having broad community interests in mind when reporting on issues such as new community-financed construction of schools, libraries, roads, and recreational facilities. These kinds of projects spend public money raised through taxes, and when newspapers examine the pros and cons of public projects, their stories are framed in such a way that the newspaper is presented as seeking outcomes consistent with the community's best interests.

But we must recall that newspapers are, first and foremost, businesses. They are expected to make profits for their owners and stockholders, just like any other business. Some money may be made by expanding circulation, but the sale of advertising space is the engine that drives newspaper profits. Thus, newspapers in the transplant cities have a vested (but typically hidden and unacknowledged) interest in growth, which they share with bankers, realtors, attorneys, construction firms, and the Chamber of Commerce. So when newspapers in the cities competing for transplants tell the story about incentives and transplant benefits for communities, it is a story spun by card-carrying members of the privileged class.

Local Spin: All the News That's Fit to Print?

We examined newspaper stories written in conjunction with the process of locating Japanese transplant firms in three midwestern communities by three different hometown newspapers—one in each community where the transplants would be located. The period of coverage for each newspaper was thirteen months, beginning with the first newspaper story that mentioned the possibility of a Japanese auto plant moving to the city or state. The purpose of the analysis was to see how local newspapers dealt with the complex task of assessing the potential costs and benefits of competing for and having a new, large manufacturing firm come to their community. Each of these projects had the potential of producing opposition from a variety of community groups such as environmentalists, organized labor, and concerned taxpayers, who might have viewed the plant as imposing unreasonable tax increases to cover the costs of the incentives and services to the plant and their employees and families. Given the potential for public controversy and community conflict, we were interested in how the local newspapers presented the story and shaped community thinking on this issue. Because local newspapers are dominated by privileged-class interests, we wondered if the content of news stories about the coming of the transplants might objectively reflect community tensions and divisions related to this story, or, on the contrary, would be more of the same of what we often saw at the national level: corporate and privileged-class propaganda masquerading as news. That is, would local news accounts reflect a pro-growth spin aimed at soothing potentially disruptive local fears and concerns and defusing potential opposition? In short, we wanted to see if local newspaper coverage of the transplant story might represent an example of the pacification of everyday life—cooling out the locals while protecting the interests of the privileged class.

The three newspapers and time periods analyzed were the *Lafayette Journal and Courier* (Indiana, December 1986–September 1987), the *Murfreesboro Daily News Journal* (Tennessee, September 1980–September 1981), and the *Lexington Herald Leader* (Kentucky, December 1985–December 1986). In all, 490 transplant stories were written by the three newspapers in the time periods we examined. All stories were read and analyzed to answer the question, Who speaks on the transplants? We ask this question because newspapers make choices about the people and organizations that will be asked to express their opinions about the transplants, incentive money, and what it will mean for the community.

In the 490 stories from the three newspapers, 1,769 persons were named and their points of view about the transplants presented. A single event could be written up under the headline, "Auto Plant Dredges Up Ill Will" or "Auto Plant: A Plan Comes Together." These stories would incorporate the views of different persons to create an impression of divided opinion, conflict, harmony, and agreement, or a mixture of costs and benefits to the community. The journalists creating these stories often knew in advance the point of view of the people they interviewed for the story. When they interviewed the city's mayor or a representative of a community development agency, they could expect a favorable attitude toward the transplant, because these community leaders had been involved in developing the package of incentives to attract the new business. On the other hand, when interviewing a labor official they were likely to get a more critical view of the transplants, because of the strong antiunion bias of the Japanese.

When we examined who the 1,769 persons were who spoke through the news stories, we found that 36 percent were from business and industry (corporate executives, representatives of the Chamber of Commerce, attorneys) and 50 percent were local or state elected officials (mayors, state representatives, congressional representatives) or officials of state or local government agencies. Only 13 percent of the 1,769 interviewees were outside of the business-political sectors, such as labor leaders, educators, and social welfare services. This meant that almost nine out of ten opinions on the transplants expressed in news stories came from persons who would be expected to be pro-business, pro-growth, or to have pro-transplant interests. In effect, representatives from the privileged class did most of the talking in the newspaper stories. This outcome hardly reflects an effort by newspapers to provide balanced information and analysis to their readers.

When we examined the content of the 490 stories on the transplants and the amount of space devoted to positive or negative accounts about the transplants, the evidence indicated a clear preference for a positive "spin" on the transplant projects. The 490 stories made up a total of 19,331 square inches of space in the three newspapers, and only 17 percent of this space was devoted to stories that could be called "negative" or "critical" of some aspect of the transplant projects. The negative stories were largely clustered around four issues. These included (with sample headlines):

1. the high cost of the financial incentives ("Two Join Suit over Toyota Plant Financing")
2. environmental issues ("Toyota Jobs vs. Environmental Impact Debates")
3. citizens' loss of property ("Path to Auto Plants Cuts across Yards")
4. legal challenges to the state's right to give land to a private corporation ("State's Plan to Give Toyota Land May Be Unconstitutional")

The other 83 percent of the total square inches written about the transplants we characterized as variations of three positive themes. These were (also with sample headlines):

1. blatantly positive ("Auto Plant Gets Community Support")
2. passively positive ("Nissan Decision Opens New Era for County")
3. human-interest positive—descriptive stories of the positive effects of the plants for people directly involved in the projects ("Japanese Family Enjoys New Life in Greater Lafayette")

The overall impact of the newspaper coverage of the transplants was unequivocally positive and supportive of the total idea of providing financial incentives to a private corporation. Rather than being objective, neutral providers of balanced information and opinion, the newspapers acted as cheerleaders for economic growth and the transplant projects. Their coverage and biased story lines concerning the transplants were consistent with the profit-oriented, privileged-class interests of the newspaper owners, publishers, and editors.

The overwhelming representation of pro-growth views in local newspapers illustrates the domination of state and local credentialed-class members in framing economic issues with class-based implications and consequences for local communities. In the case of the transplants, the actions of local credentialed-class members had the effect of reinforcing and reproducing at the local level the interests of the national superclass of corporate and political elites. As the transplant cases illustrate, many communities are caught in a corporate squeeze that starts with multinational corporations closing plants and shipping jobs overseas. Faced with fiscal crises brought on by unemployment and declining tax revenues, these communities are forced to compete with other towns and states facing the same squeeze for the "privilege" of handing out more than $200 million in taxpayer money in "incentives" to lure corporations to bring new jobs to their towns.

The New Catch-22: Private Profits, Public Costs

The all-too-familiar scenario of plant closings followed by competition for the transplants illustrates how a new kind of "Catch-22" is built into the double-diamond class structure. The essence of the catch is this: profits are private, costs are public, and both are largely underwritten by the working class. Because the profits from doing business are private, they flow largely intact back to members of the privileged class—with few dollars skimmed off by ever lower corporate and capital gains tax rates. But the social costs of plant closings, such as increased unemployment, higher welfare costs, more family violence, increased crime, and higher rates of mental and physical illness, as well as the tax-funded costs of financial incentives to attract new businesses, are public. And both kinds of costs are primarily paid for by members of the working class. The routine business practices of corporations controlled by the privileged class create social problems while generating private profits, but the working class pays—in one form or another—most of the costs associated with the corporate system. Most obviously this includes higher taxes for the working class, but it also includes absorbing most of the

Copyright © Lloyd Dangle. Reprinted with permission.

human costs associated with corporate-generated social problems: the pain of unemployment, the confusion of disrupted lives, and the frustration of diminished community services. The double diamond leads to a double deal: a winning hand for the privileged class, a raw deal for the working class.

This new Catch-22 of the new class society provides useful insights into the contradiction between class benefits and class burdens where corporate practices and public policies are concerned. But as we have seen, newspaper accounts of the coming of the transplants do not acknowledge the existence of such a catch. The win-win vocabulary that dominated much of the local reporting on the transplants helped obscure the existence of conflicting class interests and coaxed local populations into accepting the deals as being in the best interests of all parties concerned. In a sense, the newspapers were an important part of a community-wide, street-level pacification project aimed at winning the "hearts and minds" of the working class in favor of the transplant projects. No conspiracy was necessary. The routine operation of privileged-class-dominated institutions, as the newspaper coverage illustrates, was sufficient to ensure local pacification. This outcome was evidenced by the absence of significant or sustained local opposition to the transplants in the chosen communities.

DARE: BRINGING THE DRUG WAR HOME

What DARE has excelled in is promotion for their program.

—Lloyd Johnson, University of Michigan, *Youth Today,* April 2001

Symbolic politics describes the political strategy of choosing and using safe political cal issues and public policies on the part of political elites to advance their interests and those of their privileged-class supporters. This approach is safe in that it involves a focus on issues and programs that appear to address social problems— but in ways that do not threaten privileged-class interests and also have wide appeal among the working class. Symbolic politics are typically associated with at least three levels of symbolic action. First, to promote their own political interests, public office holders often "construct threats" to public well-being. This means political leaders—with the help of superclass sponsors and media attention—select social conditions widely perceived as undesirable and transform them, by policy pronouncements and the mobilization of political resources, into high-priority public "threats" requiring public policy intervention. Second, public-office holders can invoke a "scapegoating strategy" whereby social conditions publicly viewed as problematic or "constructed threats" are explicitly or implicitly linked with unpopular or stigmatized groups, which encourages public perceptions of these groups as the source of the problems or threats. Third, political leaders can propose programmatic interventions that they claim will ameliorate problematic conditions or "constructed threats" and also reassure voters that public institutions are responding appropriately to these dangers.[11]

DARE as Symbolic Politics

While the early 2000s provide many examples of symbolic politics (e.g., policies concerning immigration, gay rights, abortion, Internet pornography), we view the so-called War on Drugs as a classic example of these concepts in action. Growing out of a high-profile, politically constructed "threat" (the "drug plague"), the drug war has resulted in numerous multifaceted government programs with national and local class-related implications and consequences—such as the DARE (Drug Abuse Resistance Education) program. DARE represents a safe, programmatic example of symbolic action claiming to address a threat to the public well-being at the community level. Organized and promoted by members of the privileged class, DARE is a powerful but unadvertised and unnoticed part of the everyday cultural routines that reinforce privileged-class interests, help legitimate class inequalities, and thus contribute to the pacification of everyday life.

On the surface, it appears that DARE has everything to do with preventing youth drug use and nothing to do with social-class inequalities. But as in the film *They Live!* peering beneath surface images can open our eyes to a very different reality. What we find beneath DARE's surface is a drug education program of questionable effectiveness that over the past decade has become an institutionalized cultural and political force serving the economic, political, and ideological interests of the privileged class. Although there is no evidence that DARE was deployed as part of a conscious, privileged-class conspiracy to distract public attention from growing class inequalities and related social problems, there is evidence that the DARE program does help produce this and other outcomes that serve privileged-class interests.

What Is DARE?: A Really Brief History and Overview

DARE is a standardized, copyrighted, school-based drug prevention program that began in Los Angeles in 1983–84 as a joint effort involving the Los Angeles Police Department (LAPD) and the Los Angeles Unified School District. Following former president Reagan's launching of his antidrug "crusade" in 1986, DARE expanded rapidly. This expansion was facilitated by DARE America, a nonprofit, tax-exempt corporation formed in 1987 to promote and coordinate DARE. By the early 2000s, DARE was taught in 75 percent of U.S. school districts and in fifty-five countries worldwide.[12]

The DARE core curriculum is designed for fifth- and sixth-graders and consists of seventeen weekly lessons, each approximately forty-five to sixty minutes in length. All DARE classes are taught by uniformed police officers who have undergone eighty hours of specialized training. Classroom activities are scheduled during the regular school day, and the program encourages student involvement in exercises such as "question and answer [sessions], group discussions, and role-play[ing] activities." DARE's "major goal . . . is to prevent substance abuse among school children"; it strives to accomplish this goal by teaching students "the skills for recognizing and resisting social pressures to experiment with tobacco, alcohol, and drugs." The DARE lessons focus on enhancing students' self-esteem, decision-making, coping, assertiveness, and communication skills and "teaching positive alternatives to substance use."[13] In addition to classroom instruction, the program can involve other activities such as the use of selected high school students as DARE "role models" in the elementary grades, informal officer-student contacts, teacher orientation, parental education, and community presentations.

Although DARE's basic goals and curriculum structure have remained relatively constant since its inception, over the years DARE has also changed in several ways. During 1992–94, revisions were made in the core curriculum. Materials were added to place "greater emphasis on the prevention of tobacco use . . . normative beliefs, and on violence prevention and conflict resolution." The presentation format was also changed to make the program more interactive. The revised curriculum was phased in during 1993–94 and was fully implemented after January 1, 1995.[14] Despite the makeover, researchers continued to find that DARE had no long-term effects on drug-use rates among youth exposed to it.

Partly in response to research findings that DARE was ineffective in preventing drug use among youth, DARE America officers and critics met at a U.S. Department of Justice–sponsored meeting in 1998 to discuss ways of improving the program. Additional discussions in 1999 and 2000 involved drug education researchers, DARE administrators, U.S. government officials, and Robert Wood Johnson Foundation (RWJF) representatives (which often funds health-related projects). As a result of these developments, in 2001 DARE America received a $13.7 million RWJF grant to substantially revise the DARE curricula and to evaluate the effectiveness of the new program in reducing drug use among youth. The revised DARE program would reportedly focus more attention on students in the seventh and ninth grades, and plans were developed to evaluate it in 80 high schools and 176 middle schools.[15] It was also reported that DARE America administrators planned to implement the new program worldwide in late 2002.[16]

It is unclear if the forthcoming changes in the DARE curricula will alter the program's basic objectives or assumptions concerning drug use among youth. In the past, DARE has embraced the same "zero tolerance/no use/drug-free" orientations that have guided national drug policies. DARE has also implicitly embraced "free will" and "user accountability" principles. This means that all forms of drug use have been viewed as driven by free-willed, individual choices, and users are held strictly accountable for their choices. The DARE program appears to have assumed that it provides students with the information and life-skills resources necessary to guide them into making the "right" choices. If after DARE exposure individuals still choose to use illicit drugs, such choices are viewed as free-willed criminal acts to be condemned and punished by the legitimate application of all available legal sanctions. This logic has held despite the acknowledgment by DARE's curriculum materials that structural factors such as mass media advertising (like the $6 billion tobacco and alcohol ad budgets) contribute to public demand for drugs.

In the past, DARE has made no distinctions between legal and illegal drugs and has advocated total abstinence as the only acceptable approach to all types and categories of drugs. The program also made no real distinction between experimental and frequent drug use. An unstated assumption of DARE appears to have been that experimental use of any drug (including legal—for adults—"gateway drugs" such as tobacco) constitutes "drug abuse" or will inevitably lead to problematic drug use. More realistic approaches to drug use, such as "responsible use" or "harm reduction"—as used in drug education programs in other nations such as the Netherlands—have been excluded from the DARE program. It remains to be seen if the "new and improved" DARE program will reflect any alterations in the basic objectives and assumptions that have guided DARE in the past.

DARE: Hometown Drug Prevention or Pacification?

In 1987, DARE came to Kokomo, Indiana, a midwestern auto factory town with a population of 45,000. In fact, Kokomo was the first Indiana city to adopt the DARE program. The process that led DARE to Kokomo began in 1986, when the mayor and chief of police learned about the program while attending a conference—about the same time the War on Drugs transformed the "drug problem" into a hot-button political issue. By late 1986, local political, educational, and law enforcement leaders had decided to implement DARE in the Kokomo schools.

We were invited by school and police officials to assess DARE's effectiveness in Kokomo. Our efforts began in 1987, and by the mid-1990s we had completed several short- and long-term studies of the program. Our most comprehensive project was a seven-year study of DARE's long-term effectiveness in preventing or reducing adolescent drug use. Based on a series of comparisons between the 214 high school seniors exposed to the DARE program in the fifth grade and the 331 high school seniors not exposed to DARE, we found no significant differences in the self-reported drug-use rates of the two groups. Moreover, when we talked to seniors from both groups in focus group interviews, we heard the students saying in their own words what our questionnaire data revealed: DARE was not effective in keeping kids off drugs. Our findings paralleled those of other researchers across the United States and seemed to present us with a contradiction: Although DARE was ineffective as a drug-prevention program, throughout the nation it continued growing rapidly in size, scope, and popularity. We had to wonder why.

When we consider DARE's role in the class-based pacification of everyday life, we can see that our research findings and DARE's resilience and popularity are not at all contradictory. Viewed as a political and cultural force serving privileged-class interests, DARE's expansion and popularity make perfect sense. The following sections describe DARE's emergence as a political and cultural force and describe how the program serves the political, material, and ideological interests of the privileged class.

DARE: A Political and Cultural Force

National interest in the "drug problem" among the political leaders of both major parties crystallized in 1986 with President Reagan's televised "War on Drugs" address to the nation and the subsequent passage of the Anti-Drug Abuse Act of 1986. Once set in motion, the drug war remained a popular focus of political and media attention through the 1990s and continued as such in the twenty-first century.[17] It was also transformed into a complex and multifaceted political and organizational force.[18] The Anti-Drug Abuse Act of 1988 systematized the drug war under the Bush I, Clinton, and Bush II administrations into a "national drug control strategy" aimed at controlling both the supply of and demand for illicit drugs in the United States.[19] The latter dimension of this strategy included an emphasis on developing "demand reduction" programs of all types, including drug education. As the drug war generated more public support for antidrug programs, political interest in and federal funding for drug education programs—including DARE—increased substantially throughout the 1980s, 1990s, and early 2000s. Federal funding for youth-targeted antidrug education grew from $230 million in 1988 to $660 million in 1995 to more than $1 billion in 1997.[20] By 2001, the federal government was spending over $2 billion per year on drug-prevention education with state and local governments spending even more. "Estimates on total expenditures range as high as $5 billion annually."[21]

Increased federal funding for drug education combined with drug-war-driven popular support for such programs led to the emergence of direct and indirect "DARE stakeholder" groups. For the most part, these groups consist of privileged-class individuals and organizations with material, political, and ideological interests in DARE's continuation and expansion.[22] Direct stakeholders are those groups and individuals with explicit links to DARE in terms of direct involvement in supporting and implementing the program—such as DARE America officials and program administrators in schools and law enforcement agencies. By contrast, indirect stakeholders are those groups and individuals only loosely coupled and only indirectly involved with DARE—such as political leaders and corporate sponsors who publicly support or contribute to the program. Both groups benefit from the reflected approval, legitimacy, and widespread public support associated with a program linking a popular cause with traditional authority structures, symbolized by the involvement of schools and law enforcement agencies.

At the national level, DARE emerged as a bipartisan favorite of political leaders in the late 1980s, and strong political support for the program continued into the early 2000s. Powerful members of Congress allied with former president Bush ensured passage of a 1990 amendment to the 1986 Drug-Free Schools and Communities Act (DFSCA) mandating federal funding for DARE. As amended, the DFSCA requires that 10 percent of DFSCA "governor's funds" (30 percent of federal funds made available each fiscal year to states for drug prevention programs) be used to fund programs "such as Project Drug Abuse Resistance Education."[23] DARE was the only drug education curriculum specifically targeted for federal funding by the DFSCA, which gave the program a tremendous boost.

Over the years, national political support for DARE has included various high-profile events including several joint congressional-presidential "DARE Day" proclamations applauding DARE's contributions to the national campaign against drugs.[24] Perhaps even more important recently has been the willingness of Congress to continue funding DARE in the face of mounting studies showing the program to be ineffective. The 1998 federal budget included language that gave Safe and Drug Free Schools grantees, such as DARE, two years to show their programs were effective in order to continue to receive funding. In that same year the Department of Justice appropriations "included some unusual language about DARE crafted by the House Appropriations subcommittee on Commerce, Justice, and Judiciary." The committee essentially directed the DARE America administrators to revise the program to make it more effective. And although DARE was not on the list of "exemplary" or "promising" drug education programs issued by the Department of Education in January 2001, it appears that DARE's RWJF grant and the curricula revision efforts now under way will ensure continued federal funding of DARE for at least the next several years.[25]

These highly visible federal actions represent the tip of an iceberg of links between national, state, and local politicians and the DARE program. Federal resolutions and funding support, along with similar actions at the state and local levels, link political leaders to the program as indirect DARE stakeholders, who boost their own popularity by being identified with the popular program. At the same time, their political support further legitimates the DARE program and enhances its funding prospects, thereby benefiting individuals and organizations directly involved with its operation and expansion.

DARE's direct and indirect stakeholders have collaborated to embed the program within a complex organizational support structure that helps ensure a continuing flow of resources to sustain its survival and growth. An important feature of this structure is DARE America, a nonprofit corporation organized in 1987 as a 501(c)(3) tax-exempt organization to promote and coordinate the DARE program. Information from recent DARE America federal tax returns provides a sense of the organization's financial stake in the drug war, and it illustrates the financial interests of DARE America's top credentialed-class officers in the continuation of the program.

In 1998 (the most recent year available), DARE America reported total revenues of $243 million. This figure included "$215 million worth of labor by volunteers and police officers (whose departments pay for their DARE work)," $15 million from corporations, and $11 million from other sources, including $2.2 million in government grants. Since much federal funding is indirectly channeled to DARE programs through the states in the form of grants, the total amount of federal dollars supporting the program is much higher than the $2.2 million. "Media estimates in recent years have hovered around $650 million for the entire effort, although DARE has said that figure is probably high."[26] Also, according to information reported in DARE's 1996 federal tax return, the organization's president, Glenn Levant (former LAPD assistant police chief), was paid $232,948. Two deputy directors earned $90,000 each, and three specialized directors earned $80,000, $64,000, and $63,750, respectively.[27]

DARE America has been a potent organizational advocate for the DARE program. It has aggressively worked to expand the program by pursuing goals that include "the adoption of DARE in all states and communities . . . support [for] a national DARE instructor training program . . . [and] coordinat[ing] national fundraising for DARE."[28] The organization has also successfully recruited numerous corporate, political, and entertainment elites, such as TV personality Arsenio Hall and singer Ted Nugent, to serve as DARE spokespersons and fund-raisers.[29] The DARE America Board of Directors consists of well-known national business, political, law enforcement, educational, sports, and entertainment figures. For example, in 1996, the thirty-five-person board included Thea Adelson, Rosey Grier, Alice King, Helen Mars, Diane Disney Miller, and Willie L. Williams.[30]

Another dimension of DARE's organizational support structure consists of a network of ties linking DARE programs to various federal, state, and local government agencies. The Bureau of Justice Assistance (BJA, an agency within the U.S. Department of Justice) serves as a major organizational link tying DARE programs to the federal government. This connection dates to 1986, when former LAPD chief Daryl Gates succeeded in arranging a BJA grant of $140,000 to the LAPD "to share [the] unique DARE Program with other communities throughout the United States."[31] Bureau of Justice Assistance involvement with DARE expanded in the late 1980s and led to agency funding of five regional DARE training centers. The BJA also appoints five of the fifteen members who make up the DARE Training Center Policy Advisory Board, which is responsible for overseeing the training of DARE officers. Other federal agencies with ties to DARE include the National Institute of Justice and the National Institute on Drug Abuse, which have funded DARE evaluation research. The U.S. Department of Education also provides some program funding through the DFSCA, and the U.S. Department of Defense has adopted DARE for use in the schools it operates for dependents of U.S. military personnel. Government linkages also extend down to the state and local levels and involve law enforcement agencies, schools, and community groups.[32]

In addition to extensive public sector support, there are numerous links tying DARE to corporate sponsors at the national, state, and local levels. DARE America has been especially instrumental in recruiting national corporate sponsors. For example, in 1995 Kimberly-Clark contributed $401,505 to DARE America, and Citibank, First Interstate Bancorp, Packard Bell, Simon and Schuster, and Western Union each contributed $100,000 (or more). Other corporate contributors include Kentucky Fried Chicken, McDonald's, Toys "R" Us, Warner Brothers, and Zenith. Corporate support at the state and local levels involves hundreds of large and small firms contributing to the program.[33]

DARE: Stakeholder Interests and Pacification

Although direct and indirect DARE stakeholders have different types and levels of interest in the program, the preceding section suggests that both groups have shared and overlapping concerns in several areas including economic, political, and ideological interests. Among direct stakeholders, DARE benefits the material interests of credentialed-class members. This is the case because like many other programs devised to address social problems, DARE is largely administered, supported, and delivered by members of this class. The top DARE America officials represent one obvious example of how credentialed-class members benefit from public and private resources allocated to fund the program. Other examples are credentialed-class members who administer and coordinate DARE through the BJA-funded DARE regional training centers, the Department of Defense, and local school districts. Also, top credentialed-class administrators in all DARE-connected organizations benefit directly from DARE's popular public image. As one local DARE official confided to us, "DARE is a great PR program for the schools and the police." DARE even serves as a career booster for lower-level law enforcement officers. A police colonel from Washington state testified during congressional hearings that "a lot of DARE officers are being promoted across our state. . . . [We are] continually looking for officers to train other officers . . . because they end up getting promoted."[34]

Indirect DARE stakeholder groups, such as national political leaders and superclass corporate sponsors, have a number of class-based political and ideological interests that are served by DARE's emphasis on individuals, drugs, and authority. These features of DARE help promote privileged-class interests, legitimate class inequalities, and reinforce the pacification of everyday life in several specific ways.

First, DARE promotes the acceptance of individual-level explanations for and solutions to social problems. Second, it encourages a continuing public focus on drug-war issues while distracting public attention from social-class inequalities as sources of social problems. Third, DARE reinforces uncritical acceptance of and deference to privileged-class-controlled authority and power structures including, at the community level, the schools, the police, and corporate program supporters. Fourth, it assists in the "demonization of drugs" and helps rally public unity against a common enemy. Fifth, DARE helps legitimate a punitive law enforcement, antidrug model and harsh sanctions that are used to control drug use as well as other forms of deviance viewed as stemming from free-willed choices or "bad attitudes."

DARE's ideologically loaded lessons promote privileged-class interests because the indoctrination of working-class students, parents, and citizens to these ideas distract people from class inequalities, defuse class tensions, constrain the development of class consciousness, and reinforce the legitimacy of privileged-class-dominated social control agencies. The latter feature is especially relevant to DARE's social effects because as one arm of the larger war on drugs, the program helps legitimate that war. And as Ken Silverstein and Alexander Cockburn point out, "Domestically, the 'drug war' has always been used as a pretext for social control. . . . Essentially, the drug war is a war on the poor and dangerous classes, here and elsewhere. How many governments are going to give up on that?"[35]

Although it is a national program, DARE acts as a franchiselike operation bringing the symbolic politics, actions, distractions, and other features of the drug war relevant to privileged-class interests down to the community level. Even most "DARE-less" communities have some variation of drug education in their schools, not to mention high-profile state and local drug laws in place, so the political and cultural dimensions of the drug war have become permanent fixtures in every community. And although DARE has been subject to some criticism on the basis of its costs and effectiveness and as promoting a kind of "Big Brother is watching" mentality, only a few communities have dropped DARE. But for every community that drops out, more sign on with the program. The list now includes New York City plus three hundred new cities added in 2000.[36]

As noted earlier, we do not view DARE's pacifying effects as the result of some dark superclass conspiracy. Even so, there is little doubt that DARE's individual-level prevention focus and symbolic messages concerning the drug threat, respect for authority, and condemnation of deviance are consistent with privileged-class interests. They are also consistent with the privileged-class-supported, Rush Limbaugh-like conservative ideology regarding the causes of and "cures" for a wide range of social ills in America today. According to a number of conservative political leaders, pundits, and radio talk-show hosts, most current problematic social conditions—from poverty to joblessness to drug use—are essentially "attitude problems."[37] The routine "cure" prescribed by this group consists of a short "attitude adjustment" course (sometimes combined with a kick in the pants). DARE represents a neat fit with the conservative model of the causation of social problems. DARE's match with privileged-class interests and conservative ideology illustrates how a program seemingly far removed from the issue of class inequalities is actually not so far removed after all. By helping to keep public attention focused on winning the drug war—and not on a truly explosive issue like starting a "class war"—in hometowns across the United States, DARE contributes to the pacification of everyday life.

POLITICS AND PACIFICATION

The Democrats say one thing ("Save the planet") and then do another, quietly and behind the scenes with all the bastards who make this world a dirtier place. The Republicans just come right out and give the bastards a corner office in the West Wing.

—Michael Moore, *In These Times*, June 11, 2001

The American political system was described many years ago by sociologist William Gamson as one characterized by "stable nonrepresentation." This felicitous phrase is simultaneously a testament to the strength of the system and a condemnation of its fundamental flaw. The system is stable because almost all of its elected and appointed political officials and operatives share the same guiding premises about its economic institutions ("free-market capitalism") and its political institutions ("representative democracy"), and because they are all members of the same privileged class. Moreover, their privileged-class standing is not affected by whether they win or lose in their various political struggles over legislation or elections. The "outs" simply move on to work as consultants to corporations or lobbyists for other governments, as part of the "revolving door" government that takes care of both winners and losers. The nonrepresentative nature of the system is connected to the fact that political officials pay careful attention to the interests of powerful and influential corporations, who were not elected by anyone. The backstage influence of the unelected is part of the normal operation of the system, hidden from public view by the high-profile front-stage activities that appear to be serving the interests of most Americans.

To illustrate how this system works, let us consider the high-profile legislation on the so-called patients' bill of rights, debated in Congress in the summer of 2001, that would give people the right to sue their HMOs if they are denied services recommended by their physicians. The first intended message of this debate, as it is presented in the media, is that both political parties are concerned about protecting the rights of patients to obtain quality medical care from private managed care companies. The second intended message is that the parties differ on the best way to protect those rights, and that those differences should encourage voters to support Democrat or Republican candidates in future elections. The intensity of the debate leaves the average observer with the impression that the federal government is also the provider of health insurance, when in fact most Americans buy either directly through insurance companies, or jointly with their employers. Ironically, government-provided Medicare and Medicaid recipients, who are perhaps in greatest need of protection against denial of medical services, are excluded from the right-to-sue provisions of the patients' bill of rights.

What Congress is actually talking about is extending the right to sue by people who already have private health insurance. The legislation has nothing to do with the 42 million Americans who have no health insurance because they cannot afford to pay the premiums or because their employers do not provide health insurance. The Democrats tell us they want to make it easier for (insured) Americans to sue managed care companies when they believe that they have been denied care, and to obtain jury-awarded settlements when they win their lawsuits. The Republicans tell us that they want to enable lawsuits as a last resort and would limit settlement to half a million dollars.

This "patients' bill of rights" is about politics, not the needs of the American people, insured or uninsured. Both political parties were trying to score points with voters and protect the fat-cat contributors to their political coffers—trial lawyers for the Democrats and insurance companies for the Republicans.

After all the heat of this debate is over, and the politicians finish "huffing and puffing" about all they have done for the American people, it is the people who will pay the cost. Uninsured Americans will still be uninsured, and if the patients' bill of rights is adopted (whether the Demopub or Republicrat version) the most likely result will be an increase in the share of medical costs paid by workers, and a decline in the number of Americans who have private health insurance. Congress will not do a thing about insurance companies that raise premiums, or employers that drop health insurance or raise the cost of workers' contributions. That would be tampering with private enterprise!

Understanding the American political system of "stable nonrepresentation" requires greater attention to what is not discussed in Congress. In the case of the "patients' bill of rights," we should ask why privileged-class members of Congress will not discuss the creation of a single-payer system of universal health for all Americans, like a Medicare for all. The reason is that the Democrats' lawyer-contributors and the Republicans' insurance company-contributors, as well as most other members of the privileged class, would be opposed to a system of universal health care that would be of greatest benefit to the working class. In the case of providing prescription drug coverage for seniors (a hot topic in the 2000 presidential campaign), the two parties debate the question of how much money to provide seniors and how to pay the cost. What they don't discuss is why the cost of prescription drugs is so high in the first place, given that more than half the money spent on research to create top-selling prescription drugs comes from federal grants from the National Institutes of Health. The taxpayers get it in the neck twice: first when they pay the scientists and universities (members of the privileged class) to create the drugs, and second when the drug companies make them pay top dollar for the drugs over the counter.[38]

The alternative class-power network, described in chapter 2 and revisited in chapter 8, has a very difficult time trying to get some of the above-noted questions on the public agenda for discussion. The major mass media outlets apparently believe that stories concerning divergent class interests involving health care budgets are not sufficiently important or interesting to their readers and viewers. Without a broad-based social movement and a visible national leader to put a spotlight on these issues, the political system will continue to churn out reform after reform that will amount to little more than rearranging the deck chairs on the Titanic.

THE CULTURE INDUSTRY AND PACIFICATION

> The global media system plays [an] explicit role in generating a passive, depoliticized populace that prefers personal consumption to social understanding and activity, a mass more likely to take orders than to make waves.
>
> —Robert W. McChesney, *Rich Media, Poor Democracy,* 1999

The auto transplants, and DARE, and health care cases illustrate how projects set in motion by and for the privileged class can dominate public awareness about economic and social issues and confine policy debates to a narrow range of options endorsed by privileged-class-controlled organizations. The effects of issue framing, agenda setting, and policy making by the privileged class in these cases include deflecting public attention from class inequalities while promoting acceptance of the status quo. These outcomes are also reinforced by the culture industry, which, as the opening of this chapter suggests, disseminates electronic entertainment products that typically have the effect of distracting public attention from class issues rather than calling attention to them.

The culture industry was briefly mentioned in chapter 5 as part of our introduction to one of its major subdivisions—the information industry. As we noted then, the culture industry encompasses far more than the dissemination of information. It is a complex enterprise composed of large multimedia firms that are increasingly interlocked with even larger industrial and service corporations, advertising agencies, and nominally nonprofit groups (such as the Public Broadcasting Service). The heart of this industry consists of large firms that produce and disseminate a wide range of entertainment, information, and advertising products through television, radio, recorded music, movies, books, newspapers, magazines, and the Internet. This industry is too large and complex to be considered in detail here—but that is not our purpose. Rather, our goal here is to present a brief overview of the scope and content of the electronic-media segment of the industry—especially television and films—to provide a sense of how it contributes to the pacification of everyday life.

The massive scope and everyday reach of the electronic media are evident in the huge distribution networks that disseminate culture-industry products such as TV and radio programming, sporting events, movies, videotapes, audio tapes and CDs, video games, and Internet website materials to thousands of communities and millions of homes and consumers. In the early 2000s, the "wiring of America" provided electronic links between various media firms and seven thousand hometown movie theaters (with 36,000 screens), the 98 percent of households with TVs (85 percent of TV households had VCRs), and 67 percent of TV households with TV cable or satellite service.[39] In 2001, several firms were providing online services to 82 percent of the 66 million U.S. households with personal computers (out of 107 million total U.S. households in 2001). Moreover, in 2001, the typical family spent $595 on communications services (Internet, wireless phones, pagers), which was more than triple the $175 spent in 1995.[40] One result of this extensive penetration of communities and homes by media networks has been that Americans are spending more and more time as passive consumers of electronic media products.

Time spent by individuals on noncommercial activities such as informal socializing or critical reflection and writing produces no benefits for culture-industry profits. Only time devoted to the consumption of products generated by culture-industry firms (TV programming, movies, software, commercial websites, videogames, etc.) juices market shares, sales, and profits. The industry has an interest in channeling more and more consumer time into its commercial products.

And it is succeeding. In 1988, the average American spent 1,751 hours consuming various electronic media products (TV was no. 1, at 1,490 hours, followed by recorded music, home videos, and theater movies), with a total of 3,310 hours devoted to all forms of media consumption (including newspapers, magazines, and books).[41] By 2003, total American media consumption is projected to increase to 3,587 hours per person, with 3,261 of those hours devoted to all forms of electronic media. This includes TV (still no. 1, 1,610 hours), followed by radio (192 hours), recorded music (319 hours), online Internet access (192 hours), home video games (67 hours), home videos (66 hours), and theater movies (15 hours).[42] This means Americans—for a variety of reasons—are devoting more and more discretionary time to media consumption, and especially to electronic media consumption.

The Colonization of Consciousness

To the extent that the awareness and limited free time of nonprivileged-class members are dominated by ideas, programs, activities, and events created by the superclass-owned and credentialed-class-managed culture industry, it means that their consciousness is, in a sense, captured—or colonized—by an outside force. This privileged-class-directed "media force" is driven by class interests that are quite different from those of nonprivileged consumers. For us, then, the colonization of consciousness refers to the ongoing invasion by the culture industry—especially through electronic mass media entertainment and advertising content—of ever larger shares of peoples' time, interests, and imagination. This process is driven by many techniques, including the electronic media firms' constant tracking, creating, and linking of popular cultural trends with media content.[43] It also involves the media's use of compelling imagery (in TV programming, movies, advertising, video games, web search-engine graphics) and its constant barrage of cleverly produced ads emphasizing the prestige and novelty features of mass, niche, and (upscale and downscale) consumer products.[44] Although this process results in a number of consequences, including increases in culture-industry profits, from our perspective the reduction in time available to individuals for all other activities outside of media consumption is among the most important. Of particular importance in this regard is how the colonization of consciousness contributes to the marginalization of class-related issues and interests in individuals' everyday thoughts and discussions as more time and "thought space" are devoted to media products.

Although we may live in a "24–7" world (twenty four hours a day, seven days a week), each of us can claim only about sixteen waking hours a day—or about 5,800 hours per year. If we subtract the time devoted to work (about 2,000 hours per year), family and personal obligations, and the 3,261 hours spent on electronic media consumption, we find very little time remains each year for nonprivileged-class members to read, think, or talk about public issues—including class inequalities. Moreover, given the taboo nature of class in America and the interests of superclass culture-industry owners, we would not expect to find class-based themes, issues, or interests routinely included in the movie and television content "inserted" in consumers' minds as the colonization of consciousness process unfolds.

Movies: Class-Free Content?

Class-related issues and themes are rarely presented in movies, as revealed by a content analysis we conducted of large samples of dramas (699), science-fiction films (750), and documentaries (263) drawn from the *1995 Movie/Video Guide.* In this study we found that only about 5 percent of the films in each category (thirty-five dramas, forty science-fiction films, fifteen documentaries) included story lines or themes that could be interpreted as critiques of elite-class power or as providing sympathetic portrayals of working-class individuals or organizations (e.g., labor unions).[45] Our short list of thirty-five critical dramas that addressed working-class interests and grievances or critiqued elite-class-dominated institutions included "classics" (from the 1940s on) as well as recent films.

In many respects the findings from our study parallel what movie historian Steven J. Ross found in his review of class themes in the movies. With a focus primarily upon silent films, Ross found that a substantial number of films sympathetic to working-class interests were produced in the United States prior to World War I. However, he points out, the advent of talkies led to the demise of such movies. In a brief discussion of the contemporary period, he notes that class-critical films with "labor-capital" themes have virtually disappeared from the American cinema—reinforcing what we found in our study.[46]

The *Grapes of Wrath* (1940), starring Henry Fonda, was a high-profile, classic film from our list that we viewed as important because it helped establish and legitimate a kind of critical, sympathetic movie treatment of class underdogs in the contemporary era. Bringing the Steinbeck novel of the same title to the screen exposed millions of Americans who had not read the book to its heartbreaking portrayal of the Joad family. Tracing the family's experiences as it migrated from the Dust Bowl during the Great Depression, the movie provides a compelling and sympathetic account of how the Joads and people from similar working-class families were brutalized by the American economic and class structures of the 1930s.

Very few high-profile dramas from the recent past have followed in the class-critique, sympathy-for-the-class-underdog film tradition and also featured well-known Hollywood stars. Five recent titles illustrate as well as virtually exhaust the list of recent films with both qualities.

1. *Norma Rae:* This 1979 film starring Sally Field compassionately portrays the title character's transformation from passive worker to union activist in a southern textile plant.
2. *Reds:* Warren Beatty and Diane Keaton star in this 1981 film that presents a

sympathetic account of American radical journalist Jack Reed's career, including his reporting on the Russian Revolution.

3. *Remains of the Day:* This 1993 film starring Anthony Hopkins powerfully depicts how the British class system of the 1930s stunted and distorted servants, masters, and human relationships.

4. *Bulworth:* Warren Beatty produced and starred in this 1998 "political farce" that, although flawed in many respects, includes scenes that voice powerful critiques of current American class and race inequities.

5. *Erin Brockovich:* Julia Roberts starred in and won an academy award for best actress in director Steven Soderbergh's adaptation of a true story (2000). Brockovich, a poor single mother, lands a job as a legal aide for a small law firm. In a toxic tort case she wins the trust of working-class families, documents their health problems linked to environmental toxins, and gathers evidence on toxic chemical releases by a large utility firm. In the end, the plaintiffs receive a limited measure of justice in a legal battle pitting working-class interests against those of the privileged class. The film provides a sympathetic view of workers' interests and portrays Brockovich as a kind of working-class hero—albeit one who becomes a millionaire in the end.

A smaller number of less well known recent dramas have also followed in the class-critique, sympathy-for-the-class-underdog tradition, but with much less star power. Two examples include *Matewan* and *The Killing Floor*. The former is a 1987 film directed by John Sayles that sympathetically depicts the union side of the West Virginia "coal wars" of the 1920s. The latter title is a 1993 film that presents a historically informed account of how Chicago meatpacking firms in the early 1900s resisted unionization by exploiting racial and ethnic divisions and tensions among the workers.

Although more titles could be added to the examples listed, the entire group of class-critique dramas identified in our study makes for a very short list. Few movies in the genres we reviewed provided critiques of elite-class power or sympathetic accounts of the economic, political, social, and personal grievances of the working class. Dramas reflecting the class-critique tradition as well as science-fiction films including overt critiques of ruling-class power (such as *They Live!*) are infrequently made, narrowly promoted, and seldom viewed by mass audiences. Moreover, they are notable exceptions to the non-class-based, escapist themes and action story lines routinely depicted in most mainstream American films. In fact, we are likely to see even more escapist action movies in the future as global film-going audiences' tastes become more American-like and as the foreign market for U.S. films continues to grow—to the point where U.S. films often generate more revenue overseas than in the domestic market.[47] Moreover, it has been well documented that "violent action fare is the genre that crosses borders most easily and makes the most commercial sense.[48]

As action films and those in other escapist genres become ever more common, class themes are likely to appear even less often in movies than in the past. The film formula of the future seems to be more action equals more distraction. Speaking to the effects of movie content on culture and class consciousness, film historian Ross maintains that "American filmmakers have helped create a culture whose citizens either no longer view class as an important part of their lives or define the middle class so broadly that class no longer seems to matter."[49]

TV and ABC

So what's on TV? For openers, try advertising. A typical thirty-minute TV-network program includes at least seven minutes of advertising. Local programs have even more. American television networks now broadcast six thousand commercials per week, up 50 percent since 1983.[50] Moreover, advertisers have increased their spending on all forms of television advertising (broadcast and cable) from $29 billion in 1990 to $51 billion in 1999.[51] This nearly doubling of TV ad expenditures reflects not only the increase in broadcast time devoted to advertising but also advertisers' faith in the power of TV to sell more stuff.

What kinds of programming do the ads support? Or what else besides ads do we find on TV? The really short answer is ABC: Anything but Class. If we set aside TV news as being part of the information industry (chapter 5), we find TV advertising supports a wide range of programming that for the most part ignores class issues and trends heavily toward distraction. A tour of *TV Guide*'s daytime and evening listings for the 2001 fall season reveals recurring programming patterns, particularly for network TV. Mornings are devoted mainly to newsmagazine and talk shows. Afternoons bring soap operas and more talk shows. Evening programming is more diverse and includes paranormal *X-Files*-like series (e.g., *Buffy the Vampire Slayer*—moved from WB to UPN, *Dark Angel*, and *Freakylinks* [FOX]), "reality-based" crime shows (e.g., *Cops* [FOX]), "reality" programs (e.g., *The Amazing Race* [CBS]), sporting events, comedy series staples (e.g., *Frasier* [NBC]), Gen-X nighttime soap-like shows (e.g., *Friends* [NBC], *Pasadena* [FOX]), dramas (e.g., *West Wing* [NBC]), more newsmagazine shows, and more talk shows. Cable, satellite, PBS, syndicated programs, and movies add diversity to daily programming, but studies of TV content reveal a striking absence of programs that depict the lives or concerns of working-class Americans or that deal with class-based inequalities in ways that might promote critical reflection among viewers.

One study of four decades of TV entertainment (from 1946 to 1990) found that of 262 domestic situation comedies, only 11 percent featured blue-collar, clerical, or service workers as heads of households. By contrast, the vast majority of the series, 70.4 percent, portrayed "middle-class" families with incomes and lifestyles that were more affluent than those of most middle-income American families. In fact, in 44.5 percent of the comedy series studied, the head of the household was a professional.[52]

Another study of thirteen TV situation comedies from the 1990s found the issue of social mobility across class lines is sometimes used as a source of comic tension and moral instruction. On the rare occasions when characters in the series studied aspired to or encountered upward mobility, the outcomes reminded viewers that "achieving inter-class mobility is rare, and the rewards of any substantial social movement will likely be bittersweet." The study concluded that TV situation comedies send mixed and paradoxical messages where social mobility is concerned. On one hand, these programs typically reinforce the myth of America as a land of opportunity where hard work and persistence pay off. On the other hand, on the rare occasions when characters actually encounter social mobility, their experiences tend to be portrayed as disruptive and often undesirable.[53] The net result is the subtle reinforcement of existing class divisions, structures, and locations as normal, natural, and preferred—to the disruptive effects of social mobility.

During the 2001–2002 television season, only two prime-time network series (FOX) occasionally portrayed working-class characters, families, issues, or problems in sympathetic or positive terms. Both were animated comedies and both aired on Sunday nights: *The Simpsons* (created by cartoonist Matt Groening), and *King of the Hill* (devised by Beavis and Butthead creators Mike Judge and Greg Daniels—formerly of *The Simpsons*).[54] In contrast to the occasional sympathetic treatment of working-class concerns by these series, TV newsmagazines such as *60 Minutes, 60 Minutes II, Dateline,* and *20/20* almost never report on working-class issues or concerns—except to "expose" an occasional "bad apple" business guilty of abusing working-class consumers. The syndicated tabloid-style TV "newsmagazines" totally avoid working-class issues. The mission of these programs (e.g., *Access Hollywood, Entertainment Tonight, Inside Edition,* and *Extra!*) is to traffic in high-energy celebrity profiles and gossip about the stars—especially reports concerning sex, drugs, deviance, and opulent lifestyles. Such titillating stories appear designed to deliberately appeal to nonelite viewers by providing vicarious thrills and voyeuristic gratification. They seem to say, Maybe you can't afford it or do it or would never do it yourself, but you can watch glamorous stars own it and do it—Right here! Right now!

The themes of titillation and distraction are also staples of most daytime TV talk shows. The 2001–2002 season saw the following sampling of shows and topics: Jerry Springer on prostitution and transsexuality, Jenny Jones on people who think they're celebrity look-alikes and their friends who disagree, and Montel Williams on tough love for troubled teens.[55] Other, more "prestigious," daytime TV talk shows have adopted formats that frequently mix viewer concerns involving personal or family problems with celebrity interviews (usually TV, movie, or sports stars or the suddenly famous or infamous promoting their movies, books, or careers). A typical month of Oprah Winfrey (August 2001) included shows on how to heal a broken heart, how to age gracefully, messy home makeovers, and what kids really need.[56] Meanwhile, Rosie O'Donnell hosted an "Everybody Loves Raymond" hour including Ray Romano. Other shows included interviews with Tim Robbins, Amy Brenneman, Britney Spears, and Sarah Ferguson.[57] The pattern of TV talk show hosts interviewing celebrities also extends to nighttime TV talk shows—with talk show hosts often interviewing the celebrity hosts of other TV talk shows![58]

ABC and the Oprahfication of the Mind

In situation comedies, talk shows, newsmagazines, and other programming formats, ABC—Anything but Class—is what's on TV. "ABC" is an important factor contributing to the colonization of consciousness; and the "ABC" focus and content of most TV programming—especially talk shows and newsmagazines—contribute to another phenomena involved in the pacification process: the Oprahfication of the mind. This term refers to how the electronic media—especially television "infotainment" (superficial information presented in "information" or "news" formats but whose primary value is as entertainment)—contributes to the demise of critical thinking about current and past social, cultural, and political events and issues.

High-profile media stars (e.g., Oprah Winfrey) projected through powerful TV media platforms help establish a pop-culture conceptual framework that blends current events, celebrity, and social issues into short, seamless entertainment packages. As a result, working-class TV viewers are encouraged to concentrate on only the most dramatic or high-profile current events or the most glamorous or sensationalized personalities and issues. The September 11, 2001 terrorist attacks on the United States temporarily interrupted talk show attention to infotainment themes and story lines. For awhile, hosts shifted their focus to heroic, tragic, and touching human stories associated with the attacks. Themes of horror, heroism, the face of evil (Osama bin Laden), and the quest for justice (or vengeance), were also woven into many talk show programs—for a time.

The transient dose of reality-based content that talk show hosts delivered to TV viewers in the autumn of 2001 may well have promoted national unity and even informed viewers. But in at least one respect it was similar to the more typical content of such programs: It deflected critical attention from any consideration of class inequality issues. In fact, the wave of talk show programming devoted to the attacks and the aftermath, like the typical fare delivered to these programs, was soon depleted of novel and compelling story lines, shock value, and ratings utility. As the September 11 story lines faded, waiting in the wings were new angles on familiar infotainment topics: breathless reports on pop-culture icons (movie stars, Michael Jordan, Bill Gates, the Kennedys—our royal family, and Jackie O, Marilyn Monroe, or Lady Di—forever), breaking stories on British royalty, new serial killers, the latest movie trailers, hot new fashions, and the long-running Wall Street drama. Through such programming, American TV viewers are coached to conceptualize and think about most news and talk show topics at the most immediate, superficial, and individualized level of detail. Any sense of how social-class inequalities or wider historical or cultural contexts may be linked to current themes is lost to Oprahfication.

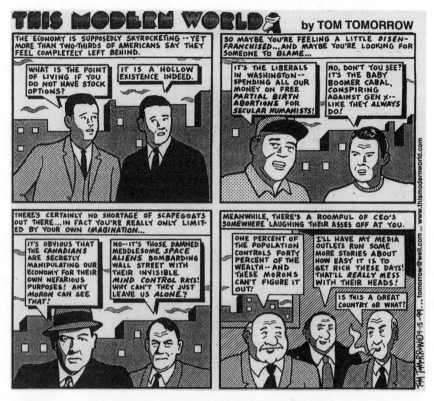

American TV viewers are also encouraged to think about social, political, and economic issues through a superficial popular cultural lens that brings into dazzling focus "SGP" (shock, glamour, and the perverse) topics while blurring the field of vision where serious issues like working-class interests, grievances, or inequalities are concerned. As our review of TV talk show content suggests, the SGP focus of these shows (and many TV newsmagazines) may sometimes be interrupted by serious events—like the September 11 attacks—but even those are channeled through and mined by the insatiable media appetite for novelty. More routinely, the SGP programming profile ranges across predictable topics with shock and novelty value such as twisted sexual practices, abuse, body piercing, satanic rituals, tattoos, racial strife, and gender bending, along with the latest medical, movie, fashion, hairstyle, and other pop-culture trends.

The SGP focus is reinforced by increasingly common "socialization to novelty" experiences among TV viewers and consumers of popular culture generally. Mass media advertising often encourages consumers to devalue stability and continuity in products, packaging, entertainment, and lifestyle trends. Much of the content and many of the commercials in the electronic media reinforce the idea that routine is boring and changes—especially fast-paced novel changes—are good. Viewers are encouraged to think that "been there, done that" experiences equal boring repetition and are to be avoided. Consumers are encouraged to pursue and prefer novel products, experiences, and activities because novelty is presented as the source of fulfillment and fun.[59] Preferences for novel products, images, and activities are driven by the mass media's recognition that speed, action, color, change, and novelty juice viewer interests as well as TV and merchandise-marketing profits.

SGP programming and accelerated socialization to novelty expereiences are key factors leading to the Oprahfication of the mind. Oprahfication is a kind of truncated and compartmentalized cognitive style that not only erodes peoples' capacity for critical thinking but also diminishes even the legitimacy of critical thought. Oprahfication reduces (1) the likelihood that people will think of social issues or current events in terms of class analysis (too boring!); (2) peoples' ability to think in such terms (they have too little practice or experience); and (3) peoples' ability to understand or appreciate a class-based analysis of problematic social conditions if it is presented to them (too confusing!). Colonization and Oprahfication are major elements in the pacification of everyday life through the culture industry.

PACIFICATION AND PROVOCATION: TWO SIDES OF EVERYDAY LIFE

Question: If men in power and younger women were all it took to fascinate media, wouldn't we see wall-to-wall coverage of the sweatshop industry?

—"Soundbites," *EXTRA!* September–October 2001

As we have shown, the pacification of everyday life is a pervasive, complex, and powerful process. The illustrations presented in this chapter suggest that it promotes privileged-class interests through a variety of institutionalized routines and practices that for the most part legitimate and reproduce existing class inequalities and at the same time distract working-class members from these issues. However, it is also important to recognize that pacification does not proceed as an unopposed process, nor is it a seamless, one-dimensional force without internal contradictions.

As we noted in chapter 2, alternative class-power networks essentially operate in ways that call attention to, challenge, and contest the pacification process. The provocation efforts of these networks typically operate outside the organizations and structures that dominate the pacification process—but not always. Some branches or substructures of mainstream organizations that drive the pacification process sometimes deliberately include people and ideas from the alternative power networks. For example, public (and on occasion commercial) radio and television broadcasters sometimes include members of the alternative power network on some programs, typically as a means of legitimating their image as providers of "open forums" for discussions of public issues. Whatever the motives of gatekeepers controlling privileged-class-dominated organizations, whenever labor leaders, consumer advocates, or elite-power critics (e.g., AFL-CIO President John Sweeney, Ralph Nader, Gore Vidal) testify at congressional hearings or appear on TV or radio talk shows and newsmagazines, their messages challenging the pacification process are heard and seen by the working class.

Perhaps more important than token mainstream appearances by members of the alternative power network are the effects that occur as a result of internal contradictions arising from institutional imperatives associated with the routine practices of the organizations that drive the pacification process. At the same time that privileged-class-dominated organizations produce pacifying "products" such as the policies, programs, and entertainment described in this chapter, some features of some products also result in paradoxical effects. That is, some products produced in the routine course of the pacification process may highlight or even challenge class inequalities rather than legitimate them. When this occurs, these features of the pacification process may actually contribute to contradictory outcomes—such as increased class tensions and resentment or even heightened class consciousness.

One illustration of how class provocation and pacification can occur at the same time as a result of routine organizational imperatives and practices can be found in the political arena. As we have seen, candidates for office are largely financed by superclass-provided funds. However, candidates must also appeal to working-class voters. The latter reality can sometimes lead even superclass-funded candidates to take public positions on some issues that appear to reinforce working-class interests at the expense of the privileged class. For example, in chapter 2 we noted Al Gore's flirtation with populist rhetoric in the 2000 presidential election. And as we saw, Green Party candidate Ralph Nader went even further. His speeches denouncing corporate greed, NAFTA, the loss of American jobs, and the growth of economic insecurity among American workers led to accusations by mainstream media pundits that he was promoting "class war." The emergence of populist and even progressive messages in national political campaigns illustrate that the routine operation of a political system that generally reinforces the pacification process has the potential to generate contradictory messages—at least temporarily and episodically.

The electronic media also illustrate how institutional imperatives can produce contradictions in pacification products. Although most media products help to distract public attention from class issues and serve to legitimate class inequalities, mass media firms are fundamentally money-making businesses. Because TV and movie corporations are driven by profit-maximization concerns, they must deliver a constant stream of novel products to attract viewer attention so as to increase sales and profits. In the absence of explicit censorship and in the routine course of producing creative and marketable products, some movies and TV programs are produced that include content critical of class inequalities or privileged-class interests.

As noted earlier, some movies include story lines that portray working-class characters and interests in sympathetic terms. Thus, studios which typically traffic in pacification products do sometimes produce provocative films that call attention to class inequalities. When viewers identify with or share the concerns of the working-class characters portrayed in such films, the stories can resonate powerfully with audiences, help legitimate class grievances, generate large box-office revenues, and even produce critical acclaim. We know movie studios are not in the business of delivering progressive political messages or stimulating class consciousness. However, if movies with such story lines generate strong profits, then they will be delivered—at least from time to time. Recent movies with big-name stars illustrating this reality include *A Civil Action* (1999, starring John Travolta) and *Erin Brockovich* (2000, starring Julia Roberts). Both films were based on factual events concerning the negative health effects of toxic waste products released into the environment by seemingly callous corporations. And while both films are flawed and send mixed class messages (e.g., rogue firms are to blame, not the larger economic system; workers need elite-class advocates; class justice is finally rendered, etc.), they do legitimate working-class grievances and expose class-based injustices.

It's clear that few movies focus on class inequalities. However, the ones that do often encourage viewers to empathize with exploited working-class underdogs or to be outraged by exposés of elite-class arrogance and power abuses. These themes are included in classic hits like *Grapes of Wrath,* and they are woven into more recent films critical of elites, such as the two just noted and others such as *Bulworth, They Live!* and *The Big One.*[60] Although we would agree that most movies are much more likely to have pacifying rather than provocative effects where class issues are concerned, the routine operation of the pacification process still produces some films that inject critical class-based themes and ideas into popular culture.

Like the movies, television is also most closely associated with pacifying effects. However, even routine television products can produce paradoxical outcomes. For example, some TV newsmagazines and talk show forums have reported on topics that do not necessarily serve privileged-class interests, such as soaring CEO pay levels, plant closings, sweatshops, campaign finance reform, capital gains tax cuts for the rich, and ethical lapses among professionals (e.g., physicians and attorneys). Such programming has the potential to fuel class tensions and resentment, increase public cynicism about mainstream institutions (especially corporations and government), and even increase class consciousness. Growing awareness of class-divergent interests is, in part, revealed by recent public opinion polls. In a 1995 Gallup poll, 58 percent of Americans said major corporations have "too much power," and 76 percent agreed "the government is pretty much run by a few big interests looking out for themselves."[61] More recently, in a 1999 Gallup Poll, 67 percent of Americans reported having only some or very little confidence in major corporations.[62]

Sometimes regularly scheduled TV programs include content that heightens some forms of class consciousness among nonprivileged-class viewers. During the 1994 (NBC) and 1995 (FOX) summer seasons, Michael Moore's *TV Nation* garnered high ratings and won awards while often featuring entertaining reports that were critical of class inequalities and privileged-class interests.[63] The series was canceled, but Moore was able to return in 1999 and 2000 with a new show, *The Awful Truth*. Shown on the Bravo cable channel, the program was similar in style and content to *TV Nation*, but it too disappeared after two seasons.

The fate of Moore's programs reveals the difficulties faced by producers and writers of progressive media products in getting and keeping their work on the air. As might be expected, progressive television programming critical of elite-class interests and sympathetic to working-class concerns is infrequently produced and aired. Even so, such TV programming does on occasion get written, produced, and aired even in a medium where pacification products, themes, and story lines dominate the airwaves.

The parade of examples illustrating the flip side of the pacification process could go on and on, but the point is that there is another side. The everyday, routine functioning of mainstream social institutions like local newspapers, drug education programs, movies, and TV programs does, for the most part, serve to distract nonprivileged groups from class issues, defuse class tensions, and legitimate class inequalities. But at the same time, the daily routines and practices of mainstream institutions occasionally can and do subvert the pacification process. On those infrequent occasions, chunks from the dark mass of conflicting interests from beneath the waterline of the class iceberg churn to the surface and produce transient episodes of inconvenience, embarrassment, and even anger for privileged-class members. Fortunately for them, such "provocations" are usually isolated and quickly smoothed over by the powerful and predictable privileged-class-controlled institutional routines that on a daily basis reinforce the pacification of everyday life. However, in the next chapter we consider the prospects for the emergence of sustained challenges to the deeply ingrained legitimating and distracting features of the pacification process and to the powerfully institutionalized and ever widening class inequalities of the early twenty-first century.

NOTES

1. Frank Newport and Maura Strausberg, "Americans' Belief in Psychic and Paranormal Phenomena Is Up over Last Decade," Gallup Poll Analyses, on the Internet at http://www.gallup.com/poll/releases/pr010608.asp (visited September 29, 2001). Also see

Robbie Fraser, "Do You Believe?" *TV Guide,* October 14–20, 2001, 56; and Greg Barnett, "Curiously, More of Us Believe in the Paranormal," *Indianapolis Star,* June 19, 2001, A1, A8.

2. Robert Goodman, *The Last Entrepreneurs: America's Regional Wars for Jobs and Dollars* (New York: Simon and Schuster, 1979).

3. Barry Yeoman, "Subsidies at Sea," *Mother Jones,* May–June 2001, 72–77, 112–13; quote, 74.

4. Joseph Weber and Blanca Riemer, "These Days Mack Trucks Isn't Built like Mack Trucks," *Business Week,* July 30, 1990, 40–41.

5. For details on incentive packages, see Peter Eisenger, *The Rise of the Entrepreneurial State* (Madison: University of Wisconsin Press, 1988); Milward H. Brinton and Heide H. Newman, "State Incentive Packages and the Industrial Location Decision," *Economic Development Quarterly* 3 (1989): 203–22; Robert Perrucci, *Japanese Auto Transplants in the Heartland* (New York: Aldine de Gruyter, 1994).

6. James Derk, "We Got It, Toyota!" *Indiana Business Magazine,* January 1996, 9–13.

7. "The New Transplants," *UAW Research Bulletin,* January–February 1995, 10–11.

8. Ibid.

9. Michelle Cottle, "The Real Class War," *Washington Monthly,* July–August 1997, 12–16.

10. "Unbalanced!: Bipartisan Budget Bill Boosts Billionaires," *Labor Party Press,* November 1997, 4–5.

11. Katherine Beckett, "Setting the Public Agenda: 'Street Crime' and Drug Use in American Politics," *Social Problems* 3 (1994), 425–47. Also see *Ageism on the Agenda,* special issue, *EXTRA!* March–April 1997.

12. Kate Zernike, "Antidrug Program Says It Will Adopt a New Strategy," *New York Times,* February 15, 2001, A1–23; Earl Wysong and David Wright, "A Decade of DARE: Efficacy, Politics, and Drug Education," *Sociological Focus* 28 (1995): 283–311.

13. U.S. Department of Justice, Bureau of Justice Assistance. *Program Brief: An Introduction to DARE—Drug Abuse Resistance Education,* 2d ed. (Washington, D.C.: Bureau of Justice Assistance, 1991), 3–7.

14. Wysong and Wright, "A Decade of DARE," 285.

15. Patrick Boyle, "A DAREing Rescue," *Youth Today,* April 2001, 1, 16–19.

16. Jason Cohn, "Drug Education: The Triumph of Bad Science," *Rolling Stone,* May 24, 2001, 41–42, 96.

17. For example, see Eric J. Jensen, Jurg Gerber, and Ginna M. Babcock, "The New War on Drugs: Grass Roots Movement or Political Construction?" *Journal of Drug Issues* 21 (1991): 651–67; James D. Orcutt, and J. Blake Turner, "Shocking Numbers and Graphic Accounts: Quantified Images of Drug Problems in the Print Media," *Social Problems* 40 (1993): 190–206; Mike Males, "Pot Boiler: Why Are Media Enlisting in the Government's Crusade against Marijuana?" *EXTRA!* July–August 1997, 20–21; Salim Muwakkil, "Just Vote No, the War on Drugs Loses at the Polls," *In These Times,* December 25, 2000, 25–26; Marc Cooper, "Plan Colombia," *Nation,* March 19, 2001, 11–18; John Nichols, "Drug Warrior Dissent," *Nation,* May 28, 2001, 8.

18. Earl Wysong, Richard Aniskiewicz, and David Wright, "Truth and DARE: Tracking Drug Education to Graduation and as Symbolic Politics," *Social Problems* 41 (1994): 448–72.

19. For example, see Office of National Drug Control Policy, *The National Drug Control Strategy* (Washington, D.C.: National Criminal Justice Reference Service, 1992), 9. Also

see Office of National Drug Control Policy, *National Drug Control Strategy: 2001 Annual Report,* (Washington, D. C. : U. S. Government Printing Office, 2001), 1–7.

20. Budget figures are from Office of National Drug Control Policy (ONDCP), *National Drug Control Strategy* (Washington, D.C.: National Criminal Justice Reference Service, 1992), 45; *National Drug Control Strategy* (1994), 79, and *National Drug Control Strategy* (1996), 61–62.

21. Cohn, "Drug Education: The Triumph of Bad Science," 41.

22. Wysong and Wright, "A Decade of DARE," 298.

23. U.S. Code Annotated, 20 U.S.C.A. sect. 3192, Amendment to Public Law 101–647, Cumulative Annual Pocket Part (St. Paul, Minn.: West Publishing, 1995), 337.

24. For examples see various issues of the Congressional Record that reference the DARE program from 1992 through 1996 (listed in the bibliography).

25. Boyle, "A DAREing Rescue," 17, 19.

26. Ibid., 18.

27. U.S. Department of the Treasury, "Return of Organization Exempt from Income Tax—Form 990, DARE AMERICA," 95–4242541 (Washington, D.C., 1996).

28. U.S. Department of Justice, *Program Brief,* 11.

29. Dennis Cauchon, "Studies Find Drug Program Not Effective," *USA Today,* October 11, 1993, 1–2.

30. U.S. Department of the Treasury, Form 990.

31. U.S. Congress, Senate Committee on Labor and Human Resources, Drug Abuse, Prevention, and Treatment, 100th Cong., 2d sess., 1988, 198.

32. See Everett M. Rogers, "Diffusion and Re-Invention of Project DARE," in *Organizational Aspects of Health Communication Campaigns: What Works?* ed. Thomas E. Backer and Everett M. Rogers (Newbury Park, Calif.: Sage, 1993), 139–62. Also see U.S. Congress, House Committee on Education and Labor, Subcommittee on Elementary, Secondary, and Vocational Education, *Oversight Hearing on Drug Abuse Education Programs,* 101st Cong., 1st sess., 1990, serial 101–129.

33. Information from various sources, including DARE America's 1995 Form 990 Income Tax Return. Also see Cauchon, "Studies Find Drug Program Not Effective"; and U.S. Congress, House Committee, *Oversight Hearing on Drug Abuse Education Programs.*

34. U.S. Congress, House Committee, *Oversight Hearing on Drug Abuse Education Programs,* 57.

35. Ken Silverstein and Alexander Cockburn, "Why the Drug War Works: It's A Money/Class Thing, of Course," *CounterPunch,* June 15–30, 1998, 4–5.

36. Boyle, "A DAREing Rescue," 16. Also see "Spokane Just Says No to DARE Program," *Kokomo Tribune,* October 6, 1996.

37. Frances Fox Piven, "Poorhouse Politics," *Progressive,* February 1995, 22–24.

38. Marcia Angell, "A Wrong Turn on Patients' Rights," *New York Times,* June 30, 2001, A25.

39. "2000 U. S. Economic Review: U. S. Theaters," Motion Picture Association of America, on the Internet at http://www.mpaa.org/useconomicreview/2000 Economic/slide.asp?ref=24. Also see U.S. Department of Commerce, Bureau of the Census, Statistical Abstract of the United States (Washington, D.C.: U.S. Government Printing Office, 2000), 567.

40. Rick Lyman, "A Partly Cloudy Forecast for Theater Owners," *New York Times,* March 12, 2001, C12; Tony Pugh, "Massive Immigration Steers Population Reapportionment," *Indianapolis Star,* December 29, 2000, A1, A21; Associated Press, "Americans Are Wired into New Bills," *Indianapolis Star,* July 7, 2001, A1.

41. U.S. Department of Commerce, Bureau of the Census, *Statistical Abstract of the United States* (Washington, D.C.: U.S. Government Printing Office, 1995), 572.

42. U.S. Department of Commerce, *Statistical Abstract of the United States* (2000), 566.

43. Tom Frank, "Let Them Eat Lifestyle," *Utne Reader,* November–December 1997, 43–47. Also see *The Merchants of Cool,* PBS *Frontline* TV Documentary, narrated by Douglas Rushkoff, 2001.

44. David Leonhardt, "Two-Tier Marketing," *Business Week,* March 17, 1997, 82–90.

45. Earl Wysong, "Class in the Movies," unpublished paper, 1996; Mick Martins and Mick Porter, *1995 Video Movie Guide* (New York: Ballantine Books, 1994).

46. Steven J. Ross, *Working-Class Hollywood: Silent Film and the Shaping of Class in America* (Princeton: Princeton University Press, 1998).

47. Robert W. McChesney, *Rich Media, Poor Democracy: Communication Politics in Dubious Times* (Chicago: University of Illinois Press, 1999), 109.

48. Ibid.

49. Ross, *Working-Class Hollywood,* 255.

50. Jerold M. Starr, *Air Wars: The Fight to Reclaim Public Broadcasting* (Boston: Beacon Press, 2000), 16.

51. U. S. Department of Commerce, *Statistical Abstract of the United States* (2000), 579.

52. Richard Butsch, "Class and Gender in Four Decades of Television Situation Comedy: Plus ça Change . . . ," *Critical Studies in Mass Communications* 9 (1992): 387–99.

53. Lewis Freeman, "Social Mobility in Television Comedies," *Critical Studies in Mass Communication* 9 (1992): 400–406; quote, 405.

54. "Returning Favorites," *TV Guide,* September 8, 2001, 4.

55. *TV Guide,* 2001, June 16–22, 145; August 4–10, 123; August 18–24, 93.

56. *The Oprah Show,* "Show Archive, August 2001," on the Internet at http://www.oprah.com/tows/pastshows/tows past 20108.jhtml (visited October 1, 2001).

57. *TV Guide,* 2001, September 10, 128; September 25, 140.

58. Sam Husseini, "Talking about Talk," *EXTRA!* May–June 1996, 20.

59. Ronald Dahl, "Burned Out and Bored," *Newsweek,* December 15, 1997, 18.

60. Jeremy Smith, "Intellectual Snobs versus Political Slobs," *Dollars and Sense,* May–June 1998, 38–39.

61. Michael Golay and Carl Rollyson, *Where America Stands, 1996* (New York: Wiley, 1996), 137, 173.

62. "Confidence in Institutions," Gallup Poll News Service, June 8–10, 2001, on the Internet at http://www.gallup.com/pol/indicators/indconfidence.asp (visited October 6, 2001).

63. Miranda Spencer, "TV Nation: A Show for 'The Rest of Us,'" *EXTRA!* November–December 1995, 24–25.

8

Class in the Twenty-first Century: Consolidation and Resistance

> Uninformed and misinformed; pauperized or over-worked; misled or betrayed
> by their leaders—financial, industrial, political and ecclesiastical, the people are
> suspicious, weary, and very, very busy, but they are, nonetheless, the first, last,
> and best appeal in all great human cases. . . . And, though each individual in the
> great crowd lacks some virtues, they all together have what no individual has, a
> combination of all the virtues.
>
> —Lincoln Steffens, *Upbuilders*, 1909

The stories of Forrest Gump and Jim Farley in chapter 1 of this volume focus attention on the intersection of social class and the American Dream. One shines as idealized fiction, the other illustrates the darkest side of reality, where privileged-class interests and power doom the dream to failure. There is no doubt which story is more popular. Grossing more than $679 million worldwide since its release in 1994,[1] *Forrest Gump* is the American Dream personified—its main character is the classic underdog achiever. But there's more. *Gump* also represents another important side of the American Dream: a commitment to the values of family, friends, community, and conscience.[2] The absence of those qualities in the hard-edged corporate boardrooms dominating the new class system of Jim Farley's world helped seal his fate. And Farley's economic free fall was not broken by a resilient social safety net. Despite popular enthusiasm for the sentimental Gump-like values of mutual compassion and shared sacrifices, these qualities are largely missing in action when it comes to providing meaningful assistance to the Jim Farleys of today's new working class. The chilling fact is that the downward mobility of Farley and millions like him actually serves the interests (at least in the short run) of those in the privileged class in the top diamond of the new class society.

Since chapter 1, we have tracked the contours and exposed the dark side of the new class society. From Jim Farley to the global economy and back to the culture industry, we have documented the corrosive effects of this system on the American Dream. And we have also tracked the processes by which privileged-class advantages have been ever more tightly institutionalized and legitimated. Our travels have taken us from Forrest Gump to the taboo land of class analysis, where the strange but vaguely familiar forms of icebergs, global sweatshops, invisible empires, stealth industries, classroom tracks, and pacification schemes cast dark shadows on the future.

So is it possible to transform the emerging new class society that doomed Jim Farley into a more open and equitable structure? Is an American class system possible that accommodates both sides of the dream: opportunities for Gump-like underdog achievement and a shared, institutionally based commitment to the values of mutual respect, support, and community? Is an American society possible where the needs of the many (the new working class) outweigh the power of the few (the privileged class)? Can we have a class structure with a human face? The current economic, political, and cultural landscape does not appear to favor any major transformations of the new class society toward a more equitable system. But lessons from the past as well as recent stirrings within the alternative power networks suggest some tantalizing possibilities.

In this final chapter we consider the prospects for continuity and change in the new class society through—with apologies to Charles Dickens—a kind of Christmas Carol–like set of Present, Past, and Future themes. The section titled "Reality Check of the Present" underscores the current imbalances in class power resources and reminds us how and why the structures of institutional capitalism, racism, sexism, and classism reinforce the new class society. In the "Past as Prologue?" section we revisit the class-based foundations of the American underdog tradition by recalling those historical moments when working-class Americans forged populist movements to contest the power of the privileged class.

In the "Future of Class Inequalities" section of this chapter, we address four future-oriented topics. We begin with a subsection on "Consolidation" that considers how the struggles between the privileged class and the new working class on issues related to investment, consumption, and social and skill capital—resources at the heart of the new class society—are likely to continue to unfold as we move deeper into the twenty-first century. Our assessment is based on the expectation that privileged-class leaders will continue to pursue policies related to these forms of capital that will further consolidate and reinforce privileged-class dominance.

The "Resistance" subsection consists of selected examples from what we see as emerging class-reform, activist coalitions committed to reversing the increasing economic, political, and cultural inequalities of the new class society. Although many groups are part of the alternative power network working for change, our selections are limited to seven cases. They were chosen because of their relatively recent emergence as reform agents and because of their shared concerns with structural reforms that unite economic, political, and cultural strands of change. Also, we see them as strikingly reminiscent of the American populist tradition in terms of their goals and the language and imagery they use in critiquing current class inequalities.

The third subsection, "Beneath the Waterline," focuses on militant resistance. Here we briefly explore the links between growing class inequalities, the expansion of powerful organizations supporting privileged-class interests, and militant forms of resistance to these developments by individuals and groups—including the use of violence. In the fourth subsection, "The Superclass Suits, the Dream, and the New Working Class," we contrast the logic, language, and tactics of privileged-class apologists attempting to mask growing class inequalities with the efforts of activists working to expose the "suits" and their message.

In the concluding subsection, we contrast the "Scrooge Scenario" for reform favored by privileged-class leaders with the populist "structural democracy scenario" favored by class-reform activists. As we will see, these scenarios represent very different approaches to reforming class inequities, with the former emphasizing the importance of individual conscience and the latter emphasizing the importance of democratic participation in developing structural changes in the economic, political, and cultural arenas of American society.

REALITY CHECK OF THE PRESENT

From the standpoint of most mainstream journalists and the sources they quote, top-down class warfare hardly exists—a fact that tells you more about the media than it does about American society.

—Steve Rendall, *EXTRA!* January–February 2001

In the early 2000s, it is clear that superclass "suits" (organizational elites typically sporting expensively tailored business suits) rule. But not in the old, easy-to-spot and deflate autocratic, robber-baron style. As we have seen, more and more, superclass "suits" affect a common touch—dressed-down, casual, and media savvy—with credentialed-class coaching and backup as needed. We're all in this together, we are told. The message in the new class society is that social class (especially privileged-class origins) does not count in the competition for success. Class divisions are passé. High-tech skills, being a team player, and having a positive mental attitude, we are told, are the keys to success today. But are they?

The analysis of class relations in this book suggests that the balance of class power has shifted decidedly to the privileged class. For the past quarter-century, starting in the mid-1970s, this class has been able to accumulate ever greater shares of income and wealth at the expense of the new working class. As we have seen, privileged-class dominance has been achieved by attacking workers' jobs and wages and by reducing spending on social programs, thereby requiring working-class members to pay more for their health care, education, housing, and retirement.

The consequences of thirty years of class warfare by the privileged against the new working class are revealed almost daily in the increasing polarization of social and economic conditions between the top 20 percent of society and the bottom 80 percent. Corporate profits in 2000 for the five hundred largest industrial and service companies were up over 1999 levels (8.4 percent), but down from the 28.7 percent growth rate of 1999. Even so, 2000 revenues hit $7.2 trillion, which represented "even greater growth than in the previous year."[3] The continued growth of both revenues and profits in 2000 among *Fortune* 500 firms occurred despite the fact that total U.S. employment in these firms was essentially flat for the year and then fell dramatically in 2001.[4]

While revenues and profits for the largest firms increased and as CEO compensation levels hit record highs in the early 2000s, most workers did not share in the prosperity bounty enjoyed by the privileged class. Instead, as we pointed out in earlier chapters, many workers experienced stagnant or declining real wages. The only increases many workers experienced involved longer hours and a faster work pace. Meanwhile, large firms benefited from lower taxes on corporate revenues and less government oversight of environmental pollution and workplace health and safety. These seemingly obvious class inequalities become much less obvious after being filtered through the information industry and other powerful institutionalized forces. The filtering processes disguise privileged-class-biased corporate practices and government policies. And they legitimate the transfer of increasing shares of all capital forms—investment, consumption, skill, and social—to those in the top tier of the new class system at the expense of those in the bottom tier.

The shift of wealth and power to the privileged class has been justified, in part, by the powerful new ideology of the global economy. This idea system is often cleverly framed in the language, symbols, and imagery associated with personal freedom and liberty.[5] Messages heralding globalized free trade as the path to liberation from the limitations and narrow constraints of the parochial past are continually communicated to national and international audiences, especially through the mass media. These ideas focus public attention on the need for American businesses and workers to accommodate new competitive forces in the global economy (e.g., workers who will work harder for less money and corporations that can invest more because governments tax and regulate them less). And the threat of global competition has been used over and over again to justify the economic changes that have led to the new class society. Superclass and credentialed-class corporate executives, politicians, media moguls, and policy experts have used the global economy mantra in the same way that the specter of international communism was used to justify repressive domestic political policies in the 1950s and 1960s. The geopolitical threat of communism has been transformed into the geoeconomic threat of global competition, which has been both created and managed by institutional capitalism.

Institutional Capitalism and Privileged-Class Dominance

The ability of the privileged class to devise, disguise, and legitimate corporate practices and government policies that serve its interests but are destructive to working-class interests is reinforced by several structures described earlier in this book. These class-biased structures and outcomes are typically both part of and also facilitated by the deeply embedded economic, political, and cultural power of institutional capitalism. This concept refers to the intercorporate-network model of business described in chapter 2—as opposed to earlier forms of family or managerial capitalism.[6] It involves large, often multinational, firms linked by numerous interlocks of directors who serve on several corporate boards at the same time. And it is driven by the impersonal principles of profit maximization, capital accumulation (especially through increases in corporate stock values), and the necessity of access to capital funds (to finance operations, mergers, and expansions). It is an institutionalized force of staggering size and power dominated by and serving privileged-class interests.

Under this system, investment, worker pay, promotion, security, and production policies of interlocked firms are dictated by how such policies can best serve the impersonal principles that drive the system—especially profit maximization. High profits maximize corporate access to capital pools controlled by investment firms and satisfy large individual and institutional shareholders' demands for the highest possible investment returns and for steady increases in the share values of the stock they hold. As the dominant form of business organization in the United States today, institutional capitalism drives the core sector of the economy and creates smaller firms in the periphery to service core needs. The result is a small number of core firms with superclass owners, major stockholders, and elite corporate managers, a relatively small number of high-paid credentialed-class positions, a shrinking number of middle-income blue-collar jobs, and expanding numbers of poorly paid positions in peripheral firms occupied by larger and larger numbers of new-working-class members.

Institutional capitalism was made possible in part by the legal standing accorded to corporations by shifts in laws governing the corporate chartering process and by the landmark 1886 U.S. Supreme Court case of *Santa Clara County v. Southern Pacific Railroad.* In that case, the Court invoked the fourteenth amendment and "defined corporations as 'persons' and ruled that California could not tax corporations differently than individuals."[7] The effect of this decision, which was made by the Court without hearing any formal arguments, conferred upon corporations the same legal rights and constitutional guarantees enjoyed by natural persons.[8] The extension of personlike legal rights and protections to corporations, combined with their huge resources (even by 1886 standards), created an enormous power asymmetry between corporations and people in the American legal system and in the society generally. The social dangers posed by expanding corporate power and their potential to dominate all other social institutions were noted well before the 1886 case—by Abraham Lincoln. In an 1864 letter he warned that "as a result of the war, corporations have been enthroned and an era of corruption in high places will follow ... until all wealth is aggregated in a few hands and the Republic is destroyed."[9]

One important result of institutional capitalism today is that the basic business practices guiding and the ideological premises underlying large U.S. corporations have spread to and infused the routine structures, policies, and practices of nearly all large-scale organizations in the society.[10] This includes government agencies, universities, schools, and even charities and churches. As massive corporations (and other types of large bureaucracies) have emerged (and merged) gradually over time, they have become an integral part of our collective experiences. Because they have such a pervasive physical presence and are often associated with the satisfaction of routine individual and social needs, it is hard to imagine how economic, political, and cultural activities—indeed, even society itself—could exist without large corporations and similarly structured nonbusiness organizations. The huge organizations located in the economy and in the political and cultural arenas have become so much a part of the routine social landscape that they seem as natural as mountains, forests, rivers, and streams.

With multiple financial, personnel, and ideological links to other large organizations (e.g., government bureaucracies, universities, churches), large corporations populate and dominate the national economy, politics, popular culture, local communities, and how most people think about the new class society.[11] One example illustrating the penetration of American culture by ubiquitous corporations and the ideology and imagery associated with them is the increasing application of the business term *bottom line* to a variety of nonbusiness topics and activities. It has become a shorthand metaphor for the core or most critical feature of almost any activity or topic, such as personal health, family life, sex, movies, politics, or drug use—and many others.

Institutional capitalism is a powerful and pervasive organizational force field. It dominates the economic, political, and cultural arenas, shapes ideas and perceptions on a wide array of nonbusiness activities, and helps conceal the power of large corporations in creating, maintaining, and legitimating the new class system. But the hegemonic dominance of institutional capitalism in American society is rendered invisible by its saturation of the total social environment.

Many activities of the large organizations that make up, serve, and legitimate institutional capitalism are organized around and guided by a wide range of routine business policies and personnel practices that can be described as "institutionalized." This simply means that the typically unquestioned and taken-for-granted assumptions, policies, and practices governing how privileged-class owners and managers attempt to achieve what they believe are optimal organizational outcomes (which serve privileged-class interests) are built into the routine structures and operations of organizations. We view institutionalized practices concerning how stockholders, employees, clients, customers, or students are routinely treated by organizations as reflecting, in part, traditional cultural norms as well as economic, political, and cultural interests of the privileged class. Thus, from our perspective, institutionalized policies and practices facilitate preferential treatment by resource-rich organizations for members of the privileged class and at the same time reinforce organizationally based forms of discrimination (often subtle) against and marginalization of groups not typically found in the privileged class (i.e., people of color, women, and members of the working class). We term the organizationally based practices that generate such outcomes as institutional racism, sexism, and classism.

Institutional Racism, Sexism, and Privileged-Class Dominance

Embedded in the history and culture of the United States are a set of beliefs, practices, and social structures that can be called institutional racism and sexism. Racism and sexism are based on beliefs that link the physical characteristics of a group—African Americans or women—to a set of psychological and behavioral characteristics that are judged to be inferior to those of other groups.[12] This is ideological racism and sexism, which, when combined with the policies and practices of businesses, schools, media, and other organizations, becomes institutional racism and sexism—a principle of social domination by which groups seen as inferior are exploited economically and oppressed socially and physically. This principle of domination is carried out in schools that fail to provide equal preparation for students of color and women to assume leadership roles in their communities and workplaces; it is reflected in the mass media that either exclude oppressed groups or depict them in unrealistic and demeaning ways; and it is revealed in organizational structures that do not provide all their employees with job ladders and opportunities to learn and grow.

The privileged class benefits from institutional racism and sexism in two ways. The first involves direct benefits associated with the ability to discriminate against Blacks and women in employment and wages.[13] Privileged-class employers can reduce labor costs by paying lower wages, denying insurance and pension benefits, and using part-time workers. Of course, privileged-class employers do not view their decisions in the area of wages and benefits as being based on ideological racism or sexism. Most would probably deny any prejudicial beliefs regarding Blacks or women. Rather, their decisions would be explained on the basis of the educational background and experience that Black or women employees bring to their job. As employers who must be interested in maximizing productivity and minimizing costs, they will take advantage of available opportunities, regardless of whether it results in a segregated workforce or the employment of vulnerable workers.

The indirect benefits to the privileged class can be traced to the more widespread and subtle forms of ideological racism or sexism found in the larger population. Although only a small proportion of Americans would endorse blatant racist or sexist statements ("Women are mentally inferior to men"), a much larger proportion are inclined to believe that racism and sexism are things of the past— that Blacks should recognize that they won the civil rights revolution, and women should acknowledge that they have come a long way, baby! Believing in the existence of major gains for Blacks and women, many Americans now feel that continuing to enforce affirmative action policies only serves to give African Americans and women an unfair advantage. The existence of subtle racism and sexism enables privileged-class employers to exclude Blacks and women from certain jobs because of the opposition to them by co-workers or customers. Employers also use the employment of Blacks and women, or the threat to do so, as a way to keep downward pressure on wages and to stifle discontent among White, male workers.

Ideological racism may give even the poorest working-class Whites the psychological gains that may come from feeling superior to others, and ideological sexism may give working-class men validation of their masculinity when they can exclude women from their jobs and exert control in the home. But institutional racism and sexism are about economic and political power. When the privileged-class Democrats and Republicans in Congress and the White House developed their color-coded attack on welfare, they were also attacking the much larger number of poor Whites who also receive welfare, but that fact was never discussed. When privileged-class parents join politicians to fight against efforts at the state level to provide equality in per-pupil expenditures for all schools, it is always a color-coded event. That is, it is presented as a way to improve inner-city schools and create equity between Whites and Blacks, when in fact there are more poor White children in resource-poor schools in rural and urban America. The debates are color-coded to ensure their defeat, but the true battle is about the privileged class maintaining its economic and political power. As long as the focus stays on race, the welfare mothers and the inner-city kids will be seen as "victims" of racism and poverty, but never as casualties in a class-based struggle.

Institutional Classism and Privileged-Class Dominance

Institutional classism is another abstract label for a powerful but hidden force field that also helps reinforce and disguise privileged-class interests. At a general level, classism refers to the unspoken but widely accepted belief in American society that the values, social behavior, language patterns, and lifestyles of the privileged class are superior to those of the working class or the lower class.[14] Compared with racism, sexism, or even ageism, classism is largely a silent, hidden "ism"— partly because of the taboo nature of class in America. But classism is similar to racism and sexism in terms of its effects. It leads to prejudice toward, stereotyping of, and discrimination against members of the nonprivileged class—especially those in the lower segments of the working class. *White trash, redneck, trailer-park low-life, welfare bum,* and *slacker* are only a few of the many pejorative terms applied to groups clustered in the lower segments of the new class system.

Classism is based on and justified by a widely shared belief system sometimes called the ideology of meritocracy.[15] This idea system views class location as a reflection of talent and effort. It encourages the view that privileged-class positions are occupied by people who possess widely valued and admired traits such as high intelligence, achievement motivation, and altruism. It also encourages viewing members of the new working class (especially those at the lowest levels) as being justly placed in lower ranks because they obviously lack the valued qualities necessary to "succeed" in a merit-based economic system. The ideology of meritocracy helps justify and legitimate class inequalities by making class divisions seem naturally ordained and views those at the top as rare and gifted visionaries. This is obviously what billionaire John D. Rockefeller Sr. had in mind when he said, "I believe the power to make money is a gift of God. . . . Having been endowed with the gift I possess, I believe it is my duty to make money and still more money, and to use the money I make for the good of my fellow man according to the dictates of my conscience."[16]

Like racism and sexism, classism is embedded—or institutionalized—in the routine practices and policies of organizations dominated by privileged-class members such as corporations, government, the mass media, public schools, the criminal justice system, and universities. As a result, the operations of nearly the entire organizational establishment of the society trend in directions that exclude, disadvantage, or otherwise marginalize people from the lower classes through everyday routine (but largely unrecognized) practices. Institutional classism refers to a form of hegemony whereby privileged-class-based ideas, values, norms, language styles, and social behaviors prevail in organizations dominated by this class. From schools to the workplace to government, the gatekeepers in privileged-class-controlled organizations actively screen out or marginalize working-class-based values, norms, language styles, and behaviors.

Such gatekeeping practices were evident in a recent study illustrating how Harvard law students "afflicted" with the stigma of working-class origins were subtly (but powerfully) encouraged to disguise this fact. In addition to their classroom work, they learned the importance of distancing themselves from the working-class stigma, as well as how to do it. This was necessary to increase their chances of being selected to join elite law firms and thereby maximize their own career opportunities. The acceptance of these students by privileged-class "organizational masters" in elite law firms required them to demonstrate an easy familiarity with elite cultural codes and conform to the cultural standards, social behaviors, style of dress, and patterns of speech of the privileged class.[17]

The hidden power of privileged-class communication styles illustrates yet another dimension of institutional classism. Teachers and professors in public schools and universities—especially those serving students where many already possess advanced levels of social capital—actively discourage working-class students from communicating in the language styles of their class and penalize their grades if they persist. The same pattern extends to hirings and promotions in the workplace—especially for positions above entry-level ranks—and to the conferring of legitimacy to political candidates by the mainstream media. The "elaborated code," encompassing more abstract conceptual references and complex sentences, routinely structures communication (written and spoken) among members of the privileged class.[18] As a kind of "gold standard," it is the only legitimate communication style or mode of expression accepted or rewarded in classrooms, boardrooms, and the formal political and policy-making arenas.

Hidden class-linked advantages or disadvantages associated with privileged-class gatekeeping practices and with the class-based hegemony of the elaborated code as a communication style are seldom noted or explored by social scientists, media commentators, or social pundits. In fact, the details of these phenomena are virtually unknown to the public. The placement of workers in advanced entry-level career positions as well as the pace of later career advancement are typically explained in mainstream academic research or in mass media profiles of "successful people" as functions of merit and talent and not as the result of class-biased gatekeeping practices. Similarly, the differential mastery by students of "proper" communication styles and forms (the elaborated code) is typically viewed as an indicator of merit and talent and not as the result of the advantages or disadvantages associated with privileged versus working-class origins and experiences.

Some features of privileged-class advantages are informally recognized among segments of the population, as in the commonly circulated aphorism (among the working class) concerning the basis of career success: "It's not what you know, but who you know." This statement reflects a kind of cynical realism among members of the working class, but it is obviously overly simplistic and misses the hidden institutional basis of privileged-class advantages.

As tips of the class inequalities iceberg, privileged-class gatekeeping practices and rewards for mastery of the elaborated code are but two examples of the myriad ways by which class-biased organizational routines, policies, and practices perpetuate privileged-class interests. They are only two of the many covert threads woven into the fabric of institutional classism. Their powerful presence as sifting and sorting instruments helps make the common economic, political, and cultural successes (and rare failures) of privileged-class offspring as well as the common failures and rare successes of working-class children within privileged-class-controlled organizations seem to be "fair" and "impartial" outcomes.

Our reality check of the present leads us to conclude that institutional capitalism and the related institutionalized patterns and practices of racism, sexism, and classism are powerful structures that reinforce the new class society in both obvious and subtle ways. Moreover, these structures are themselves embedded in the dominant power networks that span the economic, political, and cultural arenas of social life. As we have seen, the deeply entrenched force field of institutional capitalism generates an unequal hierarchy of class-based positions, rewards, and relationships. At the same time, the class-based inequalities produced by this system are reinforced and replicated by institutional racism, sexism, and classism.

The ideology of classism is particularly potent in that it encourages viewing un-equal class outcomes as legitimate, natural, and even inevitable or desirable by large numbers of people in all classes. Thus, racism, sexism, and classism as insti-tutionalized structures help to perpetuate and reinforce—while also disguising—a variety of hidden privileged-class advantages and working-class disadvantages.

THE PAST AS PROLOGUE?

> We meet in the midst of a nation brought to the verge of moral, political, and material ruin. Corruption dominates the ballot box, the legislatures, [and] the Congress. . . . The newspapers are subsidized or muzzled. . . . The fruits of the toil of millions are stolen to build up colossal fortunes. . . . From the same pro-lific womb of governmental injustice we breed two classes—paupers and mil-lionaires.
>
> —Preamble to the 1892 People's Party National Platform, cited in Howard
> Zinn, *A People's History of the United States*, 1980

How long can the intensifying inequalities between the privileged class and the new working class continue? That's akin to asking, How long can the stock market keep going up? A typical buoyant headline from the late 1990s proclaimed, "Dow 12,000?" But some analysts expressed a more historically grounded sentiment: "You'd better enjoy the party while it's going on, because it's sure not going to last forever."[19] History, like the stock market, does not move in a straight line over time. This reality was strikingly evident in the period after the September 11 attacks. The Dow Jones Industrial Average fell from 9,600 to 8,200 and then rose to over 9,000 by mid-October—certainly not a straight line.[20]

So what are the prospects that significant political or social movements will de-velop to alter the current imbalance of power that exists between the two great op-posing classes in the double diamond? To avoid utopian visions or fantasies driven by hopes or dreams more than by reality, we look first to America's past. We focus on those times when the forces for change converged on a single project—to change the structure of society in order to reduce economic and social inequali-ties. Popular movements for change have gone by many labels, but "American pop-ulism" has endured as a common frame of reference describing many movements from the past aimed at reducing material inequalities. The next section considers lessons from the American populist tradition and provides a context for under-standing contemporary reform projects aimed at reshaping the new class society.

Breaking the Taboo: The Recent Past

As pointed out in chapter 2, populist appeals have often surfaced in national po-litical campaigns. This occurs sometimes in very close election races, or when an underdog candidate must attract new voters, thereby stimulating the tendency to strike a populist chord to see if and how it takes. In the rare instances of a third-party candidate for the presidency, the basis for that candidacy is often a populist appeal to those who have been "left out" of the political system, urging them to "take back their government." One of these conditions existed in the "toss-up" 2000 presidential campaign, when Al Gore, the democrat nominee, made several efforts to reach working-class voters (without calling them working class). In his convention speech, Gore said he was on the side of "working families" and against "powerful forces and powerful interests." This is a kind of veiled populism by a candidate who was not sure how far to push the theme. Ralph Nader, the 2000 Green Party candidate, presented an explicit progressive populist message that stressed "big money" control over both major parties and highlighted their one-party similarities by referrring to them as "Demopubs" and "Republicrats."

The 1996 Republican Party primary provided another example of populist rhetoric, but then it was "reactionary populism." Pat Buchanan was a long-shot outsider who desperately wanted to defeat front-runner Senator Bob Dole, long-time member and apologist of the privileged class. Buchanan knew that in order to have any chance to win his party's presidential nomination, he would have to appeal to working-class Americans who might not usually vote in a primary or even in the general election. Perhaps thinking like his old mentor, Richard Nixon, Buchanan must have thought, "How can I appeal to this 'silent majority'? How can I mobilize them to vote for me and not for Bob Dole?" The answer must have come to him as an epiphany: With a laser-like grasp of reality, he took the extraordinary step (for a politician) of telling the truth. His sound bites at times took on an almost Marxist tone of class analysis: "When AT&T lops off 40,000 jobs, the executioner that did it makes $5 million a year and AT&T stock soars"; "Mr. Dole put the interests of the big banks—Citibank, Chase Manhattan, Goldman Sachs—ahead of the American People"; "The voiceless men and women in this country have no one to represent them in Washington because the hierarchy of both parties really argues on behalf of these trade deals, which are often done for the benefit of corporations who shut their factories and move them overseas."[21]

In a New Hampshire primary stump speech, Buchanan made a rambling allusion to earlier times when revolutionary fervor led the masses to attack elites and take what was rightfully theirs: "'You watch the establishment,' he urged supporters. . . . 'All the knights and barons will be riding into the castle and pulling up the drawbridge, because they're coming. All the peasants are coming with pitchforks after them.'"[22]

High-profile populist rhetoric, especially in presidential campaigns, usually sends shock waves through the privileged class and creates a stir in both political parties. But consistent with the class taboo principle, in almost the blink of an eye the mainstream mass media and prominent spokespersons of the political parties rushed in to denounce the class warfare in Gore's speech, challenge the legitimacy of Nader's candidacy, defuse the class content of Buchanan's campaign, and dissipate the emerging discussion of corporate profits and greed—without mentioning the superclass or its interests. As we noted earlier, the *New York Times*, in its role as premier dominator of the mainstream ideological process, took the extraordinary step of publishing the seven-part *Downsizing of America* series. Although it acknowledged some human costs associated with downsizing, the series' basic spin presented such practices as consistent with the long-term interests of all Americans. This effort—and others like it—effectively put the class genie back in the bottle and ensured that discussion of class remained verboten.

Breaking the Taboo: Lessons from History

What political candidates like Gore, Nader, and Buchanan do when they weigh in against superclass and corporate power is not new in American history. The wealthy and powerful, in the form of corporate executives, bankers, politicians, and bureaucrats, have often served as high-profile targets of criticism by individuals and groups attempting to mobilize discontented Americans for change. Historical movements condemning elite-class excesses and promoting working-class reforms have often juxtaposed obvious and easily understood class contrasts by using terms such as the *haves* versus the *have-nots*, the *powerful* versus the *powerless*, and the *fat cats* versus the *common man*. Such references have often served as the images and language of American populism. This historical tradition of protest calling for reforms to reduce economic and social inequities has periodically emerged from the class-based grievances of the working-class majority.

Populist rhetoric has been used by numerous labor organizers, social movement leaders, and even, at times, mainstream politicians to shape and mobilize public discontent. In its classic form, populist messages seek to simultaneously elevate the masses and attack the privileged for their undeserved rewards. When the People's Party was formed in 1892, it pulled together debt-ridden small farmers, hundreds of discontented workers' groups, and several minor parties—all of whom were deeply dissatisfied with how the Democrats and Republicans had been running the country. More than a century ago, leaders of the People's Party praised the virtuous small farmers and laborers as the "producers" who created national prosperity that rightfully belonged to all Americans and heaped scorn on the "plutocrats," "parasites," and "moneyed aristocracy" who were said to wallow in idleness, extravagance, and waste. The use of sharply contrasting class-based images was a central feature of the populist message. As a noted historian of this tradition recently observed, "[Populism is] a language whose speakers conceive of ordinary people as a noble assemblage not bounded narrowly by class, view their elite opponents as self-serving, and seek to mobilize the former against the latter."[23]

The populist social movements of the nineteenth century were grounded in a rhetoric and ideology based on economic grievances and a defense of those who worked as small farmers, wage earners, and small-business people. But populist attacks on corporations, monopoly, and plutocrats were not aimed at the overthrow of capitalism. Rather, the populist reform message called for greater recognition of the importance of the common man in the economic, political, and social arenas and for a fair share of the fruits of workers' productive labor to be returned to these producers of wealth. The relatively modest scope of the populist reform agenda is underscored by author Michael Kazin's point that "through populism Americans have been able to protest social and economic inequalities without calling the entire system into question."[24] Kazin also argues that early populist critiques of American society attempted to build new bonds among people by returning to the core beliefs of the new American nation—rule by the people, reward for hard work and diligence, and faith in God.

The early moments of populism experienced through the People's Party at the end of the nineteenth century found expression in the twentieth century in different bases of discontent shared by widely varied groups. Throughout the twentieth century, populist rhetoric and movements have embraced an array of moral crusades. They began early in the century with the prohibitionists' war against alcohol and closed out the century with the religious right's attacks on the amoral elites who, it was claimed, were undermining the core values of the majority. Thus, American populism began the century as a left-liberal tradition aimed at attacking economic, political, and social privileges and inequalities but was later transformed and diverted into conservative forms of moral protest aimed primarily at defending the values of the "moral majority." The targets of populist attacks are superficially the same at both ends of the century: entrenched, irresponsible elites. But for early leftist populists, elite targets were symbolized by "fat cat" and "plutocrat" labels, whereas for contemporary rightist populists, evil is represented by "cultural elites" (as in Hollywood and the media) and by governmental elites who administer the growing bureaucratic state.[25]

As history illustrates, the American populist tradition has been both a powerful and ambivalent instrument for reform. Many real or aspiring leaders have picked up the populist instrument hoping to play a tune powerful enough to stir the sleeping masses into sweeping away corrupt elites. The power of that tradition rests with its roots in the early American experience, stressing the dignity of the common man and a rejection of the "foreign" influences of aristocracy and elitism. This thread of populism can serve as a bond unifying people to act on behalf of the common good while eschewing privilege and unfair advantage. The ambivalence associated with the populist tradition stems from its majoritarian beliefs, reflected in the support for direct participatory democracy. The majoritarian emphasis does not sit well with members of religious or ethnic groups that are numerically small and therefore feel that their interests will be ignored by the usually White and Christian majority. The majoritarian emphasis also does not sit well with "privileged leftists" who support populist ideology but whose education and credentialed-class privileges make them wary of "marching with the people."

The ambivalence of the populist tradition is partly responsible for the liberal left's movement into identity movements and identity politics while seeking to give coequal standing to the three major oppressions of class, race, and gender—which still excludes environmentalists, gays, the disabled, the aged, and numerous other groups with specific forms of grievances. The challenge facing the new-working-class majority in the United States involves finding ways to invoke the sentiment opposing privileged-class power of the populist tradition in ways that join the current disparate collection of disaffected groups, movements, and parties into a unified political movement. Only through unity can the new working class pool the modest organizational and personal resources its members possess into a substantial collective force for change—as in the aphorism of the hand and power: Each finger is only a modest force, but five fingers united transform the hand into a powerful fist.

THE FUTURE OF CLASS INEQUALITIES

It would be all too easy . . . to succumb to despair or simply acquiesce to changes from which there seems to be no escape . . . [But] widespread opposition to these trends has begun to emerge.

—Robert McChesney, *Monthly Review,* March 2001

Having recounted the past, what is the future of the new class society? We believe there is no single future. Rather, there are many possible futures. The future of class inequalities depends upon the extent to which the trends presented in the following three subsections develop and unfold in the twenty-first century. It is likely that the consolidation trend will be powerful and difficult to change. We expect that privileged-class leaders will make every effort to pursue policies concerning investment, consumption, social, and skill capital that will consolidate and reinforce privileged-class dominance.

On the other hand, it is also likely that the current resistance trend to privileged-class policies that are increasing economic, political, and cultural inequities of the new class society will continue and grow. The growth of organized resistance to class inequalities may be one of the most encouraging stories (for the new working class) of the twenty-first century. Some of the groups involved in these struggles echo the American populist tradition in terms of their goals, language, and the images they use in critiquing unfair privileged-class advantages and class inequalities.

If the future does include reforms in the new class system, their substance will be critical to any meaningful changes in class inequities. Possibilities range from superficial and cosmetic to substantial and structural reforms. The final subsection, "The Scrooge Scenario versus the Structural Scenario," considers this issue.

The Future: Consolidation

> One class will have the autonomy to live how and where it wants; the other will
> be increasingly constrained and shut out. Pedigree and power, money and edu-
> cation will make the difference.
>
> —Jerry Adler, *Newsweek*, July 31, 1995

One future trend about which we are certain is that of continuity in the areas of
class domination and class struggle. As we move into the twenty-first century, we
expect the 20 million families making up the privileged class will continue to
dominate virtually all of the elite decision-making positions as well as most of the
professional and managerial information-generating and decision-executing positions in the major economic, political, and cultural institutions that make up the
dominant power networks.

The domination by privileged-class members of the U.S. institutional infrastructure means that in their personal and public lives they will continue to
make decisions that reflect institutional imperatives favoring an expansion of already concentrated wealth and power. These decisions can be expected to produce corporate and governmental practices and policies that disproportionately
benefit privileged-class interests as against those of the working class. Thus, we
expect the trend of the past thirty years, whereby ever larger shares of economic,
political, and cultural resources have been shifted to the privileged class, to continue in this century. By *continue* we mean that privileged-class leaders will pursue policies aimed at consolidating the gains made by this class over the past
thirty years.

When we speak of consolidation, we refer to efforts to strengthen, deepen, and
extend actions and policies that are already in place. We do not refer to totally new
actions or policies, such as the ongoing attempt by the privileged class to convert
the Social Security system into a private insurance scheme. As privileged-class
consolidation efforts unfold, the quality of life among members of the new working class can be expected to deteriorate even further. This downward spiral will
continue until and unless organized mass political and social resistance movements emerge—akin to those of the populist era—that will represent the interests
and press the claims of the working class for a redress of its shared economic and
political grievances.

The following five subsections consider how privileged-class-sponsored consolidation policies related to investment, consumption, social, and skill capital are
likely to continue unfolding in this new century. In focusing on the struggles surrounding these forms of capital, we expect that at least in the short term, privileged-class-controlled organizations in the economic, political, and cultural
arenas will actively support policies that will strengthen and extend the advantages, interests, and power of this class at the expense of the new working class. We
also expect that these same organizations will engage in activities aimed at con-

RALL copyright © Ted Rall. Reprinted with permission of Universal Press Syndicate.
All rights reserved.

cealing and legitimating corporate practices and governmental policies that shift increasing shares of all forms of capital to the privileged class at the expense of the new working class.

Investment Capital: Continued Export of U.S. Jobs

We have already discussed at length the loss of high-wage manufacturing jobs over the past thirty years. American corporations have moved production overseas or built new production facilities overseas in order to find lower-wage workers and governments that are indifferent to the security and safety of workers and protection of the environment. In chapters 3 and 4 we pointed out that the flight of U.S. capital has been greatly enhanced by the 1993 North American Free Trade Agreement (NAFTA), which political leaders claimed would stimulate trade between the United States, Mexico, and Canada. Although both the Democrat Clinton and Republican Bush (II) administrations have argued that it is good for the United States, there is no doubt that NAFTA has facilitated the shift of corporate production from the United States to Mexico.[26] Despite evidence that, by 1997, NAFTA had resulted in the loss of between 261,000 and 600,000 U.S. jobs, President Clinton requested that Congress grant him fast-track authority to negotiate an expansion of the treaty to other Latin American nations.[27] Since then, economists estimate that in the period from 1994 to 2000 NAFTA led to the loss of over 700,000 jobs.[28] Despite this trend, President Bush and his trade representatives strongly favored Congressional approval of the Free Trade Area of the Americas (FTAA) agreement that would extend NAFTA throughout the Western Hemisphere.[29] Any expansion of NAFTA would undoubtedly lead to more U.S. jobs being lost, as even more incentives would be created for shifting investment capital from U.S. plants to factories in low-wage nations.

As discussed in chapter 4, the Clinton administration's request to Congress for fast-track authority to expand NAFTA in 1997 was supported by major U.S. corporations and was also endorsed by virtually all major U.S. newspapers.[30] In 2001, as we discussed in chapters 3 and 4, the Bush administration sought similar trade negotiation powers from Congress (now termed "trade promotion authority") to expand NAFTA through the FTAA and also received high levels of corporate support for this effort.[31] The Clinton and Bush efforts to expand NAFTA and the corporate support they evoked illustrate how U.S. trade policy is driven by superclass interests that in turn are grounded in and legitimated by the structures of institutional capitalism. But as we also noted in chapters 3 and 4, proposals by the Clinton and Bush administrations to extend NAFTA provoked unexpectedly stiff resistance from labor-led coalitions that included public interest, community, environmental, and religious groups as well as other organizations linked to the alternative power networks.

Groups opposed to extending NAFTA throughout the Western Hemisphere have mobilized opposition to treaties such as the FTAA in part by exposing NAFTA's anti-working-class record in the United States, Canada, and Mexico. The evidence cited by opponents is compelling. From 1994 to 2000, NAFTA resulted in the loss of 766,000 U.S. jobs (affecting every state) and 276,000 Canadian jobs. Many of the jobs lost in both nations were unionized, high-paying manufacturing positions. During the same period in Mexico, overall manufacturing employment declined. Only the maquiladora plants along the U.S.-Mexico border experienced employment increases.[32]

In addition to causing job losses, NAFTA has contributed to growing economic inequality in all three nations. U.S. workers who were displaced by NAFTA-based job losses, but who found new jobs, experienced income losses averaging 13 percent. Displaced U.S. manufacturing workers who found work in the retail sector experienced a 34 percent drop in average wages.[33] Moreover, studies from the 1990s and 2000 found that substantial percentages of U.S. firms were likely to use NAFTA-related threats of plant relocations or outsourcing during contract negotiations and union organizing drives as tactics to reduce labor costs. Outside the United States, real incomes declined throughout the 1990s for most Canadian workers below the top income fifth. In Mexico, manufacturing wages declined by almost 21 percent in the 1990–99 period, and the purchasing power of the minimum wage fell nearly 18 percent.[34]

While the economic effects of NAFTA-driven "free trade" have been largely negative for most U.S., Canadian, and Mexican workers, the effects for the privileged class have been largely positive. A recent *Business Week* article, "NAFTA's Scorecard: So Far So Good," illustrated this pattern. While acknowledging some job losses, the article primarily focused on the positive investment and trade effects of NAFTA for U.S. corporations.[35] Although the article was not framed in terms of class interests, it was clear that NAFTA's positive effects were primarily experienced by corporations—and the privileged-class members who own and manage them.

By the late 1990s, the undeniably "high negatives" of the NAFTA record and the personal experiences of many U.S. workers with NAFTA's effects were major reasons that the labor-led coalition was able to effectively mobilize opposition and win the congressional vote against Clinton's fast-track request.[36] The defeat of fast track revealed that many working-class Americans believed more NAFTA-style policies would contribute to what Ross Perot called "the giant sucking sound" of more jobs leaving the United States—and that they were willing to actively oppose such policies. The battle illustrated that the continued export of U.S. jobs is not inevitable. It demonstrated that alternative-power-network organizations can successfully unite to resist privileged-class mobilization of dominant-power-network resources and policy preferences. However, despite the 1997 fast-track defeat, most privileged-class members have continued to maintain that more (not less) NAFTA-like policies are necessary to maintain U.S. competitiveness in the global economy.[37]

Events in the early 2000s have made it clear that privileged-class-supported, consolidation-style trade policies were not derailed by the 1997 vote against extending NAFTA. Privileged-class leaders have continued to press for an expansion of "free trade" in the new century through a variety of agreements and organizations. Often denoted by a confusing array of acronyms, some are already in place (and regularly updated with new arrangements and members), while others reflect new initiatives. Regional trade agreements such as NAFTA (and perhaps FTAA), the EU (European Union), and ASEAN (Association of Southeast Asian Nations) combined with international agreements such as GATT (the General Agreement on Tariffs and Trade) and institutions such as the WTO (World Trade Organization), IMF (International Monetary Fund), and WB (World Bank) all promote privileged-class interests. In each case, these agreements and organizations "are primarily concerned with granting capital the freedom to move from country to country."[38]

We are at present locked in a struggle between privileged-class determination to push globalization and the alternative power network's efforts to protect worker interests and the environment. On one side we have multinational corporations, financial institutions, and powerful governments that support unregulated free trade; on the other, there are labor organizations, environmentalists, and some

Third World countries stressing the rights of people to regulate actions of multinational corporations. Recently, the privileged class has placed its attention on the Geneva-based World Trade Organization (WTO), formed in 1994 to replace GATT. The WTO has 135 member countries, each with a representative who participates in the formulation of a general set of rules governing trade. The key body of WTO, however, is the dispute resolution committee, which handles trade disputes between nations. Corporations may use the dispute resolution process to bring claims against a country for any of their regulations that limit the freedom of corporations to buy and sell across the globe. The outcome of this struggle is uncertain, but it will shape questions of national sovereignty in the global economy.

Consumption Capital: Continued Inequality in Jobs, Wages, and Taxes

Privileged-class-based political and economic leaders argue that the U.S. economy and workers are doing fine. They point to the tremendous job growth that has occurred in the United States even while millions of jobs were being exported and while many large firms continue to report job cuts owing to corporate downsizing. Although these leaders may be correct in terms of the net gain of new jobs created versus jobs lost to export and downsizing, most of the newly created jobs are at lower wages, with fewer benefits, and with more insecure job tenure than the jobs that were lost. The overall effect of these trends has been the imposition of intense pressures by employers on workers, resulting in the lowering of workers' real wages and a substantial weakening of workers' rights and bargaining power.[39]

Privileged-class leaders also point to the very low (5 percent range) unemployment rate in the late 1990s and early 2000s as evidence that overall the economy is strong and that everyone is benefiting as corporate profits grow and inflation remains low. There are many problems with these interrelated claims. But the government's "official" unemployment rate is fatally flawed in two respects. First, it represents a serious underestimate of actual unemployment. The official estimate is based upon a monthly national sample survey of U.S. households, which asks people a series of questions about whether they are currently working or looking for work. Only those who are unemployed but claim to be actively looking for work are classified as unemployed. This approach excludes people who are unemployed but who have not looked for work in the past month. These "discouraged workers" have stopped looking for work because their experiences tell them the search is pointless. Also excluded are employed part-time workers who want full-time jobs but can't find them. The actual rate of unemployment and underemployment jumps to more than 12 percent when discouraged workers and part-time workers seeking full-time work are included.[40]

The emphasis by privileged-class leaders on expanding job opportunities and low unemployment serves to both mask and legitimate class inequalities linked directly to most workers' diminished access to consumption capital (income). The messages sent by credentialed-class professionals who manage and spin economic news to workers whose real wages have been declining for decades take one of two forms: (1) When the economy is booming (as was claimed in the 1990s), "if you can't find a good job, it must be your fault!" (2) When the economy is contracting (as in the early 2000s), "savvy workers with the right credentials can still find good jobs. If you can't, it must be your fault!" These privileged-class scripted and main-stream-media-disseminated messages concerning aggregate unemployment rates and other economic opportunities overreport the quantity of work available (creating the illusion of low unemployment) while also underreporting on the diminished quality of the jobs held by more and more members of the working class. Mainstream media reports ignore the reality that increasing numbers of jobs pay less than "living wages," provide few or no benefits, and offer little or no job security.[41]

The trends toward lower incomes and less economic security for most members of the working class are not accidental. They are the direct result of class-war consolidation practices and policies implemented by corporate and government actions throughout the 1970s, 1980s, and 1990s that have shifted consumption capital away from working-class wage earners to privileged-class groups. Examples of consolidation policies that would exacerbate current class-based income disparities and extend them into the next century are especially evident in recent governmental policy trends producing reductions in social programs for the working class and lower taxes for the privileged class.

Social Programs and the Declining Social Wage

The privileged class will continue to press for reductions in federal and state spending for programs that constitute the "social wage," which benefits all or some segments of the working class. In industrialized nations, the *social wage* refers to government policies ensuring minimum levels of citizens' material well-being through "social programs" such as health care, a mandated minimum wage, unemployment insurance, educational assistance, housing subsidies, income and food assistance to the poor, and old-age pensions.[42] Compared with that of other industrialized nations, the U.S. social wage is very modest and lacks health care guarantees. The major features were put in place in the 1930s; modest expansions occurred mainly in the 1960s with the passage of federal Medicare and Medicaid legislation.[43] However, in recent years the social wage has come under attack by privileged-class conservatives for allegedly breeding dependency on government and undercutting individual initiative.

Spending reductions have already occurred or are being planned in several areas including, for example, federal subsidies for education, housing, and welfare assistance. As a result, living costs for members of the working class are going up as real wages continue to fall (especially for the working poor), producing a free fall in the standard of living among the poorest segments of the new working class.

This process is especially evident in the "welfare reform experiment." Organized and legitimated by credentialed-class elites acting on behalf of their own and su-perclass interests, the "reform" legislation capitalized on resentment among some segments of the working class toward entitlement programs serving the poor.

At the federal level, bipartisan congressional support led to the passage of the Personal Responsibility and Work Opportunity Reconciliation Act, which former President Clinton signed into law in 1996. This measure not only sharply reduced benefits to the poor, it also imposed time restrictions on the number of years peo-ple are eligible for assistance and added training requirements that move welfare recipients as quickly as possible into low-wage jobs. The net effects of this legisla-tion include more downward pressures on wage levels (as thousands of new work-ers are added to the low-wage labor market), increases in the number of discouraged and underemployed workers, and rising levels of human misery as many of the poor lose minimal levels of support for food, housing, and health care.[44] Ironically, for the higher-wage members of the new working class who sup-ported welfare "reform," as the poor are forced into the labor market, their pres-ence helps drive down wage rates for all workers.[45]

Privileged-class leaders are also at work on two additional major policy efforts that would shift even more income from the working class to the privileged class. The first is the ongoing battle to extend the age at which retirees are enrolled in Medicare. Currently, retirees are eligible for Medicare at age 65, but superclass-spon-sored conservative "think tank" studies and policy papers are offered as justification for legislative proposals that would extend the age to 67. Such an action would delay overall Medicare costs and also reduce government spending costs as those Ameri-cans who would have been covered at 65 and 66 die before reaching 67.[46]

The second effort, which has received cheers from the privileged class, is the ini-tiative to recalculate the consumer price index (CPI), which is used by the federal government and many other governmental bodies and private firms to estimate the rate of inflation. The annual increase in the CPI is used as the basis for calculating (among other things) annual increases in Social Security checks paid to millions of older Americans. For example, if the CPI for 2001 was 3 percent, then a typical re-tiree receiving a monthly Social Security check of $850 would receive $875 in 2002. Political and economic elites know that they can reduce federal spending by billions of dollars if the CPI is "adjusted" downward by only 1 or 2 percent. Of course, if the CPI is adjusted downward, millions of low-income older Americans will lose ben-efits. At the same time, the privileged class can then make the case for further re-ductions in federal taxes, especially for high-income taxpayers.[47]

Continued Tax Inequalities: Wealth and Income

While the wages of the new working class are constrained, the income and wealth of the privileged class will continue to grow. Salaries of corporate execu-tives, managers, and other members of the credentialed class have continued to increase sharply in the early 2000s, just as they have over the past three decades. Because the privileged class owns most of the privately held stocks and mutual funds, bonds, and commercial properties in the United States, increasing stock prices during the 1990s dramatically expanded the wealth of this group, despite some shrinkage in the portfolio values during the early 2000s. The trend of increasing concentration of wealth in the hands of the privileged class is likely to continue well past the first decade of the twenty-first century. Ironically, this trend is (will be) partly fueled by increasing economic insecurity among the new working class concerning retirement income. As benefit-defined pension plans (funded by corporate contributions) have been increasingly replaced by contribution-defined plans (funded by employee's contributions from wages; e.g., 401(k) plans), new-working-class members are forced into the stock market hoping for higher returns. Their stock purchases help drive up stock prices, which disproportionately benefit privileged-class stock owners.[48]

The expansion of privileged-class wealth and income received an additional boost from the Balanced Budget Reconciliation Act of 1997, brokered by former President Clinton with the support of both Democratic and Republican members of Congress. As noted in chapter 4, this law produced multibillion-dollar windfalls for the privileged class that had the effect of extending and expanding income and wealth inequalities well into the first decade of the twenty-first century. Two features of the law discussed in chapter 4 that are especially relevant in this regard are the reductions in the taxes on capital gains and reductions in inheritance taxes.

As we pointed out in chapter 4, wealth generated from increases in stock values is subject to capital gains taxes, but the 1997 law lowered the modest 28 percent rate of the early 1990s to 20 percent.[49] Because privileged-class members are the largest holders of capital (in the forms of stocks and bonds), they will benefit the most, with the richest 1.4 percent of households enjoying an average annual "break of $21,850 apiece."[50] This change will increase the wealth and income of privileged-class members well into the next century.

A second wealth and income-extending benefit of the 1997 law involves the amount of personal wealth that can be transferred across generations free from federal taxation. In chapter 4 we pointed out that prior to the 1997 law, individuals could transfer estates valued at up to $600,000 to their children tax free (with husbands and wives permitted to transfer $1,200,000 tax free). After the 1997 law, these amounts increased to $1.2 million for an individual and $2.4 million for a couple.[51] Clearly this tax change affects only privileged-class members and will have the effect of reinforcing the intergenerational permanence of the new class system.

The 1997 tax law changes sponsored by a Democrat president ensured that, apart from all other advantages associated with growing up in affluent families, the sons and daughters of the privileged class would lead adult lives reinforced with greater economic advantages than in the past. Yet even these tax breaks were not enough. Republican President Bush made further tax reductions for the privileged class the first priority of the new administration. On May 26, 2001, the 2001 Congress passed the new tax cuts, with the House voting 240–154 in favor (with 28 Democrats joining the majority), and the Senate passed the bill by a 58–33 margin (with 12 Democrats joining the Republican majority). Among the key provisions of Public Law 107-16 were the following:

1. A reduction in all income tax rates over the next five years, with the rates of 28, 31, and 36 percent dropping by three percentage points, and the highest tax rate of 39.6 percent dropping to 35 percent.
2. Tax-deferred contributions to personal retirement plans—401(k) plans—are raised to $15,000 a year from the current $10,500.
3. Exemptions on estate taxes increase from the present $675,000 exclusion to $1 million in 2002 and $3.5 million in 2009. In 2010, the estate tax is repealed.
4. A maximum of $4,000 in college tuition expenses may be deducted for families with annual incomes below $130,000. Families with incomes between $130,000 and $160,000 may deduct $2,000 in tuition expenses.

These provisions in the new tax law are heavily weighted to benefit those Americans with privileged-class incomes. The increase in exemptions and ultimate repeal of the estate tax is a major benefit to those with accumulated wealth. The opportunity to build wealth in retirement plans will also benefit those in higher income brackets, since few Americans could afford to have $15,000 of their salary put into a retirement account. Finally, the one possible benefit to the working class, the tuition deduction, manages to draw in everyone with annual incomes up to $160,000. Not exactly working class! With tax policies such as these—as well as those from 1997—in place, to speak of equality of opportunity as the essence of the American Dream is more than a cruel joke. It approaches the Big Lie dimensions of the most distorted forms of propaganda.

Social and Skill Capital: Closing the Gates of Opportunity

Our distributional model views social and skill capital as critical factors influencing the processes through which varying levels of the other two capital forms are distributed (or redistributed) to individuals and groups. As we noted in chapter 1, social capital includes people's participation in various kinds of social networks, their acquisition of class-legitimating and class-enhancing formal credentials, and their possession of qualities valued and rewarded by various organizations (e.g., specialized talents and skills). Skill capital is closely related to social capital in that both are often linked to formal educational organizations that develop specialized talents, refine economically valued interests and skills, and help establish access to informal social and career networks of opportunities and practicing privileged-class professional mentors.

As the American economy is transformed by corporate strategies to maximize profit and market value of stocks (through downsizing, outsourcing, job transfers, globalization), the availability of "good jobs" has become increasingly problematic. The number of positions linked to high or even moderate levels of consumption capital (income) has always been finite, but in recent years those numbers have stagnated. Neither death nor retirement of current workers nor economic expansion can be counted on to produce more "good job" openings as the economy is transformed. The situation is akin to a sports team in which only a limited number of player positions are available.

Recent research evidence on the rates of intergenerational occupational mobility indicates that in recent decades it has become more difficult for young men from working-class origins to achieve the higher levels of occupation, education, and income. In 1973, 59 percent of the sons born to fathers who were in the top quartile of occupations, education, and income also became members of that quartile. A similar comparison with data from 1998 reveals that 66 percent of sons with fathers in the highest quartile also belonged to that same quartile based on their occupation, education, and income. In short, the rate of father-son inheritance among the most privileged segment of society has increased between 1973 and 1998, making it more difficult for the working class to rise into higher socioeconomic levels.[52]

So how is the limited number of "good job" positions distributed among the large pool of aspirants? We believe social and skill capital play major roles in the distributional process in terms of providing access to these jobs as well as in explaining why it is fair and right for the holders of these jobs to occupy them. But as we have shown, the past three decades have witnessed an expansion of policies, programs, and trends that have restricted opportunities for members of the working class to cultivate social capital at individual or collective levels and to accumulate advanced levels of skill capital. For the younger cohorts of the working class, the result has been a dramatic decline in opportunities to access "good jobs" and to acquire the social and skill capital necessary for upward social mobility to professional careers in the privileged class.

Several kinds of corporate practices, government policies, and social trends are consolidating higher levels of social and skill capital in the hands of privileged-class members while decreasing access to these resources by working-class members. Although the list is long, it begins with the attack on public education by conservative privileged-class members and organizations. This group advocates decreased spending for all forms of public education, including college, while also supporting an expansion of school voucher systems and privatization schemes. These privileged-class-sponsored efforts are key examples of class consolidation policies related to social and skill capital. Already partially in place, these policies are reshaping how schools influence the distribution of social and skill capital resources to students in ways that will further disadvantage working-class children and reinforce the advantages of privileged-class children.

In state legislatures and the U.S. Congress, neoliberal privileged-class leaders are currently calling for cuts in funding for urban school programs because they claim more money will not solve problems of these schools. Their claim is based on so-cial Darwinist assumptions that view the urban poor as an underclass so disor-ganized by antisocial values and hedonistic lifestyles that many of its children are beyond educational redemption—no matter how much money is spent on them.[53] Parallel to calls for deep cuts in publicly funded education are policies advocated by superclass-funded think tanks where marketplace competition for schools is viewed as a "solution" for those segments of the urban poor that might be re-deemed by education. These "experts argue that education will only improve when poor children are given vouchers to attend private schools and private groups are allowed to start and run their own schools with unregulated public funds."[54]

Policies that defund public schools restrict working-class students' opportunities to participate in the kinds of social networks that would lead to the cultivation of an expanded circle of social ties and valued individual skills essential for acquiring a "good job" or a shot at upward social mobility. As high-quality educational expe-riences are made less accessible to working-class students and as their parents ex-perience declining real incomes, the likelihood is reduced that such students will even aspire to (let alone acquire) the kinds of formal credentials and advanced skills necessary to access the declining pool of "good jobs" and professional careers.

Privileged-class efforts to defund public education also extend to the university level, as reflected in declining levels of state support for public universities com-bined with rapidly rising tuition costs. According to state higher education finance officers, between 1990 and 1998 the state and local government appropriations for current operations of public colleges and universities increased from $33.8 to $44.5 billion. However, this increase was slightly below the rate of inflation for that period.[55] This means state funding measured in real dollars (adjusted for inflation) actually fell. At the same time, tuition rates at four-year colleges increased by 71 percent (for the 1990–98 period).[56] Looking to the future, the College Board esti-mated that for a child born in 2001, four years at a public university would cost $100,000; at private institutions the cost would be $225,000.[57]

The class-based social- and skill-capital implications of the combination of state defunding and increasing costs of college to students and parents are obvi-ous. As state support drops and tuition costs escalate, fewer working-class students will be able to afford to attend college. Children from working-class families will face ever higher financial hurdles if they hope to attend college, as costs exceed the annual incomes (and maybe even the net worth) of their parents. Working-class children will find their choices increasingly limited to the cheapest forms of higher education. And these are likely to include more impersonal, technologically driven, narrowly focused, vocational-style programs that are connected to low-paid jobs with limited opportunities.

By contrast, children from the privileged class have few financial barriers to contend with when considering college attendance. Increasingly, only children from privileged-class families will have access to elite colleges and universities with programs taught by professional faculty and linked to job opportunity networks with higher starting salaries and long career ladders. Moreover, increasingly only children from privileged-class families will be able to realistically consider or afford professional degrees beyond the baccalaureate level. These factors (and others) will conspire to limit the chances of young men and women from the new working class to achieve significant, educationally linked opportunities for occupational and social mobility. Such circumstances will dramatically restrict their ability to access the formal credential dimension of both social and skill capital, but children from privileged-class backgrounds will be much less affected.

The decline of working-class access to social and skill capital resources produces less competition among privileged-class members for these resources. This means adult members of the privileged class will be able to reserve easier access to formal skills and a larger share of social capital resources for themselves and their children. These resources can then be used to legitimate a near monopoly by the privileged class on access to and legitimation of high levels of consumption and investment capital, which together almost permanently and exclusively cement membership in this class.

The Future: Resistance

> Once I saw the mountains angry, And ranged in battle-front. Against them stood a little man; I laughed and spoke to one near me, 'Will he prevail?' 'Surely,' replied this other; 'His grandfathers beat them many times.'
>
> —Stephen Crane, *The Red Badge of Courage and Other Writings*, 1960

The privileged-class-based consolidation policies and trends outlined in the preceding section are likely to produce increasing inequalities between the top 20 percent of privileged Americans and the remaining majority. Attempts by members of the new working class to increase their capital shares are likely to be kept in check by the continued mobilization of a variety of potent resources held by the privileged class and deployed along several fronts of the new class war. Any alteration in the distribution of capital resources will have to be initiated by reform-minded people, groups, and organizations grounded in the working class and perhaps linked to lessons from the progressive populist traditions of the past.

Many of the themes, messages, and images that were part of the populist tradition reemerged in the 1990s and early 2000s. But the progressive traditions of the past were not simply revived. They were revised and updated to meet the needs and conditions of a new century through the activities of a wide array of activist groups and organizations that are part of the alternative power networks. Many groups in these networks are working to reduce class inequalities such as the Nader-founded Public Interest Groups, alternative media outlets, the Democratic

The Hand That Will Rule the World—One Big Union. *Solidarity,* June 30, 1917.

Socialists of America, and others. But our focus here is on seven examples of organizational forces for economic, political, and cultural reform that emerged (or reemerged) in the 1990s and that are continuing to work for change in the new century. The revitalized AFL-CIO, United for a Fair Economy (UFE), the Program on Corporations, Law and Democracy (POCLAD), the Labor Party, the New Party, The Living Wage Campaign, and Fairness and Accuracy in Media Reporting (FAIR) all reflect shared concerns with advancing working-class interests and democratic ideals. In many ways these groups are modern heirs to the populist tradition. They can be viewed as representing a kind of emerging "class warrior" activism committed to developing class consciousness among the new working class and to actively mobilizing a variety of economic, political, and cultural resources aimed at transforming the structural bases of the new class society and the many inequalities associated with it.

Organized Labor

In the late 1990s the AFL-CIO (American Federation of Labor and Congress of Industrial Organizations) reemerged as a major working-class force promoting economic and political changes that echo the populist tradition. The federation is the organizational foundation of the American labor movement, with 13 million members and an annual budget of $190 million (in 2000).[58] The AFL-CIO shift to a more activist stance began after John Sweeney (former Service Employees' International Union officer) was elected president in 1995 over interim president Thomas Donahue in the first contested election for president of the organization in forty years.[59]

Although the AFL-CIO's highest-profile programs initiated since the mid-1990s appear to be political in nature, their goals reflect both economic and political concerns. Recent federation programs have been aimed at increasing workers' influence in the governmental and employer arenas in order to promote economic policies and business practices that will reduce class inequalities and increase workers' economic security. To achieve these general goals, the federation is focusing more of its resources on organizing new union members and increasing participation by union voters in local, state, and national elections. Other features of the federation's agenda for change reflect related economic and political priorities, such as raising the minimum wage, supporting workers' strikes, protecting American workers' jobs (e.g., working to change the WTO agenda and working to defeat new fast-track efforts and "free trade" agreements such as the FTAA), protecting Social Security, expanding public health care, increasing spending on education, and establishing closer links with trade unions on a global basis.[60]

Under Sweeney, the federation increased its support for political efforts consistent with labor's interests. An early example was the federation's "Labor '96" campaign. It involved a $35 million commitment by the AFL-CIO to mobilize union members for Democratic candidates and to pay for advertising in support of pro-union political candidates in the 1996 elections.[61] This pattern of increased mobilization of union voters and increased federation funding for political candidates sympathetic to labor continued in the 1998, 2000, and 2002 elections.[62] In 1997, this strategy was reflected in a federation commitment to register 4 million new voters from union households to support union members running for offices at local, state, and national levels. The federation slogan, "2000 by 2000" focused attention on its efforts to field 2000 union candidates for public offices in 2000.[63] Such efforts helped increase the union household share of the national vote from 19 percent of the electorate in 1992, to 23 percent in 1996, to 26 percent in 2000—"with a growing percentage of these households voting for labor-backed candidates."[64]

Another major AFL-CIO initiative, called "Organizing for Change," was unveiled in late 1996. This future-oriented program was (and is) aimed at revitalizing the labor movement by organizing thousands of new union members. The centerpiece of this effort was the federation's expansion of its organizing budget. It grew from $2.5 million in 1995 to $30 million in 1997.[65] In 2001, 22 percent of the federation's annual budget (about $42 million) was dedicated to organizing and was "scheduled to rise to 30 percent soon."[66]

In addition to the efforts just noted, in the early 2000s the AFL-CIO began to call greater public attention to economic concerns and public policy issues relevant to all workers. The federation's high-profile emphasis on what it termed a "Working Families Agenda" appeared to be designed to increase public awareness of workers' common economic and political interests and to build public support for specific policies that would advance those interests. Part of this effort was reflected in the AFL-CIO's presentation of an "alternative budget" for 2002. It criticized the Bush tax-cut plan for favoring the rich and argued in favor of real tax cuts for working families (even unions won't publicly use the term *working class*). In addition, the alternative budget plan calls for $315 billion to extend Medicaid to 12 million lower-income adults and children, $375 billion for a comprehensive prescription drug benefit, and $185 billion to extend Internet access to every school in the nation.[67] The "Working Families Agenda" is clearly an effort by the federation to transcend the narrow economic interests of unions and their members. It speaks to the needs and interests of the entire working class.

The outcomes of the AFL-CIO's revitalization and proactive strategies for change remain to be seen. Union efforts supporting economic and political changes that would advance working-class interests while challenging those of the privileged class are likely to face many stiff challenges. Union-sponsored reform efforts have been and will be opposed by a wide array of privileged-class resources—including many organizations identified in earlier chapters. Stiff opposition is especially likely to come from the little-known antiunion industry of fifteen hundred consultants who now "earn approximately $500 million each year advising corporations on how to keep unions out of their offices and factories."[68] For example, New York-based "Executive Enterprises" organized a series of two-day antiunion workshops for U.S. companies in the late 1990s around the theme of "How to Stay Union-Free into the 21st Century." Priced at $1,495, the workshops were conducted by Jackson, Lewis, Schnitzler, and Krupman, "one of the largest law firms in the country dedicated to representing management exclusively in labor, employment, and benefits law and related litigation."[69]

Apart from privileged-class challenges, labor activists long critical of the AFL-CIO are yet to be convinced that its much-publicized revitalization is more substance than sizzle. Shop-floor dissidents who favor what labor author Kim Moody calls "social movement unionism" (using democratic unions as a force to promote economic, political, and social justice) are skeptical that the sclerotic complacency of "business unionism" so typical of the AFL-CIO in the past is truly on the wane.[70] But despite criticisms from this group and from academic and journalistic skeptics,[71] the AFL-CIO remains one of the most important organizational resources within the alternative power networks for promoting the economic, political, and cultural interests of the new working class.

United for a Fair Economy

Although unions remain the most resource-rich force pressing for economic and political reforms in the United States, new organizations emerged in the 1990s that highlighted growing class inequalities and helped call attention to the structural roots of these inequalities. One multidimensional activist organization working in these areas is United for a Fair Economy (UFE). It was created in 1996 out of the merger of the Share the Wealth Project and the Joint Project on Equality, both of which were founded in 1994. UFE is a "national organization that draws public attention to the growth of income and wealth inequality in the United States—and to the implications of this inequality for America's democracy, economy, and society."[72]

The organization disseminates information on wealth and income inequality via a number of publications, including a quarterly newsletter titled *Too Much*. In addition to serving as a kind of class-consciousness-raising organization, UFE is also involved in "advocacy and political action, community organizing and coalition building, research and media work, [and] arts and culture [projects]." A 2001 UFE brochure stated that "UFE education programs reach thousands of people in religious congregations, unions, neighborhood groups, and business associations. Over 60,000 people have attended face-to-face UFE educational programs. Our core workshop, 'The Growing Economic Divide,' explores the causes and consequences of the increased wealth gap in the U.S. We have trained over 400 trainers and support a network of 175 volunteers in 35 states."[73]

Although most Americans have probably never heard of UFE, its work and messages have been the subject of reports by many national media outlets such as the *New York Times*, the *Nation*, and Jim Hightower's radio talk show (on independent stations). In fact, "in the past two years, over 2,600 media outlets have covered [UFE's] efforts to address the growing economic divide."[74]

Program on Corporations, Law, and Democracy

Another small organization working to publicize class inequalities and to reform the organizational foundations of the corporate system that promotes privileged-class interests is the Program on Corporations, Law, and Democracy (POCLAD). POCLAD is an "ongoing project" of the nonprofit Council on International and Public Affairs (CIPA), based in New York.[75] Organized in the early 1990s by labor activists Richard Grossman and Ward Morehouse, POCLAD is perhaps best known as the leader of the "corporate charter movement."[76] The purpose of the program is "to embolden citizens and lawmakers to toughen—or rather enforce—state corporate charter laws. These laws . . . give legislatures the power to limit corporations' activities and revoke their right to do business in their state."[77]

POCLAD is actively working to increase public awareness of how corporate power undermines democracy and to mobilize group efforts to challenge and change laws that grant extraordinary powers to corporations. In 1999 POCLAD began publishing a journal titled, *By What Authority*. Its three annual issues typically include articles and commentary analyzing the nature and extent of corporate power and exploring ways of strengthening democracy in the face of such power. In 2001 POCLAD's agenda and reform efforts were reinforced by a new book titled, *Defying Corporations, Defining Democracy: A Book of History and Strategy*, edited by Dean Ritz of the Jeannette Rankin Peace Center, Missoula, Montana, and published by Apex Press.[78]

Since CIPA's total annual revenues in 1999 were only $427,699 and since POCLAD is only one of CIPA's projects, it is clear that POCLAD has a limited resource base.[79] Given its limited resources, POCLAD is unlikely to function as more than a class-consciousness-raising force. However, since it often acts in concert with other like-minded reform groups, perhaps that is a reasonable goal. In its new book, POCLAD

> urges activists to learn from past struggles and to seize the offensive by [taking several actions such as]:
>
> * Defining corporations as public entities subordinate to public control;
> * Banning corporations utterly from elections, lawmaking, charitable giving, and schools;
> * Prohibiting corporations from all discussion and debate about public policy;
> * Stripping corporations of 14th Amendment "equal protection" and "due process" of law;
> * Divesting corporations of 1st Amendment "freedom of speech";
> * Denying corporations the privilege of owning other corporations.[80]

POCLAD also advocates rewriting corporate law to require a reconfiguring of corporate governance. For example, a typical twenty-person corporate board of directors could be required to include seven directors elected by shareholders, seven directors elected by employees, and six directors "elected by a number of other constituencies—such as consumers, suppliers, bondholders, and representatives of local communities."[81]

If implemented as policy, POCLAD's reform agenda would significantly constrain corporate power and impact the current ability of corporations to serve as powerful agents of privileged-class interests. POCLAD's ideas might be dismissed as unrealistic idealism, but the organization has succeeded in attracting growing public attention to an important structural dimension of class inequalities. By encouraging the growth of class consciousness and focusing public attention on a critical feature of the dominant economic power network, POCLAD adds to the legitimacy of class analysis and helps break the silence of the class taboo.

Third-Party Challenges

Within the political arena, the Labor Party and the New Party are two new organizational forces that are grounded in the populist tradition and dedicated to challenging or reforming privileged-class dominance of the current two-party system. The Labor Party traces its roots to 1991 when "delegates of the Oil, Chemical, and Atomic Workers union (OCAW) passed a resolution to launch Labor Party Advocates (LPA) and agitate within the ranks of labor for the founding of a labor party.[82] This effort bore fruit "in June [6–9] 1996, [when] 1,400 elected delegates gathered in Cleveland, Ohio, to found the Labor Party."[83]

In July 1996, the new Labor Party began publishing *Labor Party Press*, with a newspaper-like format, six times a year. The November 1996 issue of *Labor Party Press* introduced the party's campaign for a constitutional amendment (the twenty-eighth) to guarantee every American a job at a living wage. Since then, it has published updates on this campaign and has served as a platform for the Labor Party's Just Healthcare campaign—calling for universal health care and the elimination of health insurance companies. It also has reported on progress to solidify the party organization and a variety of class-based public policy issues including Social Security, NAFTA, health care, welfare reform, the Bush tax cut, and the FTAA initiative. In each instance, the focus has been on reporting how the two major parties have crafted policies advancing privileged-class interests at the expense of the working class. The reports also often emphasize that the mainstream media have assisted in the formation of such policies while ignoring or concealing how these policies have eroded the living standards and quality of life for working-class Americans.[84]

The Labor Party's 1998 Constitutional Convention disappointed many members and supporters because it adopted a narrowly drawn "Electoral Strategy" that makes it very difficult for individuals to run for public office as official Labor Party candidates.[85] The future of the Labor Party is unclear, but the AFL-CIO's increasing interest in issue-oriented politics and campaigns could provide it with a boost in future elections. However, the AFL-CIO's extensive links to the Democratic Party make it an uncertain partner. As one analyst observed, "Wary of upsetting the Democrats, the AFL-CIO and many of its major affiliates have kept their distance from the fledgling Labor Party."[86]

The New Party (NP) represents yet another recent political force organized to promote economic, political, and cultural changes that in many ways reflect the populist tradition. Growing out of Jesse Jackson's run for president in 1988, the New Party was founded in 1992, and now includes more than 11,000 dues-paying members.[87] The basic goal of the New Party is to create a grassroots, mass political movement for change.[88] What kind of change? The "New Party Principles" endorse policies that, if enacted, would reverse many of the class-based inequalities that have produced the new class society over the past quarter century and would substantially alter the institutional structure that has contributed to the development of that system. The Principles call for economic reforms (full employment, a shorter work week, a guaranteed minimum income, a universal "social wage" covering—for example—health care and childcare), electoral reforms (public financing of elections, proportional representation), democratization of banking and financial systems, urban renewal, a more-progressive tax system, a ban on discrimination (by race, gender, age, ethnicity, or sexual orientation), reduced military spending, and new trade policies (to promote higher global living standards).[89]

The New Party has pursued a much more activist electoral stance than the Labor Party. In 1992 it backed a handful of candidates for local and state offices that grew to 25 in 1993, 70 in 1994–95, and 250 in 1996–97. In 2001, the NP claimed that over the last ten years it "won more than 300 of [its] first 400 races."[90] The party's electoral successes have occurred despite extremely limited resources. For example, the six-month budget supporting the NP's 1996–97 electoral activity was only $696,598.81.[91]

The New Party is continuing to expand through aggressive recruiting programs, and it has developed links to numerous progressive and labor organizations sympathetic to its goals and platforms. But as is the case for the Labor Party, the future of the New Party is uncertain. Even so, NP leaders are optimistic, and they invoke memories from America's populist past as examples of what a "third force" can accomplish in American politics. As party organizer Dan Cantor observed, "I look at the Non-Partisan League model [of the 1915–21 era] and I think, that's what progressives need to be looking at today. . . . We need a party that breaks the barriers of conventional politics . . . so that progressive ideas and progressive candidates are no longer marginalized."[92] Jim Fleischman, current NP Executive Director says, "It's a long-term work . . . and I'm excited that the New Party is continuing to lead the way."[93]

The Labor Party and the New Party are only two of many political organizations that have emerged from the growing class inequalities spawned by the new class society. A detailed inventory of recent local and national progressive political challenges to the traditional two-party system has been compiled by David Reynolds in his recent book, *Democracy Unbound*. However, as mentioned earlier, the success of these challenges remains to be seen, and the problems they confront are many. For example, the political-party identification of the U.S. adult population (at all degrees of attachment) was distributed in 1998 as follows: 47 percent Democrat, 36 percent Republican, 17 percent independent.[94] While the percentage of people identifying themselves as independents has grown somewhat in recent years, the general distribution has remained relatively stable for the past thirty years.[95] This means that major shifts in party identification traditions would have to occur before any third party could accumulate a significant base of support . Of course, major shifts have occurred in the past (e.g., the rapid growth of the Republican Party in the 1850s and of several populist parties in the late 1800s and early 1900s) in the context of national economic and political crises. Thus, the recent growth of progressive third parties may well signal an emerging shift in the political landscape as groups organize to challenge the inequities in the new class society.

Living Wage Campaign

As we learned in the opening chapters of this book, many Americans work full time while earning incomes that put them below or near the poverty line. They are the "working poor," with earnings at the minimum wage ($5.15 per hour) or barely above that level. Growing concern over the large number of working poor in the United States has led to a coalition of groups—the New Party, the AFL-CIO, and ACORN (Association of Community Organizations for Reform Now)— working together to shape a national social movement called the Living Wage Campaign. Working at the local level in many cities throughout the country, the campaign has sought to pass local city or county ordinances requiring private businesses that benefit from public contracts to pay their workers a living wage. Thus, businesses with large city or county service contracts; or those receiving substantial financial assistance through tax abatements, loans, or tax financing, would be required to meet specified wage standards.

The justification for the Living Wage Campaign is straightforward and based on simple fairness; namely, that public tax dollars should not subsidize poverty-wage work. Allowing companies receiving public money to pay poverty-level wages presents taxpayers with a double bill. The first bill is for the cost of the initial subsidy. The second bill is for the food stamps, emergency medical, housing, and social services that poverty-wage workers require to support themselves and their families. If workers received a living wage, which might be set at $8.20 an hour (equivalent to the poverty line for a family of four) they would be better able to meet family needs without additional assistance. The actual living-wage ordinances around the country have set wage levels ranging from $6.25 to $12 an hour, depending on local economic conditions.

ACORN, the most active of the organizations involved in living-wage campaigns, is the nation's oldest and largest grassroots organization of low- and moderate-income people. It claims a membership of over 100,000 in thirty cities. ACORN chapters have won living-wage ordinances in St. Louis, St. Paul (Minnesota), Boston, Oakland, Chicago, and Detroit, and currently (summer 2001) have campaigns in process in Albuquerque, New Orleans, Little Rock, Dallas, New York City, Washington, D.C., and Sacramento. In addition to working on living-wage campaigns, ACORN helps to build community-based coalitions providing a power base for low- and moderate-income people, helps to develop leadership skills, and gets out the message that elected public officials will be held accountable.

Media Reform: FAIR

Although Fairness and Accuracy in Media Reporting (FAIR) was organized in 1986, the 1990s witnessed its emergence as an increasingly important force in support of progressive economic, political, and cultural reforms within the mass media. The nature and goals of FAIR are printed inside the cover of each issue of *EXTRA!* (its bimonthly magazine), which prints and distributes through paid subscriptions and counter sales approximately 18,600 copies per issue.[96] "FAIR, the national media watch group, has been offering well-documented criticism of media bias and censorship since 1986. . . . As a progressive group, FAIR believes that

structural reform is ultimately needed to break up the dominant media conglomerates, establish independent public broadcasting, and promote strong, nonprofit
sources of information."[97]

In addition to publishing *EXTRA!*, FAIR also publishes *EXTRA!Update*, a four-
page bimonthly newsletter, and it organizes a number of activities in support of its
goals of exposing media biases and censorship. These include maintaining a website (www.fair.org), distributing FAIR's radio program, "CounterSpin," to more
than 130 stations and making it available on RealAudio (www.webactive.com),
and selling products consistent with its goals, such as audiotapes from "Counter-
Spin" (and panel discussions), book-length compilations of selections from *EX-
TRA!* and other books dealing with media issues. Compared with major media
firms, FAIR is a small organization that relies mainly on *EXTRA!* subscriber revenues and donations to support a ten-person staff and an annual budget of approximately $1 million.[98]

FAIR is one of many organizations that populate the alternative power networks,
but it is especially significant because of its constant focus on the biases and power
of the media. FAIR is not the only progressive organization that routinely critiques
the economic, political, and cultural power of the mass media. But its consistent focus on mass media content makes it a valuable resource for understanding how
privileged-class control of the media industry assists in maintaining and legitimating the new class society. FAIR's perspective and goals are consistent with many features of the populist tradition—especially its efforts to increase public class
consciousness and critique the antidemocratic dangers and consequences of concentrated economic, political, and cultural power in the mass media.

Beneath the Waterline: Militant Resistance

> Those who make peaceful revolution impossible make violent revolution in-
> evitable.
>
> —John F. Kennedy, March 12, 1962

While the examples of class-based resistance described earlier differ in their goals
and strategies, they are similar in their use of conventional forms of politics and
protest. As such, they represent forms of institutionalized class conflict, or class
struggle played according to some accepted set of rules. At times, these forms of resistance are highly stylized and choreographed, as in the case of consumer boy-
cotts, or the arrest of prominent political figures who join in acts of civil
disobedience *in order* to get arrested and thereby call attention to the issue. Another feature of these forms of resistance is that they take place in conventional
political and institutional settings, and with the full cooperation and participation
of the media to report on the planned or actual resistance.

We can get a glimpse of the kind of militant resistance that may be submerged beneath the waterline of public awareness by looking at two very recent prototypes of radical resistance. The first is Timothy McVeigh, convicted and executed for the bombing of the federal building in Oklahoma City. The second is Theodore Kaczynski, the so-called Unabomber, who was convicted for making homemade bombs that killed three people and wounded 23 others. These two men could not be more different in terms of their backgrounds. McVeigh, a high school graduate who joined the Army, served in a combat role in the Gulf War, and returned to civilian life to work in a number of low-level jobs. Kaczynski is a graduate of Harvard University and a former mathematics professor at the University of California at Berkeley. How did these very different paths lead these two men to the same destination, believing that violent, destructive acts were necessary to call attention to the evils of "big government," in McVeigh's case, or the "industrial-technological system," in Kaczynski's case?

McVeigh can be viewed as a part of a much larger group of "the dispossessed," a generation of younger Americans with low income, no savings, and limited education and job skills. They are also without social capital, or the ties to people with more resources who may be able to help them on a path to a secure future. Their lives are going nowhere, and they have no prospects. But perhaps of equal importance to their lack of resources, they also lack a moral account for their lives that helps to explain their condition. In short, they cannot even view themselves as "victims," because they have embraced a belief in individualism and "picking yourself up by your own bootstraps." McVeigh is an example of the American Dream Betrayed, and he used this language in a 1992 letter to the editor of the *Union Sun & Journal* in Lockport, New York: "The 'American Dream' of the middle class has all but disappeared, substituted with people struggling just to get by with next week's groceries. Do we have to shed blood to reform the current system? I hope it doesn't come to that. But it might." McVeigh's hostility toward the government may have started when he failed to qualify for Army Special Forces. But his rightward drift was solidified by the 1992 battle in Idaho between Randy Weaver, a White separatist, and agents of the U.S. Bureau of Alcohol, Firearms, and Tobacco (which resulted in the death of Weaver's wife), and the siege by federal agents of the Branch Davidians in Waco, Texas that resulted in the deaths of David Koresh and 80 of his followers.[99]

Kaczynski can be viewed as representative of "the disinherited," a generation of educated young Americans from comfortable social and economic backgrounds with bright prospects for their futures. Instead of inheriting a healthy society, as part of their meritocratic birthright, they have been presented with a society that worships economic growth and technological progress while it destroys the environment and the wilderness areas. Drawing upon their knowledge of science, technology, and politics, many young, educated Americans would probably agree with Kaczynski's apocalyptic views: "The industrial-technological system is a disaster for the human race. There is no way of reforming or modifying the system so as to prevent it from depriving people of dignity and autonomy. . . . We therefore advocate revolution against the industrial system. . . . This is not to be a POLITI-CAL revolution. Its object will be to overthrow not governments but the economic and technological basis of the present society" (from the Unabomber manifesto). Kaczynski is an example of the American Dream Corrupted, leaving a generation of educated Americans with a society that limits personal freedoms and destroys the natural world.

Militant and armed resistance, which appeared as an urban phenomenon in the 1960s, has apparently shifted to rural America, home of the militia movement concerned about the growing power of the federal government, and the setting for radical environmental activists who take direct action against the commercial interests that threaten to harm the environment. What has happened in rural America to transform it from the idealized and romanticized vision of the independent farmer, steeped in values of family, community, and God?

One thing that has happened is that rural America has become corporatized just like the rest of the country. Throughout much of the twentieth century, government support and tax benefits have gone primarily to corporate farms and multinational agribusinesses like Archer-Daniels-Midland and Cargill Corporation. The pattern of income and wealth inequality that has produced the double-diamond class structure is clearly revealed in the pattern of land ownership in the United States. Land ownership has the appearance of Central American feudal agriculture—a small number of very large land owners and most small farmers either driven off the land to work on export-driven corporate farms, or left with small subsistence plots. In the United States, the wealthiest 5 percent of landowners own 75 percent of the land, while the poorest landowners (75 percent of all landowners) own 3 percent of the land.[100]

In addition to the economic impoverishment of rural American farm-dependent towns is the cultural and political marginalization of rural life and values. The privileged class in the United States dominates cultural and political life within a bicoastal, urban framework. Rural America is at best ignored, and at worst, the target of ridicule and stereotypes (has anybody seen *Deliverance*, or heard any new trailer-trash jokes?). The combination of economic impoverishment and economic-cultural marginalization of rural America has apparently found nourishment in the history of rural radicalism and populism to produce a militant "left" and "right."[101] The militia movement and the radical environmental movement are the most contemporary expressions of a long-standing suspicion of the federal government and the industrial-technological system.

The militia movement is based on a tradition of local control and suspicion of the federal government. There were reports of organized militia in the 1980s in Michigan, Montana, and Texas, and they appeared to be diverse in their degree of emphasis on military preparedness and active military maneuvers. It is difficult to obtain firm estimates of their numerical significance because they are loosely linked local groups lacking a national organizational structure. A 1994 report by the Anti-Defamation League found evidence of militia activity in 13 states, and an online publication, *Militia Watch Dog*, reports identifying at least one militia group in 40 states, with a membership ranging from 10,000 to 40,000.[102] An interesting recent development has been the use of the Internet by militia groups to get their message to a larger audience while stressing more conventional forms of activism.[103] Militia websites provide extensive information about constitutional rights, pending legislation, up-to-date accounts of government abuse, and advice on how to contact members of Congress. Some militia websites attempt to counteract their negative image by presenting inclusive statements welcoming to their cause Americans of all racial, ethnic, and religious groups. Themes that are common to most if not all militia publications and websites include discussion of constitutional rights in connection with the right to bear arms, the role of "common law" in our justice system, Christian values, anticommunism, and mistrust of the federal government. There is also concern about protecting American identity and threats to national sovereignty, leading to anti-United Nations positions and anti-immigration policies.[104]

Radical actions against corporate and industrial projects that are believed to be harmful to the environment have been called "ecotage." The actions involved include vandalizing industrial sites, burning luxury homes that intrude on wilderness areas, disabling construction equipment, driving metal spikes into trees, blockading logging roads, and disrupting land surveys. The two groups that are best known for their actions as part of the ecological resistance movement are Earth First! and the Earth Liberation Front (ELF). Earth First! was formed in 1980 and appeared to be influenced by Edward Abbey's 1975 novel *The Monkey Wrench Gang*, a romanticized account of a group of eco-raiders who used illegal tactics to stop the growth of suburbs in Tucson, Arizona. Earth First! combines an environmental philosophy of biocentrism, stressing the intrinsic worth of human and nonhuman life, with a political analysis that challenges the belief that the United States has a democratic political system. Earth First! believes that the U.S. political system is dominated by corporate economic power and will be unable to act in time to avert ecological disaster.

Although less well known, ELF was formed in 1996 and is believed to be responsible for numerous acts of destruction resulting in millions of dollars in damage. ELF is either very mobile or has a wide network of members, because it has been identified with acts of ecotage in California, Oregon, Colorado, Michigan, Indiana, and New York.[105]

The potential for militant resistance represented by militia groups and radical environmentalists appears to be serious. The fact that such groups have been operating for at least two decades suggests that they have been attracting new members and the resources needed to continue operations. This may only be the beginning of a resistance movement in the United States.[106] A more serious and deadly international threat became apparent on September 11, 2001, when four commercial passenger jets were hijacked in flight and turned into deadly missiles as two of the planes were purposely crashed into the Twin Towers of the World

Trade Center in New York, a third was flown into the Pentagon Building, and the fourth crashed as it was headed to a target believed to have been either the White House or Camp David. The grievances of the groups believed to be responsible for these acts of terrorism may be traced to the U.S. role as a global military and economic power, especially the intrusion of Western economic institutions and Western culture into societies with fundamentalists groups dedicated to resisting secular developments.

The Superclass "Suits," the Dream, and the New Working Class

In contrast with the messages of class struggle emphasized by the seven reform groups and the apocalyptic imagery sometimes invoked by militant resistance groups, the mainstream media delivers a constant win-win spin on class-based issues such as labor-management conflicts over workers' concerns with wages, benefits, and job security. "Team players will make us all winners in the global economy," workers are told. "Workers can be investors too! Think long-term and we'll share a prosperous future together." Such messages attempt to transform workers' and activists' concerns with class inequalities and analysis into the marginalized ravings of anachronistic cranks. Even so, class-reform-minded members of the alternative power networks confront the dominant-power-network players' script with an expose-and-challenge strategy, which seeks to unmask the reality of class interests and inequalities while stripping legitimacy away from the instruments of privileged-class power.

The mask-and-legitimate and expose-and-challenge approaches crash head-on today over a number of topics, but the prospects for and the means of achieving the American Dream strike especially bright sparks of conflict. The "suits" say, "The dream lives! It is alive and achievable for anyone with a positive mental attitude." How do they make the case? With the media awash in "bridge to the next century" and "information superhighway" metaphors, the new prosperity is claimed to be just around the corner. Success, as pitched by credentialed-class hucksters in the 1990s, was based in gleaming high-tech ventures where the road to the American Dream ran straight through multilevel marketing to a dot-com website. That was then. Today (the early 2000s), the same hucksters are pitching a slightly different message. Success is still out there and available to all. But compared with the recent past, achieving the Dream today requires more expensive coaching, patience, savvy investing, and long hours of work. First, pay your dues (prove you're worthy); then claim the prize (maybe).

By contrast, alternative-power-network-based class analysis says, "Welcome to the new American scheme!" Committed to exposing and challenging the mask-and-legitimate myths disseminated by dominant-power-network representatives, class-reform analysts see a different reality. This view says, "Blinded by the fast-buck light, the success-cult members of the new working class either ignore or never see the class-biased cynical deception, distraction, and exploitation inherent in 'the dream lives' schemes." Today's hucksters play on the insecurities of life in the new working class and feed on the fading memory of a more open opportunity structure that, to some extent, accommodated and rewarded the aspirations and efforts of working-class members to achieve a "good job" or even some measure of upward social mobility.

Alternative-power-network-based critics who document the realities of the new class system are unlikely to be welcome guests at the still rapidly metastasizing motivational and entrepreneurial seminars and software certification programs. These events—with their slavish odes to new opportunities for material enrichment and personal growth via "positive mental attitudes," multilevel-marketing schemes, websites, software savvy, day trading, and other cyberspace scams—typically not only charge admission up front but also close with a sales pitch at the end—often for motivational tapes, DVDs, high-tech hardware, software, and instructional CDs. Such ventures have not been deterred by the market meltdown of the early 2000s. In fact, the volatile stock market is pitched as creating even more opportunities for savvy "insiders."

This bright and shiny view of new opportunities facilitated by high-technology-based ventures today is attacked by the expose-and-challenge views of critics of the new class system. As they point out, a major function of high-tech, computer-coordinated electronic equipment is to speed-lash workers and consumers into a frenzy of tightly monitored, closely controlled, and cleverly manipulated production and consumption that perpetuates and reinforces the new class society. Moreover, the critics maintain that even as some machines are orchestrating the control processes, others are efficiently channeling most of the profits generated by computer-driven production and marketing to superclass owners and distributing generous rewards to credentialed-class "suits" in payment for their professional contributions to creating, maintaining, and justifying the new class system.

The alternative-power-network view that the privileged class oversees dominant power networks employing computer-based, worker-consumer control crashes head-on with the corporate ministry of information line that says classes do not count and computers are our pals. The "suits" say class inequalities are irrelevant, and computers are the way, the truth, and the light—and the path to economic salvation and class mobility in the new American century. And woe unto those who fail to embrace the team-player mentality and the high-tech faith—for they shall be cast into the Lake of Economic Fire—meaning especially the marginalized contingent and excluded zones of the new working class. The "suits" say team play and the high-tech computer tide will raise all boats to new levels of prosperity, save our collective economic future, and ensure the American Dream as far as the eye can see into the twenty-first century. It is a predictable mask-and-legitimate line. Alternative-power-network members disagree. Committed to an expose-and-challenge strategy but with severely limited resources, they are vulnerable to stigmatization through name-calling ("neo-Luddites") and institutional marginalization by the "suits." And they are vulnerable to the simplistic

Scrooge scenario for reform that deeply resonates within a working class that has been intensely socialized to the individualistic credo of American culture.

The Future: The Scrooge Scenario versus the Structural Scenario

> Valiant people and dedicated civic groups can do far better than invest energies and resources into abysmal regulatory swamps designed by corporate lawyers.
>
> —Ward Morehouse, co-director, Program on Corporations, Law, and
> Democracy, 2001

In the world according to Dickens, reform is a function of conscience. In *A Christmas Carol*, the ghosts of Christmas Past, Present, and Future visit Ebenezer Scrooge. This gets results. Shown the consequences of his selfishness, Scrooge is appropriately appalled and transformed. He reforms his miserly ways, and the community becomes a better place. It is a powerful and comforting morality tale grounded in an unspoken assumption that the selfish pursuit by the rich of their narrow economic interests can be blunted and redirected by consciousness-raising experiences that awaken a latent social conscience.

The "Scrooge scenario" can be seen as a kind of pattern for reform, favored and promoted by privileged-class leaders, that focuses attention on individual renewal and personal commitment. Media accounts of political corruption involving PACs, influence peddlers, insiders, and fixers as well as economic warts such as sweatshops and child labor are portrayed as bad apples. The system is sound, we are told; we just need to replace rotten apples or force the bad apples to undergo a publicly reported transformation involving admissions of wrongdoing, acceptance of guilt, and repentance—along with promises to go forth and sin no more.

The "structural democracy scenario" places little faith in the Scrooge approach. Class reformers see undemocratic political, economic, and cultural structures controlled by the privileged class and unaccountable to the public as the problem. The populist-like "structural democracy scenario" is favored by many class-reform activists. The primary aim of this view is to revitalize the practice of democratic participation in politics and government as well as extending the principles of democratic governance to the corporate structures that currently dominate the economic and cultural arenas of our society and undergird the many inequalities of the new class society.

Although the structural democracy project of resolving class inequalities is highly problematic and uncertain, we believe it can usefully serve as a point of departure for a national dialogue on the closeted, taboo subject of growing class inequalities. An increasingly class-conscious public can provide the economic, political, and human resources necessary to support existing and yet-to-be-established institutions committed to the interests of the new working class and to reforming the new class society.

As we have seen throughout this book, there is a real and pressing need for structural, not Scrooge-like, changes in our highly unequal new class system. The reforms proposed or initiated by organizations cited in this chapter provide some concrete examples of what real structural changes aimed at redressing class inequities might look like. Such reforms on a much wider scale are essential if we are to begin the process of melting the iceberg of inequality before it rips open the current version of the *Titanic* known as the new class society and sends our democratic experiment to a permanent resting spot at the bottom of history.

NOTES

1. International Media Data Base, "The Top Grossing Movies of All Time at the Worldwide Box Office," on the Internet at http://www.us.imdb.com/Charts/worldtop movies (visited October 1, 2001). *Forrest Gump* is now (2001) eighth among all films ever released in worldwide gross receipts. It is sixth among all U.S. films ever released with gross receipts of $329 million. By comparison, *The Titanic* is the number-one grossing film of all time in the United States and the world (gross receipts: $600 million, United States, $1.8 billion worldwide).

2. Charles Derber, *The Wilding of America* (New York: St. Martin's Press, 1996), 150.

3. Noshua Watson, "Inside the 500," *Fortune,* April 16, 2001, 232–33.

4. Gene Koretz, "Downsized in a Down Economy," *Business Week,* September 17, 2001, 36.

5. Naomi Klein, "Signs of the Times," *Nation,* October 22, 2001, 15–20.

6. Michael Useem, *The Inner Circle* (New York: Oxford University Press, 1984), 172–200.

7. Joel Bleifuss, "Know Thine Enemy: A Brief History of Corporations," *In These Times,* February 8, 1998, 16–17.

8. Charles Derber, *Corporation Nation* (New York: St. Martin's Press, 1998).

9. Quoted in Jim Hightower, "Chomp!" *Utne Reader,* March–April 1998, 59.

10. Paul J. Dimaggio and Walter W. Powell, "The Iron Cage Revisited: Institutional Isomorphism and Collective Rationality in Organizational Fields," *American Sociological Review* 48 (1983): 147–60.

11. Charles Perrow, "A Society of Organizations," *Theory and Society* 20 (1991): 725–62. Also see Derber, *Corporation Nation,* 172–86.

12. Joe R. Feagin, *Racial and Ethnic Relations* (Englewood Cliffs, N.J.: Prentice Hall, 1989).

13. Barbara Reskin and Irene Padavic, *Women and Men at Work* (Thousand Oaks, Calif.: Pine Forge Press, 1994); Chris Tilly and Charles Tilly, *Work Under Capitalism* (Boulder, Colo.: Westview Press, 1998).

14. Gregory Mantsios, "Class in America: Myths and Realities," in *Race, Class, and Gender in the United States,* ed. Paula S. Rothenberg (New York: St. Martin's Press, 1995), 131–43.

15. Robert Granfield, "Making It by Faking It," *Journal of Contemporary Ethnography* 20 (1991): 331–51.

16. Quoted in Matthew Josephson, *The Robber Barons* (New York: Harcourt, Brace and World, 1934), 325.

17. Robert Granfield and Thomas Koenig, "Pathways into Elite Law Firms: Professional Stratification and Social Networks," in *Research in Politics and Society,* vol. 4, *The Political Consequences of Social Networks,* ed. Gwen Moore and J. Allen Whitt (Greenwich, Conn.: JAI Press, 1992).

18. Basil Bernstein, *Class, Codes, and Control,* 3 vols. (London: Routledge and Kegan Paul, 1971–73).

19. Allan Sloan, "What Goes Up . . . ," *Newsweek,* April 13, 1998, 42–43.

20. "Dow Jones Closing Averages September 3–October 12," *Indianapolis Star,* October 13, 2001, C3.

21. Francis X. Clines, "Fueled by Success, Buchanan Revels in Rapid-Fire Oratory," *New York Times,* February 15, 1996; Elizabeth Kolbert and Adam Clymer, "The Politics of Layoff: In Search of a Message," *New York Times,* March 8, 1996.

22. James Bennet, "Patrick J. Buchanan: Harsh Language for Party Leaders," *New York Times,* February 19, 1996.

23. Michael Kazin, *The Populist Persuasion* (New York: Basic Books, 1995), 1.

24. Ibid., 2.

25. Robert Parry, "The Right-Wing Media Machine," *EXTRA!* March–April 1995, 6–10. Also see Joseph L. Conn and Rob Boston, "Pat Robertson's Media Empire," *EXTRA!* March–April 1995, 13–16.

26. Jeff Faux, "NAFTA at Seven: Its Impact on Workers in All Three Nations" (Washington, D.C.: Economic Policy Institute, May 2001).

27. David Elsila, "No More NAFTAs!" *UAW Solidarity,* April–May 1997, 10–12.

28. Robert E. Scott, "NAFTA's Hidden Costs" (Washington, D.C.: Economic Policy Institute, May 2001).

29. David Moberg, "Fast Track Is Back," *In These Times,* July 23, 2001, 17–18. Also see "Frontlines," *UAW Solidarity,* November 2001, 4–5; William Greider, "The Right and the US Trade Law: Invalidating the 20th Century," *Nation,* October 15, 2001, 21–29; Julie R. Hirschfeld, "Zoellick Pushes for Prompt Revival of Fast-Track Authority," *Congressional Quarterly Weekly,* February 3, 2001, 295–96.

30. Janine Jackson, "Fast Track 1, Democracy 0," *EXTRA!* November–December 1997, 9–10.

31. Greider, "The Right and US Trade Law," 27. Also see David Moberg, "FTAA, Eh? A Bigger, Badder Trade Deal," *In These Times,* April 16, 2001, 16–19; and Laura McClure, "Free Trade Ache of the Americas," *Labor Party Press,* July 2001, 4–5.

32. Faux, "NAFTA at Seven," 3, 16–18, 23.

33. Charles J. Whalen, Paul Magnusson, and Geri Smith, "NAFTA's Scorecard: So Far, So Good," *Business Week,* July 9, 2001, 54–56.

34. Faux, "NAFTA at Seven," 8, 19, 24–25.

35. Whalen, Magnusson, and Smith, "NAFTA's Scorecard: So Far, So Good."

36. William Greider, "Saving the Global Economy," *Nation,* December 15, 1997, 11–16.

37. Moberg, "FTAA, Eh? A Bigger, Badder Trade Deal." Also see Moberg, "Fast Track Is Back," and Greider, "The Right and US Trade Law."

38. Alejandro Reuss, Arthur MacEwan, Phineas Baxandall, and John Miller, "The ABC's of 'Free Trade' Agreements," *Dollars and Sense,* January–February 2001, 24. Also see Kim Moody, "NAFTA, WTO, MAI, IMF, FTAA, AGOA . . . Where Does It End?" *Labor Notes,* May 1998, 16.

39. Faux, "NAFTA at Seven." Also see Stacie Garnett, "It's Tough to Be Young Today," *Dollars and Sense,* September–October 1997, 50.

40. Lawrence Mishel, Jared Bernstein, and John Schmitt, *The State of Working America, 2000–2001* (Ithaca, N.Y.: Cornell University Press, 2001), 222. Also see Marc Breslow and Matthew Howard, "The Real Un(der)Employment Rate," *Dollars and Sense,* May–June 1995, 35.

41. Mishel, Bernstein, and Schmitt, *The State of Working America, 2000–2001,* 157–60, 251–54. Also see Chris Tilly, "Next Steps for the Living Wage Movement," *Dollars and Sense,* September–October 2001, 36–39, 48.

42. Walter Korpi, *The Democratic Class Struggle* (London: Routledge, 1983).

43. Vicente Navarro, "Production and the Welfare State: The Political Context of Reforms," *International Journal of Health Services* 21 (1991): 585–614.

44. Neil deMause, "A Welfare Success—but the Program Died," *EXTRA!* September–October 2000, 23. Also see Neil deMause, "Out of Sight, Out of Mind," *EXTRA!* November–December 1997, 25–27.

45. Teresa Amott, "Will the Economy Be Less Stable?" *Dollars and Sense,* November–December 1996, 22–23.

46. Robert Dreyfuss, "Neighbor to Neighbor Takes on Medicare Myths," *EXTRA!* March–April 1997, 17–18.

47. Kim Moody, "America Gets a Virtual Raise," *Labor Notes,* February 1997, 15–16.

48. Mishel, Bernstein, and Schmitt, *The State of Working America, 2000–2001,* 142–43. Also see John Leland, "Blessed by the Bull," *Newsweek,* April 27, 1998, 51–53.

49. John Miller, "Tax Cuts: Clinton and Congress Feed the Wealthy," *Dollars and Sense,* November–December 1997, 43.

50. Michelle Cottle, "The Real Class War," *Washington Monthly,* July–August 1997, 13.

51. John Miller, "More Wealth for the Wealthy: The Estate Tax Giveaway and What to Do about It," *Dollars and Sense,* November–December 1997, 26–28, 33.

52. Robert Perrucci and Earl Wysong, "Organizational Power, Generative Capital, and Class Closure," paper presented at the annual meeting of the Pacific Sociological Association, San Francisco, March 31, 2001.

53. Mike Males, "Wild In Deceit: Why 'Teen Violence' Is Poverty Violence in Disguise," *EXTRA!* March–April 1996, 7–9.

54. Noreen Connell, "Underfunded Schools: Why Money Matters," *Dollars and Sense,* March–April 1998, 14. Also see David Stratman, "School Reform and the Attack on Public Education," *Dollars and Sense,* March–April 1998, 7; "Voucher Program Fails to Deliver," *AFT American Teacher,* November 2001, 14.

55. U.S. Department of Commerce, Bureau of the Census, *Statistical Abstract of the United States* (Washington, D.C.: U.S. Government Printing Office, 2000), 190, 487.

56. Ibid., 191.

57. Don Kuehn, "Saving for College with Section 529 Plans," *AFT American Teacher,* September 2001, 19.

58. David Moberg, "The Six-Year Itch," *Nation,* September 3/10, 2001, 11; AFL-CIO, "Frequently Asked Questions," on the Internet at http://www.aflcio.org/front/fags.htm (visited October 17, 2001); Ken Silverstein and Alexander Cockburn, "How's He Doing? Has Sweeney Changed Labor?" *CounterPunch,* July 16–31, 1997, 1.

59. Janine Jackson, "Moribund Militants: Corporate Media on (Re)Organized Labor," *EXTRA!* January–February 1996, 6–7.

60. AFL-CIO, "Working Families Agenda," on the Internet at http://www.aflcio.org/front/wfa.htm (visited October 17, 2001). Also see Moberg, "The Six-Year Itch," 11–16.

61. Russ Davis, "AFL-CIO Unveils Program to Revitalize Labor Movement," *Labor Notes,* March 1997, 1, 14.

62. David Glenn, "Adding Brains to Labor's New Political Muscle," *In These Times,* December 14, 1997, 22–23. Also see Moberg, "The Six-Year Itch," 11–16.

63. Suzanne Wall, "Union Candidates Use a 'Bottom-Up' Approach to Winning Political Power," *Labor Notes,* April 1998, 3.

64. Moberg, "The Six-Year Itch," 11.

65. Silverstein and Cockburn, "How's He Doing?" 1.

66. Moberg, "The Six-Year Itch," 11.

67. AFL-CIO, "Working Families Agenda," op. cit., Internet.

68. G. William Domhoff, *Who Rules America? Power and Politics in the Year 2000* (Mountain View, Calif.: Mayfield, 1998), 304.

69. Executive Enterprises, "How to Stay Union-Free into the 21st Century," 8-page brochure (New York: Executive Enterprises, 21 Penn Plaza, 10001–2727, February 1998).

70. Kim Moody, *Workers in a Lean World: Unions in the International Economy* (New York: Verso, 1998).

71. Kate Bronfenbrenner, "Changing to Organize," *Nation,* September 3/10, 2001, 16–20. Also see Silverstein and Cockburn, "How's He Doing?" 1, 6–8.

72. "Programs and Achievements/Program Directions," brochure (Boston: United for a Fair Economy, 37 Temple Place [fifth floor], 02111, ca. 1997).

73. "United for a Fair Economy Programs," brochure (Boston: United for a Fair Economy, 37 Temple Place [fifth floor], 02111, ca. 1997).

74. "Fair Economy Resource Guide" (Boston: United for a Fair Economy, 37 Temple Place [fifth floor], 02111, Summer–Fall 2001).

75. Council on International and Public Affairs, "About Us," and "Summary Report for 1999," 1, 5; on the Internet at http://www.cipa-apex.org/home.html. Also see http://www.cipa-apex.org/anreport.htm (visited October 17, 2001).

76. Craig Cox, "Taming the Corporate Beast," *Utne Reader,* March–April 1998, 60.

77. Joel Bleifuss, "The New Abolitionists," *In These Times,* April 1, 1996, 13.

78. Council on International and Public Affairs, "Summary Report for 1999," 5; *By What Authority* 3(3), Summer 2001; The Apex Press, "New Book Urges Democratic Offensive to Purge Corporations' Constitutional Authority to Govern," September 10, 2001, on the Internet at http://www.poclad.org/news/dcdd.html (visited October 17, 2001).

79. Council on International and Public Affairs, "Summary Report for 1999," 7.

80. Apex Press, "New Book Urges Democratic Offensive."

81. Fred Block, "Toward Real Corporate Responsibility," *In These Times,* May 27, 1996, 27.

82. David Reynolds, *Democracy Unbound* (Boston: South End Press, 1997), 225, 228.

83. "Two Parties Give Us Six New Reasons for One Party for Us," *Labor Party Press,* March 1998, 1.

84. For examples see recent *Labor Party Press* issues.

85. "Set to Organize," *Labor Party Press,* January 1999, 3. Also see "Labor Party First Constitutional Convention Documents: Electoral Strategy," *Labor Party Press—Special Supplement,* January 1999, 2.

86. Glenn, "Adding Brains to Labor's New Political Muscle," 24.

87. John Nichols, "After Fusion: The New New Party," *In These Times,* March 22, 1998, 18.

88. Reynolds, *Democracy Unbound,* 186.

89. "New Party Principles," *New Party News,* Spring 2001, 7.

90. "New Party: A Fair Economy, A Real Democracy, A New Party," on the Internet at http://www.newparty.org/ (visited September 26, 2001).

91. Daniel Cantor, "New Party Membership Solicitation Letter, Pledge Form," and "It Adds Up," budget summary, September 1, 1996, 1–6 plus additional forms.

92. Quoted in Nichols, "After Fusion: The New New Party," 20.

93. Jim Fleischmann, "Where Do We Go From Here?" *New Party News,* Spring 2001, 2.

94. James A. Davis, *General Social Surveys, 1972–1998* (Storrs, Conn.: Center for Public Opinion Research, 1998), 83.

95. U.S. Department of Commerce, Bureau of the Census, *Statistical Abstract of the United States* (Washington, D.C.: U.S. Government Printing Office, 2000), 289.

96. "Statement of Ownership," *EXTRA!* November–December 2000, 27.

97. "What's FAIR?" *EXTRA!* September–October 2001, 2.

98. FAIR's activities are summarized from various issues of *EXTRA!* (its bimonthly newsletter), *EXTRA!Update,* and contributor solicitation letters. A FAIR letter to supporters in June 2001 stated that FAIR has a "media-savvy 10-person staff." A December 1996 FAIR letter soliciting donations to support the organization listed FAIR's annual budget at $850,000. Assuming a growth rate of 3 percent per year since 1996, FAIR's 2002 budget would be approximateley $1 million.

99. Barbara Ehrenreich, "The Making of McVeigh," *Progressive,* July 2001, 14–15.

100. Osha Gray Davidson, *Broken Heartland: The Rise of America's Rural Ghetto* (Iowa City: University of Iowa Press, 1996).

101. Catherine M. Stock, *Rural Radicals: Righteous Rage in the American Grain* (Ithaca, N.Y.: Cornell University Press, 1996).

102. Anti-Defamation League, *Armed and Dangerous: Militia Takes Aim at the Federal Government.* Fact Finding Report, 1994.

103. Kevin Ward, "Militia Movement and the Internet," on the Internet at http://camden-www.rutgers.edu~wood/445/ward.html (visited October 12, 2001).

104. Leisa Meyer, "Militia Movement," on the Internet at http://encarta.msn.com/ concise index (visited October 12, 2001).

105. Kevin Fedarko, "Knobby Fires," *Outside,* June 2001: 24–26.

106. Joel Dyer, *Harvest of Rage: Why Oklahoma City Is Only the Beginning.* Boulder, Colo.: Westview Press, 1998.

Bibliography

Ackerman, Seth. "Has ABC News Given Up on Accuracy?" *EXTRA!* (November–December 1999): 18–19.

———. "The Most Biased Name in News." *EXTRA!* (July–August 2001): 10–12, 14–18.

———. "Populist Rhetoric Unpopular with the Pundits." *EXTRA!* (January–February 2001): 9.

———. "Prattle in Seattle." *EXTRA!* (January–February 2000): 13–17.

———. "Surplus Shell Games." *EXTRA!* (November–December 2000): 8–10.

"Action Alert." *EXTRA!* (December 1995): 4.

Adams, Rebecca. "GOP-Business Alliance Yields Swift Reversal of Ergonomics Rule." *Congressional Quarterly Weekly* (March 10, 2001): 535–39.

Adler, Jerry. "The Rise of the Overclass." *Newsweek* (July 31, 1995): 33–46.

Adler, Patricia, Steven J. Kless, and Peter Adler. "Socialization to Gender Roles: Popularity among Elementary Boys and Girls." *Sociology of Education* 65 (1992): 169–87.

AFL-CIO. "Frequently Asked Questions." 2001. Available at http://www.aflcio.org.

———. "Social Security: Who's Behind the Private Accounts Scheme?" 2001. Available at http://www.aflcio.org.

———. "Working Families Agenda." 2001. Available at http://www.aflcio.org.

———. "Young Workers without College Degrees Are the 'Forgotten Majority.'" *High Hopes, Little Trust: A Study of Young Workers and Their Ups and Downs in the New Economy.* Washington, D.C.: AFL-CIO, 1999.

Ageism on the Agenda. Special Issue. *EXTRA!* (March–April 1997).

Aguirre, Adalberto Jr., and David V. Baker. *Structured Inequality in the United States.* Upper Saddle River, N.J.: Prentice Hall, 2000.

Akre, Jane. "We Report, They Decide: Fox TV Censors Series on Milk Hazards." *National News Reporter* (June 1998): 12–13.

Akre, Jane, and Steve Wilson. "Fox BGH Suit." 2001. Available at http://www.foxbhgsuit.com.

Alba, Richard D., and Gwen Moore. "Ethnicity in the American Elite." *American Sociological Review* 47 (1982): 373–83.

Albelda, Randy. "Farewell to Welfare but Not to Poverty." *Dollars and Sense* (November–December 1996): 16–19.

Alexander, Charles P. "To Our Readers." *Time* (April–May 2000): 4.

Alexander, Karl S., Martha Cook, and Edward McDill. "Curriculum Tracking and Educational Stratification." *American Sociological Review* 43 (1982): 47–66.

Alexander, Karl S., Doris R. Entwisle, and Carrie S. Horsey. "From First Grade Forward: Early Foundations of High School Dropout." *Sociology of Education* 70 (1997): 87–107.

Allen, Michael Patrick. "Elite Social Movement Organizations and the State: The Rise of the Conservative Policy-Planning Network." In *Research in Politics and Society*, vol. 4, *The Political Consequences of Social Networks*, ed. Gwen Moore and J. Allen Whitt. Greenwich, Conn.: JAI Press, 1992.

Alves, Wayne, and Peter Rossi. "Who Should Get What? Fairness Judgments of Distribution of Earnings." *American Journal of Sociology* 84 (1978): 541–64.

Amott, Teresa. "Will the Economy be Less Stable?" *Dollars and Sense* (November–December 1996): 22–23.

Anderson, Charles H. *The Political Economy of Social Class*. Englewood Cliffs, N.J.: Prentice-Hall, 1974.

————. *Toward a New Sociology*. Homewood, Ill.: Dorsey Press, 1974.

Anderson, Curt. "House Passes $100 Billion Stimulus Measure." *Indianapolis Star*, October 25, 2001.

Anti-Defamation League. *Armed and Dangerous: Militia Takes Aim at the Federal Government*. Fact Finding Report, 1994.

AOL-Time Warner. *AOL-Time Warner 2000 Annual Report*. 2001. Available at http://www.aoltimewarner.com.

The Apex Press. "New Book Urges Democratic Offensive to Purge Corporations' Constitutional Authority to Govern." 2001. Available at http://www.poclad.org.

Arenson, Karen W. "Cuts in Tuition Assistance Put College beyond Reach of Poorest Students." *New York Times*, January 27, 1997.

Aronowitz, Stanley. *The Last Good Job in America*. Lanham, Md.: Rowman and Littlefield, 2001.

Aronowitz, Stanley, and William DiFazio. "High Technology and Work Tomorrow." *Annals of the American Academy of Political and Social Science* 544 (March 1996): 52–76.

Associated Press. "Americans Are Wired into New Bills." *Indianapolis Star*, July 7, 2001.

"A Time for American Leadership on Key Global Issues." *New York Times*, February 11, 1998.

Bagdikian, Ben. *The Media Monopoly*. Boston: Beacon Press, 1997.

Baker, Dean. "Free Trade Fables." *Extra!* (January–February 2000): 18.

————. "Misleading Options on Social Security." *EXTRA!* (May–June 1999): 15.

————. "Generation Excess." *EXTRA!* (March–April 1996): 12–13.

"Balance This." *In These Times* (May 13, 1996): 4–5.

Barlett, Donald L., and James B. Steele. *America: What Went Wrong?* Kansas City, Mo.: Andrews and McMeel, 1992.

————. *America: Who Really Pays the Taxes?* (New York: Touchstone, 1994), 93–94.

————. "America: Who Stole the Dream?" *Indianapolis Star*, September 22–29, 1996; business section. Reprinted from the *Philadelphia Inquirer*.

Barnet, Richard J., and John Cavanagh. *Global Dreams: Imperial Corporations and the New World Order*. New York: Simon and Schuster, 1994.

Barnett, Greg. "Curiously, More of Us Believe in Paranormal." *Indianapolis Star*, June 19, 2001.

Bates, Eric. "Campaign Inflation." *Mother Jones* (March–April 2001): 47–48.

Beckett, Katherine. "Setting the Public Agenda: 'Street Crime' and Drug Use in American Politics." *Social Problems* 3 (1994): 425–47.

Beder, Sharon. *The Corporate Assault on Environmentalism.* White River Junction, Vt.: Chelsea Green Publishing, 1998.

———. "Public Relations' Role in Manufacturing Artificial Grass Roots Coalitions." *Public Relations Quarterly* 43 (1998): 21–30.

Bendix, Reinhard, and Frank W. Howton. "Social Mobility and the American Business Elite—II." *British Journal of Sociology* 9 (1958): 1–14.

Bennet, James. "Patrick J. Buchanan: Harsh Language for Party Leaders." *New York Times,* February 19, 1996.

Bernstein, Aaron. "Back on the Edge." *Business Week* (April 23, 2001): 42–43.

Bernstein, Basil. *Class, Codes, and Control.* 3 vols. London: Routledge and Kegan Paul, 1971–73.

Birnbaum, Jeffrey H. *The Lobbyists.* New York: Times Books, 1992.

Bivens, Matt. "Harvard's 'Fitting Choice.'" *Nation* (June 25, 2001): 6–7.

Blakely, Edward J., and Mary Gail Snyder. *Fortress America: Gated Communities in the United States.* Washington, D.C.: Brookings Institution Press, 1997.

Blau, Peter M., and Otis D. Duncan. *The American Occupational Structure.* New York: Wiley, 1967.

Bleifuss, Joel. "Know Thine Enemy: A Brief History of Corporations." *In These Times* (February 8, 1998): 16–17.

———. "Money Talks, Democracy Walks." *In These Times* (May 16, 1994): 12–13.

———. "The New Abolitionists." *In These Times* (April 1, 1996): 12–13.

———. "The Terminators." *In These Times* (March 4, 1996): 12–13.

———. "Warfare or Welfare." *In These Times* (December 9, 1996): 12–14.

Block, Fred. "Toward Real Corporate Responsibility." *In These Times* (May 27, 1996): 25–27.

Bluestone, Barry, and Bennett Harrison. *The Deindustrialization of America.* New York: Basic Books, 1982.

Booker, Salih, and William Minter. "Global Apartheid." *Nation* (July 9, 2001): 11–17.

Borosage, Robert L. "Scoundrel Time." *Nation* (November 19, 2001): 6–7, 23.

Borosage, Robert L., and Ruy Teixeira. "The Politics of Money." *Nation* (October 21, 1996): 21–22.

Bowles, Samuel, and Herbert Gintis. *Schooling in Capitalist America: Educational Reform and the Contradictions of Economic Life.* New York: Basic Books, 1976.

Boyer, Gabriella. "Corporate America Stacks the NAFTA Debate." *Public Citizen* (July–August 1993): 26.

Boyle, Patrick. "A DAREing Rescue." *Youth Today* (April 2001): 1, 16–19.

Braddock, Douglas. "Occupational Employment Projections to 2008." *Monthly Labor Review* (November 1999): 51–77.

Bradsher, Keith. "The Latest Fashion: Fear-of-Crime Design." *New York Times Week in Review,* July 23, 2000.

Breslow, Marc. "Death by Devolution." *Dollars and Sense* (January–February 1996): 20–22, 38.

———. "Government of, by, and for the Wealthy." *Dollars and Sense* (July–August 1996): 23–24.

———. "Job Stats: Too Good to Be True." *Dollars and Sense* (September–October 1996): 51.

Breslow, Marc, and Matthew Howard. "The Real Un(der)Employment Rate." *Dollars and Sense* (May–June 1995): 35.

Brinton, Milward H., and Heide H. Newman. "State Incentive Packages and the Industrial Location Decision." *Economic Development Quarterly* 3 (1989): 203–22.

Broder, David. "Expanded Trade Authority Faces Political Realities." *Indianapolis Star*, November 7, 2001.

Bronfenbrenner, Kate. "Changing to Organize." *Nation* (September 3/10, 2001): 16–20.

Buchanan, Patrick J. *The Great Betrayal: How American Sovereignty and Social Justice Are Being Sacrificed to the Gods of the Global Economy.* New York: Little, Brown, 1998.

Burnett, Bob. "Publisher's Notes." *In These Times* (March 19, 2001): i.

Burris, Val. "Elite Policy-Planning Networks in the United States." In *Research in Politics and Society*, vol. 4, *The Political Consequences of Social Networks*, ed. Gwen Moore and J. Allen Whitt. Greenwich, Conn.: JAI Press, 1992.

———. "The Myth of Old Money Liberalism: The Politics of the *Forbes* 400 Richest Americans." *Social Problems* 47 (2000): 360–78.

Burson-Marsteller. "Overview: Family of Companies." 2001. Available at http://www.bm.com/overview.

———. "BKSH Government Relations Worldwide." 2001. Available at http://www.bksh.com.

Bush, George W. Yale University Commencement Address, cited in "Dunce Gets Doctorate," *Nation* (June 11, 2001).

"Bush Stacks His Social Security Commission." *UAW Solidarity* (July–August 2001): 5.

"Bush Tax Plan Will Squeeze Medicare, Education." *UAW Solidarity* (July–August 2001): 4–5.

Butsch, Richard. "Class and Gender in Four Decades of Television Situation Comedy: Plus ça Change . . . " *Critical Studies in Mass Communications* 9 (1992): 387–99.

By What Authority 3(3), Summer 2001. Available at http://www.poclad.org.

California Anti-SLAPP Project. "What Are SLAPPs?" 2001. Available at http://www.sirius.com.

Canham-Clyne, John. "When Elites Say 'Cut Medicare,' Press Debates 'How Much?'" *EXTRA!* (January–February 1996): 12–14.

Cantor, Daniel. "New Party Membership Solicitation Letter, Pledge Form" and "It Adds Up." *New Party Newsletter* (September 1, 1996): 1–6.

Carlson, Matt. "Boardroom Brothers." *EXTRA!* (September–October 2001): 18.

Cauchon, Dennis. "Studies Find Drug Program Not Effective." *USA Today*, October 11, 1993.

Center for Responsive Politics. "The Calm before the Storm: Wall Street and Social Security Reform." 2001. Available at http://www.opensecrets.org.

———. *Influence, Inc., Summary.* Washington, D.C.: Center for Responsive Politics, 2000.

———. "No Recess: How the Divided Senate Has Bolstered Campaign Fund-Raising." 2001. Available at http://www.opensecrets.org.

———. "2000 Election Overview, Stats at a Glance: Congressional Races." 2001. Available at http://www.opensecrets.org.

———. "2000 Election Overview: Top Metro Areas." 2001. Available at http://www.opensecrets.org.

———. "2000 Presidential Race: Total Raised and Spent." 2001. Available at http://www.opensecrets.org.

———. "2002 Election Overview: Fundraising by Members of Congress." 2001. Available at http://www.opensecrets.org.

———. *Who's Paying for This Election?* Washington, D.C.: Center for Responsive Politics, 2000.

"CEOs Play Reporter." *EXTRA!Update* (February 1996): 2.

Chavez, Linda. "Union Workers Deserve Choice in Use of Dues." *Indianapolis Star*, September 17, 2001.

Chomsky, Noam. *The Common Good.* New York: Common Courage Press, 2000.

Church, George J. "Are We Better Off?" *Time* (January 29, 1996), 37–40.

Citizens for Tax Justice. "Final Version of Bush Tax Plan Keeps High-End Tax Cuts, Adds to Long-Term Cost." 2001. Available at http://www.inequality.org.

———. "Post-2001 Tax Cuts Offer Little to Most Americans." 2001. Available at http://www.ctj.org.

Clawson, Dan, Alan Neustadtl, and Denise Scott. *Money Talks* (New York: Basic Books, 1992).

Claybrook, Joan. "Corporate Accountability." *Public Citizen News: Special Anniversary Edition* 21 (2001): 20–21, 29.

———. "Why It's Their NAFTA, Not Ours, Not Yours." *Public Citizen* (November–December 1993): 2, 15.

Clines, Francis X. "Fueled by Success, Buchanan Revels in Rapid-Fire Oratory." *New York Times*, February 15, 1996.

Cockburn, Alexander, and Jeffrey St. Clair. "It Really Was a Coup." *CounterPunch* (December 2000): 2.

———. "Nike's New Wage Scam." *CounterPunch* (April 15, 1999): 1, 6.

———. "Real Politics and the Jeffords Jump: Was the Bush White House Truly Sorry?" *CounterPunch* (June 1–15, 2001): 2.

Coen, Rachel. "Whitewash in Washington." *EXTRA!* (July–August 2000): 9–12.

Cohen, Adam. "This Time It's Different." *Time* (January 8, 2001): 18–22.

Cohen, Jeff, and Norman Solomon. *Adventures in MediaLand.* Monroe, Me.: Common Courage Press, 1993.

Cohn, Jason. "Drug Education: The Triumph of Bad Science." *Rolling Stone* (May 24, 2001): 41–42, 96.

Coleman, Richard D., and Lee Rainwater. *Social Standing in America.* New York: Basic Books, 1978.

Collins, Chuck. "Horatio Alger, Where Are You?" *Dollars and Sense* (January–February 1997): 9.

Collins, Chuck, and Felice Yeskel. *Economic Apartheid in America.* New York: The New Press, 2000.

Collins, Randall. *The Credential Society.* New York: Academic Press, 1979.

———. "Functional and Conflict Theories of Educational Stratification." *American Sociological Review* 36 (1971): 1002–19.

Collins, Sharon M. "The Marginalization of Black Executives." *Social Problems* 36 (1989): 317–31.

"Confidence in Institutions." *Gallup Poll News Service*, June 8–10, 2001. Available at http://www.gallup.com.

Congressional Budget Office. *A CBO Study,* "Historical Effective Tax Rates, 1979–1997." (May 2001). Washington, D.C.: Congress of the United States.

Congressional Record. April 30, 1992, S5915–16.

———. July 21, 1992, H6333–34.

———. September 10, 1992, S13299.

———. June 8, 1993, S6963–64.

———. July 23, 1993, S9365.

———. September 8, 1993, E2099.

———. March 8, 1994, E373.

———. March 9, 1994, H1113–23.

———. April 21, 1994, S4598–99.

———. March 21, 1996, H2579.

———. May 8, 1997, S4236–38.

———. May 15, 1997, S4588–91.

———. June 26, 1997, H4668-H4813.

———. June 26, 1997, S6449–51.

———. June 27, 1997, S6678–79.

Conn, Joseph L., and Rob Boston. "Pat Robertson's Media Empire." *EXTRA!* (March–April 1995): 13–16.

Connell, Noreen. "Underfunded Schools: Why Money Matters." *Dollars and Sense* (March–April 1998): 14–17, 39.

Conniff, Ruth. "The Budget Surrender." *Progressive* (June 2001): 12–13.

———. "Will Democrats Abandon Social Security?" *Progressive* (March 1999): 19–23.

Cooper, Marc. "Labor-Latino Beat in CA." *Nation* (June 29, 1998): 5–6.

———. "Plan Colombia." *Nation* (March 19, 2001): 11–18.

Corn, David. "Rove-r and Out?" *Nation* (July 16, 2001): 5–6.

Cottle, Michelle. "The Real Class War." *Washington Monthly* (July–August 1997): 12–16.

Council on International & Public Affairs. "About Us," and "Summary Report for 1999." 2001. Available at http://www.cipa-apex.org.

Cox, Craig. "Taming the Corporate Beast." *Utne Reader* (March–April 1998): 60–61.

Crane, Stephen. *The Red Badge of Courage and Other Writings.* Ed. Richard Chase. Cambridge, Mass.: Riverside Press, 1960.

Crockett, Harry J. Jr. "The Achievement Motive and Differential Occupational Mobility in the United States." *American Sociological Review* 27 (1962): 191–204.

Croteau, David. "Challenging the 'Liberal Media' Claim." *EXTRA!* (July–August 1998): 4–9.

Crutsinger, Martin. "Fresh Reports Paint Picture of Recession." *Indianapolis Star,* October 26, 2001.

Cummings, Scott, and Del Taebel. "The Economic Socialization of Children: A Neo-Marxist Analysis." *Social Problems* 26 (1978): 198–210.

"Current Labor Statistics: Tables 25 and 26." *Monthly Labor Review* (May 2001): 90–91.

Dahl, Ronald. "Burned Out and Bored." *Newsweek* (December 15, 1997): 18.

Daniels, Arlene Kaplan. *Invisible Careers: Women Civic Leaders from the Volunteer World.* Chicago: University of Chicago Press, 1988.

Davidson, Osha G. *Broken Heartland: The Rise of America's Rural Ghetto.* Iowa City: University of Iowa Press, 1996.

Davies, Scott, and Neil Guppy. "Fields of Study, College Selectivity, and Student Inequalities in Higher Education." *Social Forces* 75 (1997): 1417–38.

Davis, James A., and Tom W. Smith. *General Social Surveys, 1972–1998.* Storrs, Conn.: The Roper Center for Public Opinion Research, 1989.

Davis, Russ. "AFL-CIO Unveils Program to Revitalize Labor Movement." *Labor Notes* (March 1997): 1, 14.

deMause, Neil. "A Welfare Success—but the Program Died." *EXTRA!* (September–October 2000): 23.

———. "Out of Sight, Out of Mind." *EXTRA!* (November–December 1997): 25–27.

Derber, Charles. *Corporation Nation.* New York: St. Martin's Press, 1998.

———. *The Wilding of America.* New York: St. Martin's Press, 1996.

Derk, James. "We Got It, Toyota!" *Indiana Business Magazine* (January 1996): 9–13.

Dimaggio, Paul J., and Walter W. Powell. "The Iron Cage Revisited: Institutional Isomorphism and Collective Rationality in Organizational Fields." *American Sociological Review* 48 (1983): 147–60.

Dines, Gail. "Capitalism's Pitchmen." *Dollars and Sense* (May 1992): 18–20.

District of Columbia Bar. "Attorney Resources." 2001. Available at http://www.dcbar.org.

Doherty, Brian. "Those Who Can't, Test." *Mother Jones* (November–December 1998): 68–71.

Dolan, Kerry A., and Luisa Kroll. ed. "The World's Richest People." *Forbes* (July 9, 2001): 110–24.

Dolny, Michael. "Think Tanks in a Time of Crisis." *EXTRA!* (March–April 2002): 28–29.

———. "Think Tanks Y2K." *EXTRA!* (July–August 2001): 6–7.

———. "What's in a Label?" *EXTRA!* (May–June 1998): 9–10.

Domhoff, G. William. *The Powers That Be.* New York: Vintage Books, 1979.

———. *State Autonomy or Class Dominance?* New York: Aldine De Gruyter, 1996.

———. *Who Rules America? Power and Politics in the Year 2000.* 3rd ed. Mountain View, Calif.: Mayfield Publishing, 1998.

———. *Who Rules America? Power and Politics.* 4th ed. Boston: McGraw-Hill, 2002.

Donovan, Doug, and Peter Kafka. "Hosts with the Most." *Forbes* (March 19, 2001): 164–66.

"Don't Let Them Fool You." *AFSCME Public Employee* (March–April 1998): 6–16.

"Don't Read This Soundbite." *EXTRA!* (January–February 2000): 5.

Dooley, David, JoAnn Prause, and Kathleen A. Ham-Rowbottom. "Underemployment and Depression: Longitudinal Relationships." *Journal of Health and Social Behavior* 41 (2000): 421–36.

"Dow Jones Closing Averages September 3–October 12." *Indianapolis Star,* October 13, 2001.

Downs, Alan. *Corporate Executions.* New York: AMACOM, 1995.

Dreifus, Claudia. "Interview: Gore Vidal, the Writer as Citizen." *Progressive* (September 1986): 36–39.

Dreiling, Michael C. "The Class Embeddedness of Corporate Political Action: Leadership in Defense of the NAFTA." *Social Problems* 47 (2000): 21–48.

Dreyfuss, Robert. "Neighbor to Neighbor Takes on Medicare Myths." *EXTRA!* (March–April 1997): 17–18.

Drinkard, Jim. "Lobbying Costs Hit $100 Million a Month." *Indianapolis Star,* March 7, 1998.

DuBoff, Richard B. "Globalization and Wages: The Down Escalator." *Dollars and Sense* (September–October 1997): 36–40.

———. "Social Security: Hardly Secure at the *New York Times.*" *EXTRA!* (March–April 1997): 10–11.

DuBoff, Richard B., and Edward S. Herman. "Mergers, Concentration, and the Erosion of Democracy." *Monthly Review* (May 2001): 14–29.

Dubose, Louis. "Bush's Hitman." *Nation* (March 5, 2001): 11–15.

Duka, Walt. "Panel Hypes Social Security Problems, Experts Caution." *AARP Bulletin* (September 2001): 3, 30–31.

Duncan, Greg J., and Wei-Jun J. Yeung. "Extent and Consequences of Welfare Dependence among America's Children." *Children and Youth Services Review* 17 (1995): 157–82.

Dunham, Kemba J., and Greg Ip. "Weak Economy Takes Unusually Heavy Toll on White-Collar Jobs." *Wall Street Journal,* November 5, 2001.

Dunham, Richard S. "Privatizing Social Security: Despite the Slump, Support Is Solid." *Business Week* (August 13, 2001): 41.

Dye, Thomas R. "Organizing Power for Policy-Planning: The View from the Brookings Institution." In *Power Elites and Organizations,* ed. G. William Domhoff and Thomas R. Dye. Newbury Park, Calif.: Sage, 1987.

———. *Who's Running America? The Clinton Years.* Englewood Cliffs, N.J.: Prentice-Hall, 1995.

Dyer, Joel. *Harvest of Rage: Why Oklahoma City Is Only the Beginning.* Boulder, Colo.: Westview Press, 1998.

Economic Policy Institute. "Data Zone: Historical Values of the U.S. Minimum Wage, 1960–2001." 2001. Available at http://www.epinet.org.

———. "Data Zone: Hourly Wages by Occupation, 1973–2000." 2001. Available at http://www.epinet.org.

———. "Data Zone: Income Limits for Each Fifth and Top 5 Percent of Families, 1947–1999." 2001. Available at http://www.epinet.org.

Editorial. "$30 Million Can Make Media Shy of Truth." *National Catholic Reporter* (April 24, 1998): 1.

The Editors. "The Nader Campaign and the Future of U.S. Left Electoral Politics." *Monthly Review* (February 2001): 1–22.

Ehrenreich, Barbara. *Fear of Falling.* New York: Harper, 1989.

———. "When Government Gets Mean: Confessions of a Recovering Statist." *Nation* (November 17, 1997): 11–16.

———. "The Making of McVeigh." *Progressive* (July 2001): 14–15.

"The 89 Percent Liberal Media." *EXTRA!* (July–August 1998): 10.

Eisenger, Peter. *The Rise of the Entrepreneurial State.* Madison: University of Wisconsin Press, 1988.

Elsila, David. "No More NAFTAs!" *UAW Solidarity* (April–May 1997): 10–12.

Elsila, David, Michael Funke, and Sam Kirkland. "Blaming the Victim: The Propaganda War against Workers." *UAW Solidarity* (April 1992): 11–17.

Endicott, Evan. "Musical Memento." *In These Times* (July 23, 2001): 26–27.

English, Jane. "Bush Eyes 'Fast Track' Authority." *Public Citizen News* (July–August 2001): 1, 7.

"Everyone's Rich in Media-Land . . . But You?" *EXTRA!Update* (August 1999): 4.

Executive Enterprises. "How to Stay Union-Free into the 21st Century." New York, N.Y.: Executive Enterprises, 21 Penn Plaza, 10001–2727, February 1998.

"Fair Economy Resource Guide." Summer–Fall 2001. Boston, Mass.: United for a Fair Economy, 37 Temple Place.

———, George, and Justin Elga. "Sunday Morning Political Talk Shows Ignore Corporate Power Issues." 2001. Available at http://www.essentialaction.org.

———. "What's *Not* Talked About on Sunday Morning?" *EXTRA!* (September–October 2001): 14–17.

Farley, John E. *Sociology.* Englewood Cliffs, N.J.: Prentice Hall, 1990.

"Fast Track Falters in Major House Vote; UAW Steps Up Drive." *UAW Solidarity* (October 1997): 9.

"Fast Track Media Misperceptions." *EXTRA!Update* (February 1998): 1.

"Fast Track Sidetracked." *UAW Solidarity* (November 1997): 7.

Faux, Jeff. "Beyond NAFTA: A Forum." *Nation* (May 28, 2001): 20–23.

———. "NAFTA at Seven: Its Impact on Workers in All Three Nations." Washington, D.C.: Economic Policy Institute, May 2001.

Feagin, Joe. *Racial and Ethnic Relations.* Englewood Cliffs, N.J.: Prentice Hall, 1989.

Featherman, David L., and Robert M. Hauser. *Opportunity and Change.* New York: Academic Press, 1978.

Fedarko, Kevin. "Knobby Fires." *Outside* (June 2001): 24–26.

Federal Election Commission. "Contributions from Individuals by Size of the Contribution, 1999–2000." Press release, May 15, 2001.

———. "FEC Releases New PAC Count." Press release, July 28, 1989.

———. "FEC Reports Increase in Party Fundraising for 2000." Press release, May 15, 2001.

———. "FEC Reports on Congressional Financial Activity for 2000." Press release, May 31, 2001.

———. "Financial Activity of All U.S. House of Representative Candidates—1988–2000." Press release, May 15, 2001.

———. "Financial Activity of All U.S. Senate Candidates—1988–2000." Press release, May 15, 2001.

———. "1999–2000 Financial Activity of Senate and House General Election Campaigns." Press release, May 15, 2001.

———. "PAC Activity Increases in 2000 Election Cycle: Summary of PAC Financial Activity for 1999–2000." Press release, May 31, 2001.

"Field Guide to TV's Lukewarm Liberals." *EXTRA!* (July–August 1998): 14–17.

"Fighting Permanent Normal Trade Relations Status for China." *Public Citizen News: Annual Report 2000* (March–April 2001): 10–12.

Fineman, Howard. "Move Over, Gray Panthers." *Newsweek* (September 10, 2001): 29.

Fineman, Howard, and Rich Thomas. "Snip! Snip! Snip!" *Newsweek* (February 19, 2001): 18–22.

"The 500 Largest U.S. Corporations." *Fortune* (April 16, 2001): F1–19.

Flanders, Laura. "Is It Real . . . Or Is It Astroturf?" *EXTRA!* (July–August 1996): 6.

Fleischmann, Jim. "Where Do We Go from Here?" *New Party News* (Spring 2001): 2.

Foerstel, Karen. "No Allowance, but Look at the Perks." *Congressional Quarterly Weekly* (March 17, 2001): 576.

"Fortune 1000 Industry Totals." *Fortune* (April 16, 2001): F69.

"The Fortune 1000 Ranked within Industries." *Fortune* (April 16, 2001): F45–69.

Frank, Tom. "Let Them Eat Lifestyle." *Utne Reader* (November–December 1997): 43–47.

Fraser, Robbie. "Do You Believe?" *TV Guide* (October 14–20, 2001): 56.

Freeman, Lewis. "Social Mobility in Television Comedies." *Critical Studies in Mass Communication* 9 (1992): 400–406.

"From the Left: More than a Figure of Speech?" *EXTRA!Update* (February 1996): 1.

"Frontlines." *UAW Solidarity* (November 2001): 4–5.

Gallup, George, and S. F. Rae. *The Pulse of Democracy.* New York: Simon and Schuster, 1940.

Garnett, Stacie. "It's Tough to Be Young Today." *Dollars and Sense* (September–October 1997): 50.

General Electric. *GE 2000 Annual Report.* 2001. Available at http://www.ge.com.

Geoghagen, Thomas. "Overeducated and Underpaid." *New York Times,* June 3, 1997.

Gilbert, Dennis, and Joseph A. Kahl. *The American Class Structure.* Chicago: Dorsey Press, 1987.

Gitlin, Todd. "Unum versus Pluribus." *Nation* (May 6, 1996): 28–34.

Glenn, David. "Adding Brains to Labor's New Political Muscle." *In These Times* (December 14, 1997): 22–25.

Goetzman, Keith. "Righteous Babe: Interview with Ani DiFrancio." *Utne Reader* (July–August 2001): 94–96.

Golay, Michael, and Carl Rollyson. *Where America Stands, 1996.* New York: John Wiley and Sons, 1996.

Gonnerman, Jennifer. "Media Watch." *In These Times* (December 25, 1995): 9.

Goodman, Robert. *The Last Entrepreneurs: America's Regional Wars for Jobs and Dollars.* New York: Simon and Schuster, 1979.

Gordon, David M. *Fat and Mean: The Corporate Squeeze of Working Americans and the Myth of Managerial "Downsizing."* New York: Free Press, 1996.

Gordon, Jim. "Mystery Milk, Journalistic Debate." *EXTRA!* (January–February 2001): 29–30.

Granfield, Robert. "Making It by Faking It." *Journal of Contemporary Ethnography* 20 (1991): 331–51.

Granfield, Robert, and Thomas Koenig. "Pathways into Elite Law Firms: Professional Stratification and Social Networks." In *Research in Politics and Society,* vol. 4, *The Political Consequences of Social Networks,* ed. Gwen Moore and J. Allen Whitt. Greenwich, Conn.: JAI Press, 1992.

Granovetter, Mark. *Getting a Job: A Study of Contacts and Careers.* Cambridge: Harvard University Press, 1974.

Greenberg, Edward S. *Political Socialization.* New York: Atherton, 1970.

Greider, William. "Nader and the Politics of Fear." *Nation* (March 12, 2001): 15–18.

———. "The Right and US Trade Law: Invalidating the 20th Century." *Nation* (October 15, 2001): 21–29.

———. "Stockman Returneth." *Nation* (April 2, 2001): 4–6.

———. "Saving the Global Economy." *Nation* (December 15, 1997): 11–16.

Gup, Ted. "Fakin' It." *Mother Jones* (May–June 1996): 53–54.

———. "The *Mother Jones* 400." *Mother Jones* (March–April 1996): 43.

Hallinan, Maureen T. "Tracking: From Theory to Practice." *Sociology of Education* 67 (1994): 79–85.

Hardt, Michael, and Antonio Negri. *Empire.* Cambridge: Harvard University Press, 2000.

Harris, Bob. "Everyone's Getting Rich!" *EXTRA!* (July–August 1999): 9.

Harrison, Bennett, and Barry Bluestone. "The Crisis of the American Dream." In *Great Divides,* ed. Thomas A. Shapiro. Mountain View, Calif.: Mayfield Publishing, 1998.

, Peter. "Nader the Nightmare." *EXTRA!* (January–February 2001): 11.

Peter, and Seth Ackerman. "Bill O'Reilly's Sheer O'Reillyness." *EXTRA!* (July–August 19–20.

, and Jim Naureckas. "Nader and the Press: Condescension Turns Nasty." *EX- te* (October 2000): 4.

Hart, Peter, and Steve Rendall. "Meet the Myth Makers." *EXTRA!* (July–August 1998): 26–27.

Hartung, William D. "New War, Old Weapons." *Nation* (October 29, 2001): 4–5.

Haveman, Ernest, and Patricia Salter West. *They Went to College.* New York: Harcourt, Brace, 1952.

Hearn, James. "Academic and Nonacademic Influences on the College Destinations of 1980 High School Graduates." *Sociology of Education* 64 (1991): 158–71.

Hellander, Ida. "A Review of Data on the Health Care Sector of the United States." *International Journal of Health Services* 31 (2001): 35–53.

Helwig, Ryan T. "Worker Displacement in a Strong Labor Market." *Monthly Labor Review* (June 2001): 13–28.

Henriques, Diane B. "Ties That Bind: His Directors, Her Charity." *New York Times,* March 21, 1995.

Henson, Kevin D. *Just a Temp.* Philadelphia: Temple University Press, 1996.

Henwood, Doug. "American Dream: It's Not Working." *Christianity and Crisis* (June 8, 1992): 195–97.

———. "Economic Tall Tales." *In These Times* (September 30, 1996): 32–34.

———. "TV on Social Security: It's Broke, Fix It." *EXTRA!* (May–June 1999): 8–12.

Herman, Edward S. "The Media Mega-Mergers." *Dollars and Sense* (May–June 1996): 8–13.

Herman, Tom. "Tax Report." *Wall Street Journal,* October 24, 2001.

Herzenhorn, David. "The Story behind the Generous Gift to Harvard Law School." *New York Times,* April 7, 1995.

Hightower, Jim. "Chomp!" *Utne Reader* (March–April 1998): 57–61, 104.

———. "Class War." *Dollars and Sense* (November–December 1997): 7.

Hill, Catherine. "Privatizing Social Security Is Bad, Particularly for Women." *Dollars and Sense* (November–December 2000): 17–19, 35.

Hipple, Steven. "Contingent Work in the late-1990s." *Monthly Labor Review* (March 2001): 3–27.

Hirschfeld, Julie R. "Zoellick Pushes for Prompt Revival of Fast-Track Authority." *Congressional Quarterly Weekly* (February 3, 2001): 295–96.

Hochschild, Arlie, and Anne Machung. "The Second Shift: Working Parents and the Revolution at Home." In *Working in America,* ed. Amy S. Wharton. Mountain View, Calif.: Mayfield Publishing, 1998.

Hodge, Robert W., Paul M. Siegel, and Peter H. Rossi. "Occupational Prestige in the United States: 1925–1962." In *Class, Status, and Power,* ed. Reinhard Bendix and Seymour M. Lipset. New York: Free Press, 1966.

Hodge, Robert W., and Donald J. Treiman. "Class Identification in the United States." *American Journal of Sociology* 73 (1968): 535–47.

Hodge, Robert W., Donald J. Treiman, and Peter H. Rossi. "A Comparative Study of Occupational Prestige." In *Class, Status, and Power,* ed. Reinhard Bendix and Seymour M. Lipset. New York: Free Press, 1966.

Hodson, Randy, and Teresa A. Sullivan. *The Social Organization of Work.* 2nd ed. Belmont, Calif.: Wadsworth, 1995.

———. *The Social Organization of Work.* 3rd ed. Belmont, Calif.: Wadsworth-Thomson, 2002.

Hoffman, Hank. "Time is Tight." *In These Times* (November 12, 2001): 7–8.

Hojnacki, Marie, and David C. Kimball. "PAC Contributions and Lobbying Contacts in Congressional Committees." *Political Research Quarterly* 54 (March 2000): 161–80.

Hoynes, William. "The Cost of Survival." *EXTRA!* (September–October 1999): 11–19.

———. "News for a Captive Audience: An Analysis of Channel One." *EXTRA!* (May–June 1997): 11–17.

Hurst, Charles E. *Social Inequality.* Boston: Allyn and Bacon, 1995.

Husseini, Sam. "Checkbook Analysis." *EXTRA!* (May–June 2000): 23–24.

———. "Talking about Talk." *EXTRA!* (May–June 1996): 20.

"In Fact." *Nation* (August 26–September 2, 1996): 5.

"Inside the 500." *Fortune* (April 16, 2001): 232–33.

International Media Data Base. "The Top Grossing Movies of All Time at the Worldwide Box Office." 2001. Available at http://www.us.imdb.com.

Jackman, Mary R., and Robert W. Jackman, *Class Awareness in the United States.* Berkeley: University of California Press, 1982.

Jackson, Janine. "Economic Pack Journalism." *EXTRA!* (November–December 1996): 11–12.

———. "Fast Track 1, Democracy 0." *EXTRA!* (November–December 1997): 9–10.

———. "Let Them Eat Baguettes." *EXTRA!* (March–April 1996): 14–15.

———. "Major Player or Big Bully?" *EXTRA!* (January–February 1997): 9–10.

———. "Moribund Militants: Corporate Media on (Re)Organized Labor." *EXTRA!* (January–February 1996): 6–7.

———. "Wall Street's Gain Is Journalism's Loss." *EXTRA!* (September–October 2001): 20–21.

———. "We Feel Your Pain." *EXTRA!* (May–June 1996): 11–12.

Jackson, Janine, and Peter Hart. "Fear & Favor 2000: How Power Shapes the News." *EXTRA!* (May–June 2001): 15–22.

Jacobs, David G., ed. *The Foundation Directory, 2001 Edition.* New York: Foundation Center, 2001.

Jacobs, Jerry A. "Gender and Academic Specialties: Trends among Recipients of College Degrees in the 1980s." *Sociology of Education* 68 (1995): 81–98.

Jaros, Dean. *Socialization to Politics.* New York: Praeger, 1973.

Jaszczak, Sandra, ed. *Encyclopedia of Associations.* 31st ed. Vol. 1. Detroit: Gale Research, 1996.

Jencks, Christopher, et al. *Inequality: Reassessment of the Effect of Family and Schooling in America.* New York: Harper and Row, 1972.

Jensen, Eric J., Jurg Gerber, and Ginna M. Babcock. "The New War on Drugs: Grass Roots Movement or Political Construction?" *Journal of Drug Issues* 21 (1991): 651–67.

Jezer, Marty. "The Missing Candidate." *Progressive Populist* (November 1, 2000): 14–15.

———. "Soft Money, Hard Choices." *Dollars and Sense* (July–August 1996): 30–34, 42.

Johnson, David S., John M. Rogers, and Lucilla Tan. "A Century of Family Budgets in the United States." *Monthly Labor Review* (May 2001): 28–45.

Josephson, Matthew. *The Robber Barons.* New York: Harcourt, Brace and World, 1934.

Judis, John B. "The Most Powerful Lobby." *In These Times* (February 21, 1994): 22–23.

Kadlec, Daniel. "Zap." *Time* (March 26, 2001): 26–31.

Kalet, Hank. "We Need Electoral Reform Now." *Progressive Populist* (August 1–15, 2001): 19.

Kallick, David D. "Saving Social Security (from its saviors)." *In These Times* (March 7, 1999): 10–13.

Karen, David. "Toward a Political-Organizational Model of Gatekeeping: The Case of Elite Colleges." *Sociology of Education* 63 (1990): 227–40.

Katz, Michael B. *The Irony of Early School Reform.* Cambridge: Harvard University Press, 1968.

Katznelson, Ira, and Mark Kesselman. *The Politics of Power.* New York: Harcourt Brace Jovanovich, 1975.

Kazin, Michael. *The Populist Persuasion.* New York: Basic Books, 1995.

Kerbo, Harold R. *Social Stratification and Inequality.* 3rd ed. New York: McGraw-Hill, 1996.

———. *Social Stratification and Inequality.* 4th ed. Boston: McGraw-Hill, 2000.

Kilgore, Sally. "The Organizational Context of Tracking in Schools." *American Sociological Review* 56 (1991): 189–203.

Klein, Naomi. "Signs of the Times." *Nation* (October 22, 2001): 15–20.

———. "Trading on Terrorism." *In These Times* (November 12, 2001): 9.

Knecht, G. Bruce. "Hard Copy: Magazine Advertisers Demand Prior Notice of 'Offensive' Articles." *Wall Street Journal,* April 30, 1997.

Knoke, David. *Organized for Action: Commitment in Voluntary Associations.* New Brunswick, N.J.: Rutgers University Press, 1981.

Koeber, Charles, and David W. Wright. "W/Age Bias in Worker Displacement: How Industrial Structure Shapes the Job Loss and Earnings Decline of Older American Workers." *Journal of Socio-Economics* 30 (2001): 343–52.

Kohut, Andrew. "Globalization and the Wage Gap." *New York Times,* December 3, 1999.

Kolbert, Elizabeth, and Adam Clymer. "The Politics of Layoff: In Search of a Message." *New York Times,* March 8, 1996.

Kominski, Robert, and Rebecca Sutterlin. *What's It Worth? Educational Background and Economic Status.* U.S. Bureau of the Census, Household Economic Studies P70–32. Washington, D.C.: U.S. Government Printing Office, 1992.

Koretz, Gene. "Downsized in a Down Economy." *Business Week* (September 17, 2001): 36.

———. "Downsizing's Painful Effects." *Business Week* (April 13, 1998): 23.

Korpi, Walter. *The Democratic Class Struggle.* London: Routledge, 1983.

Kozol, Jonathan. *Savage Inequalities: Children in America's Schools.* New York: Harper, 1991.

Krebs, A.V. "Court Upholds Award in Suppressed TV Report." *Progressive Populist* (January 1–15, 2001): 7.

Krugman, Paul. *Mother Jones,* November–December 1996.

Kuehn, Don. "Saving for College with Section 529 Plans." *AFT American Teacher* (September 2001): 19.

"Labor Party First Constitutional Convention Documents: Electoral Strategy." *Labor Party Press—Special Supplement* (January 1999): 2.

Ladd, Everett Carll, and Karlyn H. Bowman. "The Nation Says No to Class Warfare." *USA Today* (May 1999): 24–26.

Lavelle, Louis. "For Female CEOs, It's Stingy at the Top." *Business Week* (April 23, 2001): 70–71.

———. "Special Report: Executive Pay." *Business Week* (April 16, 2001): 76–108.

Lee, Martin A., and Norman Solomon. "Does the News Media Have a Liberal Bias?" In *Taking Sides,* ed. Kurt Finsterbusch and George McKenna. Guilford, Conn.: Duskin Publishing Group, 1996.

Lehmann, Chris. "Michael and Me." *In These Times* (October 14, 1996): 39–40.

Leland, John. "Blessed by the Bull." *Newsweek* (April 27, 1998): 51–53.

Leonhardt, David. "Two-Tier Marketing." *Business Week* (March 17, 1997): 82–90.

Levison, Andrew. "Who Lost the Working Class?" *Nation* (May 14, 2001): 25–32.

Levy, Clifford J. "New York Attorney General Remakes Staff by Patronage." *New York Times*, November 10, 1995.

Lewis, Charles. "The Buying of the President." *Dollars and Sense* (July–August 1996): 28, 41.

Lieberman, Trudy. "Social Insecurity: The Campaign to Take the System Private." *Nation* (January 27, 1997): 11–18.

Lipset, Seymour M., and Reinhard Bendix. *Social Mobility in Industrial Society*. Berkeley: University of California Press, 1959.

Litt, Edgar. "Civic Education, Community Norms, and Political Indoctrination." *American Sociological Review* 28 (February 1963): 69–75.

Lucas, Samuel R., and Aaron D. Good. "Race, Class, and Tournament Track Mobility." *Sociology of Education* 74 (2001): 139–56.

Lustig, Jeffrey R. "The Politics of Shutdown." *Journal of Economic Issues* 19 (1985): 123–59.

Lyman, Rick. "A Partly Cloudy Forecast for Theater Owners." *New York Times*, March 12, 2001.

MacEwan, Arthur. "Ask Dr. Dollar." *Dollars and Sense* (May–June 2001): 41.

Macionis, John J. *Sociology*. Upper Saddle River, N.J.: Prentice Hall, 2001.

Makinson, Larry. *The Big Picture: Money Follows Power Shift on Capitol Hill*. Washington, D.C.: Center for Responsive Politics, 1997.

———. "Business, Labor, and Ideological Donors." *Who's Paying for This Election?* Washington, D.C.: Center for Responsive Politics, 2000.

Males, Mike. "The Myth of the Grade-School Murderer." *EXTRA!* (May–June 2001): 30.

———. "Pot Boiler: Why Are Media Enlisting in the Government's Crusade against Marijuana?" *EXTRA!* (July–August 1997): 20–21.

———. "Wild in Deceit: Why 'Teen Violence' Is Poverty Violence in Disguise." *EXTRA!* (March–April 1996): 7–9.

Mandel, Michael J. "How the Super-Rich Lucked Out Twice." *Business Week* (May 14, 2001): 52.

Mangan, Katherine S. "A Shortage of Business Professors Leads to 6-Figure Salaries for new Ph.D.'s." *Chronicle of Higher Education* 47 (May 4, 2001): A12–13.

Manilov, Marianne. "Channel One, Joe Camel, Potato Chips, and ABC." *EXTRA!* (July–August, 1996): 18–19.

Mantsios, Gregory. "Class in America: Myths and Realities." In *Race, Class, and Gender in the United States*, ed. Paula S. Rothenberg. New York: St. Martin's Press, 1995.

———. "Media Magic: Making Class Disappear." In *Race, Class, and Gender in the United States*, ed. Paula S. Rothenberg. New York: St. Martin's Press, 1995.

Marable, Manning. *The Black World Today*, February 22, 2000.

Marger, Martin N. *Social Inequality: Patterns and Processes*. 2nd ed. Boston: McGraw-Hill, 2002.

Marin, Rick, and Yahlin Chang. "The Katie Factor." *Newsweek* (July 6, 1998): 53–58.

Marshall, Jeffrey. "The Buck$ Aren't $topping." *Financial Executive* (July–August 2001): 40–43.

Martinez, Theresa A. "Popular Culture as Oppositional Culture: Rap as Resistance." *Sociological Perspectives* 40 (1997): 265–86.

Martins, Mick, and Mick Porter. *1995 Video Movie Guide*. New York: Ballantine, 1994.

Masci, David. "Senate Rejects Striker Bill; More Action Unlikely." *Congressional Quarterly* (July 16, 1994): 1936.

McChesney, Robert W. "Global Media, Neoliberalism, and Imperialism." *Monthly Review* (March 2001): 1–19.

———. "Journalism, Democracy, and Class Struggle." *Monthly Review* (November 2000): 1–15.

———. *Rich Media, Poor Democracy: Communication Politics in Dubious Times.* Chicago: University of Illinois Press, 1999.

———. "The Global Media Giants." *EXTRA!* (November–December 1997): 11–18.

McClure, Laura. "Free Trade Ache of the Americas." *Labor Party Press* (July 2001): 1, 4–5.

———. "Social Security Sneak Attack." *Labor Party Press* (September 2001): 8.

McGinn, Daniel. "Weathering the Storm." *Newsweek* (March 16, 2001): 22–26.

McGinn, Daniel, and Keith Naughton, "How Safe is Your Job?" *Newsweek* (February 5, 2001): 34–43.

McKenzie, Evan. *Privatopia.* New Haven: Yale University Press, 1994.

McKinnon, John D., and John Harwood. "Wall Street Ponies Up to Back Bush's Social Security Plan." *Wall Street Journal,* June 12, 2001.

"Media Myths & Facts." *UAW Solidarity* (April 1992): 17.

Melloan, George. "Whatever Happened to the Labor Movement?" *Wall Street Journal,* September 4, 2001.

Meyer, Lisa. "Militia Movement." 2001. Available at http://www.encarta.msn.com.

Mickelson, Roslyn Arlin. "The Attitude-Achievement Paradox among Black Adolescents." *Sociology of Education* 63 (1990): 44–61.

Miller, Ellen, and Randy Kehler. "Mischievous Myths about Money in Politics." *Dollars and Sense* (July–August 1996): 22–23.

Miller, John. "Getting Back More than They Give." *Dollars and Sense* (September–October 2001): 60–62.

———. "More Wealth for the Wealthy: The Estate Tax Giveaway and What to Do about It." *Dollars and Sense* (November–December 1997): 26–28, 33.

———. "Tax Cuts: Clinton and Congress Feed the Wealthy." *Dollars and Sense* (November–December 1997): 43.

———. "When Is the Economy in a Recession?" *Dollars and Sense* (July–August 2001): 10–11, 32.

Miller, John, and Ramon Castellblanch. "Does Manufacturing Matter?" *Dollars and Sense* (October 1988): 6–8.

Miller, Mark C. "Free the Media." *Nation* (June 3, 1996): 9–15.

Miller, S. M. "Born on Third Base: The Sources of Wealth of the 1996 *Forbes* 400." *United for a Fair Economy* (February 1997).

Mines, Luke. "Globalization in the Classroom." *Nation* (June 1, 1998): 22–24.

Mishel, Lawrence, Jared Bernstein, and John Schmitt. *The State of Working America, 2000–2001.* Ithaca, N.Y.: Cornell University Press, 2001.

———. *The State of Working America, 1996–1997.* Armonk, N.Y.: M. E. Sharpe, 1997.

Moberg, David. "Fast Track Is Back." *In These Times* (July 23, 2001): 17–18.

———. "FTAA, Eh? A Bigger, Badder Trade Deal." *In These Times* (April 16, 2001): 16–19.

———. "Going Down: Congress Is Only Going to Make It Worse." *In These Times* (November 12, 2001): 20–21.

———. "The Six-Year Itch." *Nation* (September 3/10, 2001): 11.

———. "Tear Down the Walls: The Movement Is Becoming More Global." *In These Times* (May 28, 2001): 11–14.

"Monitoring Harmonization and Other Trade Issues." *Public Citizen News: Annual Report 2000* (March–April 2001): 10–12.

Monroe, Ann. "Getting Rid of the Gray." *Mother Jones* (July–August 1996): 29.

Moody, Kim. "America Gets a Virtual Raise." *Labor Notes* (February 1997): 15–16.

———. "NAFTA, WTO, MAI, IMF, FTAA, AGOA . . . Where Does It End?" *Labor Notes* (May 1998): 10, 16.

———. *Workers in a Lean World: Unions in the International Economy.* New York: Verso, 1998.

Moore, Michael. *Downsize This!* New York: Crown Publishers, 1996.

———. "Give the Devil a Bone . . . " *In These Times* (June 11, 2001): 29–30.

Moore, Stephen. "How to Slash Corporate Welfare." *New York Times,* April 5, 1995.

Moore, Thomas S. *The Disposable Work Force.* New York: Aldine de Gruyter, 1996.

Morehouse, Ward. "New Book Urges Democratic Offensive to Purge Corporations' Constitutional Authority to Govern." 2001. Available at http://www.poclad.org.

Mother Jones, "Wall Street Leads Top Campaign Contributors on *Mother Jones* 400," on the Internet at http://www.motherjones.com/about_us/pressroom/ 030501_2.html (visited July 21, 2001).

Moyers, Bill. "Which America Will We Be Now?" *Nation* (November 19, 2001): 11–14.

Murray, Charles. "The Shape of Things to Come." *National Review* (July 8, 1991): 29–30.

Muwakkil, Salim. "Just Vote No: The War on Drugs Loses at the Polls." *In These Times* (December 25, 2000): 25–26.

Nader, Ralph. "Product Libel." *Public Citizen News* (May–June 1998): 4.

National Center for Responsive Philanthropy. "$1 Billion for Ideas: Conservative Think Tanks in the 1990s." Press release, March 12, 1999. Washington, D.C.

Naughton, Keith. "Lock and Download." *Newsweek* (October 22, 2001): 61–62.

Naureckas, Jim. "Corporate Censorship Matters: The Case of NBC." *EXTRA!* (November–December 1995): 13.

———. "From the Top: What Are the Politics of Network Bosses?" *EXTRA!* (July–August 1998): 21–22.

———. "Orwell's Network." *EXTRA!* (July–August 2001): 2.

———. "Where's the Power: Newsroom or Boardroom?" *EXTRA!* (July–August 1998): 23.

Navarro, Vicente. "Medical History as Justification Rather than Explanation: A Critique of Starr's *The Social Transformation of American Medicine.*" *International Journal of Health Services* 14 (1984): 511–28.

———. "Production and the Welfare State: The Political Context of Reforms." *International Journal of Health Services* 21 (1991): 585–614.

Neustadtl, Alan, and Dan Clawson. "Corporate Political Groupings: Does Ideology Unify Business Political Behavior?" *American Sociological Review* 53 (1988): 172–90.

Newman, Katherine S. *Declining Fortunes.* New York: Basic Books, 1993.

———. *Falling from Grace: The Experience of Downward Mobility in the American Middle Class.* New York: Free Press, 1988.

"New Party: A Fair Economy, A Real Democracy, A New Party." 2001. Available at http://www.newparty.org.

"New Party Principles." *New Party News* (Spring 2001): 7.

Newport, Frank, and Maura Strausberg. "Americans' Belief in Psychic and Paranormal Phenomena Is Up over Last Decade." *Gallup Poll Analyses.* 2001. Available at http://www.gallup.com.

The News Corporation. *News Corporation 2000 Annual Report.* 2001. Available at http://www.newscorp.com.

Newsweek. Cover story. June 4, 2001.

"The New Transplants." *UAW Research Bulletin* (January–February 1995): 10–11.

New York Times. Downsizing of America. New York: Random House, 1996.

Nichols, John. "After Fusion: The New New Party." *In These Times* (March 22, 1998): 18–20.

———. "Drug Warrior Dissent." *Nation* (May 28, 2001): 8.

———. "Behind the DLC Takeover." *Progressive* (October 2000): 28–30.

———. "Policy Profiteers." *Nation* (October 22, 2001): 4–5.

———. "Real Paycheck Protection." *Nation* (March 26, 2001): 8.

Nitschke, Lori. "Coalitions Make a Comeback." *Congressional Quarterly Weekly* (March 3, 2001): 470–74.

———. "Tax-Cut Bipartisanship Down to One Chamber." *Congressional Quarterly Weekly* (March 10, 2001): 529–32.

———. "Tax Plan Destined for Revision." *Congressional Quarterly Weekly* (February 10, 2001): 318–21.

Nitschke, Lori, and Wendy Boudreau. "Provisions of the Tax Law." *Congressional Quarterly Weekly* (June 9, 2001): 1390–94.

Noble, David F. *Forces of Production: A Social History of Industrial Automation.* New York: Knopf, 1984.

Noble, Douglas D. "Schools as 'Instructional Delivery Systems.'" *In These Times* (November 30, 1992): 28–29.

Nye, Peter. "Lobbying and Gift Reform Shines Sunlight on Influence Peddling." *Public Citizen* (January–February 1996): 1, 3.

Oakes, Jeannie. "More than Misapplied Technology: A Normative and Political Response to Hallinan on Tracking." *Sociology of Education* 67 (1994): 84–89.

O'Connor, Carla. "Race, Class, and Gender in America: Narratives of Opportunity among Low-Income African American Youths." *Sociology of Education* 72 (1999): 137–57.

Office of Congressman Dick Armey. "Washington's Lobbying Industry: A Case for Tax Reform—Executive Summary." (June 19, 1996).

Office of Management and Budget. *Budget of the United States Government: Fiscal Year 2002.* Washington, D.C.: U.S. Government Printing Office, 2001.

Office of National Drug Control Policy. *The National Drug Control Strategy.* Washington, D.C.: National Criminal Justice Reference Service, 1992, 1994, 1996, 1998.

———. *National Drug Control Strategy: 2001 Annual Report.* Washington, D.C.: U.S. Government Printing Office, 2001.

Office of Technology Assessment. *Technology and Structural Unemployment.* Washington, D.C.: Congress of the United States, 1986.

Oliver, Melvin, Thomas M. Shapiro, and Julie E. Press. "'Them That's Got Shall Get': Inheritance and Achievement in Wealth Accumulation." In *Research in Politics and Society,* vol. 15, ed. Richard E. Ratliffe, Melvin Oliver, and Thomas M. Shapiro. Greenwich, Conn.: JAI Press, 1995.

Omicinski, John. "Public in Poll Supports Church, Police, Military." *Indianapolis Star,* June 26, 2001.

"The 100 Largest U.S. Multinationals." *Forbes* (July 17, 1995): 274–76.

"Opposing Harmful Trade Measure for Africa." *Public Citizen News: Annual Report 2000* (March–April 2001): 10–12.

"Opposing the World Trade Organization." *Public Citizen News: Annual Report 2000* (March–April 2001): 10–12.

The Oprah Show. "Show Archive, August 2001." Available at http://www.oprah.com.

Orcutt, James D., and J. Blake Turner. "Shocking Numbers and Graphic Accounts: Quantified Images of Drug Problems in the Print Media." *Social Problems* 40 (1993): 190–206.

Orum, Anthony M., and Roberta S. Cohen. "The Development of Political Orientations among Black and White Children." *American Sociological Review* 38 (1973): 62–74.

Pace, Eric. "B. Gerald Cantor, Philanthropist and Owner of Rodin Collection, Is Dead at 79." *New York Times,* July 6, 1996.

Parenti, Michael. *Power and the Powerless.* New York: St. Martin's Press, 1978.

Parks, Daniel J. "Bush May Test Capitol Hill Clout Early with Expedited Tax-Cut Proposal." *Congressional Quarterly Weekly* (January 6, 2001): 41–42.

———. "Under Tight Spending Ceilings, Democrats Lower Their Sights." *Congressional Quarterly Weekly* (June 9, 2001): 1362–64.

Parry, Robert. "The Right-Wing Media Machine." *Extra!* (March–April 1995): 6–10.

———. "Who Buys the Right?" *Nation* (November 18, 1996): 5–6.

Paulin, Geoffrey and Brian Riordon. "Making It on Their Own: The Baby Boom Meets Generation X." *Monthly Labor Review* (February 1998): 10–21.

"Paycheck Deception Act: Don't Let Them Fool You." *AFSCME Public Employee* (March–April 1998): 7–19.

Perkins, Joseph. "Caught in the News Media's Liberal Bias." *Indianapolis Star,* July 18, 1998.

Perrow, Charles. "A Society of Organizations." *Theory and Society* 20 (1991): 725–62.

Perrucci, Carolyn C., and Robert Perrucci. "Social Origins, Educational Contexts, and Career Mobility." *American Sociological Review* 35 (1970): 451–63.

Perrucci, Carolyn C., Robert Perrucci, Dena B. Targ, and Harry Targ. *Plant Closings: International Context and Social Costs.* Hawthorne, N.Y.: Aldine de Gruyter, 1988.

Perrucci, Robert. *Japanese Auto Transplants in the Heartland.* New York: Aldine De Gruyter, 1994.

———. "The Significance of Intra-Occupational Mobility." *American Sociological Review* 26 (1961): 874–83.

Perrucci, Robert, and Bonnie L. Lewis. "Interorganizational Relations and Community Influence Structure." *Sociological Quarterly* 30 (1989): 205–23.

Perrucci, Robert, and Marc Pilisuk. "Leaders and Ruling Elites: The Interorganizational Basis of Community Power." *American Sociological Review* 35 (1970): 1040–57.

Perrucci, Robert, and Earl Wysong, *The New Class Society.* Lanham, Md.: Rowman and Littlefield, 1999.

———. "Organizational Power, Generative Capital, and Class Closure." Paper presented at the Pacific Sociological Association annual meeting, March 31, 2001, San Francisco, Calif.

Perrucci, Robert, et al. "The Two Faces of Racialized Space in a Predominantly White University." *International Journal of Sociology* 37 (2000): 230–44.

The Pew Research Center for the People and the Press. "Journalists Avoiding the News, Self Censorship: How Often and Why?" 2001. Available at http://www.people-press.org.

———. "Economic Inequality Rising, Boom Bypasses Poor." 2001. Available at http://www.people-press.org.

Phillips, Jim. "What Happens After Seattle?" *Dollars and Sense* (January–February 2000): 15–16, 31–32.

Phillips, Kevin. "Fat City." *Time* (September 26, 1994): 49–56.

Phillips, Peter. "Self Censorship and the Homogeneity of the Media Elite." In *Censored 1998,* ed. Peter Phillips. New York: Seven Stories Press, 1998.

Phillips Peter, and Project Censored. *Censored 2001: 25th Anniversary Edition.* New York: Seven Stories Press, 2001.

"Phony Paycheck Protection: It'll Cost You More than You Think." *UAW Solidarity* (March–April 1998): 10–11.

Piven, Frances Fox. "Poorhouse Politics." *Progressive* (February 1995): 22–24.

Pohlman, Kimberly. "Solid Ratings Don't Protect Progressive Radio Voices." *EXTRA!* (July–August 2000): 22.

Polivka, Anne E. "Contingent and Alternative Work Arrangements, Defined." *Monthly Labor Review* (October 1996): 3–9.

Pomery, John. "Running Deficits with the Rest of the World—Part I." *Focus on Economic Issues.* West Lafayette, Ind.: Purdue Center for Economic Education, Fall 1987.

Postman, Neil. "Virtual Students, Digital Classroom." *Nation* (October 9, 1995): 377–82.

Powers, Richard. "American Dreaming." *New York Times Magazine* (May 7, 2000): 66–67.

Pozner, Jennifer L. "Power Shortage for Media Women." *EXTRA!* (July–August 2001): 8–9.

———. "Women Have *Not* Taken over the News." *EXTRA!* (January–February 2000): 9–10.

Press, Eyal. "Spin Cities." *Nation* (November 18, 1996): 30–33.

"Programs and Achievements/Program Directions." Boston: United for a Fair Economy, 37 Temple Place, ca. 1997.

Public Campaign. *Hard Facts on Hard Money.* Washington, D.C.: Public Campaign, 2001.

Pugh, Tony. "Massive Immigration Steers Population, Reapportionment." *Indianapolis Star,* December 29, 2000.

Purdue Research Foundation. *Home for High-Tech Business.* West Lafayette, Ind.: Purdue Research Park, 1998.

Quinn, Jane Bryant. "Private Accounts Won't Work." *Indianapolis Star,* September 17, 2001.

———. "Tax Cuts: Who Will Get What." *Newsweek* (June 11, 2001): 30.

Rampton, Sheldon, and John Stauber. "Oprah's Free—Are We?" *EXTRA!* (May–June 1998): 11–12.

———. "This Report Brought to You by Monsanto." *Progressive* (July 1998): 22–25.

Rather, Dan. *The American Dream: Stories from the Heart of Our Nation.* New York: William Morrow, 2001.

Reich, Robert B. "Broken Faith: Why We Need to Renew the Social Contract." *Nation* (February 16, 1998): 11–17.

———. *The Next American Frontier.* New York: Times Books, 1983.

———. "Secession of the Successful." *New York Times Magazine,* January 20, 1991, 16–17, 42–45.

———. *The Work of Nations: Preparing Ourselves for the Twenty-first Century.* New York: Knopf, 1991.

Renchler, Ron. *Financial Equity in Schools.* ERIC Digest No. 76. Eugene, Ore.: ERIC Clearinghouse in Educational Management, 1994.

Rendall, Steve "Media See the Poor as Aggressors in 'Class War.'" *EXTRA!* (January–February 2001): 10.

———. "Nation's Top Columnists Still Lean Right." *EXTRA!* (January–February 2000): 11–12.

Reskin, Barbara, and Irene Padavic. *Women and Men at Work.* Thousand Oaks, Calif.: Pine Forge Press, 1994.

"Returning Favorites." *TV Guide* (September 8, 2001): 4.

Reuss, Alejandro, Arthur MacEwan, Phineas Baxandall, and John Miller. "The ABCs of 'Free-Trade' Agreements." *Dollars and Sense* (January–February 2001): 24.

Reynolds, David. *Democracy Unbound.* Boston: South End Press, 1997.

"The Rich Get a Good Return on Their Campaign Investments." *Sanders Scoop* (Winter 1998): 1.

Riechmann, Deb. "Clinton Signs Measure to Open China to U.S. Goods." *Indianapolis Star,* October 11, 2000.

Rogers, Everett M. "Diffusion and Re-Invention of Project DARE." In *Organizational Aspects of Health Communication Campaigns: What Works?* ed. Thomas E. Backer and Everett M. Rogers. Newbury Park, Calif.: Sage, 1993.

Romano, Michael. "2001 Physician Compensation Report." *Modern Healthcare* (August 13, 2001): 30–34.

Roscigno, Vincent J., and James W. Ainsworth-Darnell. "Race, Cultural Capital, and Educational Resources: Persistent Inequalities and Achievement Returns." *Sociology of Education* 72 (1999): 158–78.

Rosenthal, Robert, and Lenore Jacobson. *Pygmalion in the Classroom.* New York: Holt, Rinehart and Winston, 1968.

Ross, Steven J. *Working-Class Hollywood: Silent Film and the Shaping of Class in America.* Princeton: Princeton University Press, 1998.

Rothman, Robert A. *Working: Sociological Perspectives.* 2nd ed. Upper Saddle River, N.J.: Prentice Hall, 1998.

Rousseau, Jean-Jacques. *The Social Contract.* Tr. Charles Frankel. New York: Hafner Publishing Co., 1947.

Rubin, Beth A. *Shifts in the Social Contract.* Thousand Oaks, Calif.: Pine Forge Press, 1996.

Rushkoff, Douglas (narrator). *The Merchants of Cool.* PBS *Frontline* TV Documentary, 2001.

Safire, William. "Jimmy That 'Lockbox.'" *New York Times,* September 10, 2001.

Samuelson, Robert J. "Confederacy of Dunces." *Newsweek* (September 23, 1996): 65.

———. "Down with the Media Elite!?" *Newsweek* (July 13 1998): 47.

———. "Great Expectations." *Newsweek* (January 8, 1996): 24–33.

———. "Indifferent to Inequality?" *Newsweek* (May 7, 2001): 45.

Schaefer, Richard T. *Sociology.* New York: McGraw-Hill, 2001.

Schellhardt, Timothy D. "Are Layoffs Moral? One Firm's Answer: You Ask, We'll Sue." *Wall Street Journal,* August 1, 1996: A12.

Schemo, Diana J. "U.S. Schools Turn More Segregated." *New York Times,* July 20, 2001.

Schlozman, Kay L., and John T. Tierney. *Organized Interests and American Democracy.* New York: Harper and Row, 1986.

Schor, Juliet B. "Keeping Up with the Trumps: How the Middle Class Identifies with the Rich." *Washington Monthly* (July–August 1998): 34–37.

Schrag, Peter. "Edison's Red Ink Schoolhouse." *Nation* (June 25, 2001): 20–24.

Schrammel, Kurt. "Comparing the Labor Market Success of Young Adults from Two Generations." *Monthly Labor Review* (February 1998): 3–9.

Schwartz, Felice N. "Management Women and the New Facts of Life." In *Working in America,* ed. Amy S. Wharton. Mountain View, Calif.: Mayfield Publishing, 1998.

Scott, Robert E. "NAFTA's Hidden Costs." Washington, D.C.: Economic Policy Institute, May 2001.

Seider, Maynard S. "American Big Business Ideology: A Content Analysis of Executive Speeches." *American Sociological Review* 39 (1974): 802–15.

Seldes, George. "Is the Entire Press Corrupt?" *EXTRA!* (November–December 1994): 26–27.

"Set to Organize." *Labor Party Press* (January 1999): 1, 4.

Sewell, William A., A. O. Haller, and G. W. Ohlandorf. "The Educational and Early Occupational Status Attainment Process." *American Sociological Review* 35 (1970): 1014–27.

Sewell, William A., and Vimal Shah. "Parents' Education and Children's Educational Aspirations and Achievements." *American Sociological Review* 33 (1968): 191–209.

Shaiken, Harley. *Work Transformed: Automation and Labor in the Computer Age*. New York: Holt, Rinehart and Winston, 1985.

Sherman, Scott. "An Appeal to Reason." *Nation* (March 10, 1997): 15–19.

Shuldiner, Allan, and Tony Raymond. *Who's in the Lobby? A Profile of Washington's Influence Industry*. Washington, D.C.: Center for Responsive Politics, 1998.

Sifry, Micah L. "How Money in Politics Hurts You." *Dollars and Sense* (July–August 2001): 17–20.

Silverstein, Ken. "Manufactured News." *EXTRA!* (January–February 1997): 23–24.

Silverstein, Ken, and Alexander Cockburn. "How's He Doing? Has Sweeney Changed Labor?" *CounterPunch* (July 16–31, 1997): 1, 6–8.

———. "Our Little Secret: Life on the Fast Track." *CounterPunch* (September 1–15, 1997): 2–3.

———. "Why the Drug War Works: It's a Money/Class Thing, of Course." *CounterPunch* (June 15–30, 1998): 4–5.

Simmons, Robert G., and Morris Rosenberg. "Functions of Children's Perceptions of the Stratification System." *American Sociological Review* 36 (1971): 235–49.

Sirico, Robert A. "The Capitalist Ethic: True Morality." *Forbes* (December 2, 1996): 85.

Sklar, Holly. "CEO Ponzi Scheme." 2001. Available at http://www.inequality.org.

Sloan, Allan. "A Lot of Trust, But No Funds." *Newsweek* (July 30, 2001): 34.

———. "What Goes Up . . ." *Newsweek* (April 13, 1998): 42–43.

Smith, Jeremy. "Intellectual Snobs versus Political Slobs." *Dollars and Sense* (May–June 1998): 38–39.

Smith, Wesley J. "Nobody's Nader." *Mother Jones* (July–August 1996): 61–63.

Snow, Tony. "What the Class Warriors Don't Get about $1.6 Trillion." *Lafayette Courier Journal*, February 10, 2001.

Social Security Administration. "2001 Social Security Changes." 2001. Available at http://www.ssa.gov.

"Social Security Heist." *Nation* (July 9, 2001): 3.

Soley, Lawrence C. "Corporate Censorship and the Limits of Free Speech." *EXTRA!* (March–April 1999): 19–21.

———. *Leasing the Ivory Tower: The Corporate Takeover of Academia*. Boston: South End Press, 1996.

———. "The Power of the Press Has a Price." *EXTRA!* (July–August 1997): 11–13.

Solomon, Norman. "Media Moguls on Board." *EXTRA!* (January–February 1998): 19–22.

———. "The Media Oligarchy: Undermining Journalism, Obstructing Democracy." In *Censored 2001*, ed. Peter Phillips. New York: Seven Stories Press, 2001.

Solowey, Fred J. "Selling Social Insecurity." *EXTRA!* (March–April 1998): 22–23.

"Soundbites." *EXTRA!* (May–June 1996): 5.

———. *EXTRA!* (September–October 1996): 5.

———. *EXTRA!* (September–October 2001): 5.

Spencer, Miranda. "TV Nation: A Show for 'The Rest of Us.'" *EXTRA!* (November–December 1995): 24–25.

"Spokane Just Says No to DARE Program." *Kokomo Tribune*, October 6, 1996.

Starr, Jerold M. *Air Wars: The Fight to Reclaim Public Broadcasting.* Boston: Beacon Press, 2000.

"Statement of Ownership." *EXTRA!* (November–December 2000): 27.

Stauber, John, and Sheldon Rampton. *Toxic Sludge Is Good for You: Lies, Damn Lies, and the Public Relations Industry.* Monroe, Me.: Common Courage Press, 1996.

————. "Watching the Watchdogs: How Corporate PR Keeps Tabs on Reporters." *EXTRA!* (May–June 1996): 22.

Steffens, Lincoln. *Upbuilders.* 1909. Seattle: University of Washington Press, 1968.

Stendler, Cecelia Burns. *Children of Brasstown: Their Awareness of the Symbols of Social Class.* Urbana: University of Illinois Press, 1949.

Stevenson, Richard W. "U.S. to Report to Congress NAFTA Benefits Are Modest." *New York Times*, July 11, 1997.

Stillman, Don. "The Devastating Impact of Plant Relocations." *Working Papers* (July–August 1978): 42–53.

Stock, Katherine M. *Rural Radicals: Righteous Rage in the American Grain.* Ithaca, N.Y.: Cornell University Press, 1996.

Stohl, Michael, and Harry R. Targ. *Global Political Economy in the 1980s.* Cambridge, Mass.: Schenkman, 1982.

Stone, Peter H. "The Nicotine Network." *Mother Jones* (May–June 1996): 50–52.

Stratman, David. "School Reform and the Attack on Public Education." *Dollars and Sense* (March–April 1998): 7.

Strobel, Frederick R., and Wallace C. Peterson. *The Coming Class War and How to Avoid It.* Armonk, N.Y.: M. E. Sharpe, 1999.

Strope, Leigh. "Job Cuts Hit 21-Year High." *Indianapolis Star*, November 3, 2001.

Tasini, Jonathan. "Lost in the Margins: Labor and the Media." *EXTRA!* (Summer 1990): 2–6.

————. "Media Stereotypes about Unions." *EXTRA!* (Summer 1990): 4.

"Tax Cut Madness." *Nation* (June 4, 2001): 3–4.

Thomas, Evan, and Gregory L. Vistica. "Fallout from a Media Fiasco." *Newsweek* (July 20, 1998): 24–26.

Thompson, Hunter S. *Generation of Swine.* New York: Vintage Books, 1988.

Thomson, Allison. "Industry Output and Employment Projections to 2008." *Monthly Labor Review* (November 1999): 33–50.

Thurman, Terry. "Political Action Is a Year-Round Process." (Region 3 Moving Forward Insert). *UAW Solidarity* (November 2001): 1–2.

Tilly, Chris. *Half a Job: Bad and Good Part-Time Jobs in a Changing Labor Market.* Philadelphia: Temple University Press, 1996.

————. "Next Steps for the Living Wage Movement." *Dollars and Sense* (September–October 2001): 36–39, 48.

Tilly, Chris, and Charles Tilly. *Work Under Capitalism.* Boulder, Colo.: Westview Press, 1998.

Tobiasen, Linda G., ed. *The Foundation Grants Index, 1996.* New York: Foundation Center, 1995.

Tomaskovic-Devey, Donald. *Gender and Racial Inequality at Work.* Ithaca, N.Y.: IRL Press, 1993.

"The Top Paid CEOs." *Forbes* (May 18, 1998): 224–99.

Tudor, Jeannette F. "The Development of Class Awareness in Children." *Social Forces* 49 (1971): 470–76.

"Two Parties Give Us Six New Reasons for One Party for Us." *Labor Party Press* (March 1998): 1.

"2000 U.S. Economic Review: U.S. Theaters." Motion Picture Association of America. 2001. Available at http://www.mpaa.org.

TV Guide. 2001. June 16–22, 145; August 4–10, 123; August 18–24, 93; September 10, 128; September 25, 140.

Uchitelle, Louis. "U.S. Corporations Expanding Abroad at a Quicker Pace." *New York Times,* July 25, 1998.

Uchitelle, Louis, and N. R. Kleinfield. "On Battlefield of Business, Millions of Casualties." *New York Times,* March 3, 1996.

"Unbalanced! Bipartisan Budget Bill Boosts Billionaires." *Labor Party Press* (November 1997): 4–5.

"United for a Fair Economy Programs." Boston: United for a Fair Economy, 37 Temple Place, ca. 2001.

U.S. Bureau of the Census. Foreign Trade Division. Washington, D.C.: U.S. Government Printing Office, 2000.

———. "Money Income in the United States, 1999." Washington, D.C.: U.S. Government Printing Office, 2000.

U.S. Code Annotated. 20 U.S.C.A. sect. 3192. Amendment to Public Law 101–647. Cumulative Annual Pocket Part. St. Paul, Minn.: West Publishing, 1995.

U.S. Congress. House Committee on the Budget. *Unnecessary Business Subsidies.* 106th Congress, 1st sess. Serial 106–5. Washington, D.C.: U.S. Government Printing Office, 1999.

———. House Committee on Education and Labor, Subcommittee on Elementary, Secondary, and Vocational Education. *Oversight Hearing on Drug Abuse Education Programs.* 101st Congress, 1st sess. Serial 101–129. Washington, D.C.: U.S. Government Printing Office, 1990.

———. House Committee on Ways and Means. *Comprehensive Tax Reform.* 99th Congress, 1st sess. Serial 99–41. Washington, D.C.: U.S. Government Printing Office, 1985.

———. *Impact, Effectiveness, and Fairness of the Tax Reform Act of 1986.* 101st Congress, 2d sess. Serial 101–92. Washington, D.C.: U.S. Government Printing Office, 1990.

———. Senate Committee on Labor and Human Resources. *Drug Abuse, Prevention, and Treatment.* 100th Congress, 2d sess. Washington, D.C.: U.S. Government Printing Office, 1988.

U.S. Department of Commerce, Bureau of the Census, *Statistical Abstract of the United States.* Washington, D.C.: U.S. Government Printing Office, 1995, 572.

———. *Statistical Abstract of the United States.* Washington, D.C.: U.S. Government Printing Office, 2000.

U.S. Department of Education. National Center for Educational Statistics. *The Condition of Education, 1996.* NCES 96–304. Ed. Thomas Smith. Washington, D.C.: U.S. Government Printing Office, 1996.

———. *Digest of Educational Statistics.* NCES 2001–034. Ed. Thomas D. Snyder, Charlene M. Hoffman, and Clair M. Geddes. Washington, D.C.: U.S. Government Printing Office, 2001.

———. *Digest of Educational Statistics, 2000.* Washington, D.C.: U.S. Government Printing Office, 2001.

U.S. Department of Justice. Bureau of Justice Assistance. *Program Brief: An Introduction to DARE—Drug Abuse Resistance Education,* 2nd ed. Washington, D.C.: Bureau of Justice Assistance, 1991.

U.S. Department of Labor, Bureau of Labor Statistics. "Union Members Summary." Press release, January 17, 2002.

U.S. Department of the Treasury, Internal Revenue Service. "Return of Organization Exempt from Income Tax: Form 990: DARE America." 95–4242541. Washington, D.C., 1995, 1996.

———. *The Statistics of Income.* SOI Bulletin. Washington, D.C.: U.S. Government Printing Office, Spring 2001.

Useem, Michael. *The Inner Circle.* New York: Oxford University Press, 1984.

Vanderpool, Tim. "Secession of the Successful." *Utne Reader* (November–December, 1995): 32–34.

Vanneman, Reeve, and Lynn Weber Cannon. *The American Perception of Class.* Philadelphia: Temple University Press, 1987.

Viacom Incorporated. *Viacom Inc. 2000 Annual Report.* 2001. Available at http://www.viacom.com.

Vidal, Gore. "The End of History." *Nation* (September 30, 1996): 11–18.

"Voucher Program Fails to Deliver." *AFT American Teacher* (November 2001): 14.

Wall, Suzanne. "Union Candidates Use a 'Bottom-Up' Approach to Winning Political Power." *Labor Notes* (April 1998): 3.

Wallach, Lori. "Corporate Protectionism." *Public Citizen: Special Anniversary Issue* 21(1), 2001: 10–11, 27.

"Wall Street Leads Top Campaign Contributors on *Mother Jones* 400." *Mother Jones.* 2001. Available at http://www.motherjones.com.

The Walt Disney Company. *TWDC 2000 Annual Report.* 2001. Available at http://www.disney.com.

Ward, Kevin. "Militia Movement and the Internet." 2001. Available at http://www.rutgers.edu.

Watson, Noshua. "Inside the 500." *Fortune* (April 16, 2001): 232–33.

Weber, Joseph, and Blanca Riemer. "These Days Mack Trucks Isn't Built like Mack Trucks." *Business Week* (July 30, 1990): 40–41.

Wechsler, Pat. "This Lesson Is Brought to You By." *Business Week* (June 30, 1997): 68–69.

Weissman, Steve. "Discharge Petition May Force Hastert's Hand." *Public Citizen News* (September–October 2001): 6.

Weller, Christian. "The Commission Straw Man: Social Security Well Prepared for Retirement of Baby Boomers in 2016." *Economic Policy Institute,* Issue Brief #159, July 19, 2001.

Wells, Susan J. "Looking for Trouble." *HR Magazine* (January 2001): 38–42.

Wenglinsky, Harold. "How Money Matters: The Effect of School District Spending on Academic Achievement." *Sociology of Education* 70 (July 1997): 221–37.

Whalen, Charles J., Paul Magnusson, and Geri Smith. "NAFTA's Scorecard: So Far, So Good." *Business Week* (July 9, 2001): 54–56.

"What Is the 'Paycheck Deception Act'?" *AFSCME Public Employee* (March–April 1998): 10–11.

"What's FAIR?" *EXTRA!* (September–October 2001): 2.

"The Whitening Newsroom." *EXTRA!Update* (June 2001): 2.

Wiedenbaum, Murray L. *Business, Government, and the Public.* Englewood Cliffs, N.J.: Prentice-Hall, 1977.

Willis, Derek. "Debating McCain-Feingold." *Congressional Quarterly Weekly* (March 10, 2001): 524–27.

Wohl, R. Richard. "The 'Rags to Riches Story': An Episode of Secular Idealism." In *Class, Status, and Power,* ed. Reinhard Bendix and Seymour M. Lipset. New York: Free Press, 1966.

Wolfe, Alan. *The Seamy Side of Democracy.* New York: David McKay, 1973.

Wolfe, Charles, and Kip Lornell. *The Life and Legend of Leadbelly.* New York: HarperCollins, 1992.

Wolff, Edward N. *Top Heavy: The Increasing Inequality of Wealth in America and What Can Be Done about It.* New York: Twentieth Century Fund, 1996.

"Working to Tell the Untold Story." *Too Much* (Winter 2000): 8.

Wright, David. "Changes in Hourly Earnings, 1947–2001." *Work Series.* Wichita, Kan.: Wichita State University (August 2001): A19–20.

Wright, Erik O. *Classes.* London: Verso, 1985.

———. *Interrogating Inequality.* London: Verso, 1994.

Wright, John W., ed. *The New York Times Almanac, 2001.* New York: Penguin, 2000.

Wu Dunn, Sheryl. "When Lifetime Jobs Die Prematurely." *New York Times,* June 12, 1996.

Wysong, Earl. "Class in the Movies." Unpublished paper, 1996.

———. *High Risk and High Stakes: Health Professionals, Politics, and Policy.* Westport, Conn.: Greenwood Press, 1992.

Wysong, Earl, Richard Aniskiewicz, and David Wright. "Truth *and* DARE: Tracking Drug Education to Graduation and as Symbolic Politics." *Social Problems* 41 (1994): 448–72.

Wysong, Earl, and David Wright. "A Decade of DARE: Efficacy, Politics, and Drug Education." *Sociological Focus* 28 (1995): 283–311.

Yardley, Jim. "Well-Off but Still Pressed, Doctor Could Use Tax Cut." *New York Times,* April 7, 2001.

Yeoman, Barry. "Subsidies at Sea." *Mother Jones* (May–June 2001): 72–77, 112–13.

"Yes, We Have No Bananas." *Wall Street Journal,* September 4, 2001.

Zeller, Shawn. "Thriving in a Crisis." *National Journal* (October 14, 2000): 3262.

Zernike, Kate. "Antidrug Program Says It Will Adopt a New Strategy." *New York Times,* February 15, 2001.

Zinn, Howard. *A People's History of the United States.* New York: Harper Colophon Books, 1980.

Zuckerman, Diana. "The Derailing of Social Security." *EXTRA!* (May–June 1999): 13–14.

Zuckerman, Mortimer B. "A Time to Celebrate." *U.S. News and World Report* (July 17, 2000): 120.

Zweigenhaft, Richard L., and G. William Domhoff. *Diversity in the Power Elite: Have Women and Minorities Reached the Top?* New Haven: Yale University Press, 1998.

Index

About the Authors

Robert Perrucci is professor of sociology at Purdue University. His current research examines the effects of shift work on workers and their families, and stresses the role of participatory action by workers and families in shaping work schedules. He is the author of numerous articles, book chapters, and books, including *Japanese Auto Transplants in the Heartland: Corporatism and Community; Plant Closings: International Contexts and Social Costs;* and *Science Under Siege? Interest Groups and the Science Wars.* His most cherished award is having been described as a scholar-warrior by his coauthor.

Earl Wysong is professor of sociology at Indiana University Kokomo. His commitment to critical sociology, strengthening working-class institutions, and social equity has often caused him much personal and professional grief. But he is too dumb to cure and too smart to worry about. He is currently researching the relationship between the distribution of class power resources and worker access to family-friendly workplace benefits. Although his speed-lashed prose and high-energy style have been frequently muted by mainstream editors and reviewers, he has still managed to publish several memorable articles, book chapters, and biographical profiles. He is the author of *High Risk and High Stakes: Health Professionals, Politics, and Policy,* and he expects to strike again soon as coauthor of a new book on family-friendly workplace issues.